SUCK IT UP OR GO HOME

A TRUE STORY ABOUT THE COURAGE TO STAND UP, KEEP GOING AND NEVER GIVE IN!

SIMON GRAY

SUCK IT UP OR GO HOME

Published by Career Codex Limited
First published in Great Britain in 2020

Book cover © 2020 Simon Gray and
designed by Nabinkarna
Main cover photograph by Samantha J Gray Photography
Small cover photographs taken by Simon Gray

PRAISE FOR
SUCK IT UP OR GO HOME

'As someone who completed the course 12 years prior to Simon's, I was very interested to delve into another Senshusei experience. *Suck It Up Or Go Home* is a fantastic read and an authentic account of the emotional, physical and spiritual rollercoaster that creates a Senshusei. Through Simon's eyes you are immersed in all aspects of traditional Budo training in Japan. The life lessons and character development that traditional martial arts develop are evident throughout. A captivating, informative and enjoyable read for both martial artists and normal people, too!'
– Nic Mills Dojocho Sendokan Dojo, 7th Dan Aikido Yoshinkai & 'Mad Dog' from *Angry White Pyjamas*

'Simon's story is remarkable. Set on the unforgiving Aikido mats of Tokyo it is a wider story of how we face adversity, discipline ourselves and win the inner game. How we find the courage and resilience to live out our passions, so that ultimately we can truly find the best in ourselves. If the martial arts had a Special Forces, the Senshusei course would be it. A great read that I couldn't put down.'
– Richard Mann, Ex UK Special Forces (SBS) & Host of the Mann on a Mission Podcast

'Having trained in Shotokan Karate for over 30 years I found this a fascinating read. Simon's personal memoirs give a comprehensive insight into the unique world of traditional Japanese martial arts, which very few Westerners have experienced. Simon's detailed account shows what it takes to complete the gruelling Senshusei course and earn a black belt in Yoshinkan Aikido. His story is proof that through grit and determination you can achieve whatever you set out to do in life.'
– Danielle Asano, 5th Dan, Former British Kata and Kumite Champion & European Gold Medallist

'I was excited to read *Suck It Up Or Go Home*. It is a fascinating book and will be of interest to anyone. The strong message to keep going, even when times get tough, really hit home. Highly recommended.'
– Dan Holloway, The Martial View & Empower Martial Arts Academy

For my lovely wife Samantha. Thank you for your constant support, for being by my side and for our wonderful boys.

Charles and Maximus, I hope this inspires you. Always follow your dreams and explore the amazing opportunities life has to offer.

Love always, Simon & Daddy xxx xxx xxx

For Mum and Sally to know me better. It's been a difficult year but we keep going. I love you both.

Love and miss you Dad. Forever in my heart.

Simon 9x

'To live in hearts we leave behind is not to die.'
– Thomas Campbell

CONTENTS

THREE QUOTES AND A MOTTO / MANTRA FOR LIFE

'Do not pray for an easy life, pray for the strength to endure a difficult one.'
– **BRUCE LEE**

'Perseverance in any profession will most probably meet its reward.'
– **ADMIRAL LORD HORATIO NELSON**

'Live your life while you have it. Life is a splendid gift. There is nothing small in it. Far the greatest things grow by God's law out of the smallest. But to live your life, you must discipline it.'
– **FLORENCE NIGHTINGALE**

Nana korobi ya oki (fall down seven times, get up eight).
– **JAPANESE PROVERB**

A WORD OF WARNING

This is a story about courage, determination and never giving in – are you ready?

This is a true story. It's a true story that will make you laugh, possibly even cry – but more than anything else it will inspire you to take action. Everything you are about to read happened. Some things may seem impossible, some bordering on the insane, but they happened all the same.

Whether or not you're a martial artist doesn't matter. This book, while predominantly set in a martial arts school, isn't really about martial arts at all. It's about struggle and through struggle, the ability to find strength. It's about turning a very negative experience into a positive one and not looking back. It's about what happens when you decide to step out of your comfort zone to experience something new.

I've never believed in the bucket list. I don't believe in a list of things before you die; I believe in doing things while you live. I'm just an ordinary guy but being ordinary doesn't mean you have to settle for an ordinary life. At 34 I did something extraordinary and learnt that extraordinary is always a possibility and a choice.

Be warned, as you turn the pages of this book, they might motivate you to do that thing you've been putting off, to take a step into the unknown, and to make your dream a reality. My story was a life-changing one. You might have a similar story just waiting to be written!

ACKNOWLEDGEMENTS

Through these fields of destruction.
Baptisms of fire.
I've witnessed your suffering.
As the battle raged high.
And though they did hurt me so bad.
In the fear and alarm.
You did not desert me.
My brothers in arms.
From *Brothers in Arms* – DIRE STRAITS

I am eternally grateful for the opportunity I had and to everyone mentioned in this book. You all played a special part in what was a truly enriching and life-changing experience.

Matt, thank you for joining me. Cheers mate!

A special thank you to Ronen who reviewed the first draft. My Israeli brother reminded me of things I'd forgotten and helped fill in some of the gaps. Toda raba my friend.

Thank you, too, to Inazaki-san who helped with some of the Japanese I'd long since forgotten. Domo arigatou gozaimashita!

In memory of Daniel Gainey.

INTRODUCTION

STANDING IN LINE

Standing in line, all I can think about is water. I'm not sure if I will be sick, faint or both. My mouth is dry, I can hardly swallow, and I feel like I'm swaying from side to side. I hope nobody notices. Perhaps everyone feels the same? Maybe we're all just trying to hang tough until the class is over? At last, Dave the instructor brings us to attention and shouts *'kida'*, an instruction to *bow* in Hebrew. At last I can drink, and I can't find my water bottle fast enough!

It's Tuesday, 11 September 2018 and over 10 years since I completed one of the toughest martial arts courses in the world. Finally, it's time to write this book. The *Senshusei* course, also known as the Riot Police course, is shrouded in mystery and is something very few martial artists outside of Japan have been lucky, or foolish, enough to experience. The literal translation of Senshusei is *specialist*. In its component parts; Sen (concentrate on one thing), shu (acquire scholarship and arts) and sei (student). A kind of 'special student'. The focused sort that any university professor, lecturer or Aikido teacher would want in his or her class. For 11 months you specialise in the art of Aikido and make the journey from white belt to black belt. One study, one art, and one incredible journey!

But why now, why so long? Wouldn't it have been better to write it sooner? The passage of time distorts memories. The truth is, until now, I've not been ready. I locked away the diary I wrote on the course. It's my personal time capsule buried away from prying eyes for a future generation to discover. Secrets contained within its pages speak of an experience very few have tasted. 11 years on, I'm hoping my account will finally lift the lid on what makes this course so special. My account is raw, at times unpolished, but always truthful. Those included within the pages of this book will hopefully understand that the authenticity of my words requires me to tell this story as I saw things through my eyes. My aim is not to offend or paint anyone in a negative light, but what

1

happened, happened. Everyone mentioned in what follows helped to make the experience what it was. I hold no grudges, bear no malice and hope those reading who were also there feel the same.

So why now? Standing in line as my Krav Maga (Israeli self-defence system) class ends, I'm reminded what it means to be Senshusei. What it means to be one of only 200 people or so outside of Japan who have completed arguably one of the toughest martial arts courses in the world in the physical and mental stakes and its overall duration. This 11-month bootcamp which took me from my home in Nottingham, England, to Tokyo, Japan, a unique and often strange place where traditional and old blend with the cutting edge and new. This is the place where, through my own choosing, I was thrown into a world I could never have before imagined to face the biggest challenge of my life.

This is a story of *Budo* (the path or way of martial arts), blood and bruised bodies. It's a story of training, torment and ultimate triumph. It's a story of what it takes to push yourself to the limit and then push on some more. Mine is a story of personal growth and development, and one of refusing to accept defeat. On the course we were regularly told, *'one day you'll understand'*. Now, finally, I think I do!

FISTS OF FURY

I learnt from a very young age that having the ability to fight was just as important as a good education. School can be a tough environment, and for me, it was. I was regularly involved in fights. Nothing drew a crowd more than the chant of *'scrap, scrap, scrap'*, and for a few minutes, all hell broke loose until the teacher arrived to break it up.

My Mum and Dad enrolled me in a Judo class. 'Baz' was my instructor – a small man but as hard as nails. He ruled the mats with a rod of iron. *'On your backs, move it…I'm going to put my fingers up your nose and pull your brains out!'* He wasn't a guy you messed with. I'm sure my parents wanted me to look after myself, but as the saying goes, *a little knowledge can be dangerous*. Judo for them, with no punching or kicking, was seen as the safest option. It was unlikely to result in a black eye and I wouldn't quite have enough skills to do any serious or visible damage to anyone in the school playground.

As most fights started with flying fists, I usually came off second best. Both aged 11 or 12, David Cartwright was skinnier and smaller than me, but he could throw a punch. We'd regularly fight and despite my physical advantage I'd come home with a bruised lip and scuffed knees. This frustrated me, and I pressed Mum and Dad to let me do Karate. They were adamant, though, no punching or kicking, no matter how much I pleaded.

Maybe it was frustration, maybe I was just plain naughty, but my parents couldn't control me. My Dad had been to boarding school at the tender age of seven and at 13 it was my turn. I had little concept of what boarding school was, or might involve, and I agreed to attend an open day with my parents. It all looked great. A friendly headmaster and well-mannered pupils showed us around the fantastic facilities. I was sold and agreed I would start as a full-time boarder after the summer.

Unfortunately, the reality was very different. The well-mannered pupils became my bullies and with no home time at the end of each day, there was no opportunity for escape. Not being the coolest kid – and worse still, not being selected for the First XV or Second XV rugby teams – my life was a living hell. Times were very different to how they are now. The older pupils ruled and beatings, not detention, were the force of law. Forget running to Mummy and Daddy or telling the housemaster. 'Grassing' or telling tales resulted in more beatings and social exclusion. I couldn't fight and would take out my frustration the only way I could. I'd drive my fists into a wall, chest of drawers or door until my knuckles bled. Anything to relieve the anger and sense of injustice that burned inside. I promised a sixth former and First XV player who was one of my tormentors that one day I'd pay him back. I had no plan or way to do this, at least not yet!

'Wedgies' were dished out for minor offences and could be administered by an individual at a moment's notice. If you were targeted for this punishment, your underpants would be yanked from behind and then hung on a peg. The smaller the victim, the more likely they would literally hang around for a while. 'Bog washes' were a more serious form of punishment and required considerable planning and a team to execute. They would prepare a toilet, filled with what's intended, along with bleach, toilet cleaner and anything else to make the contents more unpleasant. Ambushed by six boys, one on each leg, two at the head and two in the middle, like a funeral without a coffin, the poor victim was carried kicking and screaming to his fate. He was then dropped headfirst into the bowl, and as the toilet flushed, there was a risk of drowning in the poisonous mix or incurring serious injury.

We were all tooled up. Teenage boys wandering the school with flick knives, *balisong* (butterfly knives) and *shuriken* (throwing stars) wasn't a great idea. Metalwork was a popular option and while the teacher's back was turned, I got to work on private projects I could later use to defend myself. Teenage boys have adolescent interests and it was a rather surreal experience being pushed up against a poster of glamour model Linda Lusardi's breasts by Vincent Knight and his knife. One of the biggest kids in the school for his age he'd taken a dislike to me. Sandwiched between anyone's breasts was a fantasy I'd yet to experience. On the one hand pleasure and on the other pain, as Knight's blade pressed against my neck. I begged for mercy and survived the ordeal. The school eventually caught on and a knife amnesty was called. Some boys relinquished their weapons, but most didn't!

Sharing a dormitory with 10 to 12 other boys meant getting any sleep was difficult. The snoring, farting and messing about was relentless, much to the annoyance of the senior boys. 'Dick' Barton wasn't one for bedtime stories. One of the more brutal of the seniors he had a much better way to induce sleep. Dick by name and 'dick' by nature. While I was sat up in bed one night, he punched me so hard in the face that I fell into a semi-conscious slumber which lasted all night.

Every day started with echoes of the opening line from the book *One Day in the Life of Ivan Denisovich*. The sound of metal on metal rang out to signal the beginning of a new day. The responsibility was rotated, and I always dreaded my turn. The instrument was a hollow metal pipe, two foot in length and suspended by a length of wire attached through a hole in the top. I wandered the boarding house banging the bar with a metal rod. I had to be up first and ran the gauntlet as weary boys threw shoes, books or anything else they could find at my head. For the time it took to circumnavigate the sleeping quarters I was the most unpopular boy in the school. I wasn't imprisoned in a *Gulag*, but boarding school at times resembled a *Soviet labour camp*. I got used to dodging things and lessons were no better. My science teacher who was partial to the bottle, evidenced by his permanently bloodshot face, liked to throw, too. Usually chalk to shut up or wake up his charge, but on one occasion a kilogram weight was launched across the lab at my classmate's head. Luckily, he ducked, and it missed!

If you annoyed the prefects, you could be disciplined in other ways. I was up early most mornings, cleaning shoes that had been left outside the studies which were home to the senior boys. Frank was fat and preferred to drag me on long runs before the sun was up. He was trying to lose a few pounds and, on his journey to target weight, I was often his unwilling companion. You could be punished for a minor indiscretion and there was no regulation over the severity or frequency. The double dead leg was another favourite. Accosted either side by two assailants, a knee was driven into both thighs. With the feeling temporarily removed from both limbs, the victim collapsed to the floor unable to walk. Perhaps all were a prelude to my time on the Senshusei course?

4

The 'lamppost' was infamous. The beds were the type I'd seen on a visit to a Victorian workhouse. Black metal-framed with a paper-thin striped mattress on top. A boy with a grudge or just a warped sense of humour could easily pick up the end. Tipping the frame on its head resembled the vertical height of a lamppost and sent its sleeping occupant crashing down on his neck. It was a dangerous manoeuvre that could have killed or permanently disabled someone. Not content with this torture, one of the prefects hung one of my friends out of a first-floor window by his feet. My pal dangled there for a good few minutes before being brought back in – one slip and he'd have been dead!

One night, Tom Butler and Dick burst into the dormitory and woke everyone up. They were in the mood for trouble but, both aged 18, should really have known better. They were armed with a white powder that, according to them, they'd sourced from the Amazon jungle. The powder, if it made contact with skin, would penetrate and cause a rash to develop. This rash would be itchy, bumpy and painful. They told us, *'when the bumps burst, spiders will come out'*. Any contact with this powder meant we'd be eaten alive. We were gullible, impressionable and terrified. The powder turned out to be of the talcum variety and our arachnid friends never arrived. I didn't sleep that night; I rarely did! I struggled with asthma, a condition I inherited from my Dad. I didn't have a Ventolin inhaler, although I'm not sure why. The dormitory was dusty, and dust aggravated my condition. Cold baths and pillow fights were the stuff of boarding school legend and the latter I especially dreaded. After a pillow fight or other disturbance, my chest would tighten, my breathing became shallow and I'd spend the rest of the night wheezing – each breath was a conscious effort.

The most traumatic event of my boarding school years occurred on Tuesday, 22 April 1986. I was always close to my Nana, or 'Nansie' as she preferred to be called. She'd been ill for a while. I was stood in the matron's laundry when my friend found me. *'I've been looking for you everywhere. Your Mum and Dad are outside the school!'* I burst into tears. I knew instantly and my parents confirmed. My beloved Nansie had passed away the day before. Mum and Dad took me into the local town for lunch – I was numb, sad and angry. It was my first taste of the fragility of life and I didn't want to go back to school; I wanted to go home. I had no choice, though, and at night I cried myself to sleep. My friends didn't understand, the senior boys didn't, either. The usual chaos went on around me as I locked myself away in a private world of pain.

The sixth formers bullied the fifth formers and the fifth formers vented their anger on those in the fourth year, and so the cycle went on. There was, however, one exception to this pattern. One person somehow avoided being bullied. His name was Adrian Higgins. Only a year older and in the year above, Adrian, like me, was also way down in the pecking order, but he commanded a respect unfitting his level. He wasn't the coolest kid and was average at rugby, but he had a secret. No wedgies or bog washes for Adrian. He was exempt. In the search for a next victim, the bullies passed him by. Adrian's secret was Kung Fu. His parents had prepared him for battle. Once a week an instructor turned up at school to teach him this secret Chinese martial art made famous by the late Bruce Lee. I'd often make the journey down to the Memorial Hall. While pretending to do something else, I'd secretly watch Adrian train.

Adrian could often be found in the changing rooms punching the life out of a two-litre plastic bottle suspended from one of the many pegs that claimed the underpants of many an unfortunate pupil. If you were smart, when Adrian was training, the changing rooms were off limits. On one occasion, I passed through by accident and in his own bid to bully, Adrian instructed me to *'stand there and don't move!'* In the blink of an eye Adrian threw a series of terrifying punches and kicks within an inch of my face; such was his control. He told me that if he was attacked, he could kick someone in the head three times before the foolish assailant could get off their first punch. I had no reason to doubt him. Neither did the rest of the school. Adrian was feared, revered and left alone!

At 16 I left boarding school and came back home to finish up my education. After three years in the system, it was time to leave. The constant fear of verbal or physical assault had taken its toll. But the major factor pulling me back home was a burning desire to learn what Adrian already knew. I wanted the power and respect he had. I wanted my own fists of fury!

IT'S A KNOCKOUT

Back home in Stafford, I enrolled in a local Kung Fu school and trained relentlessly for two years. Perhaps it was a different style of Kung Fu to Adrian's, but it didn't cut the mustard for me. I couldn't understand why, to learn to fight, I had to stand with my legs apart, knees bent, and fists drawn back by my side. Also, to master the art, I had to do this for hours on end! Surely, in this position, my groin was an open goal and my head a free target for anyone who wanted to take a swing? Why, when we sparred, did we change stance and style completely? Why was I learning to do things one way, but when it came to the crunch, not using any of the techniques I spent hours practicing? This was my introduction to traditional martial arts. The legs-apart position, known as 'horse stance', was precisely that – a position warriors from the past would practice in readiness for mounted battle. I figured Kung Fu wasn't the answer I'd been looking for. I searched for something else.

Kung Fu took place in the local recreation centre, and after class, I would regularly see a group of other martial artists gathering in preparation for their class, which took place in a smaller room next door. Curious, I often stuck around, ear pressed to the door. It was the noise that first struck me. The rhythmic grunting and smashing, as fists, elbows, knees and shins met leather pads at lightning speed. I was far too scared to go in and only glimpsed the action when someone went in or out of the room. These combatants were training how they sparred, and they could hit much harder than I could, even with two years of Kung Fu under my belt. Perhaps this was the martial art I'd been looking for? Could this take me to a level past Adrian? Maybe one day I'd be able to get my revenge. I could square off against him and come out victorious. Despite my fear, I made a promise to myself to talk to the instructor after my next Kung Fu class. I roped in my best friend Anthony for moral support, and in we went. Alan the instructor invited me to give it a go, so I gloved up and got stuck in. I loved it – bang, whack, bang, whack, I hit the pads as hard as I could, but the pad holder didn't flinch. This was full contact, this was real, but I was absolutely rubbish! Still, at the bottom of a mountain, there's only one way to go, and that's up. I couldn't get any worse, and with the right discipline and training, I was confident I'd get better. As the end of the class approached, the sparring started. Students of varying abilities donned gloves, shin protectors, groin guards and gum shields and paired up. Given this was my first class, it surprised me when Alan asked me to join in. Somewhat hesitantly, I gloved up and was matched with a guy who had a fight coming up in the next few weeks. Not to worry, he knew it was my first time and was told by Alan to *'go easy!'* A few moments later, I was on the deck. Dizzy, dazed and confused I came round wondering where I was and what the hell had just happened. I found out later I'd been hit with a straight left and right cross and as I reeled back in my instinctive attempt to avoid the blows, I'd hit the back of my head on the wall behind. Apparently, my eyes had rolled back in their sockets and I'd unceremoniously slid down the wall and slumped on the floor. In my semi-conscious state, time moved quickly; and before I knew it, the class was over, and everyone had left, including Alan! Thank goodness for Anthony. They left the door of the small training room open, and he spotted Andy, one of the senior Kung Fu students leaving the training hall next door, having finished his class. Andy came to the rescue and knew what to do. He helped me downstairs to his car and took me to the

Accident and Emergency (A&E) department at Stafford hospital. My parents met us there and weren't happy. Their precious son had nearly had his brains bashed in! To my dismay, they had little sympathy and blamed me for putting myself in the situation in the first place. *'Why can't you do something safer like cricket or football, Simon? This fighting is dangerous!'* They didn't understand, and they possibly never have. They're fantastic parents, but combat sports are something they've never been able to get their heads around.

My introduction to Muay Thai, or Thai Boxing as it's more often known, had been a painful one. I felt angry, let down and not sure what to do next. I didn't know it, but revenge would eventually be mine. It's at crossroads in life that we have to make important and sometimes difficult decisions. Often through fear we take the easy road, and I now had a difficult decision to make. I knew that Kung Fu, for me at least, wasn't the answer, but on the flip side, my first brush with Muay Thai had landed me in hospital with concussion. I couldn't see the way forward. But as they say, *when the student is ready, the teacher appears.* An avid reader of *Combat* magazine and *Martial Arts Illustrated*, I'd noticed a few articles about Kru Tony Moore. His story inspired me. Tony hadn't just settled for what he could learn in Manchester; he had a dream to learn from the best and regularly acted on this dream. As Chairman of the British Thai Boxing Council and Chief Instructor of the Sitsiam Camp, he was well respected and well connected. If I wanted to learn Thai Boxing properly, perhaps this was the guy to teach me? I don't mind admitting that, dialling Tony's number for the very first time, I was terrified. It took me a few days to pluck up the courage to do it. I was only 19 and had little experience of the world. I didn't really know what to say and had no idea what response I'd get. On 9 April 1991, I caught the train from Stafford to Manchester and met Tony at Piccadilly Station. For the next 15 years, I travelled to Manchester regularly. I trained privately, which gave me the opportunity to learn quickly, but also gave me nowhere to hide when the training got tough. Tony took me under his wing and taught me Muay Thai as it should be taught. This was boxing Thailand style and not the Western interpretation. I spent hours bouncing on an old tractor tyre, legs alternating back and forth, while I fired out punches in the air with hands made heavier by weights. I hit the heavy bag and Thai pads repeatedly. Although I was doing the hitting, it didn't feel like it. They gave as good as they got! Despite training privately, I often had company. Sometimes a visiting Thai over for a fight in the UK, and on one particular day, a trio of trouble. Muay Thai was full contact, and apart from my first introduction, I'd not felt what it was like to take a full-on punch from someone who knew what they were doing.

Walking into the Fighters and Fitness Centre in Clayton on this day, I noticed three guys gloving up in the corner. Tony told me to put on my gloves and get ready to spar. He also told me the guys I was about to go head-to-head with were Moss Side taxi drivers. Moss Side had a reputation for being one of the toughest suburbs of Manchester. If your job was ferrying people to and from this area, you had to be able to handle yourself. Crack! A left hook connected with the side of my head, and I was down. I glanced up at Tony who was leaning over the ropes and into the ring, but there was no tea and sympathy. *'Get up, Simon, and keep your right hand up!'* I was back in the fight and cycled through each. As I got weaker, they seemed to get bigger and stronger. It was my first taste of proper combat, and while I didn't enjoy the experience, getting through it was an achievement.

Inspired by Tony, in September 1992 I made my first trip to Thailand. Bangkok was like nothing I'd ever experienced – chaotic, energetic and a little scary, this being my first visit to Southeast Asia. On the fighting front, the Thais were on a different level. Muay Thai was their national sport, and there were Thai Boxing camps all over the city. Clutching a picture of Tony and me, which formed my sole means of communication, I entered Carryboy gym, where they welcomed me with open arms. Nowadays *farang* (foreigners) are a regular sight in Muay Thai gyms across Thailand, but back then it was a rarity. I vividly remember being gestured to kick a heavy bag which unbeknown to me they'd filled with sand. My leg made no impact and bounced off, nearly disengaging my right hip from the rest of my body. To make matters worse, the twisting action of my standing leg on bare concrete had ripped a flap of skin off the bottom of my foot. All this was normal to my newfound training partners, but for me it was a wake-up call and a realisation that training in Thailand would be no joke. I was a tourist who wanted to get a better understanding of what Thai Boxing was all about. For everyone else in the camp, it was different. This wasn't recreation; it was much more than that. Muay Thai was an opportunity to escape poverty and to make a better life. The aim of becoming Lumpinee or Rajadamnern champion, the two main Thai Boxing stadiums in Bangkok, was their daily focus. Despite possessing lethal skills, everyone was kind and gentle, and there was none of the bravado or ego you often experience in martial arts clubs in the west. They had nothing to prove to anyone. They were the best, and they knew it – and now, so did I!

In Thailand a young man from Holland was already making a name for himself. Ramon Dekkers was someone I'd heard about from Thomas, one of Tony's senior students who had taken a couple of my private lessons when Tony was away. Thomas had fought Dekkers on a show in the Netherlands in April 1990 and come off worse. Every shot Dekkers threw was fired with serious intent. In the first and second rounds he caught Thomas with uppercuts that slipped under his leg and impacted his groin. Thomas told me after the fight that his balls had swollen up like melons. In good humour, he'd asked his doctor to remove the pain but keep the swelling! Dekkers was not much older than me and already proving his skills and abilities in the ring. Thailand had opened my eyes and Dekkers had proved that it was possible to take on the Thais at their own game and win. Known as 'The Diamond' he'd further fuelled my love of Muay Thai and strengthened my desire to fight. I didn't know it at the time, but many years later I'd see him compete in his penultimate fight before his untimely death in February 2013. In July 2005 I saw him beat Duane Ludwig in the K-1 World Max 2005 Final Super Fight in Yokohama, Japan. At 35, Dekkers was coming to the end of his career but still going strong. He downed Ludwig, nine years his junior, three times in a one-armed fight. Dekkers, having sustained an injury a few days before, only had his left punch at his disposal.

Back home, I told Tony I wanted to fight. Having experienced Thailand firsthand, for me fighting was now the only way to understand Muay Thai. I had to get in the ring and face down my opponent; I had to know what it felt like! With the memory of being knocked out in my very first class, fighting was an opportunity to exorcise my demons – demons of that night and also of the bullying I'd experienced at school. I had my first fight on 14 October 1992 at Reets nightclub in Manchester. I won! I've no idea how; it's still a blur to this day. All I know is that it was stopped 30 seconds into the fight, my opponent having sustained a bad cut above his eye. A win is a win, and it encouraged me to carry on fighting regularly to win the Northern Counties and Midlands Light Middleweight Titles.

Revenge came in the form of my third fight on 4 February 1993. I'd since moved to Nottingham and been introduced to Master Lec, a former Thai champion with a reputation for authentic Muay Thai and tough training. I started training under Master Lec at Singnakonchai and continued with Tony at Sitsiam. In Muay Thai this went against the usual convention of only training at one gym but given my geography and the good relationship between Tony and Master Lec, I got the best of both worlds. I was now training in a class as opposed to just private lessons, so I had more opportunities to spar. I could now test my skills with people of all shapes, sizes and levels of experience. I travelled up to Sheffield with Kaleem and Colin, two of my new training partners. We met Tony at the football club where the show was taking place and I headed straight for the medical and to weigh in. Glancing round the preparation area, which always felt like a cage full of lions eyeing each other up, I noticed Alan, the instructor who'd given me my first taste of Thai Boxing two years earlier. That was a taste I hadn't forgotten! When my opponent was announced as one of his students, I immediately went into panic mode. Paul was one of Alan's senior students. A tall, rangy fighter, he'd been there on the night I got knocked out. Although it wasn't Paul who had bounced my head off the wall, he was guilty by association, representing the camp, and instructor who had let this happen. I knew I had to make him pay. All the memories of that night came flooding back, and as they did, the fear inside me grew. Was I ready? Would I get knocked out again? How could I get myself out of this situation?

Tony is someone any fighter would want in their corner and he calmed me down. Whoever truly believes they can win irrespective of their physical capabilities often has the advantage, and Tony convinced me this fight was mine for the taking. This after all was personal! Paul being taller than me, my game plan was to take the fight to his body. I knew I'd struggle to reach his head. *Hit him hard in the body so he drops his head*, I thought to myself, *then bang, bang goodnight!* If only it was that easy. This was a three-round fight with each round lasting two minutes. It doesn't sound like a long time, but I can tell you it's an eternity when you're in there trying not to get hit in the face. In the first round Paul came on strong, using his range to get the better of me. I attacked his lead leg with my right low kick, which instead of slowing him down seemed to make him angry and even more aggressive. Towards the end of the first round I tested his left leg again and deadened it. Paul hopped on his right trying to regain control of his lower body and I took his right leg out from under him with my left low kick. He went down to the canvas and got up hopping. Find an opponent's weakness, exploit it repeatedly and claim the prize of victory. A strong puncher, Paul's weakness were his legs! I went to work again, again and again, every time driving my shin into the soft muscle on the side of his left leg. I hardly bothered to punch and instead, as Bruce Lee advised, fired *my longest weapon against the nearest target.* Near the end of the round, as Paul leaned in for what he hoped would be a knockout punch, I jumped up and drove my left knee into his stomach. I knew I'd hurt him when he glanced at Alan in his corner, so I hit him again with the same technique for good measure. To take the fight back to me, he came on strong again but was still reeling from the pain in his guts. As the round ended with him taking a standing eight count, he was already leaning over ropes and shaking his head at Alan. In that moment, I knew he was ready to quit, and the fight was mine. In the second round it was all Paul. He was all over me like a rash and closing the distance with his punches; it was difficult to get my kicks off. I was hanging on, but not too badly hurt. He had to burn himself out at some point, which he inevitably did. It was back to the knees and the kicks. Drained of energy, Paul was now a sitting target. In the third and probably deciding round, I stuck to the game plan and fired kick after kick into his left lead leg and body to the sound of Tony screaming from my corner. *'Come on, work him, non-stop now, Simon, again, again, again!'* Alan meanwhile screamed in desperation, *'work the hands Paul, come on!'* As the final bell rang, Alan wasn't happy and dragged Paul by the arm back to his corner. The referee called us both to the centre of the ring and raised my hand in victory. I'm not sure whether Alan was more upset about his fighter trying to quit, him losing, or the fact he'd lost to me. Justice had finally been served!

Training regularly under Master Lec helped take my Muay Thai to a new level. He was an encyclopedia of Thai Boxing. The original Thai masters who brought Muay Thai to the UK respected him, including Master Sken and Master Bob. Kaleem, my main sparring partner, and I became firm friends, and Singnakonchai's gatekeepers. Master Lec's reputation attracted visitors from across the UK, and on one particular night, two bodybuilders walked in wearing tight T-shirts to show off bulging muscles; we'd met their type before. Master Lec did what he usually did and, towards the end of the class, asked Kaleem and me to spar with our new friends. Muscles may have worked on heavy weights, but in one-on-one combat, they weren't an asset. After only a few minutes, both bodybuilders quit, and one puked in the corner. They left, and we never saw them again!

ABOVE THE LAW

I've always been a huge fan of movies and especially those involving martial arts. I'd watch anything and everything and tried to adopt Bruce Lee's advice to *absorb what is useful*. Most of the movies I saw focused on punching and kicking. Kung Fu and Karate were all the rage, and the movie producers continued to feed the craving of this genre's die-hard fans. To stand out, you have to be different; and when something new pops up, as human beings, we pay attention. For me this something was *Above the Law* (also known as *Nico*), a 1988 film starring Steven Seagal as Detective Sergeant Nicolo 'Nico' Toscani. The film opened with Nico training in Japan, throwing multiple attackers with a grace and ease I'd never seen before. The techniques were new and involved no punching or kicking. They were strange but highly effective and beautiful to watch. I was amazed, intrigued and in disbelief all at the same time. Could you really win a fight without punching and kicking? Was this real or just Hollywood make-believe? This was my first introduction to Aikido. I became a fan and rented every Steven

Seagal movie which came out, including *Hard to Kill*, *Marked for Death* and my personal favourite, *Out for Justice*. With each movie, the techniques got stronger, more brutal and appeared far more effective. I was still hooked on striking, but Aikido, thanks to Steven Seagal, had sown a seed in my head that unbeknown to me at the time would blossom over a decade later.

I'd been training in Muay Thai for over 10 years when my friend Will came over to my flat before one of our regular drinking sessions out on the town in Nottingham. I'd known Will for a while as we worked together at KPMG, a firm of chartered accountants. I'd liked his confidence and straight talking from the start. We'd become firm friends and regular drinking partners. Although not an experienced martial artist he had a discipline and strength gained from his time in the Royal Navy. The warm-up drinks on my balcony were the same as any other, but what he showed me that night would change the direction of my life for ever. Matt, Will's brother, had enrolled in the Shudokan Black Belt Academy and had persuaded Will to join him for moral support. They'd not been training long, but Will was keen to try out a move he'd learnt on me. Always keen to experience new things, I agreed. He moved towards me with his hips pivoting and his arms circling across my chest. I didn't understand what he was doing, but I felt my balance go and I stumbled backwards. Will was smaller than me, but despite this he'd taken my power and left me helpless to do anything. He'd done all of this without throwing a punch. *'What was that?'* I asked. *'That's Aikido; you should try it'*, he replied. My Aikido journey had started and within a few weeks I was training with Will and Matt at the Shudokan in Nottingham under *Sensei* Ken Robson (Sensei is the generic word for teacher in Japanese). Aikido fascinated me, particularly how it was possible for somebody much smaller to throw a bigger and more powerful aggressor. Coming from a striking background I found the movements difficult, and no matter how hard I tried I found it impossible to relax. Under Sensei Ken's direction, I worked my way up through the grading syllabus and eventually achieved my *shodan*. For many, the *black belt* is the end goal, but for me it would prove just the beginning.

On the way to attaining my black belt, I was recommended a book called *Angry White Pyjamas* by Robert Twigger. The book had done the rounds in the *dojo* (matted area and place where martial arts are practiced) and was a regular topic of conversation in the changing room before and after class. It was a tale of initiation; one man's journey on one of the toughest martial arts courses in the world. As I turned the pages of the book, the events that unfolded intrigued me along with the characters portrayed in a story of relentless and often brutal training at the *honbu* (sometimes written as hombu) dojo; the *head* dojo in Tokyo, Japan. It sounded horrendous and not something for the faint-hearted, but once again my curiosity was sparked. A fire had been lit, and I knew that at some point I wanted to experience it for myself. The only person I knew who'd trained abroad in traditional martial arts for any length of time was Dan Hardy. Dan and I first met and trained together at Master Lec's. From the start, I knew there was something different about him. With a background in Taekwondo, he'd also spent two months at the Shaolin Temple in China. Dan had a professionalism and seriousness beyond his years. A dedicated student of fighting, he trained with a discipline I'd not seen before. Many years later, ahead of UFC 111 (Ultimate Fighting Championship) and his fight with Georges St-Pierre (GSP) for the Welterweight Title, he'd referenced his Shaolin roots. Despite GSP's habit of sporting white pyjamas, his black belt and a headband adorned with the Japanese flag on his walk to the octagon, it was Dan who claimed an edge. The foundations of traditional martial arts had given him something, and it was something I wanted, too. I'd never been to Japan, but to my mind that didn't matter, I'd survived Thailand, hadn't I? I didn't speak the language, but did that really matter? What was to stop me learning? I couldn't afford it (I'd heard Japan was expensive), but yet again, this didn't worry me. Surely, I'd find a way. The seed was sown and needed to grow. I sold my house, car and other worldly possessions. In May 2005, I arrived at Narita Airport in Tokyo, Japan, to begin my adventure.

TRAIN ON THE TRACK

Imagine your opponent is a train, hurtling towards you at speed. Standing on the track, you have 10 seconds or fewer to decide what to do, or you will end up smashed to a pulp. The Judo practitioner turns in and throws the train over his or her back and walks away unscathed. The Karate expert looks the train straight in the eyes, recoils a fist and fires a superhuman punch into the front of the train, smashing it into a million pieces. The Aikido master steps off the track and lets the train fly past.

Aikido is often described as the way of harmony. Rather than meeting strength with strength, the strategy is to harmonise with an attacker's force and turn this force against the assailant.

AI – harmony.
KI – spirit or energy.
DO – path or way.

Unlike other martial arts, where the aim is to damage or injure an opponent to take away their ability to fight, Aikido practitioners sought to defend themselves without causing injury to their attacker. Though other styles of Aikido may adhere to this principle, from my personal experience, *Yoshinkan* Aikido, which means *a place to cultivate the spirit*, does not. Yoshinkan Aikido with spirit at its core combined the practitioner's technique and power with the strength and energy of an attacker to generate formidable and devastating techniques. It was as tough a style of martial art as any.

Morihei Ueshiba is widely regarded as the founder of Aikido. A man of unparalleled skill and almost supernatural power, he used circular movements to deflect and defeat would-be attackers whatever their size or experience. One of his best students was Gozo Shioda, who was the founding father of Yoshinkan Aikido. Known as *Kancho* (head teacher) his dedication to Aikido led to the creation of the International Yoshinkan Aikido Federation (IYAF). To promote the teaching of Yoshinkan Aikido, Gozo Shioda travelled throughout Japan and taught at police training colleges. His work with the police led to the development of the Senshusei programme for the Tokyo Metropolitan Police in 1957. A rite of passage for police officers looking to advance their careers, this course became popularly known as the Riot Police course. The Riot Police course ran for a gruelling nine months and helped to establish the reputation of Yoshinkan Aikido throughout Japan. Over the years, international visitors to the honbu dojo in Ochiai, Tokyo included boxer Mike Tyson and politician Robert Kennedy, brother of US President JFK. This international recognition helped to spread the message of Yoshinkan Aikido throughout the world. Due to its growing popularity, the IYAF established an 11-month course for international students, who, upon graduation, would be qualified to teach Yoshinkan Aikido in their home countries. The first international Senshusei course began on 4 April 1991 and ran with the Riot Police course. Police and international students trained alongside each other for nine months and when the police went back to full-time duty, the international students stayed on for an additional two months to gain an international teaching licence.

TOKYO DREAMING

Robert Twigger's book had gotten me Tokyo dreaming. What would it be like to train in Japan? Were the stories in the book true? Could I hack a full 11 months of blood, sweat and tears? At 34, I'd had my fair share of hardship. Boarding school had been a tough three years but couldn't really compare to what I imagined Senshusei would be like.

At school I'd enrolled in the CCF (Combined Cadet Force). When I say enrolled, I don't actually mean that, like most things at boarding school, it was compulsory alongside Saturday morning lessons and rugby twice a week. Although CCF had given me some exposure to discipline, it was intermittent and formed only a small part of the school curriculum. I have a vivid memory of falling asleep in a ditch on a 24-hour exercise. It had been a long night, and at 5am, even a cold, damp hole in the ground looked a welcoming place to rest my head. Crack! I woke up to find myself out of the ditch clutching my backside in pain. My slumber had caught the attention of Eddie Fanneran, the head of the CCF. A veteran of the British Army, he'd had most of his teeth blown out while on active service in Northern Ireland. He wasn't a guy to mess with. He'd already taught me how to skin a rabbit and eaten some of my friend's vomit to prove a point!

Although Thailand had taken me away from the UK and landed me firmly in a country and culture I didn't at first understand, it had only been for two weeks, with subsequent visits lasting a similar period. To become Senshusei would involve much more than studying martial arts. I'd have to live and work in a country I'd never visited before and knew very little about. I bought a book entitled *Culture Shock* and read it from cover to cover. It described the cultural differences I'd need to understand and respect if I were to survive and hopefully thrive in Japan. I bought a phrase book and, with the help of an audio CD, began learning and practising Japanese words and phrases that I hoped would help me make a good first impression. I practiced whenever I could. *Konichi wa* (hello), *arigatou gozaimasu* (thank you), *sumimasen* (excuse me) and *wakarimasen* (I don't understand).

Working in financial recruitment, I'd done well. It was hard work, but in a buoyant market and with no cap on earnings, I'd accumulated bonuses that I'd put aside for a rainy day. Until you're truly committed and there's no way back, it's easy to talk yourself out of any situation. I quit my job and brought the rainy day forward to train full-time in Aikido in the UK. This experiment, conducted on a much smaller scale over a few months, would tell me if I was cut out for Japan and also give me time to plan my trip. Leaving paid employment was terrifying. Without money coming in, there was only money going out, and like the fuel gauge on my car I watched it tick down with each passing day. I threw myself into Aikido and trained every class I could at the Shudokan. As the school continued to expand Sensei Ken brought over two black belts from Poland to help with the teaching. I'd first met Michal and Sebastian a year before at the week-long summer school held in Nottingham. Aikido is popular in Poland and Michal, Seb and several other Polish black belts had made the journey to the UK, where they represented in force. The Poles were tough and showcased an intensity in their Aikido I'd not seen before. As they arrived in England with little understanding of the English language and acclimatising to new surroundings, I immediately recognised the parallel with my proposed trip to Japan and sympathised with their situation. Away from their family and friends, Michal and Seb taught most of the classes. Through very broken English, they communicated instructions, but it was their powerful movements in Aikido that did the real talking. Always on the mats, I got to know both of them very well. We became friends and agreed to train together during the day while the Shudokan was officially closed. The deal was that I would teach them Muay Thai, and in return, they'd share their personal and extremely effective style of Aikido with me. I'd arrive early most mornings to teach them Thai Boxing. Skipping, pad drills, techniques and sparring to me were second nature by now, but for Michal and Seb, it was a new experience. As they were experts in Aikido, I'd put them both on a pedestal. Their techniques were fluid, powerful and beautiful to watch. Now, studying something less familiar, they were more awkward, clunky and, for the first time in my eyes at least, looked like regular human beings. After an hour of Muay Thai we switched roles, and it was my turn to look awkward. With determination, though, slowly and surely, I got better and better, not just in technique, but in mindset, too. I'd sensed that Michal was into the spiritual side of Aikido. The shape of his movements looked the same as Seb's, but something was different. An energy, a force from within, an intense focus – I had no idea what it was, but he had it in spades, and it rubbed off on me.

Having established his reputation in the dojo, Sensei Michal set up a special class. This class took place on Friday nights and was invitation only. The dojo had two floors and two matted areas. A narrow staircase sealed by a door at the bottom accessed the top floor. Up in the rafters of the building was a private area hidden away from the more accessible training hall and reception desk downstairs. Michal's idea, I would later realise, was to create an environment that resembled in part what it was like to train in Japan and specifically on the Riot Police course. Sensei Michal hadn't done the course, but I knew he'd read lots about it.

There were two rules:

17

1) The class lasted an hour and no matter what, you couldn't leave until it finished.

2) Whatever you were told to do, you had to do.

Climbing the stairs to this class late on a Friday evening, I was always scared. The training was intense and often involved repetitive and painful exercises followed by equally painful techniques. It was the class you dreaded but also the one you never wanted to miss.

I continued to train with Michal and Seb, and eventually I was ready to take my shodan test under the watchful eye of Sensei Ken. The test was tough. I'd landed awkwardly the week before. Thrown by Sensei Michal, I'd injured my left shoulder. My left collarbone visibly protrudes and has sat higher than my right since then. During the live knife section of the exam Sensei Ken produced the most terrifying knife I'd ever seen. It was more suited to John Rambo in *First Blood* and when he handed it to my partner I nearly fainted. I cut my finger during a disarm technique and heart pumping, bled all over the mats. The test had to be temporarily stopped while they were cleaned. I'd done it. I was finally a black belt, but although I'd achieved my goal, there was a nagging thought in the back of my mind that I just couldn't seem to shake off. I hadn't got my shodan in Japan, and I'd not yet trained with the legendary masters I'd read about in *Angry White Pyjamas*. I'd not yet become Senshusei!

IT'S ALL IN THE SMALL PRINT

With the Riot Police course, you couldn't just turn up and expect to join in. You had to apply and be selected. I'd read the advice on the Yoshinkan honbu dojo website, and I don't mind admitting it made me nervous. Rather than being a sales pitch for the course, the narrative seemed to do everything in its power to dissuade anyone from ever doing it. Was this its aim or clever marketing to make it sound more exclusive and appealing? I wasn't sure and had no way of telling!

Extracts from the application information read:

1) *The intent of this information is to enable prospective Senshusei to make a more informed decision about whether to come to Japan and take the course.*

18

2) *There are limits to the number of applicants we can accept. Applicants will be chosen based on their essay and the effort they have made to involve themselves in the Yoshinkan Aikido community.*

3) *Before coming to Japan and commencing the Senshusei course, it's very important to seriously consider what you are about to undertake.*

4) *The course is designed to be very exacting, both physically and mentally, so correct preparations are necessary.*

5) *The cost of living in Japan is very high. As a bare minimum you will need 250,000 Yen* (at the time c.£1,250) *per month to live.*

6) *Try and obtain a reasonable level of fitness. The first month is particularly difficult physically.*

7) *You will need to apply for a Tourist Visa. Once you've demonstrated the necessary commitment, the honbu dojo will assist you in obtaining a Cultural Visa from within Japan.*

8) *Be aware that there is a high dropout rate.*

9) *Remember that you will be living in a foreign country with different food and a different lifestyle from what you are used to. You may suffer from culture shock for a period of time.*

10) *You are advised to think carefully before committing yourself. Consider the level of commitment, the level of fitness and, in your own mind, whether you are mature enough to participate in such a specialised course.*

11) *Trainees are required to pay a monthly tuition fee of 26,000 Yen* (at the time c.£135) *upon entering the course.*

12) *The course is very demanding, physically, mentally and emotionally. Try to be in good physical condition (with special emphasis on cardiovascular training). You should try to improve your flexibility in your hips, knees, ankles, shoulders and wrists. You will also need to work on having a strong lower body and at the same time having*

soft and relaxed knees. Mental preparation is probably the most important. You need to prepare yourself, to train hard and push yourself every day.

13) *The training at the honbu dojo is hard. Most people will never have done anything like it before. Even if at your home dojo you have hard practice a few times a week, it probably will not compare with hard practice four hours a day, five days a week for 11 months. The course is truly gruelling, especially over the long run. It is expected that you push yourself to what you believe is your limit and then push yourself further.*

14) *As Senshusei you are expected to train harder, respond quicker, listen, watch and train more intensely than any other student. You are expected to show strong spirit and to try to increase your spirit through training. You are expected to follow commands given immediately and without question. When given a command or feedback on any matter the correct response is osu!*

15) *The Japanese tend to be well dressed wherever they are, if you tend to dress down you may find you are a little out of place. It is not appropriate to come to the dojo looking like a bum.*

Also, the application process was very specific in requesting the following documentation:

1) *Personal history, including education and work experience.*

2) *Letter of introduction from a Yoshinkan Aikido instructor or person of authority, including contact address and phone number.*

3) *Letter explaining the reason for making the application to be handwritten by the applicant.*

4) *Signed application form.*

And just in case I was in any doubt: *Acceptance as a trainee does not guarantee graduation.* This was no belt factory. From the information I'd digested, Senshusei would be no easy ride.

20

NOW TO NARITA

I'd left England shortly after achieving my Shudokan black belt with a plan to get to Japan and see what it was like, before committing to 11 months of intense training. Sensei Michal had given me a parting gift. His *dogi* (a traditional uniform, similar in look to pyjamas and compulsory wear for martial arts practice) top and a book called *Training with the Master, Lessons with Morihei Ueshiba, Founder of Aikido.* Inside he'd inscribed the words, *Aikido and life are one. For Simon, a great martial artist, student and friend that I was lucky to meet. All the best in the future! With deepest respect, Michal, osu!* It was a nice touch and it meant a lot. He'd signed off with, *PS: ENJOY THE FLIGHT!* This had a double meaning. I'd previously asked Sensei Michal how to fall safely from a particular throw. With a deadly serious look on his face, he'd advised, *'you can't, just enjoy the flight!'* I was humbled and felt it should have been him. Sensei Michal should be flying out to Japan, not me!

I'd not yet completed the application process to join the course, and I still wasn't sure if it was what I wanted to do or whether I even had a chance of being accepted. Although I had a black belt in Aikido, I'd not been taught in a Yoshinkan school. Martial arts can be political, and I knew I'd struggle with the letter of introduction, required as part of the application process. Just as I'd turned up in Thailand with a photo of Tony, I was reliant again on a path trodden before me by others. But this time I had no such introduction, and this posed a very real problem. This in part had fuelled my decision to leave for Japan ahead of applying. It was also the safer option. If I committed to Senshusei I'd be living in the country for a year, so it was better to find out beforehand if I liked it. I'd initially planned to be in Japan for only six months. Tokyo was a stopover on the way to Australia. One application I'd already done successfully was an Immigration Visa to the Land Down Under. I knew I could delay arriving in Australia. It was fairly flexible on my first date of entry. This meant Japan was open-ended. Provided I met the visa requirements I could extend my stay, which would give me the option to join the course.

Arriving at Narita International Airport in Tokyo was an amazing experience. For the first time in my life, I was without baggage, apart from what I'd squeezed into my backpack. It was the most liberated I'd felt in a very long time. Approaching my mid-thirties, I was free from the constraints of modern life. No mortgage, no job and nothing much to worry about apart from what would happen next. The plan was simple. Find somewhere to stay and find the dojo. I knew I'd also need to find a job at some point, but that could come later. Having found a hostel for the first night, I went to sleep full of excitement, mixed with a good helping of trepidation. I'd exchanged my country of birth for one I knew very little about. It looked different, it smelt different, and even the simplest of tasks were now hugely complicated because of the language barrier.

I remember entering the honbu dojo for the very first time on Thursday, 2 June 2005. I'd watched several documentaries on Aikido filmed within its walls, but now in person it seemed less familiar than I thought it would. I'd only seen footage filmed inside and had imagined entering a traditional Japanese building. The reality was very different, which was one reason it took me so long to find it. A short walk from Ochiai Station, the international headquarters of Yoshinkan Aikido was located on the third floor of an ordinary-looking office building. Aikido Yoshinkan Honbu Dojo, 2-28-8 Kamiochiai, Shinjuku-ku, Tokyo 161, Japan was an address I'd memorised, but the only clue to its whereabouts was the Japanese calligraphy on the windows, which spelt out AI-KI-DO. I took the lift. The first and only time they allowed me to use it. As the doors opened, a chest-high bust of Kancho Gozo Shioda immediately greeted me. I could already hear the rumblings from inside the dojo and the cries of *'osu'* (the standard response to any instruction, request or in response to feedback, used in traditional Japanese martial arts to confirm understanding and obedience), as the students on the mats gratefully received instruction. I was in no doubt I was in the right place. I removed my shoes and made myself known to the office. I'd arranged to meet Murray Sensei. Canadian by birth, he now lived and worked in Japan and was the international liaison for visiting *Aikidoka* (a practitioner of Aikido). We sat down in the tearoom and engaged in polite chit-chat for a few minutes. I explained I was in Japan to experience Aikido in its birthplace and was interested in learning more about the Senshusei course. I'd expected a grilling, given the seriousness and formality of the information I'd previously read, but Murray Sensei was very relaxed and suggested I enrol in the morning *ippan* (regular or general) classes. I'd be training on the same mats as the current Senshusei intake, but with the ability to watch from a safe distance.

And so, it began. I'd signed up, purchased a dogi and officially joined the Yoshinkan honbu dojo. I was back the next day for my very first class. The black belt they had awarded me in England was gone and I donned a white belt again. This was Yoshinkan Aikido, and although many of the movements looked the same as the ones I'd learnt at the Shudokan, it was back to the beginning for me. A summer camp was scheduled to take place on Friday, 10 June 2005 and run for three days. Chida Sensei, Takeno Sensei and Inoue Kancho were scheduled to teach, and the three-day excursion was something I just had to do. Having only just arrived in Tokyo I boarded the bus to Chiba Kujukurihama Shirasatokaigan Taiyou Sports Centre full of nervous anticipation. I might have been new to the honbu, but Chida, Takeno and Inoue were names I knew of old. The timing of my arrival in Japan was perfect. This wasn't just any old weekend away, this was the 50th Anniversary Gasshuku. *Gasshuku* was the Japanese word for *training camp* and this camp marked 50 years since Yoshinkan Aikido was founded. On Friday we trained under Chida Sensei. I had to pinch myself to make sure I wasn't dreaming; but this was no dream. My ambition to come to Japan and learn from the best was now a reality. In the evening there was a dinner and party. Not a party like I knew back home. It was more of a formal get together that involved lots of kneeling, bowing and drinking! Chida Sensei was present and, positioning myself in close proximity, he asked me, *'why do you have short hair? You look like a convict and I bet your Mum doesn't like it!'* A bit taken aback and possibly a little star-struck, I responded. *'It's good for training Sensei. My hair doesn't get in the way!'* As I was now officially in dialogue, I took the opportunity to ask the best question I could come up with on the spur of the moment. *'Sensei, what is the most important thing in Aikido for a beginner?'* Chida contemplated, reflected and responded with one word. *'Kamae!'* On Saturday, after a morning with Chida, it was Takeno's turn to teach. I liked his style and took as many videos on my digital camera as its memory card would allow. His principal uke threw me with a technique that looked vaguely familiar from my Shudokan days and her power was incredible. At night there was another dinner and party where Inoue Kancho invited questions. Seizing this golden opportunity, I went first. *'Sensei, what is your most memorable moment from your time in Aikido?'* I waited in eager anticipation for his response. As a direct student of Kancho Gozo Shioda I hoped he'd share a story about training under Yoshinkan's founder; I wasn't disappointed. He recalled a particularly punishing class as an *uchi-deshi* (inside / live-in student) when he was in his twenties and Gozo Shioda was in his forties. *'I had to rush to the back of the dojo to be sick out of a small window!'* On Sunday we trained with Inoue Kancho before heading back to Tokyo. I shook his hand and he wished me a safe trip back. On the return bus I reflected on the three days just gone. I'd trained with the masters I'd previously only read about or watched on video. The gasshuku had drawn an international audience from Malaysia, Canada, Russia, Ukraine, Australia, Japan, and with my presence, England. During the three days, I'd regularly chatted with a guy called Curtis Seeger from Canada.

He'd previously made the decision to do the Senshusei course. Back in Tokyo, I'd soon have my own decision to make.

It was great to be finally training in Japan, but after the gasshuku and back at the honbu dojo I found the classes boring. Training with the regular students was slow, and in many of the classes, I barely broke a sweat. Time with Sensei Michal back in Nottingham had prepared me well, and I realised quickly that I was training in the wrong class at the wrong end of the dojo. The current Senshusei trained on the same mats but at the far end of the training hall. The ippan class seemed tame and quiet compared to the twisting, throwing and incessant cries emanating from the far side of the room. In the regular class we shared the same mats, but that was where the similarities ended. Senshusei was a different level. The honbu also offered *kenshu* classes as something in the middle, but from what I'd seen there was still too much standing around. Described as 'intensive' they were more concerned with diving into the detail of a technique than physical exertion. Ippan was undergraduate, kenshu postgraduate and Senshusei the School of Hard Knocks. Kenshu wasn't for me and if the ippan class was a family four-door, Senshusei was the Ferrari I now longed to drive. My decision was made. I spoke with Murray Sensei and primed myself for the arduous application process. It turned out, though, because I was already in Japan, much of the formality was no longer required. Technically, I now had the introduction I needed from the Yoshinkan honbu dojo itself.

I'd now found a flat in Musashi Koyama, a small suburb a short train ride out of central Tokyo and was slowly settling into my new surroundings. The flat was basic and a far cry from the mod cons I was used to back in England. It comprised one room divided down the middle by a pull-across screen, a tiny bathroom and an even smaller kitchen. There was no bed, and in true Japanese style, I slept on a *futon* (a traditional Japanese bed), essentially a mattress on the floor which was rolled out at night and put away again in the morning to save space. Life was basic but good, and with lots to keep me occupied I rarely missed home.

April was fast approaching and with the rainy-day fund running short, it was time to find a job. The pressure to secure gainful employment was not only financial, it was also motivated by a need to stay in the country. My Tourist Visa didn't permit an extended stay, and from chatting with the current Senshusei, the promise of a Cultural Visa via the honbu dojo seemed unlikely. Most were teaching English to support themselves and received sponsorship to stay in Japan as part of the deal.

I asked around and was introduced to Berlitz, an international language school with lots of teaching locations in Tokyo. After two meetings and some compulsory form filling, I was officially employed and assigned to the Sangenjaya school. Most *gaijin* (foreigner or non-Japanese) I met were teaching English. The *Culture Shock* book I'd read while Tokyo dreaming contained a stark warning early in its pages. *Remember, Japan is for the Japanese, it's not for you.* This was sound advice and even for gaijin I met with a command of the Japanese language it appeared the only job available was teaching English.

One way round the visa issue was to leave the country every 90 days. A 24-hour trip to South Korea was a route well-travelled by foreign nationals, but the Japanese authorities were getting wise to this loophole, and the chances of obtaining a Tourist Visa again and again without question was fast becoming a thing of the past. Berlitz provided the paperwork that would keep me in the country long enough to complete the course, providing I did a good job and remained in their gainful employment. I was now set up. I had a place to stay, a visa to live in the country and a job to pay the bills. I was becoming acclimatised and by now could even navigate the Tokyo train system without a map.

Senshusei grew nearer, and with each passing day, I felt a growing sense of inevitability. There was no escape, and as if guilty of a crime and now awaiting trial and sentence, each day was becoming increasingly precious. It was at about this time I wrote a letter (a copy can be found near the end of the book). Words have power, and although I didn't know it, the words in this letter would change the recipient's life for ever. Matt had also trained under Sensei Ken back in England. Despite being younger than me, we'd got on well, and he shared my passion for martial arts. The more I thought about it, the more I was convinced that Matt should do the course. Sure, he could carry on training in England, but here was an opportunity to experience Aikido in its country of origin. Also, there's often perceived safety in numbers, and with Matt on the course, too, the prospect of doing it would feel a lot more comfortable. My letter explained how I was loving Japan and sold the idea of joining me on the course. Having posted the letter, I didn't give it another thought. Upping sticks and moving to the other side of the world was something I'd done, but this didn't mean it was for everyone. I didn't have to wait too long to hear from Matt. He was game and, like me, prepared to turn what for many would be a pipe dream into a reality. I put him in touch with the dojo and helped him secure accommodation. I reassured him that finding a job would be easy and would be the best way to secure his visa.

. I was loving Japan but decided to take a couple of breaks. On the east side of the world, Tokyo's Narita International Airport provided cheap flights and easy access. After a visit from my sister Sally, a trip to Nikko to see the Toshogu Shrine and pretending I was a Samurai (traditional Japanese warrior) at Edo Wonderland (a Samurai theme park), in October 2005 I boarded a plane to Thailand. I checked in to my usual accommodation, the Pathumwan Princess Hotel, with its luxurious rooftop swimming pool and views of the city. I visited the Grand Palace, the Temple of the Reclining Buddha and my favourite, the Temple of Dawn on Bangkok's Chao Phraya river. I trained three times at the Bangkok Fight Club before heading west and switching hotels to the less salubrious Viengtai Hotel, in the busy Banglampu area, which was much nearer the river and most of the action. I was in Thailand for a very specific reason. I was meeting Kru Tony and joining his Tracking the Warrior Tour. It was Tony who had first paved my way to train in Thailand and now I was excited to join him and other Muay Thai enthusiasts for some deep immersion in training, culture and history. In Bangkok we fitted in two afternoons at Sasiprapa Muay Thai Gym run by Master Thakoon. The heat was intense and after only a few rounds on the pads and heavy bag my energy levels were depleted. We then travelled north of Bangkok to Ayutthaya, Thailand's original capital city, and alternated two training days at the Sit-Palan Gym, run by Kru Lang who I'd previously met at Sitsiam in the UK, with a day at Buddhai Swan to study Krabi Krabong (Thai weapons). Kru Tony had broadened his study of Thai martial arts under Arjarn Samai. In the same year I started my study of Muay Thai under Kru Tony, he'd began his study at Buddhai Swan under 'Por Kru'. Being in Thailand with Tony was an amazing experience and one I had been determined not to miss.

In the spring of 2006, I took some time out again. An adventure and holiday before the course; I visited Australia, New Zealand and Thailand. In Australia I met up with former colleagues, Ben and Mandy, from KPMG, strolled across the golden sands of Bondi Beach and visited Ramsay Street, the set of the TV show *Neighbours* (a programme I'd grown up watching). To keep my hand in and in preparation for the start of the course, I trained under Sensei Joe Thambu at his Thornbury and Oakleigh dojos. In Auckland I cycled along the waterfront and to One Tree Hill. In Thailand I met up with Rob, one of my Thai Boxing friends from back home. We went ringside at Lumpinee Stadium and met Muay Thai legends, Saenchai and Samkor, backstage and also trained at Sasiprapa. It was Rob's first time in Thailand, and he wasn't quite sure what to expect. We arrived at Sasiprapa for afternoon training and began skipping. Heavy ropes and Thailand's heat didn't mix well and after five minutes Rob was flagging. *'Why is no one coming to teach us?'* Rob didn't understand what was going on. Accustomed to the ways of Thailand and after my recent visit, I urged him on. *'Keep going mate, they're watching to see if we're worth teaching!'* I was right. After 20 minutes the trainers emerged and took us in turn on the pads.

Later on, we watched fights at Rajadamnern Stadium and travelled out of Bangkok to pay our respects at the Kanchanaburi War Cemetery. Now living in Japan, it was chilling to be in a place that had seen so much suffering at the hands of the Japanese. During the Second World War, Japanese forces used prisoners of war and civilian labour to build a railway between Burma (now Myanmar) and Thailand. Sickness, malnutrition, exhaustion and mistreatment cost the lives of 15,000 prisoners and 100,000 civilians. I now found myself walking across the Bridge on the River Kwai; a place of untold suffering. After Kanchanaburi we travelled up to Chiang Mai in the northern part of Thailand to train at Lanna Muay Thai. It was a very different experience to Sasiprapa. Too many farang diluted the authentic feel of a pure Thai camp and one day was enough. Stepping out of our comfort zones, Rob and I did a day of cooking at the Chiang Mai Thai Cookery School. My diet in Japan had already gotten a little boring, so the plan was to develop some new skills for my return. We did some rest and recovery in Koh Samui and then flew back to the UK to see family and friends. With Senshusei looming, I didn't know when I'd next get the chance. Dad and I had a trip to London to take in the sights. A keen artist, Dad was eager to visit Tate Modern. A room full of polystyrene cubes wasn't art! The modern stuff didn't quite cut it and once again I found myself craving tradition; the tradition I'd found in Japan. The time passed quickly, and before I knew it, Matt and I met at Heathrow Airport. It was my return to Tokyo and Matt's maiden voyage. With the course starting soon, for both of us, it was the point of no return!

TALKING JAPANESE

Japanese is one of the most difficult languages to learn. There are three alphabets. *Kanji* (adopted Chinese characters), *hiragana* (used to write Japanese words for which there are no kanji) and *katakana* (for foreign words that fall outside of the kanji and hiragana convention). Then add into the mix romaji (Roman letters used to write Japanese) for those who can't read kanji, hiragana or katakana. On top of this, where you sit in society determines how you are spoken to. There are variations in the words and structure of language depending on your seniority and hierarchical positioning. As if things couldn't get any more complicated, there is dojo language, the words and phrases specific to Aikido and other Japanese martial arts. Some of these words, including Sensei, Sewanin and dogi in certain sentences, might seem like they should be pluralised. As the singular is the same as the plural version in Japanese, I've stuck to this convention throughout the book. Although this book isn't intended to teach you Japanese, a few basics are essential. All the Japanese words and phrases in this book appear in italics on first mention, along with a brief explanation. You will have already found and will continue to find this moving forwards. The word or phrase, if regularly cited or deemed important, can also be found at the end of the book in what I've termed the dojo dictionary. To make life easy for you (and for me, too), I've stuck to the romaji!

If you're planning to visit Japan, the 2003 film *Lost in Translation* starring Bill Murray and Scarlett Johansson is compulsory viewing. The pair form an unusual alliance to explore Tokyo, and they experience confusion and hilarity because of cultural and language differences. Throughout Japan, they teach English in schools and a large proportion of the population have a good grasp of it. It's common to be stopped in the street and offered help with directions – a valuable opportunity for your helper to practice his or her English. At the honbu dojo it was a different story. While the international instructors taught in English, the Japanese instructors made sure they taught in their native tongue. Shortly after arriving in Tokyo and having struggled with the language barrier, I'd enrolled in Japanese lessons. In the beginning these were classroom-based at Sendagaya Japanese Institute under Kato Sensei and then at MLC (Meguro Language Centre) under the guidance of Hotta Sensei. Having completed the introductory course at MLC, I'd asked Hotta Sensei to teach me privately. She'd agreed, and now once a week I made the trip to her house to take instruction. At Berlitz they did all teaching in English. They permitted no Japanese when communicating with Japanese students attending class. This was an easy rule for me to follow, as although I had some knowledge of Japanese, I had very little ability to speak it! The teaching style at Berlitz was total immersion, and it seemed to work. Hotta Sensei followed suit, and although her English was good, from the moment I arrived at her house until the moment I left, it was Japanese all the way. I'd expected that having a basic understanding of Japanese would help me on the course, and I would soon be proved right. Taking instruction would be difficult enough, but not understanding the instructions in the first place would make life at the honbu dojo much more difficult.

THE SECRET DIARY OF A SENSHUSEI

On the course it was compulsory to keep a diary, as a record of our training and all we learned. This was the official diary, the one we had to hand in at the end of every month to be signed off and graded by our superiors (you'll find my scores and feedback near the end of the book). Besides the technical elements of what we were learning, we were also encouraged to document what we were thinking and feeling. What I would think while on the course and how I imagined I would feel were not things I was comfortable sharing. Doing so, I thought, would be a dangerous strategy and potentially open me up to questioning and punishment I could do without. In part to protect my sanity, and also because I thought it would be interesting to look back, I kept a personal and very private diary. This was my record of what really went on – the good, the bad and the ugly! It was how I saw things then and not necessarily how I see things now. It remains pure, untainted and unaltered by the passage of time. It was a place for my innermost thoughts, a medium to download the day and free my mind in the hope of being able to get some sleep. The instructors never saw this diary, and no one to date has seen it, either. It's my record of what happened and a personal account of day-to-day life on one of the toughest martial arts courses in the world.

My intention was never to write a book, and I've debated long and hard whether to share my story – and now, having decided to do just that, how best to present my record of life on the course. Should I present things as a story or remain true to the diary format? *Angry White Pyjamas* told the story of the course, but in my opinion, not the details of the day-to-day grind, which is part of what being a Senshusei is all about. To give a complete and authentic insight into life on the course, to a degree I've respected the diary format and share my story chronologically as I wrote it, subject to a bit of spit and polish and some careful editing. Each heading highlights a key story or event in that particular segment. The diary starts a few days before the course officially began and culminates with the graduation day. It contains the ups and downs, the highs and lows, the sheer torment and hilarious humour that were all part of this life-changing experience I will never forget. For the first time, I tell the story of Senshusei like it's never been told before!

THE CALM BEFORE THE STORM

3...READY...

Three days to go until the start of the course. In the early hours of Wednesday, 29 March 2006, I found myself awake. It was 2am and I couldn't get back to sleep. I put it down to jet lag from the long flight back from the UK, but I also knew that although I might not want to admit it to myself, I was worried. Fear of the unknown is the worst fear of all, and apprehension about the start of the Senshusei course was kicking in. Although I'd seen the 15th Senshusei train and now graduate, watching from the stands would be a very different experience to playing on the pitch. Anyone can be an armchair warrior full of advice for those who have skin in the game, and soon I'd have a lot of skin in a game I'd never played before. Tiredness eventually kicked in, and on my journey back to full unconsciousness, I was rudely awoken by my alarm. The start of another day in Tokyo had arrived and with it another opportunity to do my best to prepare physically and mentally for the start of the course. After a quick shower, a hurried bowl of porridge and some Japanese verb practice, I packed my Aikido dogi into my bag in preparation for the day ahead.

After a short walk from my apartment to Musashi Koyama Station I jumped on the train to Meguro and then picked up the JR Yamanote Line north to meet Matt at Takadanobaba before catching the subway to Ochiai. This wasn't my first trip to the honbu – far from it. I'd been training in the ippan classes for months. But today after two months away and with the start of the course imminent, alongside Matt, I stepped into the honbu dojo with an increased level of fear. Everything felt more serious than it had done before. In signing up for the course I'd crossed a line and there was now no turning back.

In the locker room, my allocated Senshusei locker was ready and waiting. Previously I'd pick any locker that was free, but now a specific locker bearing my name was more evidence that things were different. My former

Shudokan dogi felt good but despite my best efforts I'd been unable to get rid of the red outline of the Shudokan badge, which now at the Yoshinkan I'd had to remove. I was confident I'd get away with it today but was sure that punishment would be on the cards if I turned up to my first Senshusei class in a discoloured dogi.

On the mats there were other soon-to-be Senshusei in town. Like Matt and me, to show willing and get into the swing of things, there were three guys from Israel, one from the United States and Dave from the Isle of Man, whom I'd met before. Higa Sensei, one of the Japanese instructors, took the class, and we reviewed *kamae* (ready position or fighting stance), *seiza* (kneeling position) and *rei* (bowing), in addition to what I'd already learned was a painful exercise, *shikko ho* (knee walking). I paired up with Carlos from Mexico, one of the ippan students; we'd trained together several times before. Although I was training with Carlos, I found myself going through the motions. All I was interested in doing was catching a glimpse of my soon-to-be comrades and getting a gauge on their skills and abilities. I was back in the warm-up area again ahead of a Muay Thai fight trying to spot strengths and more importantly weaknesses, I could exploit when the bell rang. Everyone looked to have some previous Aikido knowledge and Dave's technique had come on lots since he'd started training in the regular classes. When he'd first arrived in Japan, he'd never trained in Aikido before but now looked to have made at least some progress. The Israeli guys, Ronen, Dror and Boaz looked like they knew what they were doing and with Aikido big in Israel I suspected they were all at a decent level. Similarly, Clyde from the United States looked to have some experience, too. I did a double take; it couldn't be could it? From the back Clyde sporting a black ponytail looked like Steven Seagal's illegitimate son! I'd heard from the previous year's Senshusei that the worst place to find yourself on the course was at the bottom of the group. Still confused by the differences between the Shudokan and Yoshinkan, Matt and I were nervous.

After the class we chatted with Ronen, Dror, Boaz and Clyde in the locker room where a rumour was circulating that two people would arrive on Saturday who had never done Aikido. Saturday signalled the start of the course, and with no Aikido experience and having never set foot in the honbu dojo before the two new arrivals would no doubt face a rude awakening! This made me feel better. I remembered how hard getting started in Aikido had been, particularly the *ukemi* (how to fall properly and safely). My lack of specific Yoshinkan knowledge suddenly seemed a nice problem to have. At least I could take a fall. These late entrants would have to get up to speed quickly or risk injury. It looked like Matt and I wouldn't be at the bottom of the pecking order.

After getting changed, we congregated in the tearoom and met Avry from last year's course, sporting his black belt. From what I'd seen, the *Sewanin* (prior-year Senshusei graduates who stay on to manage and discipline the current year) had singled him out and made his life hell for most of the year. Given some classes and punishments I'd seen him endure, I'd no idea how he'd got through. Another native of Israel, Avry was tough, with from what I could gather, a background in the fighting arts of his home country. Despite his martial arts heritage, he'd still struggled, and as I congratulated him on his shodan and getting through the course, he hardly acknowledged me. I didn't take it personally and wondered if he couldn't bring himself to look me in the eyes, knowing the pain and torment I was about to embark on, or maybe as one of the new intakes I wasn't worthy of his attention anymore. At the honbu I'd already seen hierarchy play out everywhere, and perhaps it was now my turn to be on the receiving end?

As we chatted Malik entered the room, and after the compulsory *'osu'* all round, he told Ronen, Dror, Boaz, Clyde, Matt and me that we needed to practice. *'Your osu needs to be louder and in time!'* Malik, like Avry, had graduated from the course just finished and had stayed on as Sewanin. The Sewanin sat between the Sensei and Senshusei, and beginning Saturday, would manage our every moment at the honbu to ensure we would all toe the line. Malik was keen to start early, and the friendliness I'd seen as an ippan student had morphed into formality. I was sure it was a sign of things to come and the very different experience I was about to have. The Senshusei were the lowest form of life at the honbu dojo, lower than any other living being. We'd already been told this in no uncertain terms. A new student walking through the door for the very first time, even with no previous Aikido experience, had a higher status. The Sewanin would be the militaristic enforcement squad that would make sure we always knew our place. I already suspected that the bullied would become the bully and that Malik would have a point to prove this year.

Paul, another former Senshusei, last year's Sewanin and now an official Sensei, arrived and took us into the room just off the dojo that the Riot Police would use as their private quarters when they arrived. Several new faces had turned up for this meeting, and we all kneeled in seiza for the best part of 40 minutes while Paul Sensei ran through the International Senshusei Handbook. There had been a similar meeting on Saturday, which Matt and I had missed on account of us not being in the country. This was to be my first taste of an extended period of seiza and judging by the uncomfortable looks on everybody else's faces, Saturday's introduction hadn't done much to get them prepared. You could feel a storm was coming. Paul Sensei was nice, but as Ronen put it later, *'you could tell that in a few days we'll all be fucked!'* Nobody appeared to be listening with the pain from the kneeling position searing through all of our legs. When it was finally over, I could hardly feel my feet. Paul advised that the only safe way to recover without risking permanent injury was to fall to one side to free our legs, and only when the blood returned to our extremities should we gradually straighten them out. After five minutes lying on my side in what best could be described as the foetal position, I was finally ready to walk again! Overwhelmed by our new surroundings it wasn't clear if one guy quit. I didn't see him again and would find out at a later date that his induction to dojo life had caused him to go AWOL for a week. The story goes that his family and friends didn't know where he was. He went missing in action in Tokyo and much to the relief of the honbu, eventually turned up safe.

Everyone was already on my case. I'd had enough of my pre-course taster and put my coat on, threw my bag over my shoulder and headed for the exit. On my way out I ran into Higa Sensei, who had taught the morning class. *'No coat in the dojo, take it off and put it on outside'*, he cautioned. *'No bags to be carried on shoulders, do what you like outside, but not in here!'* This was definitely a sign of things to come and until I got used to the rules and regulations that applied only to the Senshusei, life would be difficult. I finally escaped and put my coat back on. Matt and I decided we'd head over to Jonathan's restaurant, a Senshusei favourite just up the road from the honbu. We chatted about the others we'd met earlier on that morning and wagered on who we thought had the stuff to make it to the end of the course. Pizza, pasta and the unlimited drinks bar went down well. With only a few days to the start, it didn't really matter what we ate. Anything now would burn off quickly, and a serious dose of carbohydrate loading seemed the sensible option.

Matt and I parted company, and while he went off to sort out his Alien Registration Card, which all gaijin were required to carry, I headed home. Anyone intending to stay in Japan for over 90 days had to get one. If you wanted to get a mobile phone or open a bank account, you had to have one. When I'd learnt I'd have to get one on arrival in Tokyo, I'd smiled at the thought of being termed an 'alien'. What a strange way to welcome long-term visitors to the country – by inadvertently suggesting they came from outer space! We'd agreed to meet up later at Axis. Not only had I roped Matt into joining the course, I'd also persuaded him to start Jiu Jitsu. At the end of the formal class we got into pairs and rolled. Free sparring was the bit I really enjoyed – the opportunity to see if I could catch an unwitting opponent in an arm-bar, triangle or similar. Having been away for a while, I felt rusty and took a hammering from one or two of the senior grades, which resulted in a nice bruise above my left eye. *Oh shit*, I thought to myself, *how am I going to explain that one at training tomorrow?* Axis stood for A-ction, X-perience, I-ntelligence and S-piritualism; all things we'd need in abundance once Senshusei started.

2...STEADY...

Two days to go until the start of the course. Thursday played out in a similar fashion to Wednesday. I didn't really feel like going to the honbu, and I didn't have to. The thought of the others getting ahead of the game before Saturday's start, though, was a thought I just couldn't bear. At the dojo the theme of today's class was ukemi. I thought I was pretty good at it already, having spent many hours in the UK practicing and perfecting, but the difference now was the hardness of the mats. The mats back at the Shudokan had been soft and inviting, but at the honbu landing on concrete would have probably provided a more comfortable fall. I'd now have to re-learn ukemi. It was no longer about my ability to fall safely; more serious now, I'd need to master the art of falling without killing myself. The hardest type of fall for those new to ukemi was the infamous flip. The flip was a somersault where you had to spring upwards and forwards on both feet to catapult your legs directly over your head, with the aim of landing safely on your side on the mats. All good in theory, but if done wrong, it was one of the quickest and easiest ways to get injured. Panic mid-flight and you'd land on your head, which could mean a one-way ticket to the hospital with a suspected broken neck or collarbone. Dave hadn't yet mastered the art of the flip and on every attempt, hit the mats with a deafening thud. Clyde and the Israeli guys seemed to cope better, but Dave already looked to be in trouble. The harder he tried, the worse it got, and the more he seemed to wince in pain. The more it hurt, the more he seized up ahead of his landing. In order to not hurt, the fall had to be done relaxed, and although Dave knew this, his body just wouldn't play ball.

After the class was over, we congregated in the tearoom where we were taught how to tie our belts the Senshusei way. A lesson in *origami* (the practice of folding) the Senshusei knot was supposed to be unbreakable and a physical representation of what we'd be by the end of the course. You couldn't break the knot just as you weren't supposed to be able to break a Senshusei. It seemed the two were inextricably linked. To protect Clyde from getting broken, Matt and I discreetly had a word. We'd seen a similar scenario play out back home and as Clyde seemed like a nice guy, we didn't want him to suffer the same fate. We told him about a guy from the Shudokan who had a ponytail and got smashed because of it. Like a red rag to a bull everyone seemed to go that little bit harder to make it flap in the air with the force of their throws. Clyde looked more than a little concerned. His ponytail's days were numbered and by Saturday it would be gone. No matter what grade we'd got in our home countries, we were all back in white belts. They designed the course to dismantle you piece by piece and then build you back up again. The stripping away of any previous grades, even from a Yoshinkan school, was the start of this process. As we stripped back to basics in preparation for the start, I wondered how we'd all finish. This thought was a momentary lapse of reason. To survive the course, I'd been told it was best not to look forward. The best advice I'd received was to take one day at a time. Think too far to the future or count the days to the end, and the enormity of the task would overwhelm.

After training I headed off to the Berlitz school at Sangenjaya to meet Peter my manager. I might have been able to speak English, but I was no English teacher. Although I'd never taught before I'd done a weekend TEFL (Teaching English as a Foreign Language) course back in the UK before leaving for Japan. As a native speaker, I had no clue about grammar. The past participle of such-and-such meant nothing. Verbs, nouns and tenses were lost on me at school and I had no desire to go back to basics now. The Berlitz system ran on a series of levels with each level having a corresponding file that guided learning. A fictional scenario starring a multitude of different characters, grammar focus and vocabulary, followed by a series of practical exercises, moved the students up the gears as smoothly as possible. The lessons had to be delivered in sequential order, and my students would need to trust in me to get where they wanted to go. At the honbu, starting Saturday, it would be much the same. I'd need to trust in the Sensei and Sewanin to teach me what I needed to know to get me to shodan and beyond. I only hoped that their understanding of the basics of Aikido was much better than mine in English. Speaking English as a native and teaching its complex structures and forms were two different things, and although total immersion would enable me to skip some grammar, my English-teaching house was built on shaky foundations. Advice was on hand in the form of the other teachers, some helpful and some quite the opposite. The big debate was how to get the Japanese students on side. A willing and able student was a breeze, but one who clammed up and didn't want to engage was a complete nightmare. Like a bad date with conversation that quickly dries up, the latter made for an uncomfortable scenario for both teacher and student. This was an important moment of self-reflection. Starting Saturday, I'd need to make sure I was ready, willing and able. If I wanted to get the most out of my Senshusei experience, I'd need to engage in everything I was asked to do, no matter how painful.

All the Berlitz teachers seemed to adopt a different style, with each highlighting the training manuals in his or her own unique way. As there was no student ownership, it was highly likely that I'd end up teaching their students and they'd wind up teaching mine. Shared ownership didn't sound like a great idea to me. Not only were there different teaching styles, but there were different accents, too. How would students adjust to being taught in a British accent instead of an American one and then switching back and forth as the teaching schedule dictated? It felt already that teaching English would be an absolute nightmare, particularly after a day of hard training. In case I was in any doubt, Peter wandered into the staffroom to hand me my teaching schedule. Every weeknight apart from Monday, I'd be teaching from 3:15 until 9:15pm and then all day on Sunday. This meant on Tuesdays, Wednesdays, Thursdays and Fridays, I'd be up at 5:20am in readiness for Senshusei and wouldn't get home after teaching until about 10pm. My only downtime would be between 2 and 3pm, and during this time I'd be travelling from Ochiai to Sangenjaya or wherever Berlitz sent me. Things had just gotten a whole lot worse. How was I going to cope?

1...GO...

One day to go until the start of the course. The last day of March had finally arrived and signalled the end of life as I'd know it for at least the next 11 months. With the course officially starting tomorrow, I took a break from the honbu but still woke up at an unearthly hour. I tried my best to get back to sleep, but my mind was too busy with a strange mix of excitement, fear and apprehension. My plan today was to get as much rest as possible to ensure I could survive the first day. *One day at a time,* I thought to myself. *All I need to do is get through the first, and I'll then have Sunday and Monday to recover.*

To calm my mind and save my sanity, I got up, got dressed and took a short walk down the road to Musashi Koyama park. Every day at 6:30am, a group of Japanese men and women of all ages would meet to exercise. The scene was quite atmospheric, with cherry blossom on the trees and 30 or more people flexing and stretching their muscles to what sounded like some nationalistic music played on a radio that looked like it had seen action during the Second World War. Despite the best intentions, the Japanese warm-up routine needed some serious updating, but when in Japan and all that. I stood at the back and followed along. My body didn't like it; the motions broke most of the current advice on how to exercise properly and safely that I'd regularly read about in *Men's Health* magazine back home. I decided there and then that I wouldn't be taking part again; it seemed like a sure-fire way to get injured.

I spent the rest of the day at Tokyo DisneySea, which, despite its name, was located just outside of the city. I needed to distract myself from thoughts of tomorrow and also wanted to enjoy my last day of freedom to the full. After a few hours there, I took the train to Omotesando for a quick session at Gold's Gym to rectify the damage I'd done in the park and to prime my body for the onslaught I expected it would come under tomorrow morning. By 10pm I was in bed, and as I drifted off to sleep, my mind raced again. Tomorrow was day one, and I was nervous!

PART ONE: DAI ICHI
(1 April to 7 June 2006)

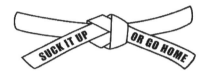

THE CHAOS BEGINS

In the words of arguably the greatest author who has ever lived – *it was the worst of times, it was the best of times*. In the opening paragraph of Charles Dickens' historical novel, *A Tale of Two Cities*, written in 1859, little did he know that nearly 150 years later, his words would be a fitting description for what was to become my experience on the Senshusei course. Filled with excitement and dread, I'd waited for this day to arrive. Day one on possibly the toughest martial arts course in the world. Saturday, 1 April 2006 had arrived, and although it was a Saturday when most of my friends back in the UK would enjoy a lie-in, I was up at 5:20am with my mind on one thing and one thing only. I'd heard so much about the Senshusei course from turning the pages of *Angry White Pyjamas*, which I'd read more than once. This was the book to read for all Senshusei and the only real account of a course steeped in secrecy and the traditions of Japanese Budo culture. Before leaving for Japan I'd presented my Mum and Dad with a copy. Dated May 2005 and inscribed in the front my message had been a farewell for now and a promise of what was to come. *Dear Mum and Dad, I am really going to miss you both while I am away. Thank you for all of your support and help with everything, I am very lucky to have parents like you. If you read this book you will understand a lot more about martial arts and Aikido in particular. This is a true story and the dojo in the book is where I am going to train in Tokyo! Lots and lots and loads of love, from Simon, xxx xxx xxx.* Dad had read it and thought I was crazy. Mum didn't want to know; it would only make her worry.

Back in the UK it would be April Fools' Day and the chance to pull a prank or two on family and friends, providing I instigated it before midday. But who was the fool now? There'd be no such fun today. I knew today would be deadly serious. As I climbed out of the shower, slightly more awake than when I'd first stepped in, a host of thoughts racing through my mind crystallised in *how am I going to survive?* I'd seen firsthand the pain and suffering the most recent graduates had gone through, and while I wanted the same experience, I didn't really want it at all. I knew enough Aikido to satisfy most people, but with my habit of seeking the most extreme form of anything, the dream of Senshusei had taken hold. That dream could very well turn into a nightmare, through injury, exhaustion or a combination of the two. Leaving the small upstairs flat in Musashi Koyama, I made the short walk to the railway station. It was still dark, and the birds in the trees were quiet. I'd always enjoyed this time of day. The rising out of bed was always difficult, but the opportunity to have a bit of the world to myself for even a moment was well worth it. Finding a moment alone was no easy feat in Tokyo, one of the world's most populated cities; but this morning I had my moment, and I enjoyed it before the inevitable chaos of dojo life began. I'd slept badly, tossing and turning with a multitude of thoughts racing through my brain. I'd never understood why, on the days when a good night's rest the night before was so important, I couldn't sleep. Anxiety or nervous apprehension was possibly the cause, but if I'm to be honest, it was much more than either of these. I was scared. Fear had taken hold, and it wasn't letting go. Although I had an inkling of what today might bring, I was about to find out I really had no idea.

Pulling into Meguro Station, I realised I was almost alone in the carriage. This was unusual in Tokyo, where the principal mode of transport was the train and where at peak times you sometimes had to fight to get on. Changing trains at Meguro, things got busier, but I found a seat. They arranged Japanese trains much the same as those on the London Underground – seats adorning each side of the carriage, with passengers forced to sit awkwardly across from strangers while doing their best to avoid any form of eye contact. I had a solution to this. With seven stops to Takadanobaba, I had time to sleep. Aside from the murmur of the train and the doors opening and closing at each station stop, I was oblivious. We passed through Shibuya and its famous crossing and Shinjuku, the world's busiest train station, but I paid no attention. My mind drifted back to childhood when my Dad would drive me from my home in Stafford back to boarding school. I'd hated boarding school and travelling back on a Sunday evening was always difficult. As if to put a buffer between myself and the inevitable, I'd fall asleep in the car, which served as a period of calm before my arrival. I'd instruct my Dad to rouse me at a certain landmark to give me a few minutes to wake up and get ready. Today I was living this experience again. The journey time on my second leg was 40 minutes, which ironically was the same for the car journey all those years ago. This time, I was alone. Dad was back in England, and the tears I'd shed as a child of 13 had no place now. I was an adult, and I'd chosen to do this thing.

I was pleased to meet Matt at Takadanobaba. I didn't have to look too hard, as, like me, he stood out. Early on a Saturday morning, you didn't see an abundance of foreigners wandering about. We made our way from the over-ground JR Yamanote Line to the Tokyo Subway and jumped on the train to Ochiai. We didn't talk much. It was far too early, and what was there to say? Deep in our own private thoughts or on a mission to save every bit of energy, we rode the final few stops of our journey in silence. We climbed the stairs out of the subway to the hustle and bustle of the city waking up. Gone was the calm of my earlier walk. We were here, and it was time. Matt and I had made a choice, and once we stepped into the dojo for the first time as Senshusei, we'd be committed for the next 11 months of our lives. I say Matt had made a choice, but I'd had a hand in his decision. I wondered if he now regretted responding to my letter and agreeing to join me in Japan.

I'd climbed the stairs to the honbu dojo as a regular student many times before but being a regular student hadn't cut the mustard, and I'd sought the extreme. We bowed before the bust of Kancho Gozo Shioda, the founder of Yoshinkan Aikido, and turned to face the office. Feet together and hands by our sides, we came to attention and bowed. 'Ohayou gozaimasu, osu' (good morning, but also used as the first greeting at any time of day) was the obligatory greeting, which was acknowledged by a rumble from the office. We took off our shoes and placed them in the cupboards provided and officially stepped into the honbu in our socks. The dojo was awake, and I could feel the tension already. 'Okagi, onegaishimasu, osu' (my locker key, please) I cried collecting my locker key from the office. My Senshusei card was ready and waiting. Number G510, a Yoshinkan membership card that the office would stamp every day to mark my attendance on the course. They'd be keeping track! In the locker room I changed into the customary uniform of every Senshusei, a white dogi and white belt. It was back to basics, because the basics were what I'd been told good Aikido was all about.

We'd already met some of our fellow Senshusei and would meet the rest today. I was determined not to find myself at the bottom of the pile in the chores and training. I'd seen what had happened to Avry the year before and didn't want the same experience. He had been a marked man, and they had subjected him to the harshest training, relentless abuse, and punishment after punishment. Graham had graduated from the prior year's course and would now sit between the Senshusei and Sensei as Sewanin, alongside Malik, to look after the new draft. When I say 'look after', I mean maintain discipline, dish out punishment and ensure that we did what we were told. I knew them already, but their personas today were very different to what I was used to. Now officially Sewanin, they were determined to make their presence felt, and I presumed all the shouting and screaming was their way of communicating to the Sensei that they were doing a good job.

Like a peacock who had just discovered his feathers, Malik was already parading around his paddock. The smaller of the two Sewanin, he was proud and purposeful. At about 60 kilograms and a few inches shorter than me, he pushed out his chest and walked on the balls of his feet to elevate his stature and status. A fellow Brit, when he spoke, he 'ummed' too much. Perhaps a sign of nervousness in his newfound position? Perhaps due to honbu dojo pressure; now an enforced need to pick and choose his words more carefully? He was pristine in his presentation with all the potential to be problematic! Graham was bigger; much bigger. With an academic, 'frat' look, he was of similar build to me. A motorbike-riding, almost monastic figure, Graham was Yin and Yang rolled into one. Canadian by birth, he was already fully immersed in the Japanese way of life. Amidst the Tokyo traffic, Graham navigated his was across the city with a composure and calmness that was lost on his fellow commuters. More experienced in Aikido than Malik, he had less to prove. Much harder to weigh up, it was clear that getting the measure of Graham would take longer. He had less to say but, when it came to Budo, I suspected much more to offer. If Malik was more yelling, Graham was much more yoga. If Malik was mayhem, Graham was definitely meditation! We'd found ourselves in our very own *Fight Club*. Like Tyler Durden, Malik was chaotic and charismatic, compared to The Narrator's calmer, Graham-like persona. Despite different motivations and the potential to disagree, like Pitt and Norton in the film, their combined fate, at least for the next 11 months, was naturally tied to one another. I was already sure it would make compelling and, for us, compulsory viewing. Like Riggs and Murtaugh in *Lethal Weapon*, with their contrasting styles; explosive and unpredictable (Malik) alongside cautious and calming (Graham). Opposites in so many ways, they'd been thrown together to learn the ropes of Sewanin, with the responsibility for whipping into shape a new and unruly batch of Senshusei!

Malik and Graham threw us into the cleaning. On the rota I'd been assigned the Sensei's locker room but at the last minute was given the men's toilets instead. In Japan everything runs to a strict code of hierarchy. I suspected the early demotion was not a good omen and a sign of things to come. The course was not just about the Aikido training. As the lowest form

41

of life in the dojo, we were responsible for all the cleaning and anything else the Sewanin or Sensei gave us. As I picked up pubic hairs, cleaned the urinals and wiped the floor, I half wondered if they had created the course to enlist a band of cleaners to get the honbu dojo sparkling for free. My wandering mind was shocked to attention when Paul Sensei burst in with a camera in hand. He wanted a photo for an article he was writing on the 16th international Senshusei for *AYI e-Magazine*. With my back to the yellow tiles I feigned a nervous smile. The men's toilets didn't make the best backdrop and I'd now be for ever pictured in the loo! Having scrubbed, shined and polished our stations, we met on the mats to clean them, too. In case we were in any doubt about how to clean, the Sewanin furnished us with a copy of the 2005-2006 Senshusei Cleaning Checklist. It was a comprehensive list comprising three sides of A4. It was detailed beyond belief and had some interesting highlights.

GARBAGE

Take the bag out of the small black wastebasket containing the chopsticks. Be careful when you place these chopsticks into the burnable garbage bin because they can poke holes very easily into the sides of the trash bags.

When taking out the trash, be careful to check for leaks. If the bag is leaking, then get another bag or use a piece of duct tape to cover the hole.

MEN'S LOCKER ROOM

Each day you should take a different section of lockers and wipe down the locker doors, paying special attention to the air vents on each locker and the handles.

Clean the zokin cloth to remove the dust bunnies, dirt, pubes, etc, but don't put it away yet.

MEN'S SHOWER ROOM

Take the Kabi Killer and spray the inside of the shower curtains, the tile floors and any black or orange mould spots you see growing on the shower walls. Make sure the windows are open so that you don't get sick from the chemicals in the Kabi Killer.

Use the vacuum to clean the entire floor, taking special care to get the grime out of the corners, the dust from under the sink and the pubes which will be everywhere.

MEN'S TOILETS

Make sure there are at least five rolls of extra toilet paper in each toilet stall. Toilet paper can be found in the storage area inside the tearoom. Neatly fold the toilet paper hanging in each stall.

Make sure the soap dispensers are full. You can use the green soap concentrate and mix it with water in the two-litre bottle, using a 70% water / 30% soap ratio.

DOJO

After each class and before the first class on Tuesday morning, you must sweep the dojo. When getting the brooms, NEVER let the cops or ippan students beat you.

When you zokin, you need to shake out your rag after finishing each column. If you put a dirty rag back into the bucket, you will just be spreading around the crap you just picked up. Shake your rag out of one of the windows, preferably one that is hidden from the view of both the dojo office and Kancho Sensei's office.

Finally, we were into the warm-up. Suddenly I was back in the park and couldn't quite believe the prehistoric exercise routine I'd experienced yesterday was the one we were doing today, minus the accompanying music. I was sure the suitability and sensibility of the warm-up had never been considered. Passed down from generation to generation, it undoubtedly had never been questioned whether the exercises served the intended purpose of getting the body prepared for class. I was certain bouncing knees and straining joints were not best practice but had no choice but to grin and bear it. This was a Senshusei's daily ritual and if I wanted an authentic Senshusei experience, then it would become part of my daily ritual, too. As I circled my arms and rotated my hips in time with the count in Japanese, *'ichi, ni, san, shi...'* (one, two, three, four), I caught myself thinking about the daily schedule from the Senshusei Handbook, which I'd no doubt know by heart soon. The Senshusei trained five days a week with no excuses. If you were injured or feeling unwell, unless it was serious, you trained. If you were tired, tough; you still trained! We'd be training with the *Kidotai* (Riot Police) in the second class during the week and would have a slightly shorter session on Saturdays, where in the last class we'd be joined by the ippan students.

Tuesday to Friday:

8:30 to 9:30am – First class. Usually a high-intensity session taught by one of the international instructors, which included some of the more junior Japanese Sensei.

10:00 to 11:30am – Second class. Often high intensity, too, and extremely repetitive. Taught by a senior Japanese instructor. In this class we'd be joined by the Riot Police.

12:00 to 1:30pm – Third class. Usually more of a technical session, again taught by a senior Japanese instructor.

Saturday:

8:30 to 9:30am – First class. Usually a high-intensity session taught by one of the international instructors, which included some of the more junior Japanese Sensei.

10:00 to 11:00am – Second class. Often high intensity, too, and extremely repetitive. Taught by a senior Japanese instructor.

11:30am to 12:30pm – Third class. Usually an easier session taught by a Japanese instructor. In this class, we'd be joined by the ippan students.

For 19 hours each week, we'd be immersed in serious, disciplined instruction. We'd be spending a lot more time at the honbu, though, outside of these times we would be cleaning, performing ceremonial duties and attending meetings. You'll find a detailed daily schedule at the back of this book. As Senshusei, we were also eligible to join any of the regular classes at no extra cost whenever we wanted. I already knew I had no plans to do this. I'd already had a taste of what they offered, and 19 hours would be more than enough.

The course was split into four parts – *Dai Ichi*, *Dai Ni*, *Dai San* and *Dai Yon*. For Dai Ichi, they partnered me with Lloyd from Brisbane, Australia. Standing in line opposite Lloyd in kamae was my first opportunity to test his mettle, something all the new partnerships appeared to be doing as we lined up across the dojo. Lloyd appeared to be a likeable fellow; tall and skinny with a top of curly hair, he had a somewhat goofy but pleasant smile.

44

Physically I was much bigger and, in my mind, had a psychological edge from my previous training. I stared intensely at Lloyd, not breaking his eye contact, and was pleased to see him look away first. I'd claimed an early victory, but as I'd come to learn, Lloyd was no pushover. The first class came and went. Shock tactics seemed to have been the order of the day, and with all the shouting and screaming most of us were messing up. This I suspected was to disorientate us and through confusion drive a wedge between any previous training we'd ever done and what we were there to do now. 200 press-ups in a matter of minutes, running back and forth to start positions and relentless backdrops were already starting to take their toll, especially on one guy from Canada. Geoff was the tallest of all the Senshusei and had never trained in Aikido before. Because of his height, he had farther to fall, and with little idea of how to do it properly, he'd already made himself known to Malik Sewanin.

Between the first and second classes, we got our first taste of Japanese formality Senshusei style, with the daily *Shinkoku*. I'd seen Shinkoku performed by the then-Senshusei during my time as a regular student, but conducted in Japanese, I didn't understand what was going on. All I knew now was that I was tired, thirsty and ready for a break, and that Shinkoku was getting in the way. The Shinkoku drill was performed by the *Shinkoku toban*. Shinkoku meant *to offer something* and toban *the person in charge of work that changes in turn*. Shinkoku I quickly learnt was a daily ritual where the Senshusei lined up outside the office to formally ask for permission to train that day. *Slightly late in the day*, I thought to myself, as we'd already done the first class. With Inoue Kancho in today, there was a huge amount of fussing. Inoue Kancho had succeeded as head of the Yoshinkan on Gozo Shioda's passing and the Sewanin urged us to make sure that our Shinkoku was perfect or there would be trouble later. We were told, *'your osu must be loud but respectful and your bow in time'*, but as the majority of us had only just met, and we were exhausted from the first class, our performance was far from perfect. I was looking dishevelled already. In the first class, I'd ripped my trousers at the knees, and following Shinkoku, I scrabbled around for some tape to fix them up as best I could. This was improvisation – and an important skill I would come to learn a Senshusei needed to develop. The tape held as well as it could in the second and third classes, before training came to a close at 12:30pm.

As the ippan students who'd joined us in the final class departed the dojo, we still had work to do. To finish, Malik and Graham stepped things up a gear and, by design or not, caused as much confusion as possible. They conducted a detailed tour of the honbu while providing specific instructions on how to clean every nook and cranny. They should know having cleaned the dojo from top to bottom during their year, and with the characteristics of a military inspection, their ability to spot even the minutest of dirt was impressive. With our newfound knowledge, it was back to our cleaning stations before a final inspection to see if we'd made the grade. While I was on my hands and knees in the toilets, Graham came in and told me not to bother wiping the toilet floor as there was no time – which, on final inspection, Malik reprimanded me for not doing!

We finally escaped at 2:15pm, much later than what I'd been led to believe was the designated finish time of 1pm. Physically tired, mentally exhausted and famished, I suggested to Matt that we grab some food. Lunch and a meet for beers at the Dubliners' bar in Shibuya later that evening was a celebration of having survived day one. As we drank, we performed a diagnostic of the day, like two soldiers conducting a formal debrief after a mission. We also speculated about what was yet to come. One beer turned into two and we finished the night on JD (Jack Daniel's) and Cokes at the HUB bar up the road. It had been a long first day, but thankfully there were now two full days before it was back to the grindstone on Tuesday. A chance to rest, recover and recuperate.

WHAT DO YOU MEAN I'M FUNNY?

Sunday arrived far too quickly, and the banging in my head and the aching in my body reminded me all too abruptly of the previous day's proceedings. While some of my fellow Senshusei would be resting, this was my first day at Berlitz. I needed the money, but more than that, I needed the visa and a reason to be in the country other than Senshusei. I started out on full-time hours, which meant I was at Berlitz's beck and call and had little choice during my time away from the dojo over when I taught or didn't. Luckily Peter was sympathetic to my cause and agreed to switch me over to a per-lesson schedule. I now had more control over when I worked and could work fewer hours, as this contract paid much better. It was a win-win all round.

I'd been warned that any gaijin I met in Japan without a specific reason for being there could be slightly odd. Tokyo, with the possibility to teach English, was rumoured to be attractive to anyone wanting to escape their native country for whatever reason. In Japan, a country fast adopting European and American fashions and trends, Western tourists were held in high regard. A geek back home could be the cool guy in Tokyo, not to mention popular with the ladies! I'd already had firsthand experience of this oddness on the course Berlitz had sent me on, which was compulsory before ever being let loose in a classroom. They held it in a large meeting room at the top of a Tokyo high-rise at Berlitz HQ. On the first day, waiting to get in, I'd chatted to a guy in the corridor called Brian, who seemed like a decent bloke. I was in Japan for Senshusei, but he was there to teach. The Berlitz training ran for a week, and I began to sense that Brian had a problem with me. Nothing was said, but I'd catch him glaring at me, and on more than one occasion, he'd made a dismissive comment on a point I'd raised with the trainer. Having been briefed and then drilled on the Berlitz method, we were asked to take turns teaching a mock lesson in front of our fellow trainees. Brian was up and delivered a comical class, which I was certain he'd purposefully made entertaining. His style of delivery and content prompted laughter from around the room, and although I laughed occasionally, I wasn't the most vocal. It turned out, though, that Brian saw things differently, and during the coffee break, he squared up to me. It was a watercooler showdown where the backdrop was a busy Berlitz office. Right up in my face he questioned why I'd found his talk so funny and wanted to know why I'd been laughing at him.

My mind connected to that famous scene in the movie *Goodfellas* where Tommy DeVito (Joe Pesci) challenged Henry Hill (Ray Liotta) in much the same way: *'What do you mean I'm funny?'* In the movie it turned out to be one massive wind-up, and replaying the scene in my head with Brian in my face, I really thought he was joking. How stupid could the guy be? Was he really putting his opportunity to work for Berlitz in jeopardy, not to mention his ability to stay in Japan? I'd seen *Goodfellas* a hundred times and responded in the spirit of Henry Hill: *'It's just that your talk was funny. It wasn't just me laughing; everyone else was laughing, too. We weren't laughing at you; we were laughing with you.'* Despite my best efforts, this didn't appease, and I sensed Brian's next response was likely to be physical. He had that look in his eye, and I didn't want to be his victim. How would I explain this at the honbu? If he caught me good and proper, and left me with a black eye which didn't clear up by the time Senshusei started, I was sure any explanation I could offer would fall on deaf ears.

I had a problem with bullies. Given my childhood, I knew there was only one way to deal with them. Bullies in my book responded to only one thing! As Brian bounced around the office, I could tell he regretted his over confidence in picking an argument with the guy probably most equipped to deal with him. I imagined a crunching of bone as his wrist was bent back the wrong way and a thud as his mass crashed mercilessly into the concrete floor. The gasps from the Japanese office workers and my fellow would-be teachers were a combination of horror and appreciation, and I felt a mix of calm and power all wrapped into one. My mind snapped back to reality. The fantasy would be much better, but my imagined course of action wouldn't have served Brian or me very well. I realised I had to defuse the situation fast and fixed a stare right between his eyes. Calmly and confidently I said, *'out of interest, do you know why I'm here in Japan?'* He said nothing. *'You should know that I'm not here to teach English. I'm here training martial arts, so feel free to make your move!'* With that I saw the confidence drain from his face; he stepped back and walked away. Brian never bothered me again. He kept his distance, and I kept mine.

A typical Tokyo office building, Berlitz Sangenjaya was fairly uninspiring. A reception desk, the manager's office and a series of small teaching rooms comprising a table, chairs and whiteboard led to a small staff room tucked away at the back. As I entered the staff room on Sunday morning, I immediately bumped into Mike. Mike, I found out, was a long-serving teacher and probably the most experienced in the school. He'd been in Japan for years, married a Japanese girl and now plied his trade as an English teacher, as so many others like him also did. He was a brash American from Brooklyn; I didn't warm to him and was put off further when he corrected me. *'It's Michael, not Mike!'* I knew, though, that he could help me, and as a fish out of water in this strange new environment, I needed all the friends I could get. My first class was not one but three back-to-back classes with the same student. I was confident I could bluff my way through 30 minutes of teaching anyone, but with three on the trot and only a five-minute break in between to regroup, I was up against it. Luckily the Japanese are very polite, and the young medical student who'd been unfortunate enough to land me just smiled and played along. He seemed to have fun, and that in my mind was the main thing. *If I can give him a good experience, this guy might forget how bad my teaching is,* I thought to myself. The five-minute break wasn't nearly enough time. I had to go to the toilet at some point, but this meant I'd really be winging it in the next class. I struggled on and slowly grew in confidence. Having started the day with a medical student, my last class was with a law professor. You could say I'd gone from one extreme to another. At 6:15pm I left for home. What a couple of days that had been. The first day of the Senshusei course followed by the first day of my new job teaching English at Berlitz. Based on the last 48 hours, I realised that the next 11 months would be no easy task, but that's what I'd signed up for – and that's what I'd got!

FEEDING FRENZY

Monday came and went, and before I knew it, I was fumbling for the alarm clock again. It was 5:20am on Tuesday, 4 April 2006, which was to be the first real test. In my eyes Saturday had been a taster session, with the second and third classes being shorter, and with the added insurance of having the regular students join us in the last one, which I'd been confident would mitigate the level of punishment. Now with Tuesday underway, I was at the start of the first full week, and I was certain that Malik and Graham Sewanin, along with the Sensei, would be ready and waiting with something special.

Today was my opportunity to get to know Ronen better. We'd met briefly before the start of the course and more formally on Saturday, but in the blur of our new surroundings, we had little time to talk or to size each other up properly. There were 13 of us on the course, and Ronen was the one I was instantly wary of the most. I could tell from the off he was tough. As one of three Israelis on the course alongside Dror and Boaz, Ronen stood out. With a calm and serious demeanour, he was soft-spoken and had a look in his eyes that said 'don't mess'. I learnt that he'd spent time in the military, was a Krav Maga instructor and had already attained a high level of skill in Aikido in his home country. In establishing the pecking order, he was the one to watch, and for the next week of our lives we'd be joined at the hip cleaning the Sensei's locker room.

The first class of the day was with Murray Sensei. He'd been in Japan for many years and was the head of the international contingent and the first person I'd met at the honbu. The Japanese, maybe to avoid having to deal with yet another group of foreign upstarts, kept a team of international instructors around. Former Senshusei themselves, their presence helped break the language barrier and maintain discipline. Instructors were what Malik and Graham Sewanin hoped to become, but the adulation afforded honbu dojo instructors was still some way off for them. For now, they were the proverbial meat in the sandwich. Mostly an international instructor ran the first class of the day, and they used this time to make it known they weren't playing second fiddle to the Japanese in the brutality stakes. I'd now gotten to know Geoff a little, too, and watching him grimace and strain through an endless series of backdrops administered by Murray Sensei was a painful experience. Geoff was tall, and his movements, I'd noticed, looked awkward. Also, he had no clue as yet how to protect himself from the impact of the mats. Every backdrop was another punishing blow to his already bruised body. There were rumours circling, possibly started by Geoff himself, that back in Canada he was a fully-fledged *Ninja*. The Ninja I'd seen

49

in the movies were always agile with an incredible ability to withstand pain. On both counts, Geoff was already failing miserably. Geoff had enrolled on the course with his girlfriend Victoria. Vic was much younger than him and, as the only female on the international course, couldn't help but stand out. Senshusei was never designed to be a course only for men, but in the 15 preceding years, our year being the 16th international course, only a small number of women had graduated. This included Takagi Sensei, who we'd heard about, but had yet to meet. Already Vic was proving that she was made of stern stuff, and I wondered what the conversation reviewing the day would be like later on back at their lodgings. To my mind, they both had a tough challenge ahead. It's one thing doing the Senshusei course, but quite another doing it with your partner, whom you also happen to be living with. I was certain that tension would show up down the line. If their relationship could survive Senshusei it probably could survive anything, but at this stage of the game only time would tell. Overall, I was feeling good. While Geoff burned his leg muscles out in getting up, I was using body momentum. While Geoff contorted his lower body in any way he could to rise to his feet, by facing forward at all times, I protected my knees. I was already starting to realise that Senshusei was about playing the long game, and that meant not getting injured and working as efficiently as possible to preserve energy.

After Saturday's shorter schedule, I'd expected a rough-and-tough Tuesday, but a welcome rumour that the first class would be today's only class, circulated amongst the Senshusei. It was early days, but it already felt that we were the last to know anything and that the lack of clarity as to what would happen next was all part of the tactics to pile on the pressure. Finally, we had it confirmed and did our best to hide our enthusiasm. It was a strange reaction; after all, we'd all willingly left our native countries to travel to a strange land to learn one of its principal martial arts from the best in the world. Surely any cancellation of classes was bad news, but we expressed relief. Geoff led the chorus and provided the clue as to why. The longer we avoided the hard training we'd all heard and read about, the longer we were likely to survive.

Good news fades fast, and in place of the second and third classes came one of our first big tests of patience and pain management. Today was the 16th Senshusei course opening ceremony. Ceremony was definitely the right word. Sitting in seiza, we were formally introduced to all the top-ranking honbu staff. Throughout each speech, all I could focus on was the pain in my legs. With the blood supply cut off to my toes, the dull ache which was essentially my legs slowly dying got stronger and stronger. As the muscles fell asleep, they were useless in keeping the pressure off my knees and ankles, which bore the brunt. I wasn't alone in my discomfort. We'd been told in advance by the Sewanin to sit still and that any movement would be punishable afterwards. We couldn't help it, though, and all took turns transferring the weight from one leg to the other. Any temporary relief was short-lived, and the pain grew worse. As the new intake of Senshusei, today was our formal introduction, and the moment came I'd been dreading. As I jumped to my feet in response to my name being called, I realised I couldn't feel my legs beneath me. For a moment I had the strangest sensation of floating in mid-air, similar I guess to what astronauts feel when they get their first taste of outer space. But I was no astronaut, and this was my moment to shine, or at the very least not embarrass myself too much. The simple task of standing up and screaming *'hai'* (yes), followed by *'yoroshiku onegaishimasu'* (please favour me) at the top of my voice while bowing a couple of times had become a hugely challenging one. As the blood surged back into my legs I winced in pain, wobbled and made the best hash of it I could. Despite the intended meaning of the phrase I'd just uttered, the thought running through my head, and what I really felt like saying, was *please help me!* I'd already learnt from Paul Sensei that moving – and especially jumping to attention from seiza – when your legs were half asleep was a potentially dangerous manoeuvre. With no feeling in your legs, there was a real possibility of breaking an ankle or twisting a knee. As I dropped back to the floor with the feeling partially back in my legs, I was relieved to find that I hadn't succumbed to this fate.

As I'd been in Japan for a while, I had a decent command of basic Japanese and, so I'd been told, a decent standard of pronunciation, but the same couldn't be said for those who'd recently arrived in Tokyo. Dave was one of four Brits on the course alongside Matt, Neville and me. I'd warmed to Dave as soon as I'd met him. Much younger than me and most of the others, he lacked maturity and had a tendency to giggle nervously. I hadn't figured out what he was doing in Japan as yet. He wasn't a martial artist; he wasn't teaching English and he hadn't really provided an explanation of why he'd enrolled on the course, let alone been selected. My money was on Dave to make the first mistake and to put himself firmly on the radar of the good and the greats of Yoshinkan Aikido for all the wrong reasons. There always has to be one, and I was certain that today it would be Dave. In the practice session we'd done before the official ceremony, the butchery of the Japanese language by most of the Senshusei had caused much amusement. Dave had brought the house down with *'gasshuku onegaishimasu'*, which translated as *'please can we have a training camp'*. Thank goodness for the practice session. Thankfully, when the real test came, he just about got his words out in the right order and in

51

understandable form. Had he instead requested a training camp, I don't think even the most serious and deadpan-faced of the Sensei could have contained their amusement.

The ceremony finally ended, and most of us were in agreement that having a second and third class would have been preferable. On instruction from Malik and Graham, our next task was to set up tables for lunch. In my previous working life, lunchtime had been a time to relax. I'd regularly been in the habit of finding a quiet spot (usually my car) for some downtime, a sandwich and a nap. Perhaps this was our first opportunity as Senshusei to relax and unwind? It was our ceremony, so with formal introductions over, I expected a chance to enjoy myself. I'd temporarily forgotten, however, the message I'd received ahead of the start of the course. *'Senshusei never relax. From the moment you enter the dojo until you leave, you should live in fear.'* It was well-intentioned but terrifying advice from one of the international instructors I'd met through the ippan classes. Sitting in a square, at tables and chairs set up in the middle of the dojo, this was like no lunch I'd ever experienced before. Presided over by Chida *Dojocho* (head of the dojo), we waited patiently to tuck into the *bento* box we'd carefully placed at each setting moments earlier. A bento box was the equivalent of takeaway sandwiches. Comprising meat, fish and vegetables alongside rice or noodles, they were a Japanese staple and mass-produced across Japan to feed its hungry workforce and now, it would seem, hungry Senshusei. I was fast discovering that even the simplest of tasks could be made complex, uncomfortable and sometimes even ridiculous by honbu dojo etiquette. Unable to start our lunch before Chida Sensei had started his, we'd been told that we'd need to finish eating ours before he was done with his. Start after and finish before were the Sewanin's instructions, and with that, once Chida had taken his first mouthful, the race was on. Luckily nobody seemed to talk, and with all the shovelling and slurping, I don't think I'd ever seen a more concentrated and focused eating session. It reminded me of the doughnut or pizza-eating competitions I'd seen before on TV, an experience that, in a way, I was now recreating for myself. Chopsticks hampered the task in hand. At Wagamama back home in England, I could request a fork, but here in Japan there was no such luxury. With some experience under my belt, I seemed to be doing better than most, but no one could match the speed of the Sensei. This wasn't their first opening ceremony, and, brought up using chopsticks from birth, they had a distinct advantage. There was really no need for them to eat so fast, and my Mum's voice echoed in my head. *'Shovelling it in is no good for your digestion, Simon!'* They were super hungry, short on time, or eager to test the resolve and resilience of the new intake of Senshusei. My right eye was on my food, and my left eye firmly fixed on Chida. A few times he seemed to be stopping, but with a second and third burst of energy, he was back to the shovelling. As he slowed, you felt the room slow, and as he tucked back in everyone and everything sped up. It was like someone had a remote control and was switching back and forth between slow-motion and fast-forward. After what felt like only a matter of minutes, his chopsticks were down. I'd anticipated him finishing and had mine on the table a few seconds before. The clatter of chopsticks being placed on wooden tables could be heard. Like a line of dominoes toppling, the noise echoed around the dojo, as those slow to catch on finally caught up. Most of the Senshusei, myself included, hadn't finished. After the morning's exertion, we were still hungry but forced to embark on the tortuous exercise of throwing away perfectly good food, which seemed a huge waste. It crossed my mind to ask for a doggy bag, but I had a good idea how that would go down. This was an early example of the honbu's way of doing things, taking precedence over common sense. The feeding frenzy had been one crazy experience, and I was sure it wouldn't be the last.

THE RIOT POLICE ARRIVE

During the first week we were introduced to several other Sensei. When I say 'introduced', I don't mean a smile, a handshake and a pleasant chat; I mean introduced honbu style. This meant one thing and one thing only; brutality on the mats, with each instructor looking to outshine the others, not in teaching prowess, but in pain and suffering. This brutality took two principal forms. There was the physical kind, which manifested itself in punishing exercises and Aikido drills, and the mental kind, which usually meant holding static positions for extended periods.

Romeo Sensei by Japanese standards was huge. A native of the Philippines, his earlier experience in martial arts had been in Filipino knife and stick fighting, which made it all the more confusing to me why he was now in Japan teaching Aikido. Japan was still a male-dominated country, and in certain circles I'd heard stories of women being treated as second-class citizens. I'd witnessed how packed the trains at rush hour could get, and apparently the groping and touching up of female passengers was a constant problem. To combat this, the train companies had been forced to create female-only carriages, which were now available on most of the commuter routes. In the work environment and the home, Japan also appeared behind the curve on equal rights and equal opportunity afforded by more modern and progressive societies. Takagi Sensei, a female instructor who had graduated from the course a few years back, no doubt had firsthand experience of this environment. As the only female on the teaching staff, she understandably seemed to have a point to prove. Her classes were some of the most brutal and always the first of the day. Romeo, too, had been handpicked for the 8:30am beasting, and interchangeably, they were a formidable pair. Seiza, backdrops, seiza, backdrops seemed to be the order of the day. *I signed up for the course to learn Aikido, not how to fall or sit on my knees,* I'd regularly think to myself. A typical Takagi class comprised 350 backdrops performed in unison, then the same again in a circle holding hands. We performed everything to the count, *'ichi, ni, san, shi...'*. Even Dave, who was no linguist, had gotten to know his numbers. Much of our debate during cleaning duty was who we had that day, and specifically, who would take the first class. If Romeo or Takagi were seen in the building, the odds of a bad day increased dramatically. We never knew for sure who was teaching until they were there on the mats. Lining up in seiza facing the *shomen* (front) which was home to a ceremonial shrine and a picture of Kancho Gozo Shioda, we'd see, out of the corner of our eye, our instructor for the class about to begin come into view. Who arrived to bow to the shomen and then turn and bow to us could make or break the day. The first class of the day was gaining a reputation as the class you loved to hate. It was the one you needed to survive and the one that usually kept me up at night worrying, and we were all finding out that it was Takagi's class that was perhaps the toughest of the tough. The physical pain was bad enough, but it was the monotony of repetition that I found I was struggling with the most. Something new and interesting was what we all craved, and I wondered if seiza and backdrops were all there was to teach.

The monotony was finally broken on Wednesday, 5 April. Rumours circulated that the second and third classes would once again be cancelled. Cancelled classes meant potentially more rest time and less chance of getting injured, but the excitement we'd all had the first time around was this time absent. Our experience at the opening ceremony had taught us that the alternative could be much, much worse. I'm convinced that fear is a close friend of uncertainty, and today the nervous tension in the air had reached a new and worrying level. Malik and Graham Sewanin gathered us together and told us that today we'd be watching the Riot Police's opening ceremony, which meant more seiza. With our long Western legs, more seiza was the last thing we needed. On the positive side, it meant we'd meet the Kidotai. Why Tokyo needed a Riot Police, I wasn't sure. Tokyo was the safest city I'd ever visited, and back home in Nottingham, where the weekend brought its fair share of trouble, we didn't have one. I wondered when Tokyo saw its last riot and what the Riot Police did while they were waiting for trouble. The word

'Riot' when attached to 'Police' conjured up a certain image – an athletic, muscular, and aggressive individual you wouldn't want to mess with. However, as the police cadets marched into the dojo for the first time, their physical manifestation couldn't have been more different. From the daily beatings, our little band of 12 brothers and one sister was becoming battle-hardened. *What have the Kidotai been doing while we've been backdropping?* I thought to myself, and I wasn't alone in my thinking. Thrown together in the face of adversity, Matt, Lloyd, Geoff, Dave, Ronen, Dror, Boaz, Neville, Clyde, Kambara, Inazaki, Vic and I, had become tight. Now, with the arrival of Chiba, Takamatsu, Kashigawa, Ikeda, Tsuji, Toya, Tsuzuku, Tachiki, Kondo and Koyasu, what could we expect? If the truth be told, we couldn't wait to get our hands on them. They were on our turf, and we had things to prove. Things were surely about to get interesting. I learnt we'd meet the cops in the second class of the day. The first class would remain the usual beasting dished out predominantly by the international instructors, with the final class again reserved only for international Senshusei. Sure, our new comrades on the course would stay behind after we'd left the honbu for the day to receive further instruction, but the consensus already was that they had it much easier.

SICKENING SEIZA

The end of our first full week was strange. I'd sold my worldly possessions to travel to Japan and learn Aikido from the masters, but here I was now playing hide and seek, like a bunch of kids in a school playground. The source of this diversion was Laurance Sensei. Laurance with an 'a' would become a regular fixture on our weekly schedule – and an annoying one at that. A former international Senshusei, he'd stuck around as Sewanin and now was determined to earn his rite of passage as a fully-fledged instructor by punishing a fresh intake of recruits. He'd been where we'd been, but rather than being sympathetic to our plight, he seemed to want to push the pain as much as possible. Laurance had a boyish look about him, and it was perhaps his youth that led to a specific form of training he deemed suitable for Senshusei. I wasn't sure whether it was a spur-of-the-moment decision, some kind of joke, or because he couldn't think of anything more appropriate to do. While Romeo, Takagi and Murray Sensei had destroyed us with harsh physical exercise, which had never-ending backdrops centre stage, Laurance instructed us to play hunt the belt. This form of hide and seek saw us run around the dojo searching everywhere for our belts, which Laurance had previously hidden. I eventually found mine and did my best to tie it before the clock counted down. Failure to do so was punishable, and by now we'd all come to appreciate what punishment Senshusei style meant. It's fair to say we were all bemused by Laurance's class and relieved when it finished early. However, when a class finished early or was replaced by something else, it didn't necessarily mean good news. The two opening ceremonies we'd endured were testament to that. Far better to know what was coming, no matter how bad, than be curve-balled by a surprise you weren't physically prepared for or mentally able to take. An early bath or change of schedule had previously resulted in seiza, and lots of it. Seiza, I was fast learning, was the static and silent enemy of all Senshusei, no matter how tough.

We were told that next up would be a meditation session with Inoue Kancho, which immediately concerned me. The last time I'd done meditation was when I was 16 on a week-long Kung Fu summer school in Torquay. We finished every day with 30 minutes of meditation, and without fail, no matter how hard I tried not to, I'd fallen asleep. I suspected that falling asleep in Kancho's session would not be good form, but in suffering from the early starts and the onset of tiredness, particularly in the third class, it was a distinct possibility. Still, life was simple on the course. There was no choice in anything. You just got on with the task in hand. My nerves didn't matter, and my apprehension made no odds. In anticipation of Kancho's arrival, we sat opposite one another in parallel lines either side of the shomen. Within minutes the initial comfort of sitting still turned to acute pain, as quite literally, the life drained from my legs and, along with it, my ability to make rational sense of the world. Seiza was a surreal experience, a game of survival and a mashup of physical and emotional turmoil. None of us had any idea how long we'd be in this position or what was about to happen. All we knew was that Kancho would arrive soon, but the clock was ticking. Where was Kancho?

Finally, Kancho arrived, and I'd never been so pleased to see him shuffle across the mats and take his position in seiza under the shomen, centre stage and facing down the parallel lines of Sensei, Sewanin and Senshusei, all lined up in grade order. Once something started, I knew it had to finish at some point. Waiting for something to start in the first place was the worst kind of pain. Kancho proceeded to speak to us about Aikido in Japanese. Dave daydreamed, and Geoff looked like he was about to pass out. Ronen maintained focus and made the job look easy. I was struggling and couldn't stop my legs from involuntarily shaking. I just prayed Kancho wouldn't notice. Despite some knowledge of Japanese, I wasn't listening and was convinced no one else was listening, either. The only person capable of understanding what was going on was Clyde, but he was too busy, along with Matt, trying not to lose composure and end up on Kancho's naughty list so early on. Kancho showed no sympathy and just kept going. Every word he uttered we hoped would be his last, but as every new sentence began, our short-lived hope of the end being in sight turned back to the fear of how long this thing might last. Our collective pain and suffering were clearly evident, but Kancho made no attempt to speed up or cut things short. I had no idea what he was saying, and with that much pain surging through my legs, even if I had understood, I'd have had no cognitive bandwidth left to take it in.

After what seemed like an eternity, but was actually about 30 minutes, the ordeal ended. While the Japanese got up with no trouble at all, it was Dave who cracked first. A quivering wreck, unable to stand or even make an attempt at it, with tears in his eyes he fell forwards and lay there motionless. For a moment I thought he was dead. The blood flowed back into my legs, shooting pins and needles relentlessly through my lower body, and as soon as I was able, I rushed to his aid. It turned out he wasn't dead, and a few of us, now just about able to walk ourselves, lifted Dave up and marched him around the dojo, hoping gravity would take effect and drive the blood back down to his feet. Luckily an emergency amputation wasn't needed, and Dave walked again. We'd all survived, and for a brief moment our collective spirits were lifted. That is, until we heard what all of us had feared. From now on this class would take place every Thursday, and its name would be *zagaku*, where za meant to *sit* and gaku to learn.

MUSICAL STATUES

The week was almost done, but there were still six classes between me and the two-day break where I'd have 48 hours to pull myself together before week two began. Higa Sensei arrived to take Friday's first session. Soft-spoken and with what I could best describe as a calming personality, he seemed to glide to the front of the class before bringing us to attention and then into right kamae. *'Migi hamae kamae!'* My *right* leg slid forward. Weight firmly over my front knee, right hand extended like a sword in front of me, mirrored by my left hand just in front of my stomach, I'd arrived in the Aikido ready position. I'd stood in this position many times before and it had never felt like a strong, ready position. I'd always felt stuck to the ground with an inability to move, and today felt even worse. My legs were burned out from yesterday's seiza marathon, and encouragement from Higa to place even more weight over my front leg was unwelcome. We stood there, eyes front, focused on the shomen wall and the windows either side, which opened out onto a busy Tokyo street – a world of normality that seemed a million miles away from my present predicament. We stood there some more in anticipation of the next command, and after what seemed about 10 minutes rooted to the spot, our collective legs shook uncontrollably. The course was already showing me a new sensation; the feeling of not being in control of my body or what it might do at any point. Had Higa forgotten his lesson plan, left the mats to take a call, or possibly fallen asleep out of sight at the back of the dojo? I glanced out of the corner of my eye in either direction. I could see I wasn't alone in wondering what the hell was going on. I couldn't see the clock, and even if I'd been able to, looking at it during class was seen as disrespectful and was punishable in some form or other. *'Ki o tsuke!'* Finally, the call came, and we broke position to come to *attention*. It didn't take a genius to figure out what was coming next, but I lived in hope. For a moment we enjoyed a small oasis in a kamae desert before *'hidari hamae kamae!'* A frightening surge of disappointment enveloped the group, as it dawned on us, we were off again, and this torture would last an hour. Our temporary respite was vanquished as we slid forwards into the clutches of *left* kamae. 30 minutes on the right would now be followed by the same again on the left. The change of side initially felt good, but within seconds it was replaced by intense pain throughout my body, and particularly my lower back. We'd been advised that moving in seiza, though offering temporary relief, made things worse; and it seemed, given current circumstances, that kamae was much the same. Not to worry; in times of trouble, you could always rely on the Sewanin. Malik and Graham shouted words of encouragement and provided the occasional and all-too-brief shoulder massage. *Give me 300 backdrops over this any day*, I thought to myself and prayed for the ordeal to be over.

I'd enjoyed the game of musical statues as a child, but this was a new and far less enjoyable way to play it. For one, there was no music, and two, it was no fun. Geoff was the odd one out. Finished off by backdrops courtesy of the past few days, he'd found himself in *mitori geiko*. Even when injured, the course provided not let-up, and mitori geiko roughly translated as *training through watching*. This didn't mean you sat on a comfortable seat at the back of the dojo taking notes on what you were missing. No, it meant sitting in seiza on your own in the corner of the dojo while trying to understand and remember what was going on. As Higa relieved our misery by calling us to attention, I looked behind and momentarily caught Geoff's eye. The look on his face told me everything I needed to know about mitori geiko, and I made a mental note to do my very best to avoid injury at all costs. From what I'd learnt today, injury meant seiza, and seiza meant potentially more injury! We were all proud; very proud. Higa had tried to drown us in a sea of physical and psychological turmoil. Despite his best efforts, we'd made it to shore.

After the monotony of the kamae class, rumours circulated around the tearoom that our next class would be with Chino Sensei. Chino had a formidable reputation for destroying his *uke* (the person receiving a technique) and was arguably one of Kancho Gozo Shioda's most dedicated students. While others favoured a softer style of Yoshinkan Aikido, I'd heard that Chino's style was as brutal as it got. Given his reputation, we all feared the worst and took our places in seiza at the edge of the mats to await his arrival to teach the second class of the day. Despite our initial terror, Chino seemed to go easy. He guided us through *hiriki ichi*, one of the fundamental moves of Aikido incorporated into the *kihon dosa*, which resembled the motion of first raising and then cutting down with a sword. The kihon dosa was something I was already very familiar with. A series of six movements, they formed the foundations of all Aikido moves and incorporated either entering or turning motions. All six movements had their origins in sword cutting, which we now drilled empty-handed under Chino's watchful eye. Practicing kihon dosa was a move in the right direction. These six movements were the bridge between kamae and *kihon waza* (techniques), and it was the waza I wanted to get to. I'd never seen Steven Seagal destroy his opponents with the six fundamental moves. It was waza, not dosa that he'd used. There was no holding of stances for long periods of time, and the Chino I'd heard about seemed very different in real life. Perhaps he was just lulling us into a false sense of security or happened to be in a particularly good mood. Despite his amicable, almost lenient induction, I felt convinced it wouldn't be long until we saw a very different side to him.

Before the first week was over, we'd also taken instruction from Ito Sensei, Naruo Sensei and Murata Sensei, three Japanese instructors who offered very different interpretations of what the Senshusei course was all about. Good, bad and somewhat confusing! Ito was Chida Dojocho's principal uke. Chida took Ito as his uke for public demonstrations, a huge honour bestowed on Ito, who in turn had adopted Chida's more fluid and less forceful style. I could tell immediately that Ito Sensei was a genuinely nice guy, and his first class with us was extremely technical and lacking in the brutality we'd experienced in other classes. Naruo Sensei conformed to type and, through shrieks and screams, used his opening class to drill us yet again on kamae, kamae and yet more kamae. He had a pitch that reverberated around the dojo with a force and intensity like no other, as if his balls were trapped in a vice! This seismic energy bounced off the walls, the mats and permeated through our quivering bodies. Higa had broken any enthusiasm I had for kamae, but Naruo mustn't have got the memo. We drilled it again and again, and while I appreciated the importance of a strong stance, if I was to ever have a chance of defending myself using Aikido in a street situation, I would need a lot more. Although our experience with Ito had been good, Naruo brought things back to bad and continued the rollercoaster of ups and downs Senshusei was already becoming. Despite appearing a thoroughly nice guy, rightly or wrongly, whenever I saw Naruo Sensei, I imagined him in the vintage green uniform of the Imperial Japanese Army. I could see him barking out orders in a Japanese POW camp, and I wondered how different, or similar, our time together might have been 65 years earlier. Murata Sensei provided something else altogether, and before the week was out, we'd learned that his classes would be some of the most relaxing and interesting on the course. Relaxing for me was always interesting. Although I was in Japan to learn all I could about Aikido from the masters, my desire for hard training was constantly tempered by my quest for survival. While we had the tearoom, the Riot Police had the *sho dojo*, a *small room off the main dojo* where they stored their stuff and took refuge in between classes. For his inaugural class, Murata Sensei took us in there and played a 20-minute video of a grading that took place back in 2003. I didn't understand why we were watching it, and to be honest, I didn't care. The opportunity to sit down free from seiza was a wonderful experience and one I was determined to savour. At the end he explained that the reason for watching was to teach us that when moving into position, we needed to move fast. As much as I'd enjoyed my 20 minutes of rest and recovery, I was certain it would have been much simpler and quicker just to tell us.

The week was over, and we'd survived. Geoff was in a bad way, but he'd not quit yet, and although all 13 of us already had our fair share of bumps and bruises, we'd proved we could get through what they had thrown at us. If we could survive the first week, then we had a chance of surviving them all. In the locker room, as Matt peeled the sanitary towels off his bleeding lower back, the British contingent on the course agreed to grab some food afterwards. Sanitary towels had become a Senshusei staple; when taped just above the coccyx, they provided some protection from the backdrops we'd all now come to know and hate. They were difficult to apply and with the time pressure to get ready, a convoy system had developed. Before class Matt had taped a towel to my back, while Clyde applied the same to Matt's ass! Matt, Dave and I were already well acquainted, and lunch would be a chance for us to get to know Neville. Neville was from Lincolnshire, which wasn't too far from Nottingham. He had a background in Aikido and, similar to Matt and me, had come to Japan for a real experience in its country of origin. But before we could sit down to lunch for a good chinwag about the week just gone, there was one important task that needed doing. As we piled into the chemist opposite the entrance to Ochiai Station, it was no doubt a strange site for the checkout staff to see Westerners out and about in this part of town. What must have seemed even stranger, was four grown men clearing the shelves of sanitary towels. On reflection, though, as we were the 16th international course and the pharmacy being near the honbu dojo, while the whole experience was unusual and awkward for us, the staff, I'm sure, had seen it all before!

AN OPPORTUNITY OF A LIFETIME

The two-day break was an opportunity to wash my dogi and try to find time to relax in between English teaching. On the way to my Sunday stint at Berlitz, I'd stopped to phone Mum and Dad, who let me know that my Uncle Frank had died that morning. My time at boarding school had removed any prospect of homesickness in my later years, but news of a family member passing brought sharply into focus how far away from home I was – over 9,000 kilometres in distance and nine hours ahead of the UK. For the first time since arriving in Tokyo, I felt the pain of separation from my family. Uncle Frank wasn't actually my uncle; in fact, he was my Mum's uncle. I didn't see much of him, and as a result, we weren't that close. His passing brought back painful memories of losing Nansie and served as a reminder of the fragility and finite nature of life. I was in Japan; I was living my dream, and here was news from home, which reinforced the importance of pursuing my passion. Life was short, and it was there to be lived! I'd left my friends at home working the nine-to-five. It was the sensible career move to get a good education, followed by a good job, and climb the greasy pole of promotion all the way to retirement. On the subway each morning, there were frequent reminders of the corporate rat race and how the majority of Japanese society – and societies across the world – followed it blindly, like laboratory rats in one huge experiment. I was conducting a very different experiment. I was miles from home, in an alien country with a very different culture and having a very different experience indeed. As I walked away from the phone box and into the Berlitz office, I reminded myself that I was lucky to have the opportunity Senshusei presented. My mind knew it even if my body, after the week I'd just had, didn't feel it.

In the UK we have pubs in every city, town and village, and while many have closed in tougher times, they still exist in abundance and are an important part of our heritage and culture. In Japan and especially in Tokyo, the abundance of the British pubs back home was matched by fighting gyms and martial arts schools, which were found all over the place. Mixed Martial Arts (MMA) was becoming increasingly popular, and between the UFC in America and the Pride Fighting Championships in Japan, the MMA scene was only set to grow. Even Musashi Koyama, a quiet suburb just off the main JR Yamanote Line was home to Sakuraba's gym. Kasushi Sakuraba had made his name in MMA as 'The Gracie Hunter'. The Gracie family had risen to fame as the kings of the fighting world when Royce Gracie won the first UFC in November 1993. Because of Royce's win, the Gracie style of ground fighting had taken the world by storm, and to cater to young Japanese fighters inspired by Sakuraba's victories over several of the Gracie family in Pride, MMA gyms were now all over Tokyo. As I rode the train lines to and from Berlitz, I'd see these gyms everywhere, alongside the traditional Karate and Judo schools normally associated with Japan. For a martial artist like me, Japan presented the opportunity of a lifetime, not just to train in Aikido but also to train elsewhere, too. Honbu rules specifically forbade any Senshusei from partaking in other martial arts or training anywhere else while enrolled in the course. As the old adage goes, *rules are made to be broken*, and for me, the risk of getting caught was worth it. What the honbu dojo didn't know wouldn't hurt them, and my only risk would be getting injured elsewhere and having to explain myself to the Sewanin. I guessed I could always pretend the injury had happened on the course. A knee or ankle injury would be easy to link to Aikido, but a broken nose or a black eye might prove difficult to get over the line.

Since arriving in Japan and while training as a regular student in Aikido, I'd been practicing Muay Thai at several gyms across Tokyo. Masato was Japan's most famous kickboxer; a K1 champion (K1 was a major Kickboxing promotion), he trained at Shin Nihon Kickboxing, Ihara Dojo near Ebisu. I'd hunted it down and been training there regularly. While home to some amazing trainers, including 'Nopadet' Chuwatana, a Rajadamnern Stadium champion, the gym often had press and media attendance ahead of Masato's fights, and I'd got bored with turning up and the place being too packed to do a proper session. I'd met Masato in the changing rooms one day. Somewhat of a pin-up and popular amongst the non-fighting Japanese populous, I'd found him more interested in the appearance of his hair than the opportunity to chat to me. I'd decided a move to Weerasakreck Fairtex was the way forward. Fairtex was a well-known and well-established Muay Thai gym in Thailand that had successfully exported its brand and training across the globe. Japan, with its obsession with the fighting arts and the country wanting to secure its homegrown fighters' dominance in the K1 and

Pride arenas, had welcomed an influx of former professional Thai fighters to teach its own. Striking was my background and Muay Thai my bread and butter; and I continued to train at Fairtex throughout the course.

Caught up with the whole Gracie, Sakuraba, Pride thing, I'd also hunted down a Brazilian Jiu Jitsu school run by Takamasa 'Taka' Watanabe, a Rickson Gracie black belt. Axis Jiu Jitsu was a few stops outside of central Tokyo at Meidaimae, and I'd tried to get across to train at least once a week since my first class on Monday, 8 August 2005. If the Sewanin found out, they found out; but once a martial artist, always a martial artist, and I couldn't help but take advantage of what Tokyo had to offer. I'd nearly got myself into trouble, though, earlier in the week. As part of the Senshusei course we'd be learning self-defence, and Takagi Sensei had introduced a self-defence element into one of her classes. I'd caught Dave in an arm-bar, much to his surprise, and then quickly remembered this was supposed to be self-defence the Aikido way. I released it quickly, and no one seemed to be any the wiser.

Training at Fairtex and Axis was a break from the monotony and a world away from the regimented and often oppressive environment that I'd experienced at the honbu. I'd realised there was a big difference between having to train (now that my decision to do the course had been made) and choosing to train in my free time!

WHAT A LOAD OF RUBBISH!

Each week we switched cleaning studies and after the men's toilets last week, week two of the course had me demoted to bins. Although it felt like a demotion, in reality it was probably more of a sideways move. Through my Japanese study it was apparent that much of Japanese English was in fact American English, I guess because of the post-war occupation by US troops. Rubbish in the dojo was in fact garbage, which made bin duty more like taking out the trash. At Berlitz I'd constantly find myself in a losing battle. With the Berlitz manuals teaching American English, I was on a one-man quest to teach my Japanese students British English. Still, when in Rome and all that; and if the honbu decreed it was garbage duty, garbage duty it was.

For garbage duty, I was reunited with Matt. Having persuaded him to join me in Japan and to embark on the course, I was now feeling guilty and wondered if he was already regretting his decision to sign up. Little pleasures meant a lot in dojo life and taking out the trash came with its own silver lining. Of all the cleaning duties, garbage duty was the only one that came with a temporary permit to leave the honbu. The bins that would be collected by Tokyo's waste management trucks were a short walk down the street. When we entered the honbu dojo, usually just after 7am, Tokyo was still asleep, and the walk down the road at 7:45am was a unique chance to glimpse regular people on their way to work. Matt and I got some stares. Who were these strange Westerners, wearing white pyjamas and carrying black rubbish bags? The rubbish run was also our opportunity to laugh and joke freely away from the reprimand of the Sewanin. Out in the real world, there was only a minimal chance of being overheard. Our laughter was just enough for those around us to hear, but never loud enough to be heard upstairs through the dojo windows.

One of the funniest things about taking the bins out were the shoes we had to wear. The honbu was a shoe-free zone, and although we'd arrive wearing shoes each morning, these were deposited in the shoe cupboards that adorned both sides of the entrance hall, not to be seen again until the end of the day. To leave the honbu or to go to the toilet, we were all reliant on the Japanese version of flip-flops. Just as the ugly sisters failed to fit into the glass slipper in *Cinderella*, the Western foot was not designed to fit into the small brown plastic slip-on shoes designed only for Japanese feet. In the toilets, too, we had to exchange bare feet for slippers. Once again these were too small, and we had to shuffle into position to answer nature's call. The removal of outdoor shoes before entering the home or dojo was common practice across Japan and was something I was in favour of. Back in the UK, I never understood why people would knowingly drag dirt into their own houses and onto their carpets by what they'd picked up on the bottom of their shoes throughout the day. Similarly, in gyms I'd trained at, running off the mats barefoot to the toilet and back was usual but no doubt brought many nasties into the training area that had no place there.

As we got to midweek, Matt and I had cracked the garbage duty. That is until Wednesday's collection. Unbeknown to us, as we'd carried the assorted sacks of refuse down the stairs, out into the street and down to the public bins ready for collection, we'd made one huge error. Walking back up the small incline to the dojo, our laughter quietened as we noticed a trail leading us right back to the honbu. These tracks got worse as we entered the entrance hall of the building and worse still on the stairs. *One bag has a leak*, I thought to myself; *we've dripped something all the way down the stairs!* We'd failed to read the Senshusei Cleaning Checklist properly and forgotten the duct tape! Matt and I in only a couple of days had our timing down to a tee. Yesterday, we'd maximised our time outside in the fresh air and returned just in time for the morning meeting. Now, on Wednesday, there was no time to clean up the mess.

Each morning Malik and Graham Sewanin hosted the pre-training meeting in the tearoom. It was a small room by any measure, especially when it needed to accommodate 13 Senshusei and two Sewanin crowded round a table and chairs. Along the near wall were shelves covered by a curtain that pulled across to hide what was contained behind. This was where we stored our food, drinks and medical supplies. This was where, when time permitted, we refuelled in between classes and prepared ourselves mentally for the next. I'm not sure anyone ever sat at the table apart from the Shinkoku (we rarely said the word toban and used Shinkoku to refer to the ceremony and also the person leading it) who had the responsibility of writing up the dojo diary at the end of the day's training. As far as I was aware, it would be bad form for any other Senshusei to be caught sitting down, and none of us had dared to try it for fear of the consequences. The table and chairs instead formed a focal point for the room and an inconvenient obstruction we had to navigate, by pushing and shoving, to get into position to await the Sewanin. The morning meeting seemed to serve two purposes, which were wholly at odds with one another. On the one hand, it was the official forum for the Sewanin to single any of us out for a verbal thrashing in front of our peers. On the other hand, it was a vehicle to motivate and mentally prepare us for the day ahead. If we looked good out there on the mats, they looked good. So far, faced with the choice between carrot and stick, they'd favoured the stick, and Wednesday morning was to prove no exception.

I already knew the Sewanin had eyes like hawks, and as they marched in, I began to fear the worst. *'Osu, ohayou gozaimasu, osu!'* Formalities over, Malik Sewanin called us out, *'Simon Senshusei, Matt Senshusei…'*. We already knew what was coming. They'd spotted the mess on the stairs, and it turned out we'd also dripped the mysterious liquid down the corridor that passed by Kancho's office. *'Osu…osu…osu'*, we cried in response to Malik's tongue-lashing. It didn't matter what he said, the response was always osu. To be honest, I wasn't really listening. The benefit of only being permitted to utter one word meant that I didn't need to follow the flow of any verbal bashing and tried my best to block it out of my mind instead. As I cried my last *'osu'* one more time for good measure, all I could think was *what a load of rubbish!*

OYAMADNESS

Oyamada Sensei had a particular reputation around the dojo. We'd heard tales from previous Senshusei about his classes, and today it was our turn to sample the real thing.

At school I'd had good teachers, and I'd had bad teachers, but as far as I could remember I'd never had a teacher that really didn't want to teach and also didn't mind letting his or her pupils know. By the time I got to Berlitz, I was usually tired, and by now I'd been through most of the material I would teach for the foreseeable future at least once. I was already getting bored but refused to let this boredom spill over into the experience of my students. I was being paid to provide a professional service. If I gave my students an enjoyable experience, my experience would surely be more enjoyable, and they'd probably learn a lot more, too. Yawning, whinging and moaning was reserved for my five-minute lesson breaks. If these made their way into the classroom, I was sure it wouldn't be long before I got fired.

Boredom was fast becoming the enemy of the Senshusei. The physical pain was one thing, but boredom impacted the mental game. Less than two weeks into the course, I'd already been tested by Higa's kamae class, and now it was Oyamada's turn. From what I'd heard, the level of boredom in his classes took things to a whole new level. Being the second class of the day, there would also be an extra 30 minutes to endure. The honbu dojo paid Oyamada Sensei; he was an experienced instructor. I decided to give him the benefit of the doubt. *'Ichi, ni…ichi, ni…ichi, ni…'* over and over again. The rumours were true, and the repetitive movements went on and on in rhythm to his uninspired and monotonous chant. Maybe he just didn't like the international students. There was still some prejudice in Japan, and I'd regularly walk past bars with signs outside forbidding gaijin from entering. Perhaps he would be better with the cops? Perhaps he would be more enthusiastic then? Perhaps he would even crack a smile? I'd been told that Oyamada was one of only a few Sensei at the honbu dojo who hadn't done the Senshusei course himself. This would explain a lot. Like a general who has never been to war leading a platoon of troops into battle, to me, based on his first outing, Oyamada Sensei's position on the teaching roster made no sense at all. What he had to teach wasn't for me, and in my mind, his lack of Senshusei credentials put him at the bottom of the pile of who I was in Japan to learn from. While the class was no surprise, the 10-minute early finish was. I'd become wary of any change in schedule, but it seemed on this occasion, it meant an extra-long tea break. I can only assume that Oyamada had bored himself, too, and, with the thought of his tea and biscuits waiting, had called time early.

BATHTIME

In Japan, and especially in Tokyo, space was scarce. As it was one of the most populated cities in the world, the majority of the population lived in apartment blocks. Traditionally, many would not have had washing facilities, and with cleanliness a top priority, the lack of space led to the creation of the *sento*, a Japanese *communal bathhouse.* Spatial challenges also gave rise to a very different type of establishment. *Rabu hoteru* or *love hotels* were all over Tokyo. Courting couples found privacy for sexual activities that couldn't be performed at home. Signage was sparse and discretion guaranteed, thanks to Japan's technological revolution.

At the sento you paid a fee to enter. Inside, crouched in front of rows of taps, you'd find Japanese men and women (segregated to protect each other's modesty) engaged in the business of washing, at all hours of the day. In modern times, the sento could still be found all across Japan. A bit like the European spa, the experience seemed to have become less about washing and more about relaxation with the availability of saunas, plunge pools and jet baths. For sweaty, battered and bruised Senshusei, washing was first on the agenda. Although there were showers in the dojo that we were free to use, we were still in the dojo and never far from the shouts and screams of the Sewanin. Even when class was over and cleaning duties done, if you were on the premises, you were still Senshusei, with the obligatory requirement to bow and scrape and perform any task asked of you without question. This made it very hard to relax, and when time permitted, the sento was a more favourable choice, as it promised a more enjoyable end to the training day.

Just across from the dojo, there was one such sento, and Clyde and I decided to give it a whirl. Thank goodness for Clyde, who, it turned out, was a very useful guy to know. Hailing from the United States, he was half Japanese with a very good command of the Japanese language. While my Japanese was good for basic pleasantries, it wasn't up to gaining entry to a sento and understanding the many formalities I was sure would accompany public bathing. Clyde got us in with no problems, and we turned immediately right into the male bathing area, where we were greeted by a line of lockers. After getting undressed, I walked nervously into the washing area. I was used to swimming pools in the UK but there I had a pair of swim shorts for privacy and comfort. Now, here I was in Tokyo, tackle swinging, completely exposed and very much out of my comfort zone. I knew the song by Sting, *An Englishman in New York*, but a naked Englishman in a Japanese sento didn't have the same ring to it. Clyde and I grabbed our stools, and, perched at the end of a long line of bathers, we awkwardly began to wash. Opposite us were several heavily tattooed Japanese men. In Japan you could be turned away from many establishments if you sported visible ink, no matter how discreet. Yet here in what was a very public place were not just small tattoos but full-body ones, on display for all to see. I'd heard the rumours and checked with Clyde. He confirmed that these were *Yakuza*, the *Japanese mafia* or *organised crime*. Apparently as a Yakuza member, if you offended your boss, you might be required to cut off your little finger as a show of loyalty and respect. I had a quick scan of the digits on display, but by my count couldn't find any missing.

Naked and in the presence of those who could do me considerable harm didn't seem like a great combination, so I changed the subject quickly. Clyde was already finding life on the course tougher than most. Besides the physical training, mental torture and constant fear of being reprimanded for doing something wrong, Clyde had another level of pressure to carry on his shoulders. When the Japanese Sensei struggled to communicate a point of detail on a technique, they'd turn to Clyde. This meant he could never switch off and always had to be ready to turn their incomprehensible Japanese into understandable English. The Sewanin hated this, as it undermined their power. It gave Clyde a different status with the Sensei, which cut the Sewanin out. I'd already heard Malik and Graham's attempts at translation, which, from my own study of Japanese, I knew occasionally to be wrong and sometimes the complete opposite of what the Sensei was trying to get across. Clyde was already feeling the target on his back. While the rest of us were trying to keep our heads down, Clyde's was well above the parapet.

The sento turned out to be an enjoyable experience with an added bonus particular to this establishment. There was a coin-operated laundry upstairs, very similar to the one I used to wash my clothes in Musashi Koyama. Like baths, washing machines took up space, and where space was at a premium, the Japanese went out to wash their clothes, too. Clyde and I had survived our first visit and exited with all of our fingers intact. With the laundry upstairs, I already knew that this would become a regular haunt. I could wash my dogi while I bathed and then grab some food at the Royal Host restaurant down the road while the dryers went to work. It was a perfect combination, and also, I wouldn't need to carry my sweat-soaked dogi home. Once the job was done, I could carry them the short walk back to the honbu and hang them up clean, dry and ready for the next day's training. There was a huge rail in the ceiling just inside the entrance to the matted area. No need to burden myself with the excess weight, I could hang them up there and travel home or onto Berlitz unencumbered.

TURNING POINT

I knew there would be pivotal days on the course from conversations with previous Senshusei – days that would break up the monotony and frustration of trying to get the techniques to work and failing miserably. The concept of *kaizen* was something I'd read about. A commitment to *continuous improvement* was at the core of Japanese business, but it also applied just as well to the martial arts. Although any noticeable improvement had so far eluded me, I tried to focus on the smallest of details hoping they might add up to something big. Kaizen was like zagaku and the practice of self-reflection to improve. *Hansei* was the Japanese word for self-reflection and acknowledgement of one's own mistake, and plan for improvement. Han meant to *change* or *turn over* and sei to *look back on, review* and *examine*. Hansei and kaizen were at the core of what it meant to be Japanese.

My Dad, as a freeman of the City of London, had introduced me to the Merchant Taylors' Company. One of the 12 great livery companies, their motto also held significance and provided inspiration to keep trying. *Concordia parvae res crescunt* meant *in harmony small things grow.* Aikido was supposed to be about harmony, and I was doing my best to get as many of the small things right. Aikido is a difficult martial art. Muay Thai is tough, but even after a little training, it's easy to throw a punch or a kick and make it look half decent. After six months of training in Muay Thai, technically you were deemed competent enough to fight. Aikido was very different. If your posture was not quite right, or your body positioning was even a few degrees off, it could be impossible to make any technique work. If the effectiveness of Muay Thai was measured in inches, in Aikido you'd need to be accurate to the nearest millimetre; you needed surgical precision to make things happen.

Until now, I'd been focused purely on survival and not getting injured, but Thursday, 13 April 2006, was to be an important turning point on my Senshusei journey. It was to be the day that I started to learn and to open up to what the course was there to teach me. The day started like any other day, and in the first class, under the supervision of Murray Sensei, we practiced our ukemi. I'd still not grasped the importance of ukemi. Martial arts had always been more about dishing it out than learning to take it. In Muay Thai I didn't stand in front of my opponent and let him hit me so I could get used to the sensation, but ukemi and learning to go with *shite* (the person applying the technique) made little sense and didn't come naturally. The flip was the nemesis of the Aikido novice. I was a lot better than most, but their repeated execution into hard mats was working to grind me down. You don't forget your first kiss, and Aikidoka never forget their first successful flip. It was easy to identify the first successful one, as it was the first one that didn't hurt you. Mine had been back at the Shudokan at the hands of Sensei Phil Musson. A black belt under Sensei Ken, he'd told me to trust in the fall and to *'go for it!'* He was right and having committed I got up to my feet with no pain at all. In today's first class, though, judging by the shouts and screams I could hear echoing through the dojo, the ability to fall safely was still eluding some of my fellow Senshusei. It had taken me months to get my first one right, and we were still only two weeks in. Murray Sensei upped the ante by placing two chairs in front of the soft mat we'd been practicing our falls on. This necessitated an extra big jump and subsequent flip to clear the chairs. A bigger jump required more commitment, which was likely to lead to more problems. I did this on both sides, left and right, but Dror, who was up next, would not be so lucky. Dror, part of the Israeli contingent on the course, lacked Ronen's toughness, and I'd sensed from the off a certain lack of confidence, possibly connected to his younger age. He made his run up. It needed a fast run up to generate the speed to jump the required height to clear the chairs. There could be no hesitation, and the lift off had to be timed perfectly. Too early and you'd land on the chairs; too late and you'd run right through them. His speed looked good, his commitment to take flight looked good, but like a racehorse pulling up at a jump, he half launched and half didn't. His moment of hesitation had cost him and, hitting his head on the top of one chair mid-flight, he was lucky not to have knocked himself out. Geoff was also struggling, so much so I couldn't bear to watch. I was certain it would only be a matter of time before he did himself some serious damage.

The next class passed without drama, and I remembered that today was Thursday. The painful experience of last week was about to happen again. A shorter last class in exchange for at least 30 minutes of zagaku was a poor deal in my book. Still, we had no choice and lined up in two lines facing one another. The Sensei filed in and took their positions closer to the shomen. I was expecting Inoue Kancho, but to my surprise Sonoda Sensei appeared and took his position at the head of the lines. The Sewanin had warned us to prepare both a reflection and habit, and thankfully I'd heeded their advice. Dror went first, and then I heard *'Simon Senshusei'* called. *'Hai!'* I bowed in acknowledgement. Everyone bowed back. We'd all grown to like bowing. It was a momentary excuse to move and relieve the pressure of weight through the knees and ankles, an opportunity to let the blood find its way back into our blood-starved legs. The bow complete, it was my moment in the limelight, my chance to shine – or, if I messed things up, to put myself firmly on the radar for future punishment. I could feel the Sewanin's eyes bearing down on me, boring a hole through my soul with a clear and precise message – *do not fuck this up!* Reflecting that I was learning about harmony and discipline on the mats, which was also making me a better person away from the honbu, was met with grunts of approval. Articulating my habit of completing my diary every night before going to sleep also, to my surprise, found favour. Bowing and uttering the words *'ijo desu'* (the end or finished), I felt a wave of enlightenment rise through my subconscious. Perhaps Aikido wasn't about fighting but about self-mastery? To gain control over my opponent, I must first get control of myself. My hollow words to please the Sensei suddenly had new meaning. Instead of battling with my opponent, my mission should be to harmonise with his or her energy, and through discipline and self-control, I had a chance of discovering how to exert martial power over others. This felt like an important turning point, and I let the moment sink in. I didn't want to forget and lose it for ever to the pain of the vice-like grip of my current sitting position. Graham Sewanin and one of the Japanese Sensei gave feedback on what Dror and I had shared. Repeating what we'd both said didn't really seem like advice of any sort, but I was good with that. After 35 minutes it was finally over. From last week, I'd learnt not to stand up immediately, and as I fell to my side to let the blood flow freely, I saw Matt and Dave in tears. The Japanese Sensei jumped to their feet. It was all in a day's work for them. Chida Sensei in his attempt at humour decided to walk on the backs of my legs. *'Itai!'* I screamed out loud. *'It hurts'* was the politer version of what I was really thinking and something I knew Chida would understand. His massage wasn't helping, and I had to let him know.

Perhaps as a reward for my performance, before the week was out, Takashima Sensei invited me along with Matt and Victoria to serve tea to Chida Sensei and guests in Kancho's office. This was hallowed turf that no Senshusei was free to tread, and I felt privileged to have been given the honour, even though I knew it would probably be an uncomfortable experience. When the time came, and with no clue what to do, I just stood at attention with a tray in hand, trying not to make eye contact with anyone. Lack of sleep and hard physical exercise didn't mix, but I seemed to survive well on only six hours each night. I'd read that Margaret Thatcher, a former British Prime Minister who was nicknamed the 'Iron Lady', had done it, and now I was following in her footsteps in forging my iron. The mind controlling the body was something I firmly believed in, but from my experience, I knew the body could be very persuasive. With no choice but to do what I was told and with no say over how far the Sewanin and Sensei would push me, my mind was getting stronger. My body could scream and complain all it wanted, but it wasn't part of the conversation.

Naruo Sensei provided a scary finish to the week. To show how to strike a floored opponent following *shihonage* (a technique known as the four-direction throw), he asked for an uke, and I volunteered. He gave me a *bokken* (wooden sword) to hold out parallel with the floor. Taking his own bokken in hand, he struck mine with a terrifying ferocity that shook me to my core. Then, to emphasise the need to hit through the target, he struck for a second time and this time snapped his bokken in half. The temptation to laugh was overwhelming, but could prove very costly, so we all internalised our laughter by gazing at the floor. Again, I had visions of being held prisoner in a POW camp during the Second World War and could only imagine what damage Naruo would have been capable of doing with the real thing!

BUSMAN'S WEEKEND

During the week I'd longed for the weekend and the opportunity to rest my aching muscles, but despite the welcome time away from the honbu, the course was never far out of sight or mind. On Saturday night, at the invitation of the Sewanin, we'd all agreed to meet up for drinks in Shinjuku. I think it was at the Sewanin's suggestion, but it's entirely possible they'd invited themselves to a meet-up we'd privately organised. I was of the view that we should keep a professional distance. In the business world, socialising with the boss was rarely a good idea, and I was sure the same advice translated just as well to the dojo. A night out should have been a chance to relax, but with the Sewanin in tow, I doubted there'd be much opportunity for that. Even if it felt relaxed, I'm sure anything we said or did would come back to bite us. I suspected that lulling us into a false sense of security over a few drinks was all part of their cunning plan.

We spent most of the evening taking the piss out of Dave. Dave, in a relatively short space of time, had established himself as the course joker. I was convinced he said and did stupid stuff just to get a reaction, as he appeared to revel in the attention and ridicule that accompanied his antics. Dave, in my eyes, was a tourist who with nothing better to do had decided to give martial arts a whirl. This was his first venture into the Budo arts, and he'd still failed to give a convincing reason why he was in Japan or had decided to do the course. Although I'd enjoyed reading *Angry White Pyjamas*, my main criticism was that the author also didn't have a background in martial arts. Had Robert Twigger done the course only with a mind to write a book, or was there some other, more compelling reason? I was at the other end of the spectrum. Having trained in the martial arts for a long time, I had every reason to be in Japan and even more reason to do the course. If Dave was there for entertainment, I, alongside Ronen, Matt and a few others, was there for enlightenment. Dave was yet to earn his place, and as in all testosterone-fuelled environments, he would pay. Luckily for him, he seemed to enjoy it!

The *izakaya* (pub or bar) presented a welcome opportunity to drink, but only half of us were on the sauce. Despite being under the watchful eye of the Sewanin, I was determined to have a good time. Five beers in, mixing Asahi and Kirin, I was forgetting my woes and that I had to be up early for Berlitz in the morning. Eventually at around midnight sense kicked in, and I headed home. I'd find out on Monday that Dave, Clyde and Matt had stayed out until 7:30am!

Sunday was a struggle with an 8:30am to 6:15pm shift. I felt tired but not as hungover as I'd expected. Luckily two of my lessons cancelled, and this, combined with my lunch, break enabled me to escape for a while. As the clouds from the night before lifted, once again the course was front and centre in my thoughts. On the way home, I bought the Yoshinkan Aikido instructional book series. I now not only had the real thing to contend with by day, I could immerse myself still further at night. And so, the busman's holiday, or busman's weekend, continued. Our night out with the Sewanin, while physically away from the honbu, had at times felt like a formal dojo event. Even my day off from the dojo and teaching at Berlitz turned out to be hectic.

On Monday I met up with Matt at Axis Jiu Jitsu. I enjoyed the sparring, which was something we didn't get to do in Aikido. The argument was that Aikido wasn't a sport and was too dangerous to use in such a way. For me the jury was still out, and catching Matt in a submission and forcing him to tap provided further evidence that Jiu Jitsu really worked, without my uke having to go with my flow.

THE GREAT CHOCOLATE DEBATE

Week three of the course started with the usual drudge. I found myself on bin duty again, this time with Ronen. Despite being the dirtiest cleaning duty, the chance to leave the dojo even momentarily always made for a pleasant experience. The Sewanin were on it, and they seemed to perform a convincing double-act of good cop, bad cop. Malik took on the role of bad cop, while Graham fell into position as his opposite number. In Tuesday's post-cleaning, pre-training meeting we were treated to one of Malik's motivational talks. I thought motivation would be the tool of the good cop and not the bad one. Malik, at least so far, had been much more stick than carrot. His sermon included encouragement to *'come out fighting'* and a specific demand in the form of *'I need more energy from you!'* Our collective and now well-timed *'osu'* echoed in unison around the tearoom, confirming our understanding and agreement. None of us felt particularly motivated, but it was Tuesday and the start of another week.

Chida Sensei had been in Canada and returned with a gift for the Senshusei. In everyday life a gift is normally welcome and a thank you is all that's required to gratefully acknowledge receipt. If only things were as simple in Japan! Chida's gift presented one huge problem. How should we thank him? Who should do it? What was the correct etiquette? We didn't know, and the Sewanin, who were probably supposed to know, seemed to have no idea, either. After the week's first day of training was over, all I wanted to do was eat my pasta while trying to relax in the tearoom, but Malik rolled in and sparked a full-on debate on how best to perform what should have been the simplest of tasks. *Chida Sensei, I hope you had a great time in Canada and thank you so much for the chocolates, they're delicious,* I thought to myself. It was clear, to the point, and worked for me. But no. That would be far too simple. And so, the great chocolate debate began. Should all 13 of us go and see him? Would one representing all be better? What should we say? When should we catch him? Where would be best? Oh, the complication of it all! We failed to reach a satisfactory resolution, and it was agreed we'd revisit our dilemma later in the week.

There was more kamae this week, with another dose of Higa Sensei's game of statues. Another 30 minutes standing still hurt both body and mind, and to relieve the boredom, I started thinking up Japanese phrases in my head. While the course required my body to be in the dojo, my mind could be somewhere else, and I thought I might as well put it to good use. Higa encouraged us to *'let energy flow from your fingers'*. I didn't understand what he meant but played along all the same. I was confident Lloyd had understood, as in Sonoda Sensei's class we went head to head on strikes. Lloyd was letting his energy flow, and I was the unwilling recipient. We practiced *shomen uchi ikajo*. This involved me chopping Lloyd with my right forearm and him blocking and rolling my elbow over to take me down to the ground. I'm sure he was trying to snap my elbow, so in frustration my shomen strikes got progressively harder as I tried to knock him over. It's hard to break steel, and Lloyd, though tall and wiry, had a core of the hard stuff. If I couldn't break him, perhaps I could at least leave a few dents! At the end of the class, his arms were noticeably bruised. Muay Thai had taught me to take a beating, and blocking kicks with my forearms for the last 16 years had helped me survive the day.

Approximately 24 hours after the debate had started, the saga of how to thank Chida Sensei was resolved. Inazaki, one of two Japanese Senshusei not attached to the Kidotai, was given the task. Inazaki was one of us and, being Japanese, was the best choice. He would represent all 13 of us with a formal thank you to Chida. How he performed would determine our collective fate and whether we'd be punished by the Sewanin afterwards. We watched from the safety of the tearoom. I could see Malik Sewanin was panicking. The hierarchy at the honbu meant that if we messed up with the Sensei, the Sewanin would get it in the neck. They, in turn, would dish it out to us. Inazaki marched up to the office window, bowed and shouted something across to Chida Sensei in Japanese. I didn't understand what he said. It was short and to the point, and of course began and finished with *'osu!'* Chida raised his head and nodded, and Inazaki made a hasty retreat to the tearoom. That was it – the problem and panic were over. We all breathed a sigh of relief. Well overdue, the great chocolate debate was finally over!

ENTER THE DRAGON

Of all the Sensei at the honbu dojo, Chino was the one who embodied the version of Aikido I wanted to learn. At our first meeting, he'd not been quite what I'd expected. He had a reputation for brutality, but on his first outing he'd been calm and compassionate. Thursday, 20 April 2006, was the day we would meet the real Chino. The dragon entered at last, and the volunteer for a dose of destruction was Graham Sewanin. Chino Sensei controlled Graham effortlessly. Despite being half Graham's size, Chino's technique cut through the Sewanin like a knife through butter. Graham resembled a rag doll as he flew through the air in a desperate attempt to survive. As Chino's uke, Graham's job was to receive Chino's technique. I'd already seen other uke comply too willingly with shite's movements, but where Chino was concerned, it was comply or die! As Graham crashed to the mats and got back up again and again to receive more punishment, an air of menace swept through the dojo. At the honbu, the lower-ranked Sensei seemed to sit in one of two camps. There was the Chida camp, which appeared to promote soft and gentle Aikido that was beautiful to watch. Then there was the Chino camp, which advocated a fiercer and far more brutal style. Although Chida as Dojocho on the face of it had more followers, I didn't care. Chino Sensei's Aikido was real. It was this style of Aikido I wanted, too.

Chino had put on a show at Graham's expense. It had been impressive and what was scheduled for the rest of the day would now disappoint. The last class with Laurance Sensei focused on ukemi but would be cut short by Kancho's zagaku class. Geoff annoyed Malik by looking at him the wrong way, so he was sent to sit in seiza and then ordered to do press-ups. *'100-press ups or get out!'* Geoff was one of us and we encouraged him to finish. *'Come on Geoff...you can do it!'* Not content with words we joined in, voluntarily banging out our own set of press-ups. It showed solidarity in front of the Sewanin and Geoff seemed to appreciate the support. The weekly zagaku was a chance to reflect on Chino's teaching. Anything to occupy my mind was always welcome. Anything to distract me from the relentless pain of the seiza position. Matt and Dave broke first and already, with tears in their eyes, hoped not to be called out by Kancho. No such luck! Poor old Dave was up first and included as part of his reflection that *'...before I started the course, I never really tried at anything...'*. Ouch! Even if it was true, this wasn't something it was wise to admit. A statement like this was like feeding a lamb to a pack of hungry wolves; and like a lamb to the slaughter, so Dave went. Takashima Sensei was invited to give a response, but he misinterpreted Dave's statement completely. He took it that Dave was admitting to not trying on the course this week and lectured Dave that he should *'be more attentive and train harder!'* Dave looked mortified. Despite being misunderstood, there was nothing he could do but *'osu'* and bear it. Even if a Sensei got something wrong, you couldn't tell them. With the strict hierarchy in the dojo, criticising or challenging a Sensei in any way would be suicide. Dave was now on record as the Senshusei who hadn't been trying. I couldn't help feeling sorry for him. Broken by seiza and by Takashima's response, his life at the honbu was now set to get harder. During this zagaku I'd had a real and pressing urge to laugh. I didn't know why, especially given my knees were shot to bits from Chino's class. Maybe it was the irony of the situation? None of us wanted to do zagaku, let alone confess to anything. Perhaps it was the looks on each of our faces? The grimaces of pain, broken up by a dash of relief provided by intermittent bows. We all had our own way of dealing with the pain. Some coped better than others, and it was Dave and Geoff that appeared to be suffering the most – Dave as the Aikido tourist and Geoff with his long legs.

As if things couldn't get any worse, after the class, Chida announced that from next week, we'd have to do our reflection in Japanese. Back in the tearoom, we were all in agreement that from next week, the Japanese would cause us a big problem. Dave wasn't happy. *'Japanese! How the hell are we going to do that?'* Chida hadn't stopped there. He'd added the icing on the cake with a further instruction that we should present our reflections with more detail. Dave really wasn't happy. *'What! More detail than we've put forward in English, but now in Japanese?'* Dave was really screwed. Next time, with no understanding of the Japanese language, he'd really be in trouble! Clyde was the only one who could help, and he was already receiving pleas and petitions for assistance.

Before the week was out, there was another opportunity to train under Chino Sensei and feel the power of his technique. I was training with a cop, who didn't seem to know what he was doing and, as we were positioned near the front of the class, Chino came over to demonstrate. As everyone dropped into seiza, I was called up to receive his *nikajo*. A painful wrist control, nikajo if applied properly, controlled uke's whole body, forcing the unwilling recipient to collapse to his or her knee. I was still wondering whether Aikido worked at all or was reliant on uke's compliance. This was my opportunity to find out. As Chino gripped my wrist and fingers, I got my answer in no uncertain terms. Though Chino was only about five feet in height and of slight build, I was amazed at his strength and gained an instant and new appreciation as to the power of Aikido in the right hands. Looking at the faces of my fellow Senshusei, I could see the relief that they'd not been picked. Staying in the shadows was surely the best way to survive the course, but was I there to just survive, or did I really want to learn? So far this had been a difficult question for me to answer, and my focus had been on getting through each class and through each day. Receiving Chino Sensei's technique for the first time seemed to shift my focus. There was clearly a lot to learn, and rather than shying away, once again in the spirit of Bruce Lee, I realised that the best way to *absorb what is useful* was to take uke. I'd stepped out of my comfort zone coming to Japan, so why stay in it while I was here? I resolved to put myself forward at every opportunity. It was my best chance of finding out what real Aikido was all about.

I got the impression that Chino Sensei wasn't a huge fan of the cops. The Riot Police had to be there; they were paid to be there. The international Senshusei, on the other hand, were a band of willing volunteers who were paying for the privilege of being tortured every day. Chino was a true student of the martial arts, and he had willingly come to the honbu many years before to learn from Yoshinkan's founder, Kancho Gozo Shioda. Maybe we had something in common after all? I was getting frustrated with the cops. They didn't train as intensively as we did, and because they didn't have the Sewanin on their case all the time, they got away with it. My wandering mind was brought back to order by Malik's bark. *'This is martial arts, you know!'* Matt and Neville had caught his attention for all the wrong reasons. With a loud *'osu'* they acknowledged Malik and picked up the pace.

THE WIZARD

Takashima Sensei spoke fluent English and carried a certain status at the honbu with his bilingual ability. He replaced Clyde for more official translation duties and seemed to be Kancho's right-hand man. Short and somewhat portly, he lacked the intensity of Chino. He also usually beamed a smile across his face, which was a rare sight amongst the other Sensei, who generally preferred a scowl. As the final week of April got underway, it was our chance to train under him, and to experience one of his classes. We all noticed it. Some of his hand movements, and the noises he made while demonstrating were slightly strange. As Senshusei we noticed everything, and just like kids in the playground, we singled out other kids for habits they possessed or the way they did certain things. On account of his somewhat theatrical way of performing Aikido, moving forwards Takashima Sensei would be known as 'The Wizard'. Aside from my brush with Chino Sensei, Aikido still felt a lot like magic, so 'wizard' seemed to fit!

In the second class during the week, we trained with the cops, and Malik instructed us in the morning meeting to *'hit them hard'*, so much so that *'at least one should go to hospital'*. I suspected it was his way of creating a rivalry that would inspire us to push harder, to create a them-and-us scenario, where we'd strive to come out on top. Although they frustrated me, I didn't dislike any of them. I felt sorry for them. We'd chosen to be there, but they had to be there to advance to the next rung on their respective career ladders. Having been bullied at school, I wasn't about to become the bully now, particularly at the instruction of the Sewanin. There would be no hospital trips; whichever cop I trained with would be in safe hands.

Sitting in seiza in preparation for Wednesday's final class, we were pleasantly surprised to see The Wizard take his spot in front of the shomen. In the first part of the class, we each held a bokken while standing in kamae. Every few minutes we were ordered to change stance, from right to left and back again, and then drop into seiza. This was a strange magic, and I didn't understand what spell The Wizard was trying to cast. Eventually, we squared off from one another and applied *yonkajo* in a series of repetitive techniques. Yonkajo, as the fourth wrist control, was by far the most difficult to master. We'd been told that good Aikido was applied with no pain, but with yonkajo inflicting pain was all I had. Lloyd looked shattered and like he was about to pass out. He was jolted back to life with Malik's cry of, *'the gloves are off,*

78

guys!' At the end of the class, Graham and Malik said we were all starting to look like Senshusei. I'd taken Malik's words to heart and was still pumped. My gloves were still off, and all I wanted to do was fight. Perhaps this was how a real Senshusei was supposed to feel?

IT'S NEARLY A KNOCKOUT

Thursday arrived, which once again meant one thing. The last class of the day would be the now-infamous zagaku and two lucky Senshusei's opportunity to deliver their reflection and habit in Japanese. I sort of wanted Dave to be called up. His butchery of the language of our host country would be something else. While he'd surely provide a level of entertainment that might just help distract us from the pain in our legs, with no ability to laugh, his selection could prove dangerous. A giggle or even a smile would be detected by the Sewanin, and in front of their superiors, they'd be under pressure to exert a level of punishment that would deter any such hilarity in future weeks.

Before we'd find out if Dave was the chosen one, there were three classes to get through. The last thing any of us wanted was an Oyamada session before the weekly torture began, but as is often the case, we got what we didn't wish for. He drilled us over and over again to a monotonous count. This repetitive training was called *hajime geiko*. Hajime meant to *start* or *begin*, and geiko meant *training*. Combined, this meant drilling the same techniques repeatedly to the count. As the count got quicker, so did the requirement to perform the techniques quicker, too. Every Senshusei feared hajime geiko, as you never knew when it would end. Designed to build spirit and stamina, in any hajime class, inevitably, someone would break, and you never wanted to be that person. As a brief respite, Oyamada called a stop to proceedings to demonstrate for Lloyd's benefit a point on *sankajo* (third wrist control). As Lloyd's partner, Oyamada asked me to attack. I did as I was told but fired a *shomen uchi* (overhead strike to the head), instead of the required *yokomen uchi* (side strike to the head). Oyamada looked shocked as I stopped my attack millimetres from his forehead. I breathed a sigh of relief. The Sewanin breathed a sigh of relief. And Oyamada Sensei, although he didn't show it, I suspect, breathed a sigh of relief, too! Still, what did he expect? He'd just destroyed us with a hajime class. I was too tired to think and made an innocent mistake. I was certain there would be repercussions but was grateful that I hadn't made contact. With my background in Muay Thai, I knew how to hit hard, and, with the top of the head being a known weak spot, things could have been a lot worse. To the best of my knowledge,

79

no Senshusei had ever knocked out a Sensei, and I really didn't want to be first. There was no precedent of what to do in such a situation. On the downside, I'd probably have been kicked off the course, but on the upside, I'd have gone down in Senshusei history.

In the weekly seiza marathon, I sat next to Geoff, who was back on his knees after three weeks standing with a lower-body injury. With long legs and a limited ability, evidenced by his performance to date, to withstand any form of prolonged pain, I feared the worst for him. Sure enough, after only 10 minutes he started to contort and writhe about. During one of the many bows, like a prisoner desperate to escape his confinement, Geoff scratched his nails across the mats in his own desperate bid for freedom. Matt was called on to read his reflection and habit in Japanese. The first of us to test out our Japanese language skills, his reflection and habit, delivered in a Mancunian twang, provided much amusement for the Senshusei. Takashima Sensei responded and said that he wanted to hear more detail about what Matt meant in his reflection. It seemed the Japanese Sensei, once the course was over, didn't just want a bunch of hard-core disciples to spread the word of Yoshinkan Aikido across the globe. No, it seemed they also now wanted a bunch of self-reflecting linguists. Matt hadn't started studying Japanese and had only been in the country for five weeks!

IWAMA DAY OUT

The end of the week couldn't come quick enough. But before that there was Romeo, Chino and Murata Sensei to get through. Chino Sensei, from what I'd seen already, was the best living practitioner of the art. Tiny but deadly, he moved with an intensity and purpose that no one else at the honbu had. Romeo had started Friday with more hajime geiko. Despite his name and links to Shakespeare's most famous lover, there was no love lost when it came to teaching the Senshusei. His class was brutal. Murata Sensei concluded what would be a shortened week. With a growing reputation for delivering the strangest of classes, he wasn't about to disappoint. He had us snatching coins out of open palms before the holder could make a fist. I'd played this game at school, and now I was playing it again! This was followed by escapes from a rear headlock, which was much more up my street. Murata's first mistake was asking Dave to apply a headlock on him. Dave hung on for dear life, clearly as yet not having understood the importance of ukemi and going with the flow. After nearly decapitating Oyamada, I was pleased to see a fellow Senshusei make his mark. Like an angry lion on the back of its prey, Dave wouldn't let go. Back in the tearoom after class, we wound Dave up, telling him that in the process of rag-dolling Murata, he'd left a huge dogi burn on his head.

We were all excited by the prospect of Saturday – no training, a trip out, with a full week off from training to follow courtesy of Golden Week. The day began early with a 7:15am meet at Shinjuku Station. Shinjuku was unlike any other railway station I'd been to before. The biggest and busiest station in the whole of Japan and the world, it made meeting anyone a logistical nightmare. Having found the Sewanin and each other, we were all set for our Senshusei excursion, and I have to say I was pretty excited. It was a casual affair, out of our dogi and in civilian clothes for the day. Inazaki and Kambara were smartly dressed, each sporting a jacket and trousers, with the rest of us wearing whatever we'd dragged out of the wardrobe that morning. The application information was right. The Japanese tended to dress well. *It is not appropriate to come to the dojo looking like a bum*; luckily the rest of us had just made the grade!

Saturday, 29 April 2006, was to be a day to remember. I'd read lots about the origins of Aikido, and now I was off to Iwama, its birthplace. This was no ordinary day, either. Not only were we visiting this iconic place, we were doing it on the anniversary of Morihei Ueshiba opening his first dojo. Ueshiba, known as O-Sensei, was the founder of Aikido and Kancho Gozo Shioda's teacher. From O-Sensei to Gozo Shioda to Chida Dojocho, Chino and several others, as Senshusei tracing our family tree, we were three generations down the line in lineage terms from Aikido's founding father. After a three-hour journey, we finally arrived. Despite being away from the formal setting of the honbu dojo, we remained on our guard. The Sewanin had been in our shoes last year, so on the one hand, they could be regarded as friends in more relaxed surroundings; but now, responsible for our discipline and development, the foe element of the relationship never seemed far away.

At the Aiki *jinja* just across from O-Sensei's dojo, we watched a ceremony that saw a long procession of people place a small fern on the *shrine* and then, moments later, remove it. It didn't make the best viewing, and after 90 minutes, any novelty had long worn off. With no real concept of what was going on and being tired from the week just gone, I felt like I would collapse. Matt must have sensed this and suggested we explore the dojo instead. Unfortunately, it was off limits as it had been set up for what looked like a dinner that I was certain would involve yet more ceremony. However, what we could see from the outside looking in gave a real sense of history. This was the place I'd seen on the black-and-white footage of many an old film reel. This was the place where O-Sensei had experimented, developed and mastered his craft. Somewhat disappointed not to be granted access, we headed back to the shrine, this time to see Moriteru Ueshiba Sensei, the Aikikai *Doshu* (hereditary head) and O-Sensei's grandson, give a demonstration. The equivalent to Inoue Kancho he was head of Aikikai Aikido. It was interesting to watch, but it wasn't Chino, and for me it lacked the raw power of Yoshinkan.

We'd all heard stories of O-Sensei's teaching methods and a set of legendary steps that had served as a training ground for his students. After a quick lunch courtesy of a local convenience store, we set off in search. On the way, and by pure accident, we happened across another shrine and were invited inside for an audience with a group of old men. Thankfully Clyde was on hand to translate, and we learnt that these men were guardians of the shrine. It turned out that one man had trained directly under O-Sensei for five years. He reminisced about being thrown around on the hard-wooden floor of the dojo and how it was difficult to learn because he was in so much pain. To heighten the intensity, O-Sensei had ordered his students to remove the mats! Malik Sewanin asked with Clyde's help, *'having trained with O-Sensei, what do you think the meaning of Aikido is?'* It was a great question. The man replied, again with Clyde's help, and said that Aikido was a martial art and that he wasn't sure how to explain it, but it was all circles. It was a flow of energy that redirected any attack. I made a mental note. So far, my Aikido had been more about hard angles and brute force. Circles sounded like something I should try! The man also said that in Aikido there was really no kamae, just the natural state. I wasn't sure how to break this to Higa Sensei when I got back. In the spirit of Aikido, the conversation was redirected towards the shrine and we were escorted outside to pay our respects. A coin donation, a ring of the bell, two bows, a wish, two claps, followed by one further bow each. Blessed with luck and good fortune we said our goodbyes and headed off in search of the famous Aikido steps.

Naively, I'd pictured a leisurely ascent when we found them, with an opportunity to soak up the heritage and history. No such luck! Malik Sewanin thought it would be a good idea to run, so run we did. This wasn't just any run it was a timed one, and stopwatches out we began to sprint. On the way up, I just missed treading on a big green snake that poked its head out from the undergrowth. It looked as frightened as me and we got out of each other's way just in time! The steps were steep and arriving at the top we were all exhausted. At the summit of Mount Atago we found yet another shrine, where for some unknown reason Malik Sewanin decided it would be a great idea for us all to strip down to our underwear and perform press-ups, kihon dosa and some kihon waza techniques. I didn't know if this was a spur-of-the-moment decision or something he'd planned. Luckily, we seemed to have the place to ourselves, as parading around in my underwear was only one step up from the tackle swinging I'd done at the sento. It felt a little uncomfortable, not to mention somewhat inappropriate, given that the shrine was a place of worship. None of us was sure if Graham Sewanin was complicit or not, but as we finished up our unusual and impromptu training session, he looked to be getting uncomfortable, too. Beer had been available when we arrived in Iwama. Alcohol and decision-making were not always the best companions. Had Malik been drinking, had he lost command of his senses? It was a difficult dilemma. By now we all knew about the hierarchical workings of the honbu. Questioning Malik Sewanin on his course of action wasn't the best idea. In a society that rarely questioned authority, and given that Graham, who had so far positioned himself as the less extreme of the Sewanin, had done nothing to challenge Malik's judgment, we'd all gone along with it. The highlight or lowlight of the whole unfortunate proceedings was Lloyd's horrendous red underpants, which provided some amusement in a less than amusing situation.

The spirits of the shrine must have been watching. Almost as soon as we'd begun, it started to rain, which thankfully called time on our spontaneous, semi-naked training. Somewhat bemused by what had just happened, we got dressed quickly and headed back down the steps to catch the train. On the descent I spotted Boaz picking up random bits of rubbish. *The course and cleaning must have really gotten to him*, I thought to myself. It was a sign he might be taking his Senshusei duties a bit too far if that was even possible, or perhaps it was just his way of apologising for desecrating the shrine? The journey home felt much longer than the journey earlier that morning. Malik was being annoying and holding court with anyone who cared to listen. I took this as further evidence that alcohol may have had a part to play. He enlisted Clyde's help to translate for his unwilling non-Senshusei audience, which finally caused Graham to publicly break rank. It was *Mutiny on the Bounty*, with Fletcher Christian challenging the authority of Lieutenant William Bligh. I wondered if Graham would shortly set Malik adrift, but he settled for a stern word in his ear instead. '*Calm down*', Graham urged, and Malik sat down and fell fast asleep. I wondered what the Sensei back at the dojo would think of the afternoon's activities if they ever found out. Surely any leak wouldn't be good news for Malik and could have presented an opportunity, if any of us was brave enough, to have him relieved of his Sewanin duties.

GOLDEN WEEK

Golden week meant one thing and one thing only – no training! No requirement to be at the honbu dojo and no punishing regime. Instead, the chance of freedom and an opportunity to rest and recover. In the UK, I was used to the odd bank holiday dotted throughout the year, but in Japan they did things in style. Golden Week comprised a series of four national holidays within the space of one week. I didn't really care what the holidays were for; I was just glad to have them. After four weeks on the course, things were already getting monotonous, and any opportunity for a change of schedule, and scenery, was very welcome.

So, what does a martial artist do with his days off? He trains in the martial arts, and in my case, this meant Brazilian Jiu Jitsu. With Aikido, I had no choice. Committed to the course for 11 months, the experience of training for the love of training had been taken away. If Aikido felt like work, which it did, Jiu Jitsu was leisure, something I could still do for fun.

Golden Week was also an opportunity to catch up with jobs. Cleaning, tidying, washing clothes and the day-to-day administration of normal life were always second to my duties at the dojo. This week was a chance to put my life away from the honbu back in order. Working at Berlitz I needed a means for them to pay my wages, and this meant opening a bank account. To do this, I'd been told I needed a *hanko* stamp. A simple signature wasn't enough, and as if a nod to bygone times, a *name stamp* was still a necessary requirement. Not the wax version used by letter writers of the past to seal private thoughts away from prying eyes, but a modern ink version that held nothing together. It seemed like a bit of a racket to me when a simple signature would have sufficed. Still, I was in Japan for the culture and had no choice but to get one made. I found a little place in Shibuya and placed my order. A visit to one of the busiest parts of Tokyo meant a compulsory visit to the world's busiest Starbucks, which overlooked the world's busiest pedestrian crossing. This had featured in *Lost in Translation*, and now I had my opportunity to experience it firsthand. Maybe distracted or possibly just tired, I'd inadvertently missed some of my lessons at Berlitz. A call from Michael (not Mike) at Sangenjaya to tell me I was absent without leave was an unwelcome disruption to an otherwise calm and relaxing week. It turned out I'd checked the wrong schedule. I phoned Peter, Berlitz's answer to the Sewanin, to apologise and make good. Making a mistake without being punished was unusual, and I felt like I probably owed him 50 press-ups at the very least.

By now, the international Senshusei or *Kokusai* had already formed close bonds, and a week apart was just too long. On Thursday we met up at the HUB in Ebisu first, followed by Gas Panic in Roppongi. Only in Japan would you even think of naming a pub after the 1995 Sarin attacks on the Tokyo Subway. Dave was on his usual form and, while playing to the crowd, decided it would be a good idea to forward roll in the subway station. Full of booze, he went over hard and was lucky not to break his ankle.

PARTY PIECE

Golden Week seemed to end before it had even begun. Before I knew it Saturday arrived, and it was back to the 5:20am wake-up call. We were all expecting a hammering, but classes with Murray, Ito and Sonoda Sensei thankfully passed without incident. I was relieved, as I'd noticed how quickly my knees had stiffened up after only a few days away. After training we all headed home briefly with strict instructions to be back at the honbu for 4:30pm. We would mark the end of Golden Week with a celebratory party for all the Sensei, and the Senshusei would provide the entertainment.

The first Riot Police course had taken place in 1963 as an intensive course lasting two years for men and women holding at least a *nidan* (second dan and one grade up from shodan) in another martial art. Initially, 20 students joined the course, and after one month, only the best 10 were kept. In keeping with this tradition, we'd be having our welcome party one month into our own course. The other theory on the timing of the welcome party was to give us time to get used to the madness of the dojo, so that the craziness of the evening's proceedings wouldn't come as too much of a shock. The Sewanin had warned us we'd need to come up with a skit or short comedy sketch, which we'd have to perform for the Sensei's amusement. The Sewanin had also advised that to get the best response from the Sensei didn't require us to be funny. What they really wanted to see was us in pain, and the more pain the better!

We set up the dojo with lines of low-level tables parallel to the shomen, with a red carpet and cushions on the side the Sensei would be sitting. The party started at 6pm and I found myself opposite Graham Sewanin and Murray Sensei. Nothing is simple in Japan, and I'd already experienced the complications associated with dining etiquette at the Senshusei welcome party. It turned out the challenge at this gathering was pouring the beer. It was bad form for anyone to fill their own glass, and for the Senshusei, this meant no Sensei's glass could ever become empty. Once you'd topped up their glass, they in turn would fill yours. This meant the drinking was

85

relentless and non-stop. Probably a good thing, given that we were due to perform, as the drunker the Sensei got, the greater the chance they'd find our skits funny. Inoue Kancho was piling back the beer and getting redder and redder by the minute. He appeared to be enjoying himself, which meant that everyone else, aside from the Senshusei, could enjoy themselves, too.

The skits started with the cops doing a karaoke (literally *empty orchestra* or amateur singing to music) performance with bare chests and ties on. The audience seemed to enjoy it, and despite it all being very bizarre, it had served a purpose, as a warm-up act for the rest of us. Ronen and I had teamed up and come up with a race to eat five green chillies while Matt and Dror beat us on the back with belts. To further intensify the pain, and therefore amusement for the Sensei, we'd attached clothes pegs to our nipples and ears. I won the race for the bottle of water and, five chillies in, couldn't work out why my mouth wasn't on fire. What we'd bought in the supermarket looked like chillies, but the lack of fire in my mouth told a very different story. It turned out they were peppers with no heat at all, but Ronen and I, remembering the Sewanin's advice, played up to the crowd, pretending one almighty inferno had taken up residence in both of our mouths. The Sensei and Sewanin seemed to fall for it, and I could only presume they didn't know the difference between a chilli and a pepper, either. The worst skit was Geoff's. He did a *Monty Python* sketch, which was completely lost on the Japanese. The Sewanin panicked and signalled the rest of us to drag him off after five minutes, which we quite literally did. Matt and Dave had thought along the same lines as Ronen and me. They'd asked me to act as referee and, having necked a shot of sake each, spun round to disorientate themselves before beating each other with foam swords. Our parting piece was a group role play set in a fictional Japanese restaurant. Our interpretation of how Senshusei indoctrinated in the ways of the dojo dined out was no climatic end to the evening's performances. We weren't sure what we were doing, and I'm not sure our audience knew how to take it. Still, we did what we always did when we weren't sure what was going on. *'Osu, osu'* and more *'osu'* broke the deafening silence. To finish, Kancho told a story about a peach that apparently, he'd told in previous years. Most of it was lost in translation, but we laughed and showed our appreciation. He then did a dance to accompany Chida Sensei's singing. Neither was particularly good, and my advice, had I been asked, would have been to stick to the day job. They were much better at Aikido than entertaining.

Having tidied up, we headed off to the HUB in Takadanobaba for the after party. We were joined by some of the Sensei and, along with Ronen and Clyde, I got talking to Murata. I liked Murata Sensei. He hadn't brutalised us yet in any of his classes, and I knew he'd trained in other martial arts and took a Jiu Jitsu class once a week. In our conversation he said that seiza had no meaning and only stopped you from thinking clearly. Wasn't that the truth! It also stopped you from doing anything much after a prolonged session until the blood flowed back into your legs. We drank to the extremism of zagaku, in the most extreme way we could – by necking back 90-proof shots. Ronen's good looks caught the interest of a local in the bar who seemed to be set on making an approach. Despite Tokyo's status as Japan's capital city with a stream of international visitors, Westerners in certain locations were still a novelty. Luckily, I caught wind of the situation and advised the unwelcome guest to *'keep walking'*. My interception was less about shielding Ronen and more about protecting the advancing party, who was most definitely about to mess with the wrong guy. We were all smashed, and I was relieved that there was no training tomorrow. But wait, the realisation dawned on me and spread throughout our group of hardened drinkers. It would soon be Sunday, and we had Senshusei duties to perform!

URAYASU ENBU

Another day and another meet at the world's busiest railway station. Shinjuku had been our embarkation point a week ago for the Iwama expedition, and today it was the start of a day from hell. It was *Enbu* (sometimes written as Embu) day, and with some of the Sensei from the honbu demonstrating their techniques, it was compulsory for Senshusei to attend. This was to be my first experience of an Aikido Enbu, which was essentially a large gathering of Aikidoka, who each took turns centre stage to showcase their abilities in front of everyone else. En meant *performance* and bu *martial arts*. Our meet was set for 10am, and like a good Senshusei, I arrived at 9:30am. I'd factored in the logistical nightmare that Shinjuku always presented, and the extra time needed to locate the meeting point. Through the haze of my hangover I knew this would be tricky but somehow found everybody else well ahead of schedule.

At the honbu you could never be late, and the same applied for excursions. Just like the trains in Japan, we as Senshusei had to run like clockwork. British Rail back home was known for frequent delays and an inefficient service. On the Tokyo Metro, the opposite was true. At 9:55am, my phone rang. It was Matt, in a panic, on the other end. *'Mate, I'm running late and have missed my train!'* There was nothing I could do, and unfortunately, as I'd been standing next to Malik when I answered, I couldn't hide Matt's predicament from the Sewanin. I wasn't surprised Matt was set to be late. The last I'd seen of him; he was chatting up a Japanese girl he'd bumped into as we left the HUB. However, with his very basic command of Japanese, there was only so far '*ohayou gozaimasu*' could take him! Malik intercepted my phone and thankfully, this morning, Matt was more articulate in his native tongue. Somehow his story passed muster. Malik bought in and instructed Matt to make his own way to the Enbu, which was being held at Urayasu in Chiba Prefecture, near Tokyo Disneyland.

After what seemed like an endless train journey, we were sat in our seats at 11:30am. Why we'd got there so early, I had no idea, as the event didn't start until 1pm. I'd anticipated our early arrival and the monotony of what was to follow. As Senshusei there was no relaxing in our seats and the fact that most of us were nursing hangovers from hell was of no consequence. For Senshusei, there was a certain way of doing everything. There was a right way and a multitude of wrong ways that would just never do. Sitting meant positioning yourself bolt upright. It wasn't permitted to allow your back to touch the rear of the seat. It was a form of seated seiza and, I was sure, yet another way to inflict torture. A chair had a back for a reason, but we couldn't use it. Apparently resting your back encouraged slouching, and Senshusei were never allowed to slouch. Ando, Chino and Takeno Sensei performed their magic, much to the appreciation and applaud of the crowd. Ando and Takeno had also been students of Kancho Gozo Shioda but taught at their own schools away from the honbu. I'd read about both, and the only bonus of today was that I'd got to see them in action. Like Chino, Ando and Takeno possessed a hard, often terrifying style of Aikido, and for me, this was what Yoshinkan was all about.

Four long hours of demonstration after demonstration eventually passed. I could barely stand by the end; my back was so stiff. Since the start I'd been fighting the constant urge to fall into what could best be described as an upright coma, but through sheer willpower, I had made it through to the other side. Before we could go, there were still jobs to do. All Sensei wore a *hakama*, a type of traditional Japanese clothing. To those unfamiliar with the martial arts, it looked to some extent like a long dress. Hiding an Aikidoka's legs, it made his or her Aikido look more graceful, and signified the wearer's Sensei status. It meant a Sensei's movements couldn't be copied or anticipated. Although they looked nice, folding them was incredibly difficult, and this job, like all jobs, inevitably fell to the Senshusei. There was one way to fold them, and the Sewanin had shown us how. Given enough time and practice, we could probably have made a decent job of it, but for Senshusei there was no such thing as a leisurely pace, and the more time pressure and panic that went along with any activity, the better. As we frantically folded, tucked and folded some more, Malik Sewanin shouted words of encouragement. *'Do it softly but firm'*, and *'don't let the hakama control you. You control it!'* I didn't understand what he was talking about. His advice was less than helpful and even contradictory. As usual, the response was *'osu'*, which could mean many things depending on the situation. I really didn't care. I was tired, drained and ready for my bed!

ALWAYS ON EDGE

As Senshusei, we were supposed to always be on edge. There was in fact no 'supposed to' about it, as that's exactly how we felt. Even when I wasn't at the dojo, I felt the looming presence of the course. It governed what I ate, drank and pretty much anything else I did.

Tuesday, 9 May 2006, arrived; and with the onset of another week, I caught up with some Japanese on the train ride in. I figured that while living in Japan, I might as well learn some of the language, and with the added pressure of zagaku, some knowledge of vocabulary and pronunciation was now a necessity. Assigned to cleaning duty this week, in the corridor connecting all areas of the honbu, I discovered was no easy task. The sweeping, scrubbing and polishing were regularly disturbed by the requirement to bow to any superior who might be passing. Given that Senshusei were the lowest form of life in the dojo, this meant acknowledging anyone and everyone. I overhead Graham Sewanin talking to Geoff. At Sunday's Enbu Geoff had apparently enquired as to the order of proceedings by saying to Murray Sensei, *'hey, big boss man, what's up next?'* Not a wise move given that Murray Sensei was the head instructor for the Kokusai and one of the most senior non-Japanese Sensei at the honbu.

Graham reminded us in the morning meeting that we should be on edge and used an interesting analogy to get his point across. He advised that being a Senshusei should feel at all times like loading a musket we'd just shot. With the enemy fast approaching, the tension associated with the threat of being killed, was the way we should feel from the moment we entered the honbu until the time we left. I don't mind admitting that at times I wished I had a loaded musket. For the most part this would have been pointed at the Sewanin's heads, and if I fired, I wouldn't have missed. The day passed without further incident, and having stowed my imaginary firearm safely at the honbu door, ready for collection tomorrow, I headed off to Berlitz.

UPS AND DOWNS

The course was a series of ups and downs. When I woke up in the morning, I never knew if the day would be a good or bad one. Much depended on my state of tiredness, physical energy and who walked out in front of the shomen to teach. Waking up on Wednesday, I had a feeling that today would be one of the downs and, although I didn't know it on entering the dojo, it would be the hardest day of the course for me so far. For some reason I felt lightheaded, like I was drunk and not fully aware of what was going on around me. My peripheral vision was dark and cloudy, but I had no recollection of banging my head or anything else that might have caused the problem.

In the locker room, Graham and Malik Sewanin were getting changed. They both looked a little jaded, too, after an audition with Chino Sensei that had taken place yesterday. Chino was off to Russia and needed an uke to accompany him. This didn't just mean taking his techniques, it also meant waiting on him hand and foot throughout the trip. Chino's patronage was the kind of thing you needed to advance your honbu career but didn't really want. He had a reputation for brutalising his uke and, in the downtime between the seminars he would teach, I didn't imagine he would make the best company. Aside from the language barrier, he, like most of the greats in any pursuit, had one sole focus. Chino rarely spoke about anything other than Aikido. Both Sewanin had taken a beating, and Malik appeared to have come off worse. His elbows were red with visible signs of bruising, and his mouth was split inside. It was nice to see him on the receiving end of some pain for once, instead of dishing it out! Graham had won the audition and been selected for the Russia trip. Chino favoured the bigger uke, and Malik, being the smaller of the two, had been benched. I could tell Malik was disappointed and was doing his best to hide it.

The first class was with Takagi, and we started on *tenchinage ichi*. The so-called *heaven and earth throw* was a difficult one to master, and I wondered if it would have any practical application at all in the street. Chida Sensei arrived for the second class and decided it would be a good idea to ask us questions about the kihon dosa in Japanese. Even in English we would have struggled to answer, but the Japanese made things impossible. He got us doing an exercise which incorporated the fourth move from the kihon dosa. This involved a 180-degree pivot while coordinating the hips and hands in unison. This move was also brutal on the knees, and with Thursday once again looming, any additional strain in this area was particularly unwelcome. Uke had been instructed to resist shite's movement, and Chida acknowledged my efforts with *'sugoi chikara'*. Roughly translated, this meant *'good strength'*, which I took as a compliment. However, on later reflection I realised I might have got this wrong. Chida Sensei's Aikido was the softer style of Yoshinkan, where any use of force was frowned upon. If Chino had uttered the same, it would have had a very different meaning, and I reminded myself that I was in the Chino camp when it came to the style of Aikido I wanted to emulate. The last class of the day was with Miyakoshi Sensei. To date, he hadn't taught us much, but when he arrived on the mats at the start of a lesson, it was always a welcome sight. One of the nicer, less brutal Sensei, his classes were steady. They lacked the boredom of Oyamada and the terror of Chino, and on the day where I was struggling for energy the most, I was very happy to see Miyakoshi.

As usual, I had minimal time between Senshusei finishing for the day and my shift at Berlitz starting. All I wanted to do was go home and sleep, but I had students to teach. In the four classes on my roster, I was dead on my feet. I felt like I'd hit a wall, and for no identifiable reason, today had been the hardest day so far. The physical exertion was one thing, but what I was finding harder was the endless repetition of techniques. If I believed in the technique, I could get with the programme, but a day focused primarily on tenchinage and kihon dosa had sucked the life right out of me. Back at Musashi Koyama later that night, I couldn't wait to get into bed. I didn't need any rocking and was out for the count when my head hit the pillow.

The latter part of the week passed relatively smoothly, apart from a nasty fall I took at the hands of Lloyd. He'd thrown me with *kotegeashi*, which bent my wrist back and forced me to flip to save it from snapping. As my feet flew over my head, my right leg caught in his dogi, which forced me to attempt the splits mid-flight. I came crashing down on the mats with my leg still entangled and an excruciating pain in my groin. Fortunately, I was flexible from my Muay Thai training, and I'd landed before the point of no return. If Geoff had been on the receiving end, his chances of procreating would have taken a severe turn for the worse. Friday was Matt's birthday. I'd popped into Meguro and bought him a book on Japanese and a card. As I'd been responsible for persuading him to come to Japan, I thought the book would help him pick up a few useful phrases. There was no time for celebration, and at the honbu, it was business as usual. After having one of my legs nearly ripped out of its socket, I'd also woken up with a stiff neck. I applied a couple of heat patches, a staple of all Senshusei, and was surprised when both Laurance and Oyamada Sensei asked me what had happened, while expressing genuine concern. After class and a quick bite to eat at the Royal Host in celebration of Matt's birthday, Matt and I headed off to Axis Jiu Jitsu. I wasn't up to it, but Matt was keen to go. It was his birthday, so I couldn't really refuse.

BAD ATTITUDE

We'd been told on multiple occasions already that Senshusei should display the right attitude at all times. None of us had yet figured out what this meant, and in Saturday morning's meeting Malik Sewanin took it upon himself to explain. Attitude wasn't something tangible like a technique it was a way of being that none of us was getting right. It appeared our attitude around the dojo was giving Malik attitude. He said we were welcome to *'bring it on'* and promised, *'I will break you!'* My mind triggered the scene in *Rocky 4* when Ivan Drago, facing off against Rocky Balboa in the final fight of the film, utters the immortal words, *'I must break you!'* It didn't turn out too well for Drago, and by the end of class, it hadn't turned out too well for Malik, either. Matt, maybe with the same scene in his head, had thrown Malik with *shomen iriminage* and split the Sewanin's lip open. *Iriminage* was one of my favourite moves. It was a Steven Seagal favourite and therefore one of mine, too. Every time I drove my arm across uke's chest I was Nico in *Above the Law*. As I rotated my fingers down and elbow up to drive uke's head into the mats, I was Detective Gino Felino in *Out for Justice*. I nodded at Matt approvingly, and he tried to hide his smile. It was nice to see someone stick one on the Sewanin, and if Matt's actions weren't attitude, then I'd no idea what was!

It worried me that there would be comeback, and sure enough, there was. Monday was a day off, but on Monday, 15 May 2006, the Sewanin summoned us to Yoyogi Park. Our collective attitude, and Matt's especially, was worse than we'd thought, and for two hours they forced us to run through techniques. Malik was determined to break us, and taking our valuable free time was definitely one way to do it. The rift between the Sewanin and the Senshusei was growing wider, and it wouldn't be long before Malik and I would bump heads!

MIND CONTROL?

Aikido was a relationship between shite and uke. Shite performed the technique, and uke received it. I'd watched the Sewanin and other senior rank and file take uke from the top dogs at the honbu, and I'd always wondered if they just went with the techniques so as not to make shite look bad. Aikido looked beautiful, but my experience to date of real fighting was that it rarely looked pretty. Whether Aikido was practical and would work in a real confrontation was a question I'd asked myself many times. I wanted my Aikido to look good, but more than that, I wanted it to work. As a kid I'd also read articles in *Combat* magazine and *Martial Arts Illustrated* about *dim mak*. A Chinese term, as opposed to Japanese it was known as the *death touch*. Dim mak was a style of fighting that used pressure points to control and disable an opponent. The slightest touch could cause an aggressor to collapse in a heap or be thrown across the room. There were other styles that didn't even touch. A look from the 'master' or a flick of the head were enough to incapacitate uke and send him or her flying off, as if by magic! Like many others, I was sceptical, and despite being on the course for over a month now, I was still sceptical about Aikido. I'd read the stories of Kancho Gozo Shioda's fighting exploits in and around Shinjuku, and I believed his style was the real thing. But what of Yoshinkan's second generation? Did their interpretation and application of Aikido really cut the mustard? For me Chino Sensei's Aikido was the closest to Kancho Shioda's, but what about Chida Sensei, the head of the dojo? I was soon to find out!

I'd always been a firm believer that the mind controlled the body, even though it often seemed like the other way around. Another week began with cleaning duties, and this week I found myself with Matt in the locker room. Following Lloyd's attempt to split me in two mid-flight, my hip was in a right state. The last thing I wanted was four hours of mitori geiko, which would only make matters worse, so I resolved to struggle on and put my mental strength to the test. Graham Sewanin must have read my mind as in Thursday's morning meeting, he told us that when we line up in kamae opposite our partners, we should try to read their thoughts. I wasn't sure I was ready to explore the depths of Lloyd's mind, but we decided to give it a go. In the first class, we agreed to each think of a colour and then check if we'd guessed right in the first break. Despite concentrating as hard as I could on what might be going through Lloyd's brain and specifically what colour, I was none the wiser. It turned out the same was true for him, too.

In the second class, Chida Sensei arrived on the mats. He was never alone and instead was always surrounded by a group of adoring disciples. In part I suspected they were there not only to learn as much as they could from him but also to act as his personal security detail. He toured the mats, throwing everyone with kotegeashi while Laurance and Kanazawa Sensei stood either side to make sure there was no trouble. We weren't yet fully indoctrinated into the ways of the honbu, and resistance to Chida's technique from Dave and Geoff was highly likely. Any difficulty could embarrass the Dojocho and lead to a world of trouble for any would-be rebel. Eventually it was my turn to receive Chida's technique, and as he took hold of my right wrist, I was in half a mind to resist just to see what would happen. I was already getting a reputation on the course for having very stiff shoulders and was curious as to whether Chida could budge them. His grip felt soft and the application smooth and efficient. I flipped over my head as gracefully as I could and landed on my side on the mats. I wasn't sure whether he actually threw me or whether, like a good uke, I just went with it because it was Chida Sensei doing the throwing. The omnipresent Laurance and Kanazawa may have had something to do with what could have been a theatrical descent, but I couldn't be sure. When Chino Sensei had applied his nikajo on me I'd had no choice but to move. Move or risk a broken wrist or worse. With Chida, things had felt different. In fact, I'd not felt very much at all. Perhaps this was the real Aikido? Perhaps it was a form of mind control resulting from the non-questioning obedience in the face of superiors that existed throughout the honbu? Was I part of a cult? Had I been immersed in a new belief structure that would see me twist, turn and crash to the mats at the will of any Sensei? Or had I just experienced the magic of Aikido; had I just felt the power of a true Aikido master? The jury was out, and with a long time left to run on the course, there was still plenty of time to find out.

I'd taken to wearing knee pads; in fact, we all had. Dave's were a luminous shade of orange, but the rest of us opted for something more subtle. Dave liked to stand out and his knee pads did, too. Still, they at least matched his hair. With a padded front and elasticated back, they protected the knees from impact with the mats and, psychologically at least, seemed to hold joints together that were already becoming fragile. They could also be worn discreetly under white, baggy and often blood-stained dogi bottoms. In the weekly zagaku class, I took on the role of test pilot, wearing my knee pads around my ankles. I'd hoped that elevating my feet and tilting my weight forwards into my knees might help with the pain. How wrong could I be? In a matter of minutes my legs went to sleep, and I promised myself that I'd never make the same mistake again. Senshusei was an exercise in trial and error. Any slight advantage or improvement in our circumstances to take the edge off a punishing class or to survive a little longer was worth the effort to find out. Just as we were accumulating the Aikido techniques we were required to master, we were also guinea pigs running our own scientific experiments in pain avoidance. Neville was called upon to give his reflection and habit. He'd forgotten his habit so made something up on the spot about trying to speak Japanese to shopkeepers. He did well, and with my limited command of the Japanese language, I understood a fair bit of what he said. I was confident that he didn't in fact speak to shopkeepers, but it didn't really matter. Noriki Sensei was called upon by Inoue Kancho to formally respond, and the nonsense of this weekly exercise once again became apparent. '*Sukoshi wakanakatta*', Noriki began, which meant he hadn't really understood what Neville said. Perhaps Kancho hadn't, either, which is why he'd passed the buck? Geoff was sat to my left and once again was in real pain. I felt sorry for him. With the longest legs in the dojo, seiza for any length of time would never be easy. During Tachiki's reflection I heard a loud farting sound and was convinced he'd shit himself. In a white dogi there'd be no place to hide, and luckily for Geoff, if it was indeed Geoff, he'd not followed through!

Any doubts about the power of Aikido were put to bed in Friday's class thanks to Chino Sensei. He taught us to connect our arms to our body, to move uke. He got Graham Sewanin out and threw him around mercilessly, and at one point I thought he would break Graham's wrist with his nikajo. Chino's style wasn't mind control; it was raw power! After class I headed off to the sento with Ronen, Dror, Clyde and Lloyd. The post-training bath was catching on, and we were fast enlisting new recruits. It was a great way to relieve the constant knee pain that was ever-present, both on and off the mats. For a short time, alternating between the hot and cold pools, my knees breathed a sigh of relief. Once again, we were in the presence of the Yakuza. The tattoos were a giveaway in a country that frowned upon ink. I avoided eye contact as usual and tried to stop staring at what looked like two knife wounds visible on the back of one scary-looking individual. I wondered what scrape this guy had been in to sustain such an injury and pondered whether in the same situation, armed with my Aikido skills, I'd have fared any better.

SECURITY DETAIL

When a Sensei asked you to do something, the answer was always yes. This was never actually communicated in the affirmative, as all responses for the Senshusei were limited to the compulsory osu. Interpretation of what this meant was anyone's guess, but it usually confirmed an agreement with whatever was being asked.

The weather was turning, and Japan being a land of extremes had a climate to match. Despite still being May the temperature had reached a stifling 30 degrees. This was beach weather and definitely not weather to be running around in sweat-laden dogi to the shriek of '*hajime!*' In the hajime geiko classes we'd had to date, all technique seemed to go out of the window. Hajime combined with heat made things even more challenging. Back home, if I needed a drink during class, I could have one, but in Japan no drinking was permitted during class, no matter how hot the weather got.

Dehydration impaired judgment and the ability to think straight, which made our Aikido even worse than it already was. What's more, with so much sweat it was hard to grip, so applying any technique became even more difficult. In between classes was the only time to hydrate, and often this time was limited because of lectures from, or punishment dished out for an infringement of dojo etiquette, by the Sewanin. Drink too much and you'd spend the next class with a bursting bladder with no opportunity to relieve yourself. Drink too little and you'd run the risk of collapsing. Water wasn't sufficient, either, as given the amount we were now sweating, we were losing salts our bodies needed for proper muscle and nerve function. In the summer months, cramp was the enemy of the Senshusei and could be an incredibly painful experience. The honbu staff came to the rescue and recommended that we add salt to our drinking water to reduce the risk of doing our bodies irreparable damage, but in the same breath, they also warned of the dangers of drowning. This was new to me. Apparently drinking too much water could be just as dangerous. Excessive fluid intake could mean water intoxication, also known as water poisoning. Diluting the electrolytes in our blood by drinking too much could disrupt brain function and result in brain damage, coma and even death. It turned out you didn't need to immerse yourself in water to drown, you could do it from the inside out! None of us was a qualified nutritionist or medical practitioner, so the right intake of water was once again an exercise in trial and error. I erred on less over more. I'd weighed up the pros and cons of collapsing from dehydration, with the risks of pissing myself in class and self-inflicted drowning. The first option seemed like the lesser of three evils.

Drenched in sweat and in desperate need of a drink, Murray Sensei interrupted rehydration by calling Ronen, Victoria, Matt and me into the office to ask us to do security work. A native of the country, Murray Sensei had been asked to provide an elite team of well-trained personnel who could handle things in case something kicked off at a party being held at the Canadian Embassy next Saturday. *'Osu, osu, osu, osu'*, was our response. Security detail – what did I know about security work? I'd done a brief stint on the door at a student party while at university, but that was about it. Still, every day on the course presented a new challenge, and I felt pleased to have been asked. Had Murray Sensei selected us for a reason? In his eyes, were we showing the most promise on the course? The fact that he hadn't asked Geoff or Dave was clue enough. I decided I'd embrace the opportunity when it arrived. There was still a week to get through, and for the moment, that had to be my focus. In the last class, Dave threw me with his feet the wrong way round and got my leg caught in his dogi. It wrenched my already damaged hip in the wrong direction. It turned out he'd done me a favour, as after class the pain I'd experienced since Lloyd had done his worst seemed to have subsided.

After class, I headed to Shinjuku to meet Nate at Starbucks. Nate and I had been in the same Japanese class together when I first arrived in Japan, and it was a refreshing change to meet up with someone who wasn't on the course and had no interest in martial arts. He was in Tokyo teaching English and had hooked up with a Japanese girl. He was in Japan for the long haul and, being a non-native speaker, was destined for a career in teaching English. Although I was suffering daily, in conversation with Nate I realised I was doing something special. Yes, by night I was teaching English like all the other gaijin, but by day I was a warrior, immersed in an experience that went way beyond anything recommended in the guidebooks or offered by tour operators. It was a welcome reminder of my privileged position and what a great opportunity Senshusei was. That evening I met Andy in Shibuya for his birthday celebration. Andy was a student from Sitsiam in Manchester, and although we'd never trained together or even met back in the UK, we'd become friends in Japan. My neck was hurting, and I hadn't really felt like going out but had made the effort. Senshusei was always on my mind, and although spending time with people not on the course served as an important reality check, those outside the honbu didn't really understand. I had a couple of beers, made my excuses, and caught the 10:30pm train home. Everyone else was heading off to a nightclub, but I knew my days of clubbing were over, at least for the next nine months. The price of a good night out was a painful week ahead, and more pain was the last thing I needed.

I taught my usual classes at Berlitz in the week and noticed that a sign had gone up in the staffroom warning of an assault that had taken place at the Otemachi school. Brian, a Berlitz English teacher, had taken a dislike to a fellow teacher and stormed into the classroom while his colleague was teaching a Japanese student and laid him flat out with a punch. The Japanese student was unsurprisingly distraught, and no one had seen or heard from Brian since. The notice warned that he was not allowed in any Berlitz school and that all Berlitz employees should be on their guard in case he turned up. I thought the name sounded familiar and then it hit me. Brian was Tommy DeVito, who had threatened me on the Berlitz training course back in January. It turned out that my boss Peter had hired him, and I was lucky not to have crossed his path since. The guy obviously had issues, and I was pleased that I'd stood my ground in my brush with him. Bruce Lee had described his Jeet Kune Do as *the art of fighting without fighting*, and perhaps what I'd learnt from my Aikido training prior to the start of Senshusei had also instilled this philosophy in me. I'd found the more I trained, the less I wanted to fight or partake in any form of conflict, physical or verbal. I was learning to step off the train track and let the train pass by. If they ever caught up with Brian, the solution to his anger issues could very well be a dose of Budo training.

The week presented very few highlights apart from Thursday's seiza class when Kancho requested a blackboard to make a point, which none of us understood. Kanazawa Sensei was asked to fetch one from the office. Staggering to his feet, he could barely walk and stomped off the mats like an elephant. Perhaps the Japanese also found seiza painful but just hid it better, which begged the question – why bother to do it at all?

Nearly two months into the course, we were now approaching our first grading, and with this in mind in Friday's class, Paul Sensei put us through a mock test. Much to my surprise, I was feeling good and thought I'd turned in a good performance with my techniques. I was brought back to earth with a bump. Paul's feedback included the observation that I wasn't extending my feeling and energy enough, and that my *kiai* (the shriek we made when initiating an attack or finishing a grounded uke) had to come from inside. Malik Sewanin summed up; *'this isn't a play garden, it's Budo!'*

Saturday finally arrived, and I was looking forward to my stint at the Canadian Embassy. Being asked to join Murray Sensei was a message to those not invited that Ronen, Victoria, Matt and I were in favour. The last place you wanted to be on the course was at the bottom, and this was reassurance that the four of us were near the top. We left class early to travel across to the Embassy, which was a short train ride away at Akasaka. Romeo Sensei joined us, too, which was good news. With his background in Filipino knife fighting, if things really kicked off, we'd have someone to stand behind. We arrived at about midday, had a tour of the place, and, to mark us out as the official security detail, were each given a red baseball cap to wear. Having done some restraint and removal stuff in the last class with Murray Sensei, we were all very excited about the prospect of having to eject someone, even if our Aikido skills to date ultimately proved not quite up to the task. My default in any situation was always Muay Thai, but punching, kicking, kneeing and elbowing, while very effective for removal, had very little to do with restraint. Restraint was where Aikido came in, and the security detail presented a golden opportunity to test it. Ronen and I manned the door first and then walked around, trying to look mean and threatening. Ronen made good company. As an army officer and platoon commander back home he'd been in command of men and tanks. He'd also learnt Krav Maga in its birthplace from the most senior instructor in Israel. Unfortunately, the afternoon passed off relatively smoothly. The non-stop rain seemed to have curtailed the drinking, and with less alcohol ingested, there was a reduced possibility of trouble. There was only one minor incident, which Murray Sensei dealt with swiftly, and the time dragged to the 6pm finish. Murray Sensei rewarded us with a bag of beer and 8,000 Yen (at the time c.£40). Not a huge amount of money, but it was nice to be appreciated for our time.

With two days off until another week began, I decided it was time to get my neck sorted. I'd injured it a couple of weeks back at Jiu Jitsu, rolling with a guy twice my size. He'd doubled me back, feet over my head, and I'd heard a crunch that seemed to emanate from somewhere inside my vertebrae. I'd thought no more about it, but a pain in my neck had developed and was getting progressively worse. I phoned the Tokyo British Clinic in Ebisu and booked an appointment for Monday afternoon. Doctor Gabriel Symonds was friendly and examined my back and neck. Thankfully, he pronounced a clean bill of health and charged me 12,000 Yen (at the time c.£60) in return. I'd explained what I was doing in Tokyo and that this would probably be the first of many visits. I also agreed that I'd send across other Senshusei as and when they became injured, which could provide a lucrative boost to his business. I should have worked out a commission structure but was just glad to have confirmation that I was still in one piece. Injury was never far away on the course, and injury and illness were the two things we feared the most. The screaming, monotony and exhaustion we could get through, but injury and illness would make things a thousand times worse. Both meant mitori geiko, which could mean more injury. It was a route you didn't want to go down, and my visit to Ebisu was time and money well spent.

In celebration I took the train to Akihabara, which was known as 'Electric Town' on account of the sea of neon lights and electrical shops selling everything from computers to the latest novelty gadgets, which greeted you on disembarkation from the platform. I'd been keeping in touch with Mum and Dad back home in the UK by phone and decided I'd surprise them with a Skype call, for which I'd need a webcam and headset. There was no shortage of shops to buy such equipment, and it didn't take me long to find what I was looking for. I hurried back to Musashi Koyama to catch them waking up, and it was amazing to hear and now see them for the first time in what seemed like an eternity. My Dad had been especially upset the last time I'd flown out to Japan, and, having a close bond with both parents, this would now be my preferred means of communication. All I needed was my laptop and a reliable broadband signal. Since moving into the apartment, I hadn't paid for a Wi-Fi connection. I would have been more than happy to subscribe to my own dedicated service, but the complexities of gaining such a connection back in the UK paled into insignificance compared to the same task in Japan. Despite taking Japanese lessons, I could barely ask for directions, and anything more complicated, like arranging utilities, was still well out of reach. Luckily someone in a neighbouring apartment was paying for a Wi-Fi signal that wasn't password protected, so I'd been taking advantage and would continue to take advantage as long as I possibly could. The only other alternatives were the Internet cafes, which were dotted all over Tokyo. You hired a booth by the hour and, as part of the deal, could help yourself to drinks and sometimes snacks until your time ran out. I regularly used these for an alternative purpose – not just for surfing the web or checking email but as a place to sleep between the end of training and the start of teaching at Berlitz. In a private booth, I wouldn't be disturbed, and Japan being one of the most technologically advanced countries in the world, most of the chairs had reclining and massaging capabilities!

WHITE RABBITS

As month three started, I was looking for divine inspiration. Saying *'white rabbits'* on the first of any month was supposed to bring good luck, and as June crept in, I did just that. I needed all the luck I could get. My body was struggling, and Malik Sewanin was already on my case, telling me I needed to work on my fitness. I told him my fitness was fine, but my knees were knackered! As a graduate of the course, he knew where I was coming from and let my comment pass. Like him or not, he'd earned his stripes, and he seemed determined that we'd earn ours, too.

Shower duty was one of the least-favourite cleaning jobs. To clean the showers properly required the use of chemicals. I had an aversion to chemical cleaners back home, which was exacerbated by the cleaning products available at the honbu. As I couldn't read the labels, I had no idea what was in them, which made using them properly and in line with their caution instructions another game of trial and error. Kabi Killer was the worst, with the clue being in the name. It was supposed to kill mould, and I hoped in the process it wouldn't kill me! I knew it was dangerous, having now studied the Senshusei Cleaning Checklist properly. I made sure the windows were fully open!

I'd regarded myself as pretty tough before the course. Muay Thai was brutal, and conditioning was critical. If you were going to dish out the punishment, you had to be prepared to take it, and I'd taken my fair share of beatings over the years. Senshusei, though, was instilling a whole new level of toughness. There was no escape. No missing training if you felt tired. No early exit. Just the relentless march of the course, whatever the weather, whatever the day, and however you happened to be feeling. Naturally we started to look down on non-Senshusei. Although we were the lowest of the low in terms of the honbu pecking order, in our minds we were the best of the best. My experience of the Yoshinkan ippan classes hadn't been great, and this had been one reason I was so eager to take the course. I wanted to sweat, I wanted to be pushed, and for whatever reason, the regular classes hadn't satisfied, either. Of course, on the surface we respected all in the dojo and greeted everyone politely, but there was a distinct divide between the current intake of Senshusei or those who had already done the course and those who hadn't done it or had no intention of ever doing it. This disdain continued outside the honbu dojo's walls. Others didn't understand and were weak and inferior. I now could imagine how military personnel dropped back into civilian life might feel about those around them. Being Senshusei was something special and, as a unit, we formed closer bonds as the days advanced. These closer bonds were measurable by the intensity of the mickey-taking. A renewed belief in the course and a pride in being Senshusei began to fill me with an increased level of energy and determination. I wondered if this was a positive turning point that would last for the nine months the course still had to run. In contrast, Lloyd was struggling, and the hard exterior he'd possessed to date seemed to be disappearing. I suspected it was a lack of sleep, and I had to drag him through several classes. Gone was the bravado of the initial staredown when we'd met for the first time in kamae across the mats. Our job was to get each other through, and although it was now my turn to help Lloyd, I was sure he'd be in a position to return the favour at some point soon.

Though my body felt great, my eyes were suffering. They'd begun to itch like crazy and were really painful, gunky and watery. I was convinced I'd got conjunctivitis but didn't really want the expense or inconvenience of another doctor's appointment so soon after my first. Our daily routine involved cleaning the dojo mats with the *zokin* we'd used to clean our respective stations at the start of each day. A zokin was a *floor cloth*, similar in size to a duster back in the UK. They had started out life as white, but through relentless use, they'd all turned a sorry shade of grey. We ran the lines, or 'columns' as the honbu called them, before and after training. This involved all the Kokusai Senshusei, wet zokin in hands, running from one side of the matted area to the other, until all areas glistened with a surface layer of moisture that caught the light shining in through the windows. It reminded me of the wheelbarrow race at school, without the assistance of someone holding my ankles. Bottoms up, hands pressing the zokin down with feet driving hard was how the Senshusei cleaned the mats twice a day. The problem was the zokin were never washed. They never saw the inside of the washing machine which lived next to the showers just off the locker room. The washing machine that was reserved only for the Sensei's dogi. The zokin were used to clean the toilets, floors, showers, bins and everything else. You name it, and they were used to clean it, and the only cleaning they got was a rinse under the taps. After each cleaning session, we gathered side-by-side in front of the long sink opposite the showers and in full view of the washing machine we couldn't use. With taps running, each zokin was stretched out and rubbed by hand to remove any visible dirt – and usually an assortment of pubic hairs – before being hung up to dry in readiness for the next cleaning session. The production line was one Adam Smith, the author of *The Wealth of Nations,* would have been proud to witness. It was the division of labour at its best, with each Senshusei performing a specialised task that served the next Senshusei in line. I'd studied Adam Smith's work at university, where I'd graduated in economics. I knew my degree would come in handy one day but hadn't quite expected this. I was convinced my eye problem was a direct result of the dojo cleaning practices. What looked visibly clean probably wasn't, and through cross-contamination, the mats were probably home to all manner of bugs and bacteria.

As the weather warmed up, sweat was everywhere, and although in class we were prohibited to wipe sweat, when the Sensei and Sewanin's backs were turned, we did it anyway. The worst type of sweat was the stuff that ran off our heads and into our eyes. There was no choice. At the risk of being punished you had to wipe it, as it was the only way you could see. The sweat ran freely, and hands that touched the mats after every throw were used to rub our eyes. My itchy eyes were keeping me awake at night and making every waking moment a living nightmare. I tried to put the problem to the back of my mind and focus on each class, but it was proving impossible.

EXCUSES, EXCUSES!

As Senshusei we'd learnt early on that it was always advisable to be ready for questions. *'Are you working tomorrow? What are you doing after class? What are you doing on Sunday afternoon?'* You never wanted to be caught off guard, so having a list of believable excuses in your back pocket was essential. Laurance Sensei was looking for an uke for Carlos' 3rd kyu test and asked if I was available. Though I liked Carlos, and we'd trained well together in the ippan classes, agreeing to uke wasn't as simple as taking a few of his techniques; it meant at least two hours of seiza, a mandatory part of any formal grading. Luckily, I was prepared. I was working and therefore unavailable. Work was really the only acceptable excuse. The roster was made at least a week in advance, and dojo requests usually turned up the day before. The Sensei recognised work as a necessary part of life in Japan. It not only funded our ability to live and pay the honbu fees, but it was also linked to the all-important visa to stay in the country – a visa I needed to see out the end of the course. Lose your job, lose your visa and then lose your right to stay in Japan. The honbu dojo wasn't stupid. Yoshinkan Aikido was a business. We paid fees to train, and a key reason for running the Senshusei course was to create a pool of international instructors, who on returning to their native countries would start their own schools. More schools meant more students and more fees kicked up to Yoshinkan's head dojo.

No job meant no excuses, and when the dojo called, I was glad I had my ties to Berlitz. Malik Sewanin didn't like excuses of any kind. He'd established a reputation as a hard taskmaster, and staying off his radar was a skill we were all doing our best to master. Privately I'd started to refer to him as 'Mallet'. It seemed an apt description, given a mallet's purpose was to beat things into shape. Malik was beating us all into shape, and while I knew that deep down, he had our best interests at heart, I hated it all the same. Ahead of Friday's first beating he'd told us, *'you shouldn't be able to walk off the mats after each class!'* I was confused. *Does he want us to crawl?* I thought to myself. After the first class was done, he called us back into the dojo to further his earlier point. *'Why, despite my earlier instruction, were you lot able to walk off the mats after the first class?'* I knew we were supposed to give our all in every class, but giving everything in the first class of the day, evidenced by our inability to walk, seemed a tad extreme, not to mention bloody stupid. What were we supposed to do in the second and third classes? We couldn't just sit about; Malik wouldn't let us! We needed gas in the tank, not just for one but for all three sessions.

The last class of the day provided considerable amusement. Luckily, Ito Sensei was in command. As Chida's principal uke, he had a calmness about him and a relaxed demeanour both on and off the mats. Lloyd had been eating peanuts in the break, and after completing one of the techniques, I noticed he was distracted by something on the mats. Ito approached with an amused look on his face, picked up a stray peanut and, laughing, handed it to Lloyd. The rest of us, now aware of what was going on, hid our smiles. While Ito had found the whole incident funny, it was unlikely the Sewanin would have. Lloyd sheepishly tucked the peanut inside his dogi and carried on. Later on, during the class, Ito came over again, this time to check on my technique. Either I was deep in concentration or he'd crept up with Ninja-like skills without me knowing. As I turned to my left to discharge one almighty sneeze, I caught him head on, nearly knocking him off his feet. He appeared as shocked as I was, but again, in good humour, began laughing. I was sure the Sewanin would now have my card marked, too, but thankfully Lloyd and I escaped without punishment.

After class I bagged up my dogi and headed off for the washing and sento ritual that was becoming a very convenient habit. Ronen, Dror and Clyde accompanied me, and afterwards we dined at the Royal Host. We were all in agreement that Malik's behaviour and advice at times bordered on the ridiculous. Even Clyde who out of all of us was the biggest buy-in to the honbu's hierarchy, etiquette and formality, for once was in agreement. After much debate we could find no excuse for Malik Sewanin's conduct and resolved it would be something we'd just have to put up with.

DAI ICHI TEST

Everything was now building towards our first formal test. Somehow, we'd survived this far and were approaching the end of Dai Ichi, the first phase of the course. This meant a formal test of techniques – techniques we'd drilled repeatedly to iron out any mistakes. Our performance on test day would be carried out under immense pressure. Do a good job, and the Sewanin looked good; mess things up, and they wouldn't take kindly to how this reflected on them and would make us pay the price.

Lloyd and I had worked well together, and I was sorry I'd soon have to say goodbye to him as my training partner. For each phase of the course, we'd be allocated a new uke, and speculation began about who would next be paired with whom. As a parting shot or goodbye gift the day before the test during a hard hajime session, I'd messed up a technique and accidentally smashed Lloyd in the chops. My strike resulted in a mouth full of blood, which Lloyd was forced to swallow for the rest of the lesson. In typical Lloyd style, he didn't seem fazed and just carried on. To add insult to injury, in an unusually energetic Higa class, we were instructed to work on our shomen uchi strikes. After about 10 strikes to Lloyd's forehead, I left him with a big red mark. Again, he took it in his stride. Whoever got Lloyd next had best be prepared. Everyone had a limit, and I'd probably pushed him as far as he was prepared to go without firing back!

Test day arrived. Wednesday, 7 June 2006, was possibly the most important day on the course so far, and an air of nervous apprehension descended on the tearoom. The usual chatter was quieter than normal, and the Sewanin urged us to perform to the best of our ability. This was our opportunity to show the Sensei how far we'd come, and it was an opportunity Malik and Graham strongly encouraged us to grab with both hands. Spirit was everything, and what we lacked in technique we could make up for in effort. There were a few different interpretations as to what spirit actually meant – a loud kiai applied at the start and finish of every technique, quick and purposeful movements back to starting positions or a kamae that meant business. It was probably all wrapped into one, but for me it was all about the power in the techniques. I sensed that Lloyd shared my view, and as this would be our last dance together, we both intended to make our mark. Malik Sewanin told us to *'make the dojo shake'* and reminded us that our *atemi* (strike), *shime* (tighten / control uke's arm into position) and *oase* (hold down / pin) must be strong and committed. When we moved we should move as one unit. He told us, *'blend from the first bow, into kamae, sekkin* (advance / move together)*, to the final osae'*.

Before the test we had to endure the first class and slightly shortened second class. Paul Sensei beasted us, as usual, and built our confidence by telling us, *'you have no energy or spirit'*, precisely the things we needed in abundance if we were to have a successful afternoon. Ito Sensei in the second class helped us polish our techniques, but it was too little, too late. The hard work had already been done, and under the pressure of exam conditions, we'd only remember what we'd drilled multiple times already. The gloss of the last class would be wasted effort; when it came down to the test, it would be muscle memory that we'd be relying on.

The test officially began at midday, but typical of all Senshusei events, we had to be ready far earlier. At 11:30am, after a quick water break, we were back on the mats, practicing the formalities of where we needed to be and what we needed to say, under the supervision of Miyakoshi Sensei. We then lined up and sat in seiza to await the senior rank and file of the honbu who would conduct the test. After what seemed like ages, Chida, Chino, Sonoda, Oyamada and Inoue Kancho himself strode out onto the mats, clipboards in hand. The order was everything. If you were up first you got to perform on reasonably fresh legs, but then a long seiza beckoned while everyone else took their turn. Being called up near the end meant a short post-performance seiza but one hell of an ordeal beforehand and the challenge of executing the first few techniques on jelly legs. I struck lucky and was selected for the middle group, along with Lloyd, Matt and Neville. It appeared the Sensei, given Thursday's exploits over recent weeks, had realised that any extended seiza was likely to result in a disastrous performance all round and permitted a short period of warming up ahead of our individual slots. As the preceding group started their kihon dosa, Lloyd, Matt, Neville and I crawled out of the dojo to stretch our legs. We were under strict instructions that we were to be back in position before the fifth kihon waza technique was underway, which gave just enough time to banish the pins and needles and inject life back into our aching limbs.

Back in the dojo, we were called to attention and ran to our positions. I stared at Lloyd, and he stared back at me. We had no means of communication, but we both understood what needed to be done. To the command, we executed the techniques with force and vigour while trying to ignore the Sensei who were milling around us and watching our every move. The test seemed to go well and with no mistakes; none that I was aware of anyway. We were both confident of a good result. I wasn't sure if anyone had failed this stage of the course in previous years or what the consequences might be. I didn't want to find out and was sure none of my fellow Senshusei wanted to, either. Chida, Chino, Sonoda, Oyamada and Inoue Kancho left the dojo to review what they'd seen and to consider their verdicts. I imagined this was how a prisoner on trial felt when the jury retired, nervously waiting and wondering when those in power might return and with what decision.

Finally, Chida shuffled back onto the mats. As Dojocho, it had fallen to him to deliver the good or bad news. I was surprised and pleased to be the only one he gave a positive comment to. *'Good kamae'* was praise indeed, and I couldn't hide my smile. We'd all made the grade and, depending on our pre-Senshusei Aikido experience, along with our performance today, were awarded 5th or 4th kyu. Dror, Boaz and I received 4th kyu with everyone else getting 5th. I was happy; 4th kyu was one step closer to black belt than 5th, but in the great scheme of things, it really didn't matter that much. Kambara, Inazaki, Neville and Lloyd already held higher grades in Yoshinkan Aikido from outside of Japan, so they weren't officially graded. I guess it would have been unfair to downgrade them, so they kept their current grades safe in the knowledge that we'd all catch up by the end of the course. In the tearoom, we congratulated one another. After two months of hell, we'd finally received some recognition that we'd advanced on our Senshusei journey in some small way, but there was no time to celebrate. It was just another day at the office, and I had English classes to teach. I stumbled out of the honbu dojo and headed off to my other life at Berlitz.

PART TWO: DAI NI
(8 June to 3 August 2006)

NEW KNEES

Thursday, 8 June 2006, was the first day of Dai Ni. We'd all been keen to get through the first stage of the course but had been secretly dreading the second. Dai Ni's reputation had preceded it and was already firmly written into Senshusei folklore. To all Senshusei, past, present and future, Dai Ni meant 'die knees'! It meant all the techniques we'd learnt previously would now be practiced kneeling. If seiza was bad, which it was, the requirement to now perform all techniques in a seiza position promised an elevated level of torture and pain. Snap, Crackle and Pop! My knees were already shot. When I moved, they made the sound of cold milk on Kellogg's Rice Krispies. I was still struggling with my eyes, which were relentlessly itching like crazy. After the first class of shuffling across the mats on my knees, enough was enough. I sneaked into the locker room at first break and booked my second doctor's appointment.

We hadn't swapped partners as Chida Sensei had yet to sign off the new pairings. Just when Lloyd and I thought we'd escaped one another, we were thrown back together again. The new partner allocation was a bit of excitement away from the monotony of the daily routine. We'd been looking forward to it and wasted hours debating who might get whom, usually over food and drinks at the Royal Host. Unfortunately, we'd now have to wait a bit longer, as Chida was not one to be rushed. Despite yesterday's grading, there was no reprieve from the weekly zagaku. After two classes of *suwari waza* (techniques performed kneeling), seiza was the last thing any of us needed, and I was certain that today would be a difficult session. Victoria was tough; she had to be, I guess, to put up with Geoff. I'd yet to see her show any weakness. We all had a breaking point, though, and today was to be her day. Fighting off the pain in her legs as best she could, she couldn't stem her floods of tears. I was also really struggling and kept having to put my hands down. We were all suffering – a suffering made all the worse by Kancho's sermon on *Bushido* (warrior path or way of the warrior) and the benefits of enduring pain! Dror's face was the funniest. Shortly after kneeling down, he'd started to contort and shake. To the untrained eye it looked like he was having some sort of fit. I half expected him to start foaming at the mouth, but luckily for everyone, he stopped just short of this!

The whole obsession with seiza and suwari waza was, in my book, tradition gone too far. Fighting on your knees provided no practical benefit and was something I was never likely to do in a real-life situation. The Samurai had learnt combat techniques on their knees in order not to cause offence by raising their heads higher than their superiors. As we were no longer living in feudal times, the relevance of knee fighting was lost on me. The Sewanin had tried to convince us that practicing techniques from a seated position would enhance our Aikido. It would strengthen our hips and make our techniques more powerful. I wasn't convinced, and the jury was most definitely still out as to what benefit, if any, could be derived. By the end of the course, I was sure we'd all need a new set of lower hinges and made a mental note to consult my doctor. Later that day, back at the Tokyo British Clinic, I found out I had conjunctivitis and was prescribed some eye drops. Now on first-name terms, Dr Gabriel could fix my eyes but unfortunately said he could do nothing for my knees.

The rest of the week comprised more and more suwari waza, and it was only in Murata Sensei's Saturday morning class that we had any reprieve. For me, Chino Sensei was pure Aikido, whereas Murata Sensei was a martial artist through and through. Chino was obsessed with Aikido and had it as his sole focus, whereas Murata, while a dedicated student of the art, opened his mind to other martial arts and what they could teach him. Before the course we'd been told that training in other martial arts was strictly forbidden. Senshusei by definition was one focus, not two or three. I wondered if this was because having a sole focus on one Budo art was necessary to get through the course, or because the powers that be were worried that we might find something more interesting and practical in another martial art and have our heads turned. I was still ignoring this advice. Training in Muay Thai and Brazilian Jiu Jitsu, it appeared I had a kindred spirit in Murata Sensei, and as a result, I'd warmed to his somewhat unorthodox style of teaching. His classes were very popular for two reasons. First, he didn't believe in unnecessary seiza, and second, because he sent the Sewanin off the mats. It seemed he wanted to engage with us directly without the watchful eye and often inaccurate translation abilities of Malik and Graham. I knew they hated being dismissed, but for obvious reasons we loved it! In

Saturday's class, Murata confided in us that he really didn't like suwari waza or zagaku. Apparently, he knew this German guy whose leg had swelled up so badly after an extended period of seiza that he'd nearly had to have it amputated. He explained that because we were foreigners, we weren't used to some of the bacteria knocking around the dojo, so we needed to be careful. He wasn't kidding; I knew how we cleaned the mats, and although visibly clean to the naked eye, thanks to my recurring eye problems, I knew they were home to an unpleasant smorgasbord of nastiness. Murata Sensei's words, while honest, were far from reassuring. Even if he didn't believe in seiza, every other Sensei did, and we'd only just begun Dai Ni. I made a mental note to watch out for any unusual swellings and was pleased to have an English-speaking doctor saved as a favourite in my phone. I didn't know when I might need him again! Murata continued and said that suwari waza didn't really help with *tachi waza* (standing techniques) but gave you a strong base on the ground which could prove useful in Brazilian Jiu Jitsu if you were caught in someone's closed guard. With the popularity of MMA in Japan, which had ground fighting at its core, I wasn't surprised that Murata had experience in Brazilian Jiu Jitsu. So as not to disappoint, he demonstrated what he was talking about on Ronen. No wonder he sent the Sewanin out. Practicing another martial art within the dojo walls was a breach of honbu dojo policy. Murata didn't seem to care, and to be honest, I didn't, either.

THE NAIL THAT...

Life at the honbu was strict, and the constant routine and discipline was already feeling overwhelming. Even when there was an opportunity to let our hair down, it usually wasn't an opportunity. Iwama had been one such occasion, but under the constant and watchful eye of the Sewanin, there was no chance to relax. We'd planned a night out to celebrate the completion of Dai Ichi and our successful graduation from the first stage of the course. Etiquette dictated that on such occasions we should invite the Sewanin. I was sure, deep down, that Malik and Graham were good guys, but they had a role to play. They had to keep up a front, and this meant their attendance at any social occasion was certain to impose a degree of formality that we were all temporarily trying to escape.

I met Matt at 7:30pm in Takadanobaba for a coffee before meeting up with the others. It was a chance for me to check in with him on a one-to-one basis to see how he was getting on, not only on the course but also how he was settling into Japanese life. He hadn't been forced to accept my invitation to join me, but as he had, a weight of responsibility still rested firmly on my shoulders. Thankfully, he was in good spirits and seemed to be enjoying his time in Japan, but I'm not sure any of us could really say we were enjoying the course. Senshusei was probably something we'd look back on with fond memories in later life, even though real-time immersion had, so far at least, rarely provided any form of pleasant experience. We were due to meet at an izakaya round the corner from the station. Malik Sewanin, having accepted our invitation, had taken it upon himself to take charge. He'd instructed us not to be late but then turned up 30 minutes late himself! In my book, good leadership was always by example, and Malik's tardiness was yet another reason for us all to dislike him, and the list of reasons was growing. The Riot Police had also joined us, and it was a good opportunity, through broken English and pidgin Japanese, to get to know them a bit better. Clyde was always invaluable in such situations and on this occasion, like many others, provided his translation services for free. The only benefit he derived was an unrivalled level of popularity, but with that came increased visibility – and in the dojo standing out was the last thing you wanted to do. *The nail that sticks out, gets hammered down* was a well-known Japanese saying, and Clyde's cheque was already written, even if it was yet to be cashed. The Sewanin didn't like the power his language abilities gave him and wouldn't hesitate to deal with any infringement of correct behaviour with excessive punishment.

Matt was my mate from back home, and Ronen and I had already formed a close bond, so it was no surprise to find them on either side of me at dinner. My mission in these situations was to sit as far away from the Sewanin as possible, and on this occasion, I'd achieved my goal. There was no point trying to befriend them. While there could have been a potential upside, I saw only downsides and was resolute in my decision to stay off their radar as much as possible. It turned out Clyde wasn't the only nail in town. Malik started a drinking competition with Lloyd. Lloyd, while hard as nails, as one of the youngest participants on the course, was easily influenced. Malik was taking advantage, and things were about to turn sour. Sure enough, it wasn't long before Lloyd turned white and beads of sweat appeared on his forehead. His joviality stopped, and he sank into silence. This was the calm before the storm, as moments later, he was sick into one of the empty dishes on the table in front of him. Back home, puking at the dinner table wasn't best manners, and I was certain the same was true in Japan. While slurping noodles was considered a compliment in polite society, vomiting at the dinner table was most definitely not. Lloyd couldn't walk, and as fellow Senshusei, we came to his rescue. We supported him down the stairs, and Ronen and Dave agreed to walk him home. This was just the start of his troubles. Lloyd was legless and not in control of his body or bodily functions. He was caught short and with no other option took a massive 'dump' in an alley just up from the izakaya. Emptying his bowels whilst providing relief was an act that if the honbu ever found out could cause him some serious grief! It was an unfortunate incident and one he regretted. Recounting the story later, he admitted, *'it was the lowest point of my existence. The poor bastard that had to deal with it the next morning. It's a debt I can never repay and carry to the whole of Japan!'* He was right; some debts can never be settled, and it was a secret he'd need to keep, or risk being dumped from the course! Malik was a nail who had ruined what could have been an enjoyable get-together. Unfortunately, given the strict pecking order in the dojo, we didn't have a big enough hammer to hammer him down!

Matt, Neville, Geoff, Vic and I headed off to the HUB bar to watch the end of the England versus Paraguay football match. This was England's opening World Cup game, and as a member of the Senshusei British contingent I was keen to catch it. As usual, the pub was packed, and it was difficult to get a clear view of the TV. Geoff for some reason was wearing an England football shirt. While I'd never been a big football fan, on the international stage I was patriotic about my home nation, and Geoff's attempt to hijack this national pride was winding me up. A Canadian national, Geoff tried to justify his attire by telling us that on account of his surname, he was really British. To confuse matters still further, his rather lame explanation was communicated in his very poor attempt at an Irish accent! England won the match, but the press reported that they'd *stuttered to victory* and that there would *undoubtedly be tougher tests ahead*. This sounded familiar. As Senshusei we were hobbling along, and there was absolutely no doubt that the worst was yet to come!

SHINKOKU

Tuesday, 13 June 2006, was the start of a new week and my first stint in the hot seat to perform Shinkoku. Shinkoku happened every day and as a formal ceremony conducted after the first class, and before we left for the day, we were already used to it. In our precious first break, the international Senshusei lined up in the corridor in between Kancho's office and the main office to formally ask Inoue Kancho, or the most senior Sensei at the honbu that day, for permission to train. The same happened after the last class, but this time a formal thank you was given for the day's training. Faced with the punishing regime, offering a thank you was usually the last thing on anyone's mind, but the honbu dojo had rules and observing Shinkoku was one of them.

111

Being Shinkoku involved more than just the formal ceremony. It meant you had to coordinate *taiso*, the *warm-up exercise routine* we did every morning before class. Rooted in tradition instead of modern sports science, I was sure it was damaging my body. Back home at the gym, I distinctly remembered being strongly discouraged from rotating my knees in a circle, which was a key component of the daily routine. To make matters worse, we performed taiso when our bodies were cold. Comprising stretching and straining, it failed to raise the heart rate and therefore failed to get the blood pumping. Stretching was best done when the body was warm, but we invariably did it cold. The Shinkoku also had responsibility for writing up the dojo diary after class. In addition to the personal diary we were required to keep for the scrutiny of the Sensei and Sewanin, the dojo diary was a public record of the techniques we'd performed and the key points we'd learnt. If our personal diaries came under intense scrutiny, the dojo diary took things to another level. This meant you had to think long and hard about what to put down in writing, in case anything came back to bite you on review. I was also keeping my very private diary, which provided most of the content for this book. This meant, as Shinkoku, I was writing three diaries, and it was important not to get them mixed up! My biggest worry, though, was the ceremonial duties I had to perform. I'd seen those who had gone before me in previous weeks mess up occasionally and knew from the reprimands a few of them had received from the Sewanin afterwards that there was no room for error. Things had to be done in a very strict and specific order, and what's more, the request had to be made in Japanese! The timing was interesting, too, as the request came after the first class. We were technically asking for permission to train after training had already begun. I didn't understand the rationale behind this but could only presume that Inoue Kancho and the other senior Sensei didn't like the early starts, and a request ahead of the 8:30am class was just far too early.

After the first class with Murray Sensei, we lined up. My moment in the spotlight had finally arrived. I marched up to the office door, knocked, and waited for an invitation to enter. *'Osu, shitsurei shimasu...Shinkoku onegaishimasu...shitsurei shimashita!'* Roughly translated, this meant, *'sorry to disturb you... Shinkoku please...sorry to have disturbed you!'* My entry and exit were sandwiched by the obligatory bowing. I shut the office door and rushed back to my place at the head of the line. All I could think about was not messing up. The order of what I needed to say to get things right was swirling around my head, and the more I thought about it, the more confused and stressed I felt. To my right I could feel Malik and Graham Sewanin observing my every move. I was determined to avoid the punishment I knew they'd already be planning, as my reward, if I made even the slightest of mistakes. After what seemed like an eternity, Inoue Kancho came out of the office. *'Inoue Kancho ni rei!'* I cried in the loudest voice I could muster, the call that instructed us all to bow in unison, and then stepped out of line to face the head of the Yoshinkan for the most difficult part of the exercise. I bowed. *'Simon Senshusei, hoka juu ni mei, hon jitsu no keiko onegaishimasu!'* Roughly translated, this meant, *'Simon Senshusei* (me) *and the other 12 Senshusei, request permission to train today, please!'* I bowed again. Then having stepped back in line, *'Inoue Kancho ni rei!'* We bowed again as one. *'Osu!'*

My first taste of Shinkoku was over, and I'd done a good job. However, there was still Shinkoku to perform after the last class and another four days before I could pass the burden to somebody else. After classes with Noriki and Ito Sensei, I rounded off the day's proceedings. *'Simon Senshusei, hoka juu ni mei, hon jitsu no keiko arigatou gozaimashita!'* This roughly translated as, *'Simon Senshusei* (me) *and the other 12 Senshusei, thank you for today's training!'* As the rest of the Senshusei ran to their cleaning stations for the final scrub and polish of the day, I sat down alone in the tearoom to write my first entry!

DIE ANOTHER DAY

I'd always enjoyed a good James Bond film, and being overseas in a strange country doing strange things felt like the kind of mission 007 might just get assigned. *Die Another Day*, released in 2002 and starring Pierce Brosnan, marked the franchise's 40th anniversary. Only six years away from my own 40th milestone, I felt like I was dying a little, as the course progressed and got harder and harder.

There had been rumours that in the dim and distant past, someone had died on the course, but nothing had been officially confirmed. With all the throwing and landing on unforgiving mats, which were much harder than anything I'd fallen on before, there was a constant fear that something terrible could happen at any moment. The mats were traditional Japanese *tatami*. With a core of rice straw, landing on them felt like landing on concrete. Back home, the mats may have looked the same, but with a foam interior, the act of crashing into them was a much more pleasant and far less scary experience than the brutal welcome tatami presented. In Thursday's morning meeting, Malik reminded us of our commitment to the course. *'You should be prepared to die on the mats'*, he said. I had no intention of doing any such thing. If I was going to die, today was not the day. In the spirit of James Bond, I'd much prefer to die another day, far off in the future!

CHANGING OF THE GUARD

We'd still not changed partners, and Lloyd and I were getting sick of the sight of each other. Although we'd all feared the start of Dai Ni, the one saving grace was that we'd all have a new partner to train with. Although long overdue, it was still somewhat of a surprise when, in Thursday's first class, Laurance Sensei announced our new pairings. Chida Sensei had taken his time, and over a week after our Dai Ichi test, he'd finally decided on who would match best with whom. I had no idea how the decisions were made, but it didn't appear to me to be that tricky. We were all pretty bashed up by now, all consistently making mistakes, and all terrified of getting sick or injured. Geoff and Dave sat near the bottom of the group and came under the most scrutiny of the Sewanin, so a pairing with either of them would prove to be a short straw, but aside from that, we were all pretty similar. We all had our good days and bad days – mostly the latter.

I was called out opposite Boaz, Matt got Ronen, and Geoff stared into the eyes of Malik! With an odd number on the course, one of us would always pair with the Sewanin. This meant training with both Malik and Graham, who could switch roles as and when it suited. It wasn't clear whether Malik had advance news of Chida's decision, but he didn't look happy. Neither did Geoff, and I feared for him. It was one thing being under the constant scrutiny of the Sewanin, but with the 12 other people they also had to watch, not to mention the cops when they were on the mats, they couldn't spot everything. Training with a Sewanin, however, took things to a whole new level of exposure. They'd pick up on everything, no matter how small. *'Suck it up or go home'*, I told Geoff in the tearoom. This was a phrase we directed at anyone whinging or complaining about conditions on the course. I'm not sure who first coined the phrase or where they got it from, but it was uttered regularly, often in the direction of Geoff or Dave who between them had a reputation for whining the most. Geoff would really need to suck it up now, or there was every chance Malik would find a way to send him home. Geoff was the biggest guy on the course but often the most fragile. He was struggling with the techniques and especially the ukemi. Malik was technically strong, and there was every chance Geoff could find himself slow to react to a technique and forcibly retired from the course because of injury.

Although I was relieved to have dodged Geoff, Dave and the Sewanin, I wasn't best pleased to be paired with Boaz. Boaz by day trained in Aikido and by night frequented the Salsa bars of Tokyo. He was a dancer, while I was a fighter. Lloyd was made of tough stuff and had been a worthy partner for the first phase of the course. The respect I had for Lloyd didn't immediately translate to Boaz. Boaz had developed a reputation for being a know-it-all; I wasn't sure how long it would be before I did him some damage that I might live to regret. I wanted the brutality of Chino's Aikido, and from what I already knew of Boaz, I was concerned that his style was more of a coordinated dance. I had no interest in dancing and suspected that Boaz had very little interest in fighting. Although, in truth, Aikido probably lay somewhere in between, I had no desire to just go with the flow. It would be an interesting match-up, and only time would tell how we would get on.

WHAT'S THE POINT?

By the end of the week, I was really struggling. I'd survived Thursday's zagaku and seemed to be getting used to the pain, but what was proving the most challenging was my mental state. If I believed in something, I'd always put the effort in. I'd always trained hard in Muay Thai because I knew if applied properly, it would be effective in a real situation. The same went for Jiu Jitsu. Making my opponent tap was proof that my technique worked, and if it worked in the gym, it had a good chance of working in the street.

The catalyst for starting my journey in martial arts was being bullied at school. I didn't have much interest in belts; for me, it was always about the practicality of the technique and whether it would work in a real confrontation. As far as I could see, suwari waza had no place in the modern world and no practical application in real life. I just couldn't see the point, not unless a group of midgets attacked me; but even then, I'd stand up and use my height advantage to good effect. Being forced to do something repeatedly you don't believe in is hard on the grey matter between the ears, and I was feeling mentally tired in class, which in some ways was worse than the physical tiredness. I understood the power of mind control, but because my mind was in a bad place, it wasn't doing a great job of running my body. I was finding it harder and harder to push on, not because I was hurting but because my cognitive function was suffering.

Murata Sensei without doubt was the most streetwise of all the Sensei, and I hoped that at least in his classes, we'd get back to something practical. I hoped he could get me to believe in what I was doing and stoke the fading fire of my dwindling enthusiasm. Lined up in seiza for Friday's last class of the day, I was relieved to see Murata stride out onto the mats and take his position in front of the shomen. The previous classes had been back-to-back suwari waza at the hands of Takagi and then Oyamada Sensei. My brain was fried, and I needed a bit of Murata magic to get me back on track. His class, though, was to prove one of the weirdest classes of the course so far. Murata

115

tried to explain the meaning of *kokyu ryoku* power. Kokyu ryoku translated loosely into English as *breath power* and was a concept I'd come across before in Aikido. I hadn't understood it then, and Murata Sensei's explanation wasn't helping much. He guided us in a series of exercises, which in part mirrored Aikido techniques. For all movements of the kihon dosa, we'd been told time and time again to keep our rear heel firmly connected to the mats. Apparently, this was one way to tell someone who had taken the course from someone who hadn't. A connected rear heel was the sign of a Senshusei. It was therefore surprising when Murata Sensei's exercises encouraged us to alternate heel up, heel down, and then he told us, *'you should imagine roots sprouting from your heels!'* The best was, however, yet to come. Murata informed us he could teach us how to hide behind a sword! Fortunately, there were only ten minutes of the class left. I was at breaking point, and it appeared Dave was, too. Despite his best efforts, Dave just couldn't keep a straight face, and although we didn't all show it, I knew none of us had a clue what was going on. Was I slowly going mad? Was this really what I'd signed up for? Was there any point to Dai Ni, and could I take another six weeks, quite literally, on my knees? I couldn't wait for the class to end, the day's closing Shinkoku to be done and to chat over everything that had just happened with my fellow Senshusei, to try to make sense of it all.

I desperately needed the weekend but had to get through Saturday first. Unfortunately, it was to be more of the same. The Wizard had us sliding about on our knees, and Murray Sensei had us doing *kokyu ho* (kneeling techniques to build kokyu ryoku power). As I headed back to Musashi Koyama for two days of respite, I was at my lowest point of Senshusei since the start and seriously thinking of packing it all in.

THE DOCUMENTARY

Music had always been an important part of my life, but it began to play an even more significant role in my attempt to get motivated for the day ahead. I found myself listening to a lot of American rap, particularly anything by The Game. The combination of heavy beats and explicit lyrics seemed to be the perfect boost I needed on the train journey to Ochiai each morning. The Game's debut album, entitled *The Documentary*, had become my go-to listen to and from the honbu and one track seemed to sum up in its title how I was feeling about the course – *Hate It or Love It*. Like The Game, I couldn't make up my mind, either. Was I enjoying the course, or was I hating every minute? I felt privileged to be in Japan, to be training at the head dojo of

Yoshinkan Aikido, but the brutal training was taking its toll on both my physical and mental well-being. It was the proverbial double-edged sword, and I hadn't decided which edge was winning out.

The Game had his documentary, and I didn't realise that I was about to get mine. In Aikido circles, the Senshusei course was famous worldwide, and had grown in infamy due to the publication of *Angry White Pyjamas*. There were regular visitors to the honbu dojo, and those passing through invariably wanted to tread on the hallowed green tatami. Training in the odd class wasn't Senshusei, and the regular visitors were a reminder we were doing something extraordinary. Even Mike Tyson, arguably one of the greatest pound-for-pound boxers the world has ever known, while heavyweight champion, had made his own pilgrimage. The story goes that he was especially fascinated by Aikido's footwork and the flexibility in the knees of its practitioners. On the day of his visit, I could only presume that seiza had been kept to a minimum, because flexibility was not something I associated with the feeling in my own knees. Unfortunately, a few days after meeting Kancho Gozo Shioda, he'd lost his heavyweight crown at the Tokyo Dome to Buster Douglas, a 42-1 underdog. I'd always been a Tyson fan, and knowing he'd set foot in the very place I was training was further confirmation that the experience I'd signed myself up for was revered around the world. As further evidence of this, on Wednesday, 21 June 2006, as I arrived at the honbu dojo, a guy with a video camera greeted me. I'd not seen him around before, but we immediately hit it off and started chatting. His name was Robert, and he was over from the United States and in Japan to make a number of documentaries on the Japanese fighting arts, including Yoshinkan Aikido and specifically the Senshusei course. He was planning to sell his videos, which he'd badged *Fight! Japan,* to interested parties for airing on cable TV across America. He appeared to have been given free rein at the honbu and followed me into the locker room and then onto my cleaning station, which happened to be the women's toilets. It was at this point that I suggested he might want to film someone else! I had my duties to perform, and a distraction, while welcome, would no doubt catch the unwanted attention of the Sewanin. Also, I wasn't sure scrubbing the toilet floor and emptying the sanitary bin would make very entertaining viewing. In the corridor he chatted with Vic who shared the challenges of integrating dojo and daily life. *'It takes a lot of time to get established here. I just recently got another two jobs and, even though I'm working four days a week now, it's still not enough to live, eat and pay tuition here* (honbu dojo fees). *I need to get my act together if I plan to continue taking this course!'*

In the morning meeting, Robert's spotlight was literally on Malik Sewanin. Aware of the expression *playing up to the camera*, I was now about to witness this play out right before my eyes. It began with Malik's pre-training sermon and extended into the first class where Paul Sensei lined us up and demanded that we drive our yokomen uchi strikes as hard as we could into each other's forearms. We did this to the count, only pausing to rotate partners every so often. I was well versed in Lloyd's ability to dish out pain and went easy on him, but with the next change of partner, finding myself opposite Malik was an opportunity too good to miss. The Sewanin wanted spirit, and today I decided that the best measure of my spirit was how hard I could hit. I went mad and smashed Malik's forearms as hard as I could. I noticed when we broke off that his fingers were shaking, while mine weren't. *Got him good and proper*, I thought to myself.

Before the last class, Malik called us into the dojo for punishment. Why, I wasn't sure, but once again Robert's camera was rolling. We did two sets of *usagi tobi* (bunny hops) around the perimeter of the mats. This was a painful exercise that inflicted even more discomfort and suffering on our already battered knees. There was the additional requirement to perform this exercise with our hands behind our backs. This added an extra layer of hardship when inevitably, from time to time, we'd each fall flat on our faces, without the protection of our hands to brace our fall. As we got tired the action became more difficult. It reminded me of one of the pop-up toys I'd buy on holiday as a kid, having browsed the toy shop for over an hour. I'd press the novelty top down on its spring to engage the suction cup to the base. When the suction failed the toy would spring up in the air and topple over. With each turn it was back to square one. This childhood toy provided hours of amusement, but the same could not be said for bunny hops! Everyone was toppling and struggling to keep going. I was determined not to give the Sewanin the satisfaction and maybe playing up to the camera myself, I got on with the job in hand. Unfortunately, the reward for being one of the first to finish was seiza. One type of pain was replaced with another, which was a frequent occurrence at the honbu. The last thing limbs pumped full of blood needed were the brakes applied sharply. This stop-start was always the catalyst for suffering in the form of painful cramps. Suffering that would now be captured on film for ever, for all to see. Geoff was dying. Three hops and he was down; three hops more and he was down again. Long limbs and usagi tobi didn't mix, and while on the one hand I sympathised with his situation, on the other I resented the fact that he was taking so long. In his fruitless bid to ease his own pain, he was making mine worse!

When the punishment was done, Ronen as the week's Shinkoku performed the day's closing ritual. Malik Sewanin wasn't happy again and called us all into the tearoom. Ronen's volume hadn't been up to scratch, and Malik intended to find out why. *'Shinkoku...that was like a mouse...I rehearsed it with you, and it was like a mouse...are you a mouse or a man?'* Malik fired into Ronen, and then into us all. *'You're Senshusei; don't be mice, be men!'* I had a feeling that Malik might live to regret the words he'd just uttered. The look of displeasure on Ronen's face was plain for all to see. I knew he'd file that comment away and make a mental note to deliver payback in the future.

We were finally dismissed and headed off to our respective cleaning duties. My fellow Senshusei were laughing at me, as in conversation earlier in the day, we'd identified that in my free time away from the honbu I drank whisky and brandy, watched war films and also listened to highly offensive rap music. Not the healthiest collection of pastimes – and possibly a sign that I was slowly losing my mind! With one-to-one time now available with Malik Sewanin (MS), Robert Clyne (RC) probed further into his teaching philosophy and personality.

RC: *'Technically, you're probably the most talented teacher. You have the most focus, you've got the thing going on, but in terms of rapport with students, I'd have to say you're the worst!'*

MS: *'Yeah, I think my role as Sewanin has two sides. First of all, I have to instil a sense of hard discipline, the experience of what it's like to be taken to the max; what it's like to get punished. They have to experience the hard as well as the good.'*

RC: *'We've seen how you show the hard. People are doing a lot of bunny hops; they're getting chewed out a lot. How do you show the good, what's the good side of you?'*

MS: *'The good side I think is mainly through the motivational talks I give.'*

RC: *'Ok, so you're not particularly concerned that you're not that popular?'*

MS: *'No, not really. You know, as long as they understand that my intention is not to be evil.'*

RC: *'And why is hardship so important?'*

119

MS: *'Because we face it every single day in life, and it's easier to run from hardship and it's easy to quit, and what this course helps us to understand is to go on, to keep going. So, my job is to make sure that they get hardship every single day and that they get through that hardship every single day.'*

RC: *'So you're saying that in the end if they like you, but they don't really experience hardship, you've failed.'*

MS: *'Yeah!'*

GOING COMMANDO

The rules at the honbu dojo were strict, and what made matters worse was that they were also strictly enforced. Simple things most people do without thinking were banned in the dojo. No wiping of sweat and no adjustment of clothing while on the mats had been drummed into our heads repeatedly. While some rules seemed ridiculous, there was never any questioning them. Constantly reminded that we were the lowest of the low, our role was always to do, with no opportunity to ever discuss. Rules were made to be followed, and as Senshusei we had no alternative but to do just that.

Boaz and I were getting used to one another. Boaz lacked Lloyd's toughness, but made up for it with his agility and flexibility. As a Salsa dancer, his style of Aikido, as far as I was concerned, looked like, and felt more like a rehearsed set of moves. There was definitely a divide at the honbu. There were those who wanted their Aikido to be smooth, flowing and to look nice at all times. This required complicity from uke, which was not something I was particularly interested in. If I had to rely on my partner moving the right way to make my technique work, then at best I was involved in a coordinated dance, and at worst I was kidding myself that my techniques had any practical value out on the street. I just wanted my Aikido to work. I didn't care how it looked, but it had to result in the desired outcome no matter what uke did. Anything less than that, and I'd be setting myself up for trouble down the line and one huge wake-up call. I didn't imagine Geoff offered much in the way of compliance, and the Aikido I wanted had to work on a bigger guy like him even when he wasn't playing ball. Although our styles of Aikido were very different, I liked Boaz. You could have a laugh with him, and away from Salsa, he didn't appear to take himself too seriously. The day after the filming was one such occasion, and what a shame not to have captured it on camera.

I wasn't feeling good and knew I was coming down with something. The soreness in my throat and aching in my ears were red flags that all was not well. I knew it would be a hard day. I'd need an extra injection of motivation to get through or something to lighten the oppressive environment in the dojo. Thankfully, albeit unintentionally, Boaz came to the rescue. Sonoda Sensei presided over the second class of the day – the class when Boaz's trousers came loose. Training with him I had a bird's-eye view, and after each technique, they inched lower, lower and then even lower. It wasn't long before they were round his knees, and in his undressed state, Boaz's predicament finally caught Sonoda's attention. Sonoda sent him to the edge of the tatami to pull and then tie them up, and with his modesty restored, Boaz returned to training. It was only after the class that I learnt what a lucky escape we'd all had. Boaz, recounting the tale in the tearoom, explained that he'd planned to 'go commando' that day. For those not familiar with the term, this meant wearing no underwear under dogi bottoms at all, a common practice amongst many students of traditional martial arts. The rationale was to allow freedom of movement and to avoid the rubbing and chaffing that fabric close to the most intimate parts of the body might cause. We were all in hysterics at the thought of Sonoda Sensei's face, having caught sight of Boaz's bits bouncing around freely. It would have given a whole new meaning to the term 'free practice' and was something we'd thankfully all escaped!

The last class of the day was not without further incident. Laurance Sensei taught *jo* techniques, which I'd had some previous experience of at the Shudokan. The jo was a *long staff* that could be used to throw your opponent, particularly when he or she was stupid enough to grab the end. Dave who was gaining a reputation for being clumsy, tripped while he was throwing me and buried my head unceremoniously into the mats. Luckily the soft practice ones. were out, so I avoided any serious injury. Lloyd, too, was on form and exerted his surprising strength to snap his jo completely in half while throwing his uke.

GROUND ZERO

Ground zero is defined as the point directly above, below, or at the point at which a nuclear explosion occurs, and before the week was out, the honbu dojo was to have its very own. The men's toilets had two cubicles, or traps, as we preferred to call them. Entering the mats in a white dogi without emptying your bowels beforehand was a potential recipe for disaster. This meant both traps were extremely busy before the 8:30am class, and to avoid getting caught short we'd each developed our own specific routines and timings. Through another process of trial and error, and out of frustration from queuing, we'd informally and unconsciously come up with a schedule that worked for all. Leave it too late, and you might face a queue. If the queue was long, and the Sewanin called the morning meeting, you could be in trouble. Go too early and you might have unfinished business brewing that you'd then at least have to carry through the first class. It was a delicate balance, and a balance it had been worth taking the time to get right. The routine was made more complicated, not to mention time-consuming, by wearing a dogi along with the honbu stipulation that all Senshusei had to fold the end of the toilet paper into a nice, neat *sankaku* (triangle), on completion of business.

On Friday morning I was minding my own business, getting changed in the locker room, when Dror in a state of shock burst in. Dror had a preference for trap two and hurriedly explained that, having flushed the toilet post-dump, the contents of the bowl had failed to drain and instead overflowed, spilling its gruesome contents all over the floor. In times of crisis it's best to run. I'd learnt this in self-defence training, and the situation that now presented itself, courtesy of Dror, required every bit of defence I could muster. Thankfully, Ronen took charge and designated the site 'ground zero' in his deadly serious, but deadpan tone. *'Ze ha hara selha, kanes pnima acshav, ve tenake et ze. Anahnoo nispog et ha mayim bachhoz. Yalla zooz!'* He sternly ordered Dror in Hebrew. *'This is your shit, get in there now and clean it. We will soak up the water outside. Now go!'* Dror jumped inside the trap like he'd been jump-started back to life! For the next 20 minutes, endless newspaper went in folded, only to emerge moments later in a crumpled, soggy, discoloured state. Time was of the essence to get the horrible mess cleaned up before the Sewanin found out, and under Ronen's direction, things were back to normal quickly. By now we were a tight-knit unit and resolved to keep the matter under wraps. I didn't dare ask if any of the zokin had been used in the clean-up. I suspected after the initial dirty work had been done with the newspaper that they had, but it was best not to know!

Graham Sewanin was now back from Russia. He didn't say much about his trip with Chino Sensei but appeared to be in one piece. He'd described the audition as *'just like doing the whole Senshusei course in one hour'*, so I didn't dare imagine what a three-day seminar must have felt like. I know from reading an article in *AYI e-Magazine* that he'd waited on Chino hand and foot. *'Coffee always ready after his shower and breakfast on the table before he was ready.'* Rustam Sensei, the Russian host, had noticed that Chino Sensei was always in kamae. As Graham Sewanin noted, *'he had form in everything he did. The way he moved, ate, brushed his teeth and folded his clothes'*. On the mats, *'he was on fire! This was the closest I'd ever get to being with Gozo Shioda'*. The Sewanin were a constant thorn in our sides. With two of them, it was impossible to get away with anything, so with Graham away, we had hoped for a reprieve in the frequency of punishments dished out. How wrong we were. With Graham in Russia, Malik had been on a mission and had a licence to do what he liked. This had resulted in more severity, increased frequency and far too many usagi tobi. We knew Graham didn't approve of bunny hops, and we were glad to have him back!

I wasn't sure if Dror's misfortune had impacted me somehow, but after the first class, I had a word with the Sewanin to put them on alert that I was feeling sick. This didn't mean I'd have the option to miss the second and third classes – far from it. The dojo had a strict policy on everything, including vomiting. I was fine to continue training, safe in the knowledge that should things turn sour, I had four legitimate options at my disposal.

Option 1 – ask permission to leave the mats.

Option 2 – run to the toilet if time allowed (no permission needed).

Option 3 – grab the blue dust bucket, which we used as part of our dojo sweeping ritual, and do it in this while running to the toilet (no permission needed).

Option 4 – pull open my dogi top and puke my guts up in there, then revert to option 2 (again, no permission needed).

Which option I selected would have to be made in a split second, as there would be no time to think. The preferred course of action was option 1, but if time didn't permit there was no choice but to trigger options 2, 3 or 4 in that order. Option 4 was always the last resort! Luckily, I didn't have to exercise any of the options but felt dreadful all day. The last thing I wanted to do was puke in front of a Sensei. Although Dror had shared his bodily fluids earlier in the day, I had no intention of sharing mine!

DOWN WHEN OUT

Ronen with his military background had told me stories about soldiers who, on leaving the army, had struggled to adapt to normal life on civvy street. Without direction and with the freedom to direct their own lives, they'd become depressed and craved the organisation and discipline they'd left behind. I'd never understood this, but on the last Monday of the month, which was a day I had completely free with no requirement to train or teach, for some inexplicable reason, I was miserable. I'd noticed my Monday blues in previous weeks, and this depressed state seemed to be getting worse the deeper I got into the course. I couldn't explain why and could only presume that the control and discipline the honbu dojo provided was something I was starting to enjoy. With no enforced direction to my day, Mondays were becoming a challenge. I didn't feel the same on Sundays. Sundays were a good day and even if I was working at Berlitz, they still gave me a chance to rest bruised, aching muscles that had been punished all week. Mondays, though, were altogether different. Perhaps it was the routine I was missing? Perhaps I felt down because Monday was the precursor to a brand-new week? In my previous life, Sunday evenings ahead of going to work on Monday mornings had always been a bit depressing, so it was likely the latter was the more rational explanation. All I knew was that for some reason, I felt down when I was out of the honbu dojo. Despite the pain, suffering and general discomfort I experienced within its walls, while I was there, I generally felt happy.

I still wasn't feeling well, and although I'd shaken off the sickness of last week, a cold seemed to be on its way, and I'd also started coughing. Another week began, and despite feeling run down on Tuesday's train to Ochiai, I was looking forward to the week ahead. The suwari waza was getting monotonous, and with over a month left of Dai Ni, there was a lot more shuffling around on my knees still to come. Despite this, Senshusei was teaching me something. It was something you couldn't learn in a classroom or get from a book. When I thought I couldn't do something or got to a point where I felt like I couldn't go on, Senshusei was teaching me I could. The course was continuously pushing me out of my comfort zone. It was testing boundaries that I'd never tested before. I was relishing the pain and hardship, and although I hated to admit it, I was beginning to understand what Malik was on about.

SUCK IT UP

I had two very contrasting lives. At the honbu dojo, where there were no excuses, you got on with the job in hand. You could whinge and whine, but nobody was listening. If there was any complaining, it was usually rewarded with punishment. At Berlitz it was a different story. My colleagues at Sangenjaya, while I liked them, were weak. In the staff room, there was regular moaning about the crowded train on the way in, allocated shifts and irritating students. This was civvy street, and my experience on Senshusei was as close to military life as I could get. I was becoming immune to pain, detested weakness and had developed an attitude that wouldn't suffer fools. I'd already upset a couple of my students with my straight-talking, no-nonsense approach. Although I hadn't been formally reprimanded, it had been suggested that I remember where I was and to tone things down a little. My attitude was to suck it up. Whatever life or the course threw at me, Senshusei was giving me the confidence to take it on the chin and get on with things no matter what. Suck it up or go home! This was my new mantra, and anyone around me who didn't conform to this way of thinking, too, was no longer worthy of my time.

Ahead of the last zagaku class of the month, I told Neville that I would be like a rock and show no emotion. I wouldn't move or put my hands down even for a moment to relieve the pain. I'd set my stall out, and my promise served as motivation when the pain in my knees became almost too much to bear. I didn't move, showed no emotion and even managed to get up fairly quickly at the end. Dror, by contrast, was in absolute agony. During the class he moved around, trying to control the pain, but with little success. Afterwards, as I helped him to his feet, he could barely walk!

My mental state seemed to be getting stronger and stronger, and seeing weakness in others served as fuel to this ever-increasing feeling of fortitude. I was starting to really believe that the mind controlled the body and not the other way around. We were all getting physically tougher; we had no choice. Mental toughness was something we had to work at individually, and some were better at this than others. Ronen was a kindred spirit, and although I'd been wary of him at the very beginning, I now felt closer and more aligned with him than anyone else on the course. Ronen hadn't been wary of me, but as he'd put it, *'in my mode of operation I needed to be careful of assholes and people I don't trust'*. He hadn't stopped there. *'I immediately knew that you're not one of those, despite being a tough-looking British bald guy and Jason Statham wannabe!'* Matt and I were friends from back home, but Ronen possessed that inner strength that is a very rare find. You become who you surround yourself with, and the more I'd gotten to know Ronen, the more I think we'd both benefited from our growing bond. He reminded me of Sensei Michal from my time at the Shudokan, whose enquiring mind and dedication to discover the real Aikido had in many ways motivated my trip to Japan. Ronen had experience as a diver, and in diving speak, having a 'buddy' was critical to your safety and ultimate survival underwater. The term described the scenario when two people operated together as a single unit. 'Buddy system' had become our rallying cry, a verbal determination to complete the course and a unified commitment to support each other. Buddy system became our greeting in the morning and encouragement as we marched onto the mats for yet another class. Osu meant obedience and subservience in the dojo; buddy system meant something very different. Osu was the honbu dojo's word; buddy system was ours. Like prison slang, we'd developed a line of communication to protect our independence and confuse the guards! When we cried buddy system, it meant don't let the bastards grind us down, take all they can give and keep going, and it was our own special version of suck it up or go home.

Japan is a country of extremes, and the temperature in Tokyo was now regularly above 30 degrees, which, within the confines of the dojo, felt more like 40! I was still feeling rough and sweating buckets in every class, but my suck-it-up attitude was carrying me through. I hoped I could retain this feeling. Had I really changed, or was I just very good at self-deception? Either way, it didn't matter, as long as I could just keep going. In the last two classes of the week, we had Sonoda Sensei. I threw Ronen to the mats, and before he could get back up, Neville, who was training alongside us, threw Inazaki right on top of him. Classes with the cops were crowded, and space on the tatami was limited. It wasn't necessarily Neville's fault, but Ronen wasn't happy and promised me in private that *'Neville's day will come!'* Watching Sonoda, I realised the importance of Senshusei training. Like Oyamada, he wasn't a graduate of the course, and when he moved, his back heel rose and his posture looked wrong. Compared to Chino, it was chalk and cheese!

Another week was in the bag, and three months in, over a quarter of the course was now complete. After class I went with Clyde to FamilyMart, a convenience store just up from the honbu, and celebrated with a ChocoBari. It was roasting hot, and with a big sweet tooth, I couldn't resist this cookie-coated ice cream treat. Having said my farewells to Clyde, I wandered up to Ochiai Station, where, to my surprise I bumped into Malik. We chatted for about 10 minutes, and for the first time I saw him in a different light. Out of his dogi and away from the dojo, he was just another guy who, like me, had come to Japan to study martial arts. He had a role to play as Sewanin and a very specific job to do. While I didn't like much of his conduct and how he treated us, along with Graham, he was an essential component of what made the course, the course. Yes, he'd called my buddy Ronen a mouse, which was something he'd probably live to regret. But with that all said, for the first time, I felt an overwhelming sense of gratitude for his presence at the honbu and for his role as Sewanin.

HAJIME GEIKO

Hajime geiko was an integral part of Senshusei training. Performing the same technique repeatedly to a monotonous count that seemed to get quicker and quicker was apparently character building. Oyamada Sensei had given us a taster already, and other Sensei had also followed suit. It may have been character building, but in my opinion, it was technique damaging. What resembled a technique at the start of a hajime session, five repetitions in bore very little resemblance to any technique at all. Hajime was a flurry of arms and legs. It was a test of endurance rather than concentrated practice. It was something we all hated but knew we'd have to endure. Being slow at hajime geiko was like sinking in quicksand. The more you fell behind everyone else the less time you had to rest and compose yourself before the next repetition of the technique. The more you sank, the faster you sank, and the quicker your breath was taken away. It was grasping, choking and debilitating training that all of us dreaded. Survival depended a lot on uke. There was no time to do the technique properly like you would if your life depended on it. Hajime was making the shape of a technique and conserving as much energy as possible. A bad uke was like driving uphill with a boot full of luggage. A good uke was like the cleaner I'd hired on securing my first full-time job. I'd arrived home early one day to find her sat on the sofa. It turned out I'd been fooled. Her idea of cleaning was moving a few bits of furniture around. Minimal effort made to appear like maximum output. It looked the same, but it most definitely wasn't! The main problem with hajime geiko was that you never knew when it would end. It was a sickening test of commitment to keep going when you didn't know how long you'd have to keep going for. It was like driving a car foot to the throttle. The fuel would run out quicker, and you'd hope and pray to get to your destination before you found yourself running on fumes or, in a worst-case scenario, coming to a complete standstill. The constant screaming of the Sewanin and the crushing count of the Sensei were always geared up to full throttle. First gear was unacceptable, second gear not tolerated. Top gear at full pelt was the only acceptable speed.

Now into July we'd yet to personally experience a serious beasting at the hands of Chino Sensei. We'd seen him destroy Malik and Graham Sewanin in the audition for Russia and knew of his love of brutality, but so far, we'd not had the pleasure ourselves. Friday, 7 July, was to be the day we'd experience hajime geiko the Chino way. Romeo Sensei had warmed us up in the first class with an assortment of suwari waza techniques, and in the second session of the day, like lambs to the slaughter, we were thrown to the wolf. At once the hajime geiko began, and to the count, we ran through all the Dai Ni techniques. Despite the mental strength I'd found last week, about 20 minutes in, I felt worryingly drained. All of my energy seemed to be leaving my body. I was at full throttle with a hole in my petrol tank that I had no way of plugging. I looked around for inspiration to see Matt and Ronen going strong. Ronen gave me a knowing look, which meant buddy system, and a surge of energy fired back into my body. Unfortunately, this was short-lived, and like a sugar surge from a fizzy drink, moments later I crashed. I felt lightheaded and was certain I would pass out. The heat was unbearable. Japanese humidity was here, and with all the body heat, entering the dojo felt like walking into a house in the middle of summer with all the radiators on full blast. Chiba, one of the cops, was next to me, paired up with Neville. He was gagging and looked like he would puke at any moment. *I wonder which option he'll take*, I thought to myself. I didn't have to wait too long to find out. Malik could see the signs, too, and before the ripcord of option 2 was pulled, Chiba was dragged unceremoniously off the mats by the Sewanin. Down the corridor and into the toilets he went, where he deposited the contents of his stomach into the bowl of trap one.

I've no idea how I kept going. I was running on fumes by the end. Finally, and not a moment too soon, what amounted to the best part of an hour of torture thankfully ended. There were still 30 minutes left of the class to run, and Chino Sensei focused in on *kata mochi nikajo*. Whatever the technique, anything applied by Chino was bound to hurt, and after the beating I'd just taken, I wasn't too thrilled when he called me up as uke. Chino Sensei motioned for me to grip his dogi at chest level. As uke you often had to do things you really didn't want to do – things you knew were a mistake the instant you'd done them. Willingly giving your body to a psychopath to do with it what he wanted wasn't a smart move, and as raw power surged through my body I was reminded why. My wrist, elbow, shoulder and rear leg buckled in that order, and I felt Chino's energy explode out of the back of my knee as I crashed to the tatami. This was Gozo Shioda's Aikido; the real Aikido I was in Japan to find. In my mind I forgave Chino Sensei for the beasting he'd administered and trusted in the fact that if I wanted a nikajo like his, then there was probably method in the madness that was hajime geiko. The class ended, and I staggered off the mats. I knew I'd need every minute of the break to recover. My dogi was soaked through with sweat. It was too wet for the final class, so I headed into the locker room to make a quick change. I disrobed and jumped on the scales in my pants. I'd done the same thing before the first class and was shocked to discover that, thanks to hajime geiko, I'd lost just under four kilograms in weight. I jumped off and out of curiosity threw my soaked dogi on the scales instead. This now weighed over four kilograms. I'd lost over half a stone in fluid. No wonder I'd felt like I would pass out! With no opportunity to drink during class, dehydration was a constant threat, and there was no better catalyst than a Tokyo summer combined with good old hajime geiko. After the last class of the day, I travelled across the city for a Japanese lesson with Hotta Sensei. Having exchanged Japanese pleasantries on her doorstep, she broke her own rule to ask in English, *'have you lost weight?'* She wasn't kidding. I'd lost more weight in three hours than I'd cut to make weight for a Muay Thai fight over three days. I was lucky to still be alive!

BIRTHDAY BOY

On Saturday I was still recovering from the effects of yesterday's hajime geiko, and my knees and ankles were in a right state from all the shuffling about. Lloyd's knees were shredded, and in the first class, he'd left a trail of blood spots all over the tatami. He'd well and truly marked his territory, and at first glance it looked like a murder scene. Luckily there were 13 Senshusei armed with zokin to clean up. The blood would add to the mix of other things they'd absorbed during the previous months, and Lloyd's DNA would now spread far and wide around the dojo during next week's cleaning duties.

I chatted with Ronen and confided in him that I was struggling. The buddy system was in full effect, and he suggested I start taking amino acids. He'd been taking them since the start of the course and said he felt strong all the time. He promised to pick some up for me and bring them along to his birthday celebration that night. Ronen had been a regular at the pharmacy since injuring his shoulder. After a nasty fall thanks to one of Laurance Sensei's classes, he'd taken Clyde with him to a pharmacy in Takadanobaba to translate. High-strength painkillers were handed over without a prescription. Ronen took them on an empty stomach before training and wondered why he felt so good. With a smile on his face he'd thrown people around and taken whatever the Sensei threw at us. Investigating the cause of his euphoria he enlisted the help of Google. The tablets contained taurine and an opioid that was illegal everywhere else in the world apart from Japan. Ronen had been high as a kite! Ronen's birthday was an opportunity for us all to get together in more relaxed surroundings. Inevitably the discussion would turn to the course; it's the one thing we all had in common and was something never far from our minds. We agreed to meet up at Shamaim, an Israeli restaurant Ronen, Dror and Boaz knew well. The food was great and a welcome change from rice. With a few beers to wash everything down, I put the trauma of the week just gone behind me. Our little band of brothers and one sister toasted Ronen and also Dror, who'd just become an uncle. There were no late nights as a Senshusei, and I wasn't stupid enough to drink so much that I'd risk waking up with a hangover. That was Dave's territory, but he was young enough to shake it off. I said my goodbyes, caught the train home, and was in bed fast asleep by 10:30pm.

WORLD CUP BUTT

I'd caught a fair few of the Word Cup matches but was far too tired to get up at 4am to watch Italy versus France in the final. Monday was a day off from the dojo, and an early start would never be high on my list of priorities. I found out later that Italy had won, beating France on penalties after a 1-1 stalemate existed after extra-time. Zinedine Zidane, France's captain and star player, having scored for his country, was sent off after an altercation that saw him head-butt one of the Italian players.

Violence never seemed to be far away from any situation. If it could happen in the World Cup final, it could happen anywhere. Now, as Senshusei, I hoped it would knock on my door and give me the opportunity to test my skills. Away from the honbu, I found myself acutely aware of others. I'd constantly analyse my immediate surroundings to determine what I would do if something kicked off. Would my Aikido training save me? What a story I'd have to tell my fellow Senshusei, having applied one of my techniques on a would-be assailant! Any story would be solely reserved for them. The Sewanin and Sensei would be kept in the dark. I was sure that the majority had never tested their skills in the real world, and my search for combat would surely be frowned upon. I felt like a coiled spring that could be unleashed in a split second to do untold damage to anyone who crossed my path. Training all day and thinking about training all night had given me a one-track mind. The transition from honbu life to Berlitz life was always difficult. I bit my tongue regularly, and in one particular lesson, my patience was tested to the limit. In the dojo you did as you were told no matter what, but in the classroom, every now and again, the usually subservient Japanese student turned into a monster that needed taming. I had one student who was extremely difficult and hated studying from the file. I had to teach from the Berlitz manual, though, or risk losing my job – and with it my right to stay in Japan. This particular student was having none of it, and when I attempted to correct him, he'd frequently challenge back, *'why are you asking me stupid questions?'* I wasn't aware my questions were stupid and momentarily imagined launching him across the classroom and through the nearest window. Luckily for him, my temperament was better than Zidane's. I made a mental note and reported his rudeness to Peter. I didn't see the student again. Lucky for me and very lucky for him!

HOT, HOT, HOT!!!

The song by The Cure I'd spent many hours listening to back in the late eighties became the background music to the second week of July. The temperature in Tokyo was stifling. I'd trained in Muay Thai in Bangkok in similar heat, but there I'd be wearing shorts, water could be drunk as and when I wanted, and if it all got a bit too much, I could always take a break.

On the Senshusei course, the dogi was better suited to winter training. Like a sponge it absorbed as much sweat as I could produce, and from previous experience at the hands of Chino Sensei I already knew that in a 90-minute class I could produce a lot! I imagined how knights of old must have felt dragging themselves around the battlefield in suits of chain mail and armour. By the end of class, I regularly had my very own version! More sweating meant harder training, and more washing. It was compulsory to wash a dogi you'd sweated through. Hanging up a soaked dogi in the dojo overnight usually ensured it would dry, but the stink the next day would be unbearable for the wearer and anyone in close proximity. When time permitted the sento visit was a lifesaver. After a hard day of training, lugging three wet dogi on three trains across Tokyo, with all the walking in between, was extra training I didn't need. Dogi were bulky and on crowded trains finding room for myself, never mind my huge bag, was not only impractical, it was virtually impossible. Berlitz made life difficult. An early afternoon teaching slot killed any chance of sento time and made lugging the only option. Dogi would be hauled to the Berlitz school and then home again at night. This usually involving catching the last train which was always the busiest.

Hajime geiko was becoming an all-too-frequent dish on the menu of honbu dojo life. In Wednesday's second class, The Wizard cast his spell; a 50-minute beasting to the incessant count. It was a massive struggle and far too hot and humid to perform even the simplest of tasks – like breathing! I was sweating so much I thought I would faint. When hajime geiko was over, there was little reprieve as for the last half hour, we took turns performing *jiyu waza*. Jiyu waza lay somewhere between a coordinated dance and the practical application of techniques. It was one step up from kihon waza but fell short of free fighting. A set attack was initiated by uke repeatedly and dealt with by shite using a variety of techniques until the Sensei on duty called time. We practiced jiyu waza on only one side. In Muay Thai I'd trained hard to be able to fight in either stance. If my left leg got smashed up,

I could change sides and continue the battle. With jiyu waza things were different. If I ever met an Aikidoka who attacked with their left, I'd be well and truly screwed! Dripping with sweat, we lined up and patiently awaited our turn to demonstrate. Boaz and I were called out for shomen uchi jiyu waza. Boaz ran in as fast as he could, attempting to strike me on the forehead with the blade of his right hand. As this was his only permitted attack, I knew what was coming, and threw him again and again until I heard 'yame' (stop) called. Standing in line afterwards, watching the other pairs perform, was the worst I'd felt on the course to date. I thought I was going to collapse or puke my guts up right there and then. My mind wandered back to an incident at boarding school. A hot day, and an introduction to the CCF in the Memorial Hall, saw Oliver Terry fall flat on his face. Tiiimmmmbbbeeer! His head bounced off the concrete floor and he spent the next few days in the sanatorium (the school's medical facility). Back in the present, no one was felling my tree – head up and back straight, I held on!

I was still feeling destroyed while sitting in seiza, awaiting the start of the last class. As the sun beamed through the windows, dazzling my vision, I was sure things couldn't get any worse. My heart sank as I made out the silhouette of Oyamada Sensei. My least-favourite teacher was about to take his position under the shomen, and that could mean only one thing. Yet more hajime geiko was on the cards. Wednesday was turning out to be one hell of a tough day at the office. For 45 minutes we went at it, repeating the same series of techniques over and over again, with no variety and no respite. Finally, it was over, and Oyamada gave us a free pass to practice any techniques we wanted in pairs. There was still another 45 minutes to go, and glancing round, we all looked far too tired to do anything. Even staggering into bed would have been an effort, but bed was a long way off. Being given free rein to decide on what to practice and then getting on with it was far too taxing for both body and brain. In times of trouble, I could be resourceful and reverted to a strategy I'd used in the past to great effect. My plan caught on, and soon we were all asking Graham Sewanin questions. Standing still even for a minute was a precious gift! Clyde was in the worst shape I'd ever seen him. By his own admission, he was probably one of the weakest on the course. I didn't think it was a physical thing but more of a mental one. A life in martial arts and especially time in the ring had taught me the importance of mental toughness and also provided the environment to develop it. Clyde was some way behind in his development, and after the day's training, it showed. He could hardly speak and sat drinking water in the tearoom. Having come to the sensible realisation that the tearoom was too visible from the office, he clambered to his feet and staggered into the locker room. There he crumpled to the floor and sat in silence.

The week only got worse. Thursdays were always a challenge and today the Sewanin had warned us that Chino would take the second class. Chino Sensei was like chocolate. While I enjoyed the experience, I knew too much of it wasn't good for me. As advertised, Chino was in the building, and he parked the physical torture only to replace it with a mental one instead. He repeatedly told us how bad our techniques were and, almost comically, demonstrated how we performed certain moves while mumbling to himself in Japanese things we didn't understand! Dave volunteered to explain the right and wrong versions of a *sankajo suwari waza* technique. Applying Aikido's third control on your knees was no easy task. I knew Dave was already an expert in getting it wrong but wasn't convinced he had much of a clue how to do it right. When Dave did anything, there was usually a comic element, and we braced ourselves for what was about to happen. Both of Dave's explanations sounded exactly the same. It was clear he didn't understand the technique at all. What he thought was good and bad were one and the same. Chino looked confused and had every reason to be! Ronen had escaped the class. He was there in body and spirit but had been prevented from taking part. The Sewanin were in a strange mood and had punished him with 90 minutes of seiza for talking directly to Murray Sensei during the first class of the day. Ronen had broken the strict hierarchy of the honbu. His reward for missing out middle management and going straight to the top was a loss of feeling in his legs. He explained later. *'It's rare for me to break rank mate, I was semi-conscious. My head felt like it was in a furnace. They closed the windows and the heat was inhumane!'*

The summer heat provided little reprieve, and we were all acutely conscious of the dangers of dehydration. Light-headedness, cramps and constant weakness were some of the symptoms. It wasn't a game, and from the reading I'd been doing on the subject, I knew if it got out of control, it could cause increased pressure on the heart which could prove fatal. I for one already had enough pressure on my heart from hajime geiko! I had an incessant fear of excessive exercise from years before. In my Midlands Light Middleweight Title fight, I'd fought probably my toughest opponent. 'NEB', as he liked to be known, had a good 10 years on me, was heavily tattooed and ripped. He wouldn't be top of anyone's list to get into a ring with. I'd fought him at Perry Barr in Birmingham on a K-Star promotion organised by Steve Logan. Steve had made a guest appearance in one of my private lessons with Kru Tony at Sitsiam, and now I was fighting on his show. NEB gave me a five-round war. It was back and forth until, 10 seconds before the end of the fifth, I caught him with a Master Lec special. As my right shin connected to the left side of his neck, NEB's lights temporarily went out. He crucifixed to the canvas, and the belt was mine! I asked him after the fight why he was called NEB. With a grin on his face, he said, *'I Never Eat Breakfast!'* My left knee swelled up, and I couldn't bend it for two weeks. The fight had been close, and Steve was keen to set up a rematch. I heard on the grapevine that NEB was training hard, which meant I'd need to train even harder. I knew in a second outing, he'd be wary of my kicks, and without the element of surprise, I would be in for a tougher night. A few weeks before the fight, NEB pulled out. He'd been out running in the cold, arrived home and sat down in front of a warm fire. The combination of cold, heat and physical exertion caused him to have a minor heart attack. As far as I know, he never fought again. In Japan, I was exerting myself in extreme weather, and NEB's story was always at the back of my mind. The fluid loss from constant perspiration was difficult to counteract with only a small window of drinking time after every class. The dojo was like a sauna, and the mirrors we cleaned as part of the morning routine were regularly misted over. We were leaving the tatami steaming. I knew we had to keep our bodies cool. Fluid loss and a rapidly rising body temperature made for poor company. The 30-minute break between classes that had to accommodate sweeping the mats, Shinkoku, punishments, lectures from the Sewanin, going to the toilet and drinking time now included dogi changes and cold showers. This break was under attack from all directions, including the requirement to be sat in seiza five minutes ahead of the next class. Dunking my head under a cold shower for a few seconds was a surprisingly pleasurable experience and now an important ritual to reduce the risk of death!

MITORI GEIKO

An ache in my right knee was gradually getting worse, and seiza wasn't helping. Thursday's zagaku class with Inoue Kancho had been painful, and with little chance to rest, my knee had no chance of recovery. During zagaku, Kancho in a rare narrative in English had advised, *'when in Rome, do as the Romans'*. It wasn't clear what he'd meant but, as we were in Japan, I'd taken it to mean we should do whatever he or any of the Japanese Sensei told us to do, however difficult things got. No matter how strong the mind is, we're only flesh and bones. There was only so much my knee could take. Pushing on might set up a permanent injury I'd then have to endure for the rest of my life. Although it sometimes felt like it, I wasn't in a war zone fighting for my life. Senshusei wasn't supposed to be a game of life or death. I had to weigh up the situation. Was it worth doing myself irreparable damage? Perhaps it was time to put the bravado to one side?

By Friday morning any movement of my right knee sent shooting pains up my leg. The principal area of pain was to the back on the left side, and with a rudimentary knowledge of human anatomy I concluded that I'd probably damaged a ligament. After cleaning and the morning meeting, I requested an audience with Malik Sewanin. To my surprise, on inspection of my knee he agreed there was a problem and prescribed a dose of mitori geiko, to be taken three times a day until my symptoms cleared up. I wouldn't be taking part in any of the classes and would be protected from hajime geiko, but this was no welcome break. This was no lottery win where I'd be exchanging the drudge of work with a holiday in the sun. Arguably, mitori geiko was more brutal than any exercise or type of training the Sensei could throw at us, because mitori geiko was performed in seiza. It was zagaku on steroids! For all the classes I'd now have to sit at the side of the mats, back straight, head up, in the kneeling position all Senshusei hated. No wriggling permitted and no standing up to relieve the onset of pins and needles that would signal my legs had started to die under the sheer weight of my body. Mitori geiko would be four long hours, broken up only by the 30-minute breaks between classes. The breaks were precious time, not now for rehydration, but to try to get the blood back to the extremities of my toes. I knew that cutting the blood supply off to any part of the body was never a good idea. A limb starved of blood and oxygen would eventually die, and I really didn't fancy having one or both of my legs amputated. The whole concept of mitori geiko was ridiculous, particularly for anyone with an injury to the lower half of their body. It would only make matters worse. The more mitori geiko you did, the more injured you became, and therefore the more mitori geiko you'd have to do. It was a downward spiral of stupidity. Only if your lower body injury was deemed serious enough, might you escape to a standing position. A broken bone, possibly a dislodged kneecap – but as I'd found out during Malik's diagnosis, unfortunately not a strained ligament!

In the blistering heat, I started my journey. Four hours was 240 minutes, and 240 minutes was 14,400 seconds. The latter didn't sound that bad, and I resolved to count, at least for a time. The whole concept of learning through watching was wasted on me. The pain in my feet, ankles, knees and legs was intense. Pain has a concentrating effect, and blocking it out takes practice. I had to try, and like a prisoner who uses his or her imagination to escape the confines of the prison walls, I attempted to do the same to escape my prison of pain. It didn't work. I clearly needed more practice. Watching training was

135

obviously a skill in its own right, and sadly my skill level was well below par. As the seconds and then minutes marched on, the battle against pain subsided and was replaced with a very different enemy. I was permanently tired – we all were – and my static state appeared to be encouraging my need for sleep. Falling asleep in mitori geiko, as far as I was aware, had never been done by a gaijin. I dreaded to even consider the consequences. Back in the UK, while training as a chartered accountant at KPMG, James, one of my colleagues, had fallen asleep in a seminar. His snoring had given him away, and his life had been made a living hell for several weeks thereafter. He was finally absolved of his crime, having written a letter to the person presenting, which put the matter finally to bed. I didn't imagine I'd get away with a letter. I was in Japan and under the control of a punishing, unforgiving regime. Sleeping or any thought of it was definitely out of the question.

Remembering Paul Sensei's advice, at end of the first class, I fell sideways to relieve the pressure on my lower legs and then reeled in pain as the blood returned. I hobbled back into line to finish the class and then to morning Shinkoku. The regular Shinkoku took place and then, to comply with honbu etiquette, I tagged my own special version on the end. The Shinkoku for wounded soldiers! Shinkoku over, there was only one thing to do. I grabbed my phone from my locker and called the doctors. Luckily, I secured an appointment for later on. After another three hours of hell, the day was finally done, and I made my way again to the Tokyo British Clinic. Dr Gabriel examined my knee and said I had probably done something to the cartilage. He also said that since my last visit, being curious about my plight, he'd read *Angry White Pyjamas*. While it wasn't the diagnosis I'd gone for, now equipped with more understanding about the course and all it entailed, he confirmed I must be crazy and said he looked forward to seeing me again soon.

Saturday was probably the hottest day so far, and walking into the honbu dojo, I was already feeling sorry for my fellow Senshusei who would train today. While mitori geiko was not helping my knee, on the upside it was giving me an opportunity to rehydrate properly. Because I wasn't sweating, I wasn't losing salts, and as a direct result, my strength that had been lacking for a while now was slowly coming back. Nobody seemed to care if you were injured. Positioned at the side of the mats, the Sensei, consciously or unconsciously, gave you the cold shoulder. Not only was I in constant agony, I felt like a leper. I was an outcast, left on the sidelines, and was missing the bond of brotherhood that came from shared experience. After two days in mitori geiko, I couldn't wait to get back to training!

I now had the weekend to try to recover, and after training, I paid a visit to Oshman's, a sports outlet in Harajuku. I bought a pair of knee supports, which could hold ice packs in place. I'd need to wear one of these for most of the weekend and stay off my knee as much as possible. Monday, 17 July, was the 12-year anniversary of Kancho Gozo Shioda's death. A special Memorial Day was planned, which included a pilgrimage to his grave in Saitama. Some of the Senshusei were intending to go, but attendance wasn't compulsory. Saitama was an hour by train out of Tokyo, and I could only imagine the formality and waiting about that would accompany such an event. Most of the Sensei were going, and the Sewanin would surely be there, too. I already spent more than enough time with both and concluded that attendance wouldn't make my Aikido any better. I decided to give it a miss.

. I'd done quite a bit of sightseeing already, but with the constant requirement to be at the honbu, there was still a lot of Tokyo I hadn't seen. Thanks to the ice, my knee was feeling a little better, so I decided to do some exploring. The Yasukuni Shrine was something I'd read about but had yet to visit. Built to commemorate Japan's war dead, it had been the subject of much controversy over the years. In the grounds there was a museum with a diverse collection of Japanese artefacts ranging from authentic Samurai armour to a Word War Two *kamikaze* torpedo. A torpedo with just enough space to hold a human body made a chilling spectacle. I couldn't imagine what would possess anyone to climb into such a thing, to take a one-way ticket to their death.

SHOCHU GEIKO

My command of the Japanese language was slowly getting better thanks to my lessons with Hotta Sensei. I was doing my best to keep these going despite my commitment to the course, Berlitz, and my constant tiredness. A cancelled class at Berlitz was an opportunity to get the Japanese books out, and as I wasn't allowed to speak any Japanese to my students, the staff on reception became my practice partners. Grammar was a challenge, and vocabulary was, too. While I could read hiragana and katakana, kanji still eluded me. *Why have one alphabet when you can have three?* I'd regularly think to myself. The Japanese seemed to enjoy making things as difficult as possible, and the honbu dojo was no exception. If anything, my vocabulary was strongest in Aikido terminology. I knew more word combinations ending in geiko than anything else. All I did was train. When I wasn't training at the dojo, I was training myself in Japanese or training others to speak English.

Shochu geiko, though, was a new one on me. We'd been forewarned that this would begin on Thursday, 20 July. What they called it didn't matter to me, but what it meant most definitely did. Shochu geiko was *early morning summer training*. Held in the hottest season, it was designed to build physical strength and a never-give-up attitude. It was open to all students at the Yoshinkan honbu dojo, and that meant the Senshusei had no choice but to take part, too. The night before had been a long one. Berlitz had sent me to Mizuho Bank. The students didn't have to come to me. Instead, I'd gone to meet them at their headquarters in Otemachi. I'd taught four back-to-back lessons in an office that resembled a prison cell. My CD player hadn't worked, and neither had the whiteboard marker pens. It was problem after problem. The excursion, though, had given me a unique insight into the unpleasant life of the Japanese worker. Lines of drab offices down endless corridors of cream walls, with no pictures or plants, made for an oppressive, not to mention depressing, environment. In comparison, the honbu dojo looked appealing. During the summer months with the windows open it was a light, airy space, even if the air was a little too humid and hot. I was also doing something I'd chosen to do, something I'd regularly have to remind myself was actually the case. Although it didn't always seem like it, I wasn't a slave to the system, and I made a mental note to be grateful for my situation no matter how difficult things got.

When my alarm went off at 4:05am on Thursday morning, all thoughts of being grateful had faded into a dim and distant memory. My body clock, which had been programmed to wake up at 5:20am, was now jolted into life 75 minutes early. I hadn't slept properly, in part because of my late finish at Berlitz and from also knowing I had to get up earlier. To make matters worse, for some strange reason, when I'd finally fallen asleep, I'd dreamt I was translating kanji; something I had very little ability to do. I was at the honbu and in my dogi by 6am. Bin duty called, and the regular cleaning duties had to be completed before the ippan students arrived. Summer training started at 7am under the watchful eye of Inoue Kancho. The only benefit of the early start was the promise of an earlier finish. We'd all been concerned that shochu geiko would mean an extra-long day, and we were relieved to learn that it wouldn't, at least for now. Behind the scenes an agreement had been reached with Chida Sensei, the terms of which were yet to become clear.

Laurance then Ito Sensei taught the only Senshusei classes of the day, and it was then time for zagaku, which began an hour early, at midday. Given my

138

knee problem, I was extremely worried about another extended seiza session. Deciding whether to wear knee supports was a science in itself. It involved an ongoing process of trial and error, each week. Varying the position of the pads or discarding them altogether to find out what worked the best usually lent on the side of error. The continual experimentation was more pain than gain, and none of us had yet developed any method that consistently worked. Today everyone was in agony, and I had my hands down after 10 minutes. I was called to share my reflection and habit, with the latter being that I thought about Aikido when I cleaned. The feedback was that when I was cleaning, I should make more effort to think about cleaning and not Aikido. Try as I might, I couldn't win! When it was done, it took me longer than usual to get back to my feet. Even Malik appeared concerned and came over to see if I was all right. His concern was temporary, and after the closing Shinkoku, I was back on the bins. While emptying the bins in the Sensei's kitchen, Oyamada complimented me on my Japanese pronunciation and said he'd understood what I'd said during zagaku. I bowed in appreciation and, to the call of *'osu, shitsurei shimashita'*, made a hasty retreat to the door. I was so shocked by Oyamada Sensei's positive comment that I was oblivious to Noriki Sensei, who had crept in behind me. Bin in hand, I crashed into him, nearly knocking him off his feet. He'd previously taught us the concept of *tai sabaki* (body movement) to avoid an attack. *Where was his Aikido? Where was his tai sabaki?* I thought to myself.

Leaving the dojo an hour early felt like a luxury, one that, because I'd been in sleep mode during the first class of the day, I'd forgotten I'd paid for the privilege. I caught the three trains home, put a wash on at the laundry a short walk from my apartment, ate lunch and then fell asleep with ice packs strapped to both knees. My knees were in such a state that strapping ice packs to them at every opportunity was becoming common practice. I had no idea if this treatment was helping, but it temporarily alleviated the aching. I'd strap the ice packs to my knees before I went to sleep at night and come round with bags of water in their place. Occasionally the bags leaked, and I'd wake up soaked. My first thought was that I'd pissed myself. It was always a shock, and as I stumbled into another day, my predicament reminded me of the scene from *The Godfather* – thankfully without the blood and severed horse's head!

Summer training went on for 10 consecutive days. This meant that on Sunday and Monday, we'd all have to be at the honbu for 6am, and ready for class at 7am. It seemed ridiculous to get up at the crack of dawn and travel across Tokyo for only one hour of training, but rules are rules, and Senshusei did what they were told. Before the weekend – or what would now be left of it – could kick in, there were Friday and Saturday still to get through. Although I hated the early starts, the fact we were training with the regular students provided some variety and a reduction in pace.

LAND OF CONFUSION

During shochu geiko, music was even more important to me than usual. I carried my Apple iPod everywhere. Strung around my neck, it gave me instant access to my favourite songs, and at the scroll of the wheel, I could find something suitable to match my mood. Separated from my iPod at the honbu didn't mean the music stopped playing. My back catalogue could be called upon at any time. Without Apple's help the clarity was less clear, but my memory made its best attempt to recall songs that summed up any situation or to help me through a difficult time. *Land of Confusion* by Genesis was a song I'd grown up listening to, and it seemed to sum up the activities in the dojo as shochu geiko progressed. Saturday provided a whole new level of confusion. After the first class, I ran to the office to collect the hakama. The Sensei wore the hakama on the mats but not usually off them, and we were required to collect and fold them once a Sensei had finished teaching. Malik had told us the previous day that Senshusei always ran, so as soon as the class was over, I ran and knocked on the door of the office, arriving before the Sensei had time to take his off. Folding the hakama was one of the most difficult and confusing tasks we had to perform. There was a set way to do it and no room for error. The Sewanin had shown us once. But observing once wasn't enough to capture all the intricate folds and tucks that made a good job. The practice after the Urayasu Enbu had helped, but we'd continually forget some of the steps. As a result, hakama folding became a group exercise. The plan was that the more Senshusei we threw at the job, the better chance we'd have of getting it right. We'd watched the Sewanin's hasty demonstration and hopefully each of us had committed to memory at least part of the procedure, which as a group we could piece together. It was like a jigsaw puzzle, with each person holding a specific piece. For reference we only had a distant memory of the picture on the box and now would have to communicate and coordinate to complete the task in hand. The proverb states that *too many cooks spoil the broth*, which was most definitely the case. Hakama folding made another dent in our precious break time, so doing it quickly and right took on even more importance. Fumbling about and making mistakes could mean no time to drink or go to the toilet. The Sensei's priority might have been a neatly folded hakama, but ours were hydration and answering the call of nature.

I'd heard something that morning that had also confused me. After yesterday's class, apparently a few of my fellow Senshusei had approached the Sewanin to ask if they could use the mats after class to practice for the upcoming Dai Ni test. Were they mad? Did they not get enough training already? This request made no sense to me, and I suspected it was a way to curry favour. This had Boaz's name written all over it, and I made a promise to myself to throw him that bit harder in the next class. A request like this was dangerous. What could start as an optional extra-curricular activity could fast become enforced routine. If Boaz and others were doing more, the Sewanin could get the idea that we all should do more. I was already training more than enough, and every moment away from the honbu dojo was precious time to eat, sleep and work. Granting permission was not as simple as the Sewanin agreeing. Chida as Dojocho had to be consulted. He was overseas teaching a series of seminars in the USA and Canada. When permission came back as granted, I could only presume that someone had made a call to trouble the dojo head, who was in a different time zone, about the most trivial of matters.

It was impossible not to like Sonoda Sensei. He was one of the friendliest Sensei, and from what I'd seen so far, he possessed a gentle nature and a genuine interest in the well-being of the Senshusei. Much to my surprise, having already taught the first class, Sonoda arrived on the mats to teach the last class of the day. He treated us to an hour of nikajo techniques and then progressed to instruct us in the finer details of *katate mochi jiyu waza*. I'd never gotten my head around the idea behind *katate mochi* (wrist grab). I knew it had its origins in stopping a Samurai from drawing his sword, but I wasn't a Samurai and hadn't seen any knocking about downtown Tokyo. Thinking about it, I'd never really gotten my head around the whole concept of jiyu waza itself. Who in their right mind would attack you by grabbing your wrist? In the real world, if someone grabbed my left wrist, I'd punch them with my right fist. What's more, if I grabbed my opponent's wrist and he threw me, the last thing I'd consider doing was grabbing his wrist again. The confusion on the mats rose to a whole new level at the hands of Sonoda. From what I'd seen already, he had a tendency to overcomplicate even the simplest of tasks. He took too long explaining, which meant extended seiza as we listened attentively, and then, with little understanding of the explanation, nobody had a clue where they should be positioned or what they should be doing. He provided encouragement to *'do it justice'*, when 'correctly' would have done. His English, too, was more complicated than it needed to be. *'He must be an early adopter of Google Translate!'* Ronen might just have hit the nail on the head! We looked around at one another, hoping someone had got it, but they hadn't. We looked to the Sewanin, who shouted at us to move quickly but offered no guidance on what we should be doing at speed. They were as confused as we were. Not for the first time, and not for the last, the Senshusei were in a land of confusion.

NO REST FOR THE WICKED

Sunday didn't offer the usual break from the honbu that we'd all be craving during every Saturday's last class. There was no rest for the wicked – or was it no rest for the weary? Our two days of rest were to be rudely interrupted by the demands of shochu geiko, and we were due at the dojo not at the regular time, but the hour earlier that summer training demanded. There was only one hour of training on both days, but the damage had been done. My body had been shocked out of bed just after 4am, and by mid-afternoon I knew I'd be feeling it. Eight hours of teaching at Berlitz finally ended at 6:15pm on Sunday evening.

I'd been missing my Muay Thai training and not having stepped into the ring for what seemed like ages, I was determined to get a Monday session in at Fairtex. Although I didn't feel like it, I needed to hit something; and getting back to striking felt slightly intimidating, but great at the same time. According to Woody Allen, *'80 percent of success is just showing up'*. I'd shown up and brought Dave along for company. Three rounds on the pads with 'Choke' the Thai trainer was exhausting, and I realised my fitness level was probably not being helped by the course. Hajime geiko was probably maintaining it, but Senshusei had never been the intensity of a hard Muay Thai session. What made Senshusei hard wasn't any individual class but the three training sessions, five days a week, for 11 months.

My train from Meguro pulled into Takadanobaba Station at about 5:40am on Tuesday morning. Having not quite woken up, I had to do a double take to be certain I'd seen Chino Sensei walking down the platform to catch the next train to Ochiai. Finding his chosen place from which to embark, he stood in position facing the tracks. He looked like a security guard; legs wide and hands clasped in front. I half expected him to be in kamae, but in his present stance he still exuded the menace he did in and around the honbu dojo. As had been observed in Russia; Chino was always in kamae, even when he wasn't! It was one thing running into a Sensei in the dojo, but it was quite another outside in the real world. I wasn't sure what the required etiquette was and had no intention of endeavouring to find out. A brush with Chino Sensei on civvy street offered no upside but plenty of potential downside. Head down, I kept walking to find my position at the other end of the platform. Arriving at Ochiai, I followed him out of the station at a safe distance. I was on the Riot Police course and now felt like an undercover cop in hot pursuit, but with no intention of catching my quarry. I hoped Chino wouldn't sense he was under surveillance. If he did, it would make for a very awkward situation. One of the smallest of the Sensei, he appeared to move on hydraulics. When he connected with your wrist, arm or other extremity, this system sprung into life and created an incredible power that I couldn't imagine coming from a middle-aged man. Like the T-1000 in *Terminator 2: Judgment Day,* although cloaked in flesh, there was much more to Chino Sensei than met the eye. He wasn't hard to follow. It was impossible to miss his very distinctive and purposeful walk. Almost robotic in movement, he had me convinced he was more than human. But today he showed his human side, swinging his umbrella without a care in the world. He looked more like Charlie Chaplin than a complex machine controlled by a supercomputer. Perhaps Chino was human after all? As I exited the station, I thought I'd lost him. This was a risky business. Had he spotted me? Had my surveillance been the catalyst to his countersurveillance? Was I about to be ambushed? After a moment of panic, I finally spotted the honbu's most dangerous Aikidoka. In the newsagent opposite the exit to the station, the great Chino Sensei stood reading comics!

VENDETTA

With the Dai Ni test not far away, tension on the tatami and in the tearoom between classes was rising. We were living in each other's pockets, and this week, without the separation of Sunday and Monday, familiarity would only make matters worse. On the course, no man or woman could afford to be an island. We were all doing it for individual reasons, and we all faced our own personal challenges, but we collectively recognised the importance of working as a team. The team didn't always work, but we did our best. It was us against them, and it had to be – us against the Sensei, us against the Sewanin, us against the cops, and us against the ippan students. Having a common enemy united a fragmented group of individuals with very different backgrounds and from a variety of different countries. Inazaki and Kambara, although Japanese, were not cops. Like us, they'd signed up to the course to better their Aikido and were paying for the privilege. While we bickered and argued amongst ourselves, anyone bumping heads with the international Senshusei faced the united wrath of us all. It was common for ippan students to take liberties with us. They knew, as the lowest of the low, that we had no voice. No one was interested in our complaining, moaning or allegations of mistreatment. In Saturday's last class, where we mixed in with the regulars, some of them went too hard. I wasn't sure why, but some of them did. They threw us that bit harder or held painful wrist controls and pins for just a little too long. Perhaps they thought we could take it? We could, but that wasn't the point. Perhaps they did it because they knew we wouldn't complain? We didn't complain, but that wasn't the point, either. Perhaps hurting a Senshusei was a badge of honour? It may have been, but it was a badge that would come at a price. Shochu geiko provided more opportunity for the ippan students to test their mettle, and on crowded tatami, anything could happen.

In Wednesday's class, Inazaki accidentally banged his foot into one of the ippan students. Taking offence, the regular communicated to Inazaki in Japanese that he was *'going to be a bully'*. He then stamped on Inazaki's foot in retaliation. Senshusei feared injury and illness the most. Here an ippan student had wilfully wounded one of our brothers and thought he could get away with it. Inazaki recounted the story of what had happened as he iced his foot in the break. The regular could go home, but Inazaki had two more classes today and another six months of intense training to get through. The tension in the tearoom turned to united anger. Lloyd vowed vengeance and promised, *'I'll get hold of this guy tomorrow morning'*. In the spirit of one of my favourite Steven Seagal films, the regular student was *Marked for Death*. This was a personal vendetta that would be acted out by one of the toughest, yet most unassuming guys on the course. It wasn't clear what Lloyd had meant by 'get hold of', but all of us couldn't wait to find out. Lloyd was true to his word, and in Thursday's class, he orchestrated his inclusion in the same group as the ippan student who'd injured Inazaki. As each group practiced *hijishime*, we all kept one eye on Lloyd's group with eager anticipation. Hijishime was a brutal *elbow lock* that, if your ukemi was not quite up to scratch, could cause serious injury. Every time the regular student took his turn opposite Lloyd, Lloyd tested the regular's limits and cranked on the pain. Mess with the Senshusei, and the Senshusei will mess with you. Justice had been served!

Boaz had hurt his ankle and, for the last day of shochu geiko, requested mitori geiko. Boaz and I weren't the best of partners, and I would normally have welcomed any break, but not so close to the test. Geoff, who had been partnered with the Sewanin, was now given to me. At over six feet tall, he presented a new challenge. If Boaz was light and fluid, Geoff was heavy and fixed. I already knew from the group training we'd done that he was a difficult customer and that training with him meant awkwardness and rigidity. Saturday's mock test was awful. Geoff and I didn't gel, and our techniques looked clumsy. In testing, how the technique looked seemed to take precedence over whether it would work in practice. I'd had my taste of

Geoff, and I didn't like it. Boaz's state of health took on a whole new level of importance. An injured Boaz meant a potential test with Geoff, which was a test I didn't want.

Finally, shochu geiko was over, and 12 consecutive days of training without a break ended. I couldn't wait to leave the dojo. A much-needed rest was long overdue. I didn't want to wait a minute longer and after class was disappointed to learn that before cleaning could begin, we'd need to attend a meeting called by Ito Sensei. None of us had any idea what the meeting was about, but there was a united expectation that it wouldn't be good news. The chances of Ito offering an extended break as a reward for our efforts in the week was minimal. It was much more likely that we'd done something wrong and could expect to be punished, or that the honbu needed something unpleasant done, for which we'd be put to task. We filed into the sho dojo to find out. The Kidotai's room was very different to our private space. For one, it was private. The tearoom was open to the gaze of any passing Sensei or Sewanin and technically was available to any student at the honbu dojo who wanted to use it before or after class. The sho dojo was hidden in the corner of the main dojo, and to see what was going on inside, any interested party would need to open the door. The cops had a TV and a few chairs to lounge about on. It was a space where relaxation in between classes was possible, which was a far cry from what the tearoom offered. Instead of the usual seiza, Ito told us to relax, and as a welcome change, we sat cross-legged as he explained our fate. The good news was that we were going on a training camp. Gasshuku, directly translated into English, meant 'lodging together', and we didn't have to wait long to find out who we'd be lodging with. The bad news was that this gasshuku would be a three-day excursion attended not just by the Senshusei but also by the honbu's ippan students, including the kids. For three days the Senshusei would be unpaid childminders, and it sounded like it was going to be a nightmare!

The meeting finished, and after a quick clean round I would be free to go; or so I thought. Malik Sewanin wasn't happy and called Geoff and me into the dojo. He said that we hadn't been sitting properly. *'When Sensei says relax, he doesn't mean relax!'* Malik shrieked. I got 50 press-ups and Geoff got 100. I wasn't sure what we'd done wrong or why everyone else who had also sat cross-legged weren't joining us. I was more than a little confused. I thought we had to obey the Sensei at all times and without question. We'd done what we were told and were now being punished. Malik seemed to be saying that Ito Sensei didn't know his own mind. This was the only logical explanation if Ito had instructed us to do something, he really didn't want us to do. What did this mean moving forwards? Should we do the opposite of what any Sensei asked, just in case he or she didn't mean it? *What complete and utter nonsense*, I thought to myself as I banged out my 50; *I'm sick of the whole thing!*

PINCH PUNCH

Pinch punch, first of the month, and while I didn't partake in any salt grabbing to stave off evil entities, I wondered how the weekend had come and gone so fast. The first day of August had arrived, and with it, we'd officially completed four months of the course. I was reminded of the film *Pulp Fiction*, where Winston Wolfe rather poetically advises, *'well, let's not start sucking each other's dicks quite yet'*, we still had another seven months to go, and I suspected things would only get harder!

I'd rested on Sunday, but a glutton for punishment had been back at Fairtex on Monday. Now on Tuesday, I faced the prospect of another week of hard labour, and I really didn't feel up to it. As was the requirement, I handed in my diary to be reviewed by the Sensei. Not the one you're reading now, but the one where I documented the instruction we'd had and the intricacies of the techniques we'd learnt in class. I included a few bits and pieces on my feelings about the course, which were always positive. It was best to feed the Sensei what they wanted to hear, instead of what they perhaps needed to. Shochu geiko must have got the better of Malik, as he'd called in sick. Graham was left alone to manage the fort and, on seeing our sorry state, said he wasn't sure why we all looked terrible. It really wasn't hard to figure out. Summer training had a lot to do with it. Not that we needed reminding, but Graham did so anyway. Our Dai Ni test was now only two days away. We had 48 hours to pull ourselves together as we were expected to turn in a strong performance. Anything less would reflect badly on the Sewanin, and Graham, even in the absence of Malik who was the principal enforcer of law and order, was not about to let that happen.

Boaz was still in mitori geiko and, much to the resentment of the rest of us, was allowed to stand. As his injury was to his lower body, seiza was waived. His ankle had got him off the hook, and I wondered why my knee injury hadn't done the same. Even with a basic understanding of the human body, it's clear that the knee joint forms part of what we would describe as the lower body, but maybe it wasn't low enough? I'd been given seiza while Boaz got to stand. It was another wedge between our increasingly fragile partnership, which was potentially about to be weakened further. After the day's training was over, I decided it would be a good time to share my thoughts with Boaz on the differences between our respective styles of

146

Aikido. Ronen, who was within earshot, was already trying to suppress his laughter. *'Boaz, your Aikido is a lot like a shotgun, whereas mine is more like the sawn-off variety.'* My use of this analogy may have appeared slightly strange, but it was deliberate. Boaz often went off and didn't care who got hurt. I'd since had it confirmed that he was one of the culprits who'd asked for more time on the mats, the request that had disturbed Chida Sensei in North America. He regularly said stupid things in front of the Sensei or Sewanin and as such could be dangerous to be around. A sawn-off was dangerous, too, but far more efficient. It was easily concealed, better at close quarters, and a lot more destructive. It was a triple threat! *'Your Aikido might be more precise and better to look at. Mine might not be as pretty, but it's a lot more practical!'* Much to my surprise, Boaz agreed. He said that my Aikido was a lot more practical and that he would hate to get into a street fight with me. Being a dancer, I suspected in his mind, his response was pitched as a negative. In his world, Aikido had to look beautiful, and beauty trumped practicality. In my mind, though, his acknowledgement was a compliment and confirmation that I was on the right track to develop the style of Aikido I wanted – the Aikido that would work in a street fight and the type that would surely gain Chino Sensei's seal of approval.

In need of food and fluids, Ronen, Matt, Dave, Clyde and I headed up to the Royal Host. We did our usual moaning about the course, moaning that we could only do once we'd left the honbu for the day. The Royal Host provided the sanctuary to review and try to make sense of everything. Matt seemed keen to test his Japanese. *'Watashi wa pizza desu!'* Telling the waiter he was a pizza, instead of ordering one, had us all in stitches! I complained about Boaz and shared my worries about Thursday's grading, where Boaz and I would be reunited to perform together. I was keen to get Ronen's take on it all. We had our buddy system, but he shared the same nationality as Boaz. I wondered where his loyalties lay. He reflected. When Ronen spoke, he did so quietly, but people listened. He took a sip of his drink and clarified his position. *'Israelis stick together, but sometimes…!'* It was clear to me where he stood. The buddy system was still intact.

DEALBREAKER

Always be careful what you to agree to. It's tempting to trade a potentially painful experience now in favour of something more pleasurable. But, so often, the other side of the trade is that the painful experience has to be picked up and dealt with in the future when the benefit derived has long been forgotten. This is exactly the set of circumstances we found ourselves in on the second day of August. Summer training was over, but today I was up again just after 4am.

Ahead of shochu geiko a loose agreement had been made with Chida Sensei, the terms of which now became clear. In return for ditching the last class on our regular training days we'd saved ourselves a lot of pain. Five hours of training on weekdays and four hours on Saturdays, in the middle of summer, hadn't sounded like a good idea. Taking into account the decision to ditch the two 45-minute classes ahead of zagaku in favour of the regular 90 minutes, we'd shaved 10 hours off what would otherwise have been an extremely gruelling schedule. We'd successfully secured an early departure. I'd gotten used to this early finish. I think we all had. Now throughout August on Wednesdays and Fridays we'd face a five-hour day. Despite the hardship this would inflict, we'd be paying six hours to save 10. The numbers made better reading than they might have done thanks to the forthcoming gasshuku and Obon Festival. This double windfall (if you could call the former that) combined to decrease our debt. Good deal or not, as I entered the honbu dojo at 6am, if I'd had a choice in the matter, it was a deal I'd be inclined to break. Oyamada Sensei took the 7am class, and much to my surprise, it was great. The classes he'd overseen for the Senshusei had been dull, repetitive and boring, which contrasted with his performance for the ippan students, where it appeared variety was the spice of life. We got into groups to do jiyu waza. Lloyd, Matt and I found ourselves in a group with probably the oldest guy in the dojo. A black belt, he must have been in his mid-sixties. He didn't look in the best of shape and it wasn't long before we'd christened him 'Old Father Time'. We were all concerned that a mistimed throw could finish him off and went extra gentle. I didn't want someone else's demise on my conscience. As far as I was aware, a Senshusei had never killed anyone on the mats. It was actually more likely you'd be on the receiving end of a terminal throw. The prospect of landing on your head and never waking up again was never far away, or collapsing from dehydration, heat exhaustion or a combination of the two. Despite our delicate treatment, Old Father Time decided he had something to prove. We were taking it in turns to throw everyone in our group. After your series of throws were over, you'd step back into the group and wait to be thrown. Although the ippan students often took liberties, I was shocked that a man in his gentler years had made the decision to mess with the Senshusei. Old Father Time threw each of us as hard as he could. This wasn't on. I had respect for my seniors, but he'd crossed the line. My turn arrived, and I smashed him into the tatami. As he staggered to his feet, I knew he'd got the message and wouldn't trouble us again. My fighting mentality has been instilled in me by Master Lec in my early twenties. He'd told me I should fight like a bank. If someone made a deposit, it was my job to pay them back with interest. Old Father Time had entered my bank and had come away with a credit on his account. The rest of the class passed without incident, apart from Old Father Time being taken off the mats. No one had seen what had happened, but the result was a nasty cut on his chest. Bleeding heavily, he was escorted to the office to receive first aid. Back in the tearoom after the class, Matt, Lloyd and I reflected on what had gone off. Lloyd was never loud but seemed even quieter than usual. It didn't take me long to work out why. As we chatted, I noticed blood on the end of his sleeve, and there was only one way it could have got there. Had Senshusei's silent assassin been at it again?

To finish the day, we devoted our attention to test training. The Dai Ni test was almost upon us, and none of us felt ready. We knew the techniques but were exhausted from the relentless training. The mind knew what to do, but the battered and bruised body just wasn't playing ball. Oyamada Sensei graced us with his presence again for the third class. He'd surprised me with his enthusiasm and variety of teaching at the start of the day, and I was hopeful we'd now get more of the same. No such luck. It was back to the repetitive, monotonous and monotone training we associated with his classes. He'd proved earlier that he had much to offer, but perhaps as he had never been Senshusei, he now carried a grudge for Senshusei? His mission was to both beat and bore us into submission. My mind always wandered in his classes. It was the only way I could get through. Breakfast was a dim and distant memory, and I was hungry. I could have murdered a Big Mac, but there was no escape from the dojo to get a McDonald's, at least not yet. Come to think of it, Oyamada's classes were a lot like McDonald's. There was a limited menu, and I often felt sick afterwards. Although I liked McDonald's, I rarely visited the golden arches. I'd seen the movie *Super Size Me*, a documentary about a guy who solely ate McDonald's food for 30 days. By the end of the month, it was clear that excessive fast food was bad for your health. I felt the same about Oyamada Sensei's classes. They were very bad for my health, not to mention my sanity.

Ahead of the last class I was praying for a mock test. A mock test meant no hajime geiko and would ensure a level of variety that had sadly been lacking under Oyamada's watch. We were all exhausted. The maths behind Chida Sensei's deal had been good, but the reality of five hours of training was much worse than expected. The deal was slowly breaking us. Thankfully, Takashima Sensei entered the dojo and told us we would be doing a series of mock tests to prepare for the forthcoming grading. As only a wizard could, he encouraged us to extend beyond ourselves to connect with uke. With Boaz still benched, I was paired once again with Geoff. Malik Sewanin stated the bleeding obvious. *'Simon, Geoff, you have no connection!'* For once I couldn't disagree!

The longest day was not yet over. After the train ride across to Berlitz, I taught four classes, which included a group session that proved particularly challenging. The three students didn't appear to interact and stared blankly at their files. Like Senshusei, maybe they were just keeping their heads down. The best way to avoid the attention of the teacher was to avoid any eye contact and keep quiet. In desperation I changed the role play in the book and came up with my own version. I told them to imagine I was Brad Pitt, which raised a smile, but not much of one!

DAI NI TEST

The day of the second test had arrived. Thursday, 3 August 2006, was the day we went on record again in front of the Sensei to show what we'd learned over the past two months. June and July had been painful. We'd spent most of our time on our knees in both the physical and literal sense. The techniques of suwari waza and the extensive hajime geiko we'd endured in the summer heat had both taken their toll.

The grading was scheduled for midday, and before then we had classes with Murray and Murata Sensei to get through. Thankfully Murray Sensei didn't kill us but focused instead on the technical aspects of several techniques we would be tested on. Today Murata, with a growing reputation for off-the-wall classes, once again didn't disappoint. After giving us free time to review our own choice of techniques, he took us into the sho dojo and asked us individually to share publicly what our hopes for the test were. I said I hoped I'd be a good uke for Boaz and that I could relax, so that my body would work without me thinking too much about it. This was lip service to the question I'd been posed and my way of putting any animosity to bed that had developed between Boaz and me. Boaz was in earshot and seemed to welcome my sentiment. I'd set the foundations for what I hoped would be a smooth and trouble-free grading.

I'd taken my video camera in, and Graham Sewanin kindly offered to record the test. He was doing me a favour but, I suspected, also using my request as an excuse to stay standing throughout. Graham and Malik were both Senshusei, and I knew they hated seiza just as much as the current year's intake. Finally, the test was here. Boaz and I had to sit in seiza through three tests before we could crawl out of the dojo to warm up. We graded alongside Vic and Inazaki, and the test seemed to go really well. We avoided making any major mistakes but were required by the Sensei to do one technique again. Yonkajo was particularly fiddly, and when Boaz tried to apply it on me, my wrist had slipped free, prompting the required restart. Watching the video back later on, it surprised me to see that despite banging heads regularly in the lead-up to test day, when it counted Boaz and I had found a real connection.

Though we were relieved to have finished, the ordeal wasn't over yet. We lined up and sat down in seiza again to watch the final few Senshusei complete their tests. My knees were burning, and looking around, I noticed everyone who had already tested had their hands down, to relieve some pressure. The blood flow had been restricted to our lower extremities prior to being called up. Blood had then pumped hard around our bodies from the physical exertion and stress of the test, only to be shut down again sharply once our individual tests were over. The body had no time to adjust, making this the worst kind of seiza, even worse than zagaku. The blood was still pumping in our feet, calves and knees but had no means of escape. The pressure built and built to create the most excruciating pain. Chida Sensei took his time, and we waited patiently and with much anticipation to hear his feedback. At last he reentered the dojo to deliver his verdict. As judge and juror, he had the power to progress us to the next phase of the course or deem that we weren't fit to carry on. As he passed sentence, it was difficult to make out what he said. He spoke into his notes in a muffled voice, which was entirely at odds with how a Senshusei was required to communicate. Everything we did had to be loud and purposeful, yet here was Chida delivering quite the opposite impression. With ears on stalks to catch any hint of our respective names, we learnt that Boaz and I had made 1st kyu. Chida was all about connection, so our connection must have been good!

SUMMER GASSHUKU

MEGA MOAN

The high of completing Dai Ni and graduating to the third phase of the course was short-lived. Before we could officially get to Dai San, there was the small matter of the summer camp to get through, and arriving at the honbu dojo at 7:30am on Friday morning, none of us had any idea what to expect. I was especially apprehensive about the gasshuku. Although I'd attended one shortly after arriving in Tokyo, now as Senshusei, I knew the 2006 version would be a very different experience. We'd be away for two nights and in the company of the Sensei and Sewanin without a break for the best part of 60 hours. This gave me flashbacks to my time at boarding school. After a difficult day, there was no escaping to home at night, and now, once again, what would undoubtedly be difficult days of my adult life would be made even more unbearable by my inability to escape back to Musashi Koyama.

As Senshusei we were early for everything, and having arrived at Ochiai, there was a lot of time to kill, not to mention messing about, before we could board the buses and be on our way. It was a welcome change to turn up at the honbu and not get into our dogi to clean and train. We arranged ourselves in lines outside the dojo – lines that comprised not just Senshusei but also regular students, including children. There were loads of kids who had no idea where they were supposed to stand or what they were supposed to do. It was our responsibility to get them into some sort of order. The average age was no more than 10, and given their exuberance and energy levels even at this unearthly hour, I knew it would be a long day. Despite their children's tender years, the parents seemed to have delegated all responsibility to a bunch of Westerners they might have seen knocking around the dojo but really didn't know. I didn't realise it, but this was the tip of the iceberg in terms of our babysitting duties; things would soon get a whole lot worse. Ito Sensei had brought his megaphone and enjoyed using it far too much. Little did I know that it would be glued to his mouth for the entire weekend. As Camp Commandant, he had to get his troops in line and ready for inspection. His usually quiet voice, now amplified to a new and excessive level, blended with the sound of children screaming to form an intolerable fog of noise. We swapped lines, changed positions and repeated the exercise over and over again in response to Ito's commands and the Sewanin's interpretation. Like headless chickens, we scurried about, trying to get into the right positions. Positions none of us were clear on and therefore unsurprisingly got wrong. It was the very definition of organised chaos.

The Senshusei travelled to 'destination unknown' on a minibus with Naruo Sensei. I imagined he was now in his element, transporting his group of captives to a remote location where they'd be subjected to hard labour and poor rations. Ito may have had his megaphone, but the journey was a chance for us to catch up and have a 'mega moan' about the course and the prospect of three days away with no time off for good behaviour. Although we'd started off in convoy with the regulars who travelled on the larger and more comfortable bus, we'd become disconnected. The connection that I'd learnt was so important in Aikido had been lost by our driver, who didn't seem to know where he was going. Eventually we arrived at base camp two hours late. The three-hour journey out of Tokyo had become five. We'd not been driving, so it was not our fault, but as usual the Senshusei paid the price, this time with a rushed lunch. No sooner had we sat down to eat than we were required to be in our dogi for the short but very coordinated 10-minute walk down the road to the dojo. Ito shouted into his megaphone all the way. There was really no need, but I figured he was relishing in the responsibility and increased sound of his own voice.

The training was boring and reminded me of why I'd signed up for the course. I'd tried the ippan classes back at the honbu, but they were too slow and staid. I now found myself missing the intensity of Senshusei, even though the slower pace was much kinder on my body. The training on Friday and Saturday comprised two classes each day, with one class scheduled for Sunday to give us time to travel back to Tokyo. The training was easy. As Senshusei we were used to three punishing classes a day, and as part of Chida's deal were now used to four. We hated training with the regulars for two reasons. First, we had to go easy. It would be very bad form for a Senshusei to injure a regular student. I didn't like to imagine the consequences but was certain any misdemeanour of this kind would be communicated up the ranks to the top echelons of the honbu hierarchy. With seven months to go, there would be multiple opportunities for reprisal, but at whose hands? What if Chino learnt of the incident? Would the offending

Senshusei be cordially invited to be Chino Sensei's uke? None of us wanted to find out, which meant handling any ippan student with kid gloves even if we thought they could take more of the rough stuff. Soft and gentle would be the order of the day, broken up only by the opportunity to smash when, on rotation, we came up opposite one of our own. Second, the ippan students still seemed to regard hurting a Senshusei as a badge of honour. As the lowest of the low, our physical well-being really didn't matter. The Sensei showed very little interest in the injuries we'd sustained so far, and I didn't expect they would care very much if a regular student with a point to prove did us some harm. We were supposed to be tough and ready for anything. If we got hurt, it would be our own fault. Training with the regulars was like turning up to a street fight with one hand tied behind your back. You couldn't give the best account of yourself and had to take anything that was thrown your way. Still, we had the Senshusei enforcer on hand. Lloyd had proven his worth on two occasions already. Mess with any of the Senshusei, and it was highly likely that Brisbane's finest, like a laser-focused missile, would seek out and destroy. Ronen and I didn't wait for Lloyd and, after extreme provocation, took matters into our own hands. The class was a mix of men and women and a young male black belt was trying to impress the ladies. He had a black belt but that meant very little to Ronen and me. We'd clocked him earlier on, parading around like he'd just strolled off the set of *Masters of the Universe*. He had a badge, but no balls – 'He-Man' went out of his way to be as awkward and obstructive as possible. He threw too hard and wouldn't be thrown. Anything he could do to disrupt the Senshusei, he would do, and now, his time was up. Ronen and I were next to one another near the edge of the mats. Ronen would be first and me second in a payback mission that was long overdue. This time our awkward friend had no choice. I watched Ronen launch him with such a ferocity that the black belt missed the tatami completely and landed on his back on the hard-wooden floor. He looked up at Ronen in shock, but his ordeal wasn't over yet. *Two heads are better than one*, and his was set to roll again. His ego had gone head-to-head with the Senshusei and come up short!

BABYSITTING

It wasn't the training that made the gasshuku worthy of report. Instead, a whole host of other things that went on as part and parcel of the whole very strange experience. The parents had ditched their kids at the bus stop back in Ochiai and appeared to have no regard for the welfare or whereabouts of their children from that moment on. The kids were now the Senshusei's responsibility. Morning, noon and night they would be under our charge. Where we went, they went, and what we did, they did. What's more, where they went, we'd have to go, and what they wanted to do, we'd have to do, too. None of us had any childcare experience and none of us had kids of our own. What did we know about looking after a bunch of Japanese children, most of whom we couldn't even communicate with, because we didn't speak their language and, despite some schooling in the intricacies of English, they didn't really speak ours?

The accommodation was basic. A dining room and a common area had some stairs leading up to the sleeping quarters and washing facilities. We were split between two large tatami-lined rooms that we'd be sharing with the kids. Lined up along each side of our respective lodgings, we'd be bunking down in our sleeping bags and playing mummy and daddy to two groups of energetic and mischievous Japanese schoolchildren whose mission seemed to be to do anything and everything apart from what we instructed them to do. Perhaps the Sewanin had briefed them to make our lives as miserable as possible? Like mini Sewanin, they now had responsibility for administering the hardship that Malik had highlighted was an essential part of the course. We quickly learnt that the rules of summer camp meant that as Senshusei, we could never be seen without a group of kids in tow. If you were spotted in the common area by one of the Sewanin or Sensei without at least one child by your side, there would be trouble. There was no solo mission to one of the vending machines downstairs to grab a quick snack. An entourage was a compulsory requirement to move anywhere or do anything. The kids became our passport to move around the complex in freedom, free from hassle from the Sewanin or Sensei. For three days we'd have to walk around with a group of kids glued to us. The ability that I enjoyed back in Tokyo to pop to the convenience store for refreshments once class was over was no longer an option. The effort and logistics of organising and policing the kids just wasn't worth the trouble. When we weren't training, it was simpler to stay in the dormitories and do our best to keep the children entertained and calm.

Dave was worried, and I mean very worried. Back in the honbu, we'd take a shower after class to remove the sweat and stench of training. At the honbu there were three shower cubicles arranged side by side, all with a curtain which could be pulled across to protect the user's modesty. On the gasshuku, after two training sessions and before bed we'd need to wash, but our accommodation, being very traditional, provided no private shower facilities. Instead, there was a communal bath with open, exposed showers lined up alongside. Whatever you did or didn't have in abundance, however big or small, your physique and personal effects would be on full display for all to see. I was used to this arrangement from boarding school, and also from my frequent visits to the sento, but as bathtime approached, for some reason, Dave was becoming more and more twitchy. I hadn't previously questioned why he'd never joined us at the sento, but the closer we got to the scheduled wash and brush up time, all started to become clear. When bathtime arrived, I was shocked to learn that we'd be bathing with the kids. I'd thought the parents would finally make an appearance, but no; as we marched off to the washroom, they were still nowhere to be seen. Back in the UK, bathing with a group of naked kids you didn't know while naked yourself would never be allowed, and rightly so. Back home before you could be entrusted with responsibility for a minor, you'd need to possess the right qualification or qualifications and have a specialist check carried out to ensure there was nothing in your past that would bar you from working with young people. In Japan it appeared that none of this mattered. There was nothing to suggest that any of the Senshusei shouldn't be near kids, but that wasn't the point. We shouldn't have been babysitting in the first place and certainly not bathing, but as we were, the proper checks should have been carried out. Dave entered the washroom in his pants. We were all naked and he was the odd one out. Despite encouragement to remove his garment, he remained reluctant. We wondered what he was hiding under there, and our imagination of what this might be was probably far worse than the reality. Had Dave been at the back of the queue when it came to the size of his soldier? Was he secretly a woman? Eventually he confided the source of his worry. Dave was ginger and the prospect of exposing his pubes publicly filled him with dread. Senshusei weren't good at sympathy. Crying with laughter, none of us could speak!

FIREWORKS

Saturday began with a bang...the banging feet of kids rushing round our accommodation ready to start the day. I had been hoping for a lie-in, but our new companions had other ideas. The complex overlooked a beach – not the kind of beach you're probably imagining. It wasn't the type of beach you'd fly off to for your summer holiday. There was no stretch of golden sand, there was no crystal-clear water, and sadly, there was no beach bar serving ice-cold beer. This was a beach in the loosest sense of the word! We exited the rear of the building and walked across a large concrete terrace to catch our first view of the sea. There were no sunbeds or parasols and no shops to buy ice cream or sun protection. This was definitely no tourist spot; it appeared more industrial than anything else. There was no chance I was going in the sea. It looked polluted. That assessment was supported by the assortment of rubbish that had been washed up. Ito Sensei, megaphone in hand, summoned us all onto the beach. There we began the morning warm-up, which was even more primitive than the taiso we did every day back at the honbu. I was ready for breakfast, but breakfast would be some way off. I should have seen it coming. At Ochiai we began our day with cleaning, so why on vacation, if you could call it that, should things be any different? The beach was littered, and the Senshusei were a team of trained cleaners. Two plus two, unfortunately, made four; and between us and breakfast stood the mammoth task of collecting the vast array of junk that was dispersed across it. Where we went, the kids followed. Litter picking could be fun, and encouraging our young companions to get involved meant the job was done quickly.

After the day's training, we found ourselves back on the beach again. The kids wanted to go for a swim, and that meant the Senshusei would have to swim, too. I really didn't relish the prospect. The sea wasn't sanitary, and even a drop of water swallowed could spell future trouble. None of us could afford to be ill, and after my brush with mitori geiko, I wanted no part of the same again. I paddled instead. My explanation was that someone should keep watch to ensure none of the kids drowned. If I was immersed up to my neck, keeping track of what was going on would be an impossible task. I'd instead put others first, miss out on all the fun and take on the role of lifeguard close to shore. I felt like Mitch Buchannon in the hit TV show *Baywatch*, with the theme tune on repeat in my head...*I'll be ready...(whenever you fear) oh don't you fear...(I'll be ready)...forever and always, I'm always here*...I strolled back and forth along the beach, praying nobody got into difficulty. Ito was also on hand, shouting instructions in Japanese to any of the kids who messed about. He was joined by Takagi Sensei, who'd made the trip from Tokyo to support Ito in his lead role as Yoshinkan's answer to *The Pied Piper of Hamelin*. Takagi had been a thorn in the Senshusei's side since, through no fault of our own, we'd arrived late. She seemed to take pleasure in constantly telling us how disappointed she was in our performance and had spent the whole day walking round with a face on her like a wet weekend! By comparison, Malik and Graham had kept their distance. They'd had a word or two on several disciplinary matters but for the most part had left us alone. I was sure they were as sick of us as we were of them, and that they probably felt a reduced level of pressure to continually pressure us, given the absence of Inoue, Chida and Chino.

As it grew dark, after a barbecue served up by the Senshusei, there was another surprise in store. In Tokyo, any street repairs were carefully cordoned off, with numerous attendants in place to ensure the general public navigated any obstacle safely and without issue. I'd regularly see this safety-gone-mad on my travels around the capital and as a result had gained the impression that the Japanese were a safety-conscious people. At night this belief was shattered, as Ito, once again megaphone in hand, arrived on the beach with a large box of fireworks. The kids went crazy and wrestled each other to be the first to get hold of one and to secure the biggest and best for themselves. The matches were handed out, and with all the usual organisation parked, the fireworks were lit and launched in all manner of directions with no regard for who might be in the line of fire. I couldn't believe it. Kids and matches didn't mix, and children, matches, and fireworks would never be a good combination. The scene unfolding had the makings of a Molotov cocktail of chaos that I wanted no part of. There were kids and smoke everywhere, as bangs, cracks and whizzes flew all around. The sight resembled a battle scene, and the prospect of someone losing their sight to a stray incendiary seemed like a very real possibility. To add to my stress, Matt reminded me of the warnings they'd always aired on UK TV ahead of Bonfire Night. One from his childhood had left a lasting impression, and I remembered it, too. In the public information film, a kid was seen talking about the dangers of playing with fireworks. Everything seemed fine until he turned to look at the camera to reveal that half of his face had been permanently scarred! One kid set off a firework right next to me. I dived out of the way only to be hit moments later by a piece of red-hot material from the same firework which crashed down to Earth, narrowly missing my head. It was a struggle to breathe; it was a struggle to hear; and, in the fog of war, no one, not even Ito, was in control. As always, the parents were visible by their absence, and it was left to the Senshusei to deal with the fallout. Thankfully, no one was injured, with the only casualty being the beach, which, after our cleaning efforts that morning was now strewn with an assortment of firework wrappers and burnt-through embers.

THE ROAD HOME

I couldn't wait for Sunday morning to arrive, and when it did, I was ready – ready to get back to the harsh regime of Senshusei training and ready to ditch the kids. I was in Japan for one reason, and that was to complete the course. The weekend's activities had been an eye-opening and very worrying diversion, but they were just that – an unwelcome diversion from the Senshusei course, which I now couldn't wait to get back to. Everything in life is relative, and the madness of the weekend was a stark and useful reminder that the course was special. The course was a unique opportunity to experience what it meant to train in the martial arts, Japanese style. The monotony of shochu geiko was a distant memory and the torment of hajime geiko long forgotten. The weekend had put things into perspective, and I couldn't wait to get back to business. After morning taiso, tidying the beach and breakfast, it was almost time to depart. Beforehand, though, there was an opportunity for some impromptu sightseeing, and, led by Ito and his trusty megaphone, we walked in our dogi to the local fish market. While on holiday I'd regularly see Japanese tourists herded from tourist spot to tourist spot by an overeager, enthusiastic tour guide waving an umbrella or flag, and now I was experiencing the phenomenon for myself. It felt like herding cattle, but we were the cattle. The visit to the fish market made little sense. It wasn't Tokyo's Tsukiji, of international fame; it was more like an urban market I'd find back in England, but packed full of fish.

Back at barracks we had lunch and then sat down in the dining area to write an essay on the positive experiences the gasshuku had provided. The title was a little presumptuous. *Who's to say I've had any positive experiences?* I thought to myself. Catching a glimpse of Dave's pubes had been one significant low point and nearly having my head blown off by a stray firework, another one. Essay writing and diary keeping seemed to be the honbu's way of making you relive an unpleasant experience by committing pen to paper. The diary was difficult, but this essay looked to be an impossible task. The only positive that I could think of was the fact that we'd soon be leaving. Before we could get started, Graham Sewanin pitched up to enquire why none of us had offered to move any of the Sensei's bags from the sleeping quarters down to the dining area. We jumped to attention to put matters right but were intercepted by Malik on our way upstairs. He told us to sit back down and get on with our essays, as Ito Sensei hadn't told us to do anything. It was history repeating itself. It appeared that when Graham Sewanin said something, he didn't mean it, either. You just couldn't win! Back with pen in hand, I was still struggling to think of anything positive to write that would appease the Sewanin and secure my ticket home. In the spirit of zagaku, I eventually wrote that I'd not been looking forward to taking care of the kids but had enjoyed the experience. What a load of nonsense, and who was I trying to kid? It had been a complete nightmare from start to finish.

Essays written, and this time to appease Malik, on the instruction of Ito Sensei, we'd packed, cleaned and tidied our rooms and were now lined up in the common area to await Ito's further instructions. The scene was reminiscent of how we'd left Tokyo only a few days earlier. Nobody knew which line they should be in or what to expect next. The honbu seemed to run on a need-to-know basis. Information was provided only at the moment it was needed, which was one reason we were always on edge. At the start of each day, we'd never be sure who would be teaching us until they strolled out onto the mats and took up position under the shomen. On the gasshuku it had been exactly the same, and although we knew we were going home, we didn't know how, when, or what else might be in store ahead of our departure. Megaphone still in hand, the Camp Commandant proudly performed one final inspection of his troops. Walking back and forth astride the lines, he finally arrived at the front, where he was joined by a Japanese gentleman I'd not seen before. As he was in civilian clothes, it was immediately obvious that this man had no connection to the honbu dojo and looked as bewildered as we regularly did to find himself in his present position. As always, Clyde was on hand to translate what was going on. It turned out the gentleman was the hotel manager. This came as a surprise, as I for one hadn't been aware we'd been staying in a hotel. The complex had felt more like a maximum-security prison than any hotel I'd ever stayed in. On Ito's command we were brought to attention and instructed to show our appreciation for the hospitality we'd received, which we did in the usual manner, through a coordinated bow and ceremonious *'osu!'* The manager, looking slightly uncomfortable, bowed in return. Ito thrust the megaphone in front of him and invited the man to say a few words in response. The manager, stunned into silence by what had just taken place, awkwardly declined the invitation.

The return journey turned out to be much quicker and much more fun. Dave was on form, telling stories and reliving some of the crazy antics of the weekend. We stopped at a service station for petrol. Naruo Sensei got out to refuel, and to give his ears a break from the madness inside. Dave's jokes were getting too much for him. Having filled and paid, Naruo got back in, put his wallet in his bag and fastened his seat belt. He paused, took a deep breath and then with a serious look turned to Dave. In perfect English, he asked, *'are you on drugs?'* It was a good question. The minibus erupted. The laughter was uncontrollable, and Dave didn't know what to say! The good humour was abruptly brought to a halt as we pulled up outside the honbu dojo. We couldn't escape just yet to reclaim the small amount of time that was still left of the weekend. There was a requirement to perform Shinkoku. Not only had we been the dojo's unpaid slaves and unqualified babysitters, but now we'd have to line up and formally thank Ito Sensei for the privilege!

Back in Tokyo, Ronen called his Mum and Dad and was surprised when his brother answered. We all had family and friends back home and from time to time the lives we'd temporarily left behind were brought into sharp focus. Last month a war had broken out between Israel and Lebanon. Serving in a unit of the Special Forces, Ronen's younger brother was preparing for battle. There was a very real chance he'd be called to the front line. Although Ronen hadn't shown it, the end of Dai Ni had been difficult for him. The reports from the fighting were horrific, and he did his best to put the conflict to the back of his mind to detach himself from worrying about home. The gasshuku had been a welcome distraction, but back in Tokyo it was time to check in. Hearing his brother's voice on the end of the line he was initially relieved, but the reason for his brother's leave was not a good one. Ronen's grandmother had passed away and his brother had returned to attend the funeral. A few months after the war was over, Ronen learnt that his own army reserve unit had contacted his parents to find out when he was coming home. A platoon commander, as the war progressed, he was required on the front line. Ronen felt a sense of guilt not because he'd missed combat, but because he was needed. His Mum and Dad had kept it from him because they knew he'd get on a plane. Out of reach in Japan, the Senshusei course may have saved his life!

PART THREE: DAI SAN
(8 August to 23 December 2006)

WHERE'S KANCHO?

Tuesday, 8 August 2006, marked the first day of Dai San. The third part of the course was underway and with it the longest phase. Dai Ichi and Ni combined had spanned four months, with Dai San scheduled to last for just under five. Things got off to a relatively good start. There was the usual excitement about the new pairings, and we hoped that Chida Sensei would make his mind up quicker this time. Boaz and I were ready to sign our divorce papers and keen to go our separate ways. The locker room was a favourite cleaning assignment. This was our territory, where we felt at home. This contrasted drastically with the Sensei's locker room, where your heart would race in panic whenever the door opened. Even better, I was on cleaning duty with Matt and Malik Sewanin had returned to the UK. His absence was set to reduce the level of hardship we could expect for at least two weeks. Things were good; things felt very good. After the gasshuku, it actually felt great to be back at the honbu, and back into the routine.

For the first class of Dai San, we had Murray Sensei. Jiyu waza was a key part of the Dai San syllabus, and Murray Sensei wasted no time in getting started in teaching us the finer points. We learnt six basic techniques and threw each other around. With no ippan students, there was no going easy. It was nice not to have to pull our throws and be back at full pelt! Despite being glad to be back in the mix, I was feeling exhausted. Yet again, and in breach of honbu rules, I'd trained at Fairtex yesterday, and my body had yet to recover. By the first break, I was desperate for a drink and to sit down, but there was still Shinkoku to get through. We lined up outside the office and waited. Graham Sewanin would get a nod from the office staff when Kancho was ready for the knock on the door and would then motion to the week's Shinkoku to get on with it. We waited and waited some more, but the nod didn't come. We stood there sweating, not able to move or speak. This was another form of torture. With our break slowly slipping away, there'd be very little time to rehydrate and empty our bladders before we were thrown at the mercy of the second class. I was stood next to Dave, who also stood next to Matt. Flanked in a British sandwich, Dave was at our mercy. Out of sight of Graham Sewanin, we nudged and pinched him, trying to force him to break rank or burst out laughing. This was Senshusei humour – anything we could do to brighten the day where Dave was always a willing participant. Ronen, on my other side, had perspiration dripping from his nose. Wiping sweat was strictly prohibited and as the beads dropped rhythmically to the floor, one by one they formed a puddle at his feet. *More cleaning,* I thought to myself. *I'm glad I'm not on corridor duty!* After 20 minutes, enough was enough. Where was Kancho? Nobody seemed to know. After a lot of fuss and nonsense, Ito Sensei took the initiative, and Shinkoku was finally over. At 9:55am there was no time to do anything, and we were straight into the second class. It was clear why Ito had taken matters into his own hands to get Shinkoku underway. He was teaching the second class, and without Shinkoku complete, he'd have been teaching an empty room. To date, I'd always been indifferent about his classes. He rarely hammered us and usually focused more on the technical side of a technique. As Chida Sensei's senior disciple, his style of Aikido was a softer one, very different to the brutal, crashing style of Chino Sensei. While I feared Chino's classes I loved them all the same. Fear and love, as natural human emotions, made me feel alive. In Ito's classes I felt emotionless, and after three days of megaphone madness, I just couldn't take him seriously. In addition to the green megaphone, over the course of the weekend he'd sported matching green camouflage trousers and a Sakuraba T-shirt. Sakuraba as an MMA superstar was a world away from Ito Sensei's Aikido. As a huge Sakuraba fan, I took offence at Ito's choice of wardrobe, which had further tainted my view of him. Ito's trousers were already the stuff of legend. He'd often arrive at the honbu dojo in his army fatigues much to mine and Ronen's delight. *'Shhh, he's just back from another operation. Another combat mission in the bag!'*

I was glad to be standing again. The non-stop knee walking of Dai Ni was over, and my body was enjoying working and moving as designed. Suwari waza had no place in the modern world, and the argument that its practice benefited standing techniques just didn't wash with me. The best way to develop tachi waza was to perform techniques standing. Relieved to be back in a position that allowed the free flow of blood through my lower body had lifted my spirits. The course was a long-haul flight, and during my flights from Heathrow to Narita and back again, a few hours in, I'd already be feeling the effects. The free drinks and a good film would get me through to the other end, but on the course, there was no such entertainment on offer. You had to make your own entertainment and grasp any motivation or encouragement in whatever form it took. Graham Sewanin provided just this in the third class of the day. A witness to my spirit and endurance during a fairly intense jiyu waza session, he'd privately confided in me, *'I don't know where you get your strength from. By this stage on my course I had no strength left!'* The amino acids supplied by Ronen appeared to be working, but no type of supplement seemed to be able to conquer the exhaustion brought upon by the intense heat of Japan's summer months.

The first day of Dai San had been a blast, and heading off to Otemachi to teach English at Mizuho Bank, I felt happy. Before my lessons got started, I phoned Robert, who'd filmed the documentary for American TV, and he told me he'd like to do a spotlight segment on me for his *Fight! Japan* series. We'd gotten on well, and he was curious about how and why I was training in other martial arts while on the course. The second documentary sounded interesting, and although I was up for it, I was concerned that the honbu might find out about my extra-curricular activities. He agreed to keep my secret safe and said that he'd be in touch soon to get started.

BODY CLOCK

In practice, Chida Sensei's deal was proving to be a bad one. The Wednesday and Friday early classes were playing havoc with my body clock. I'd become a well-oiled machine that could wake up at 5:20am with no alarm. I'd always have one set, but it was now very rare for it to catch me asleep. I'd be awake and have it turned off well before its buzzer had the chance to shock me into a new day. On the second day of Dai San, I caught the 5:07am train out of Musashi Koyama, changed lines at Meguro, and arrived in Takadanobaba some 30 minutes later to change once again for the short hop to Ochiai. It was the journey I made pretty much every day, but twice a week now, I was making it an hour earlier. What has the world come to when you consider 5:20am a lie-in? Normality had well and truly been turned on its head, and life back in the UK seemed even further away. In my working life, I'd found getting out of bed at 7am a struggle, and on the weekends, I would regularly stay hidden under the duvet until well past midday. By 6:20am at the honbu, I was in my dogi and cleaning, and at 6:50am, the Senshusei morning meeting took place in the tearoom, as an appetiser to the 7am class. In this first class, Takashima Sensei presided, as we mixed amongst the regular students once again. Lloyd seemed relieved to see Old Father Time back on the tatami. Sporting a big plaster on his chest to cover a rather large wound, Old Father Time seemed in surprisingly good health. Just when we'd had our fill, suwari waza was back on the menu, and my knees were struggling to cope. After each successive throw from my crouched position, I struggled to get to my feet. I had a feeling already that it would be a long day in more ways than one.

In the second class and the first Senshusei class of the day, Paul Sensei turned into a maniac. The friendship several of us had developed with him away from the honbu counted for nothing during one of the worst beasting sessions we'd had the misfortune to experience. He found any excuse to punish us repeatedly. After making us stand in line in a squat position, he then instructed us to run from one side of the dojo to the other and finish in a crouched position again. Lloyd and I were struggling near the back, and Paul sent us into the corner to do alternate press-ups, sit-ups and backward ukemi. As more people fell behind, more people joined us, and the rest running the lines got usagi tobi for their troubles instead. It was a cull, and the feeling amongst the Senshusei was that it didn't really matter what we did or didn't do. Today, for whatever reason, Paul Sensei had it on him, and we were bearing the brunt. Was this his belated welcome to the Senshusei course or a rite of passage to Dai San? He'd gone hard before, but today was on a whole new level. We'd been forced to suck it up or risk going home, and having come so far, I had no intention of going home just yet. As we lined up for Shinkoku, I felt destroyed and couldn't imagine how I would get through the three hours of training yet to go. There was no choice. I was Senshusei and would have to dig deep to find a way. It was at times like this that you needed the group, the band of brothers and one sister. We'd started the course together and were determined to get to the end together, no matter how tough things got!

ALL CHANGE

As Dai San had officially begun, we were all expecting an imminent change of training partners and knew each other well enough now to know who we did and didn't want. The last pick was always paired with the Sewanin. Geoff had endured this for the last two months, and from his moans and groans in the locker room, we knew it hadn't been an easy ride. Geoff himself came in a close second to the Sewanin as the least desirable partner. He was just too tall. With a mandate that your Aikido should look good, partnering with Geoff would be a crushing blow to even the most beautiful form. Malik Sewanin had beautiful Aikido and moved with a fluidity and grace that made it look easy, but paired with Geoff during Dai Ni, even his technique had looked bad. It wasn't all Geoff's fault. He couldn't help his height, body type or the fact he had no pre-course experience. What he could help, though, was his mouth. His habit of asking stupid questions and making ridiculous comments brought unwanted attention on all of us and, with it, the distinct possibility of punishment. Anyone allocated Geoff would be well and truly in the line of fire!

Thursday was D-Day, as Chida Sensei had decided. Lloyd, expecting a staredown, had arrived at the honbu with a shaved head. I suspected the new look was a message to his new training partner that he was the boss. From our time together on Dai Ichi, I was well aware of his physical capability, and he now had a look to match. Like a football draw, we all held our breath as Geoff's name was called. But whose name would be called next? *'Simon Senshusei'* came the cry; and with Chida's words, my fate was sealed. For the next stage of the course, I'd be teamed up with Geoff. My renewed optimism at the start of Dai San was crushed in that moment. Things were about to get much more difficult. The only sweetener, if there could ever be such a thing, was that Boaz, my Dai Ni allocation, got paired with Lloyd. This would provide an interesting spectator sport over the coming months, which I looked forward to watching. In addition, Matt was called up opposite Dave. Knowing Matt's sense of humour of old and having gotten to know Dave and his comical tendencies more recently, watching this latter match unfold would also make for some very entertaining viewing. It was all change, but only time would tell if it was a change for the better!

ANY QUESTIONS?

We'd seen very little of Chida Sensei in a teaching capacity. He was usually at the honbu dojo but seemed to spend more time in the office than on the tatami with us, even though, as head of the dojo, responsibility for our success or failure ultimately rested with him. As a parallel to the business world I'd come from, Kancho was the Chairman and Chida the CEO. Inoue was the figurehead, but Chida ran the show. Despite his lack of attention, I was sure the Senshusei show was one he wanted to, and needed to, run well.

Chida Sensei had a personality and sense of humour I couldn't work out. He was popular and appeared friendly and sociable with the ippan students, but as Senshusei, we'd never been allowed to get too close. He was somewhat of a mystical figure who'd been a direct student of Kancho Gozo Shioda. We'd all read articles about Chida Sensei and watched interviews and demonstrations he'd given long before coming to Japan. His public profile had given him an almost legendary status. As if curious to know how the pairings he'd selected would work out, Chida took my first class opposite

Geoff. I'd heard that he had a reputation for inviting questions and, in return, would regularly offer answers that left the questioner even more confused about a technique than they were before. The Dojocho began the class by teaching *eri mochi* techniques. Eri mochi was a *collar grab* from the rear that I struggled to see any practical need to defend. I'd never been grabbed by the back of my collar, not even by my housemaster at boarding school. In the real world, it was more likely I'd be grabbed around the throat in an attempt at strangulation, something which had happened in my lifetime a few times already. Still, the rear collar grab was on the syllabus, and Chida Sensei showed us how to deal with it, just in case it happened. We were all struggling with the technique, and to move things forward, Chida threw the floor open to us. *'Any questions?'* Immediately I was on my guard, and although I had many questions, I wasn't about to fall into Chida's trap. Matt, on the other hand, dove right in and asked a very valid question about how to make a specific element of the technique he was struggling with work better. Chida smiled, paused and then imparted his advice. *'Just train harder!'* Matt looked bewildered. And with that, any questions that anyone else had were filed away for another Sensei.

In the final part of the class, we practiced jiyu waza footwork. Dress rehearsal over, we were split into two groups, and the first group was called out to perform in front of the second, who would be up next. The challenge was to perform a four-technique set routine twice, change over shite and uke and do the same thing again. There were 16 techniques, eight as shite and eight as uke. Also, to make things interesting, after a series of eliminations, the bottom pair, out of all of us, would be punished in front of everyone. It sounded simple enough. What could possibly go wrong? The short answer was quite a lot. We were new in our pairings and to date had had little jiyu waza practice. Matt and I had done lots of jiyu waza at the Shudokan to prepare for our black belt tests, but that was a while ago. Now paired with Dave and Geoff, respectively, any pre-existing knowledge Matt and I could muster was likely to count for very little. Add to this the pressure of performing not only in front of our peers but also Graham Sewanin and the Dojocho himself, and the whole thing had all the hallmarks of being a disaster. I was fighting a losing battle. Geoff as shite hadn't even finished his eight techniques before the other pairs in our group had completed the whole sequence. Dismissed before I'd even got started, we were sent into the far corner of the dojo to practice more in preparation for the losers' heat. To cut a long story short, in the losers' heat it was more of the same. Geoff and I were declared the overall losers and claimed our prize of 30 backward ukemi, which we performed in front of the whole class. I was annoyed and embarrassed. While I felt for Geoff, I didn't like losing at anything. With my previous Aikido experience, we'd probably been paired with the idea that I'd bring Geoff up, but on our first outing together, all he'd done was bring me down. Working with Geoff would not be easy!

FR-EEEEEEEEE-DOM!

What does a Senshusei do when he or she has a break from being a Senshusei? I was about to find out. Dismissed from the dojo without the usual zagaku class, Thursday's early finish was a very welcome surprise. There was even more reason to celebrate. For the next seven days, we were free for Obon. The Obon Festival was a special Japanese holiday where people reunited with family members, often returning to ancestral homes or travelling to visit relatives across Japan. I felt like Mel Gibson as William Wallace in the 1995 film *Braveheart*, thankfully without the castration or beheading. In one of the final scenes, as his end closes in, he lets out an almighty roar in defiance of his persecutors and tyranny, a cry that I'd also made when leaving the honbu – *'Fr-eeeeeeeee-dom!'* Freedom was all mine for the next seven days, and with my tackle and head intact, I intended to use it wisely. That night I rented two DVDs in Musashi Koyama and reviewing my diary to write this book, it intrigued me to see the titles of the films I'd chosen. *Firewall* starring Harrison Ford, about a man whose family is kidnapped and as a result is forced to take extreme measures to secure their release, followed by *The Exorcism of Emily Rose*, with the eradication of evil spirts central to its plot. Looking back, I suspect my state of mind influenced my choices. At times I felt like I'd been kidnapped by the honbu dojo, and now for a week I'd been exorcised, at least temporarily, from its control over my life. But what to do with my week off? Relax too much, and all the hard work I'd put in on the course to date could be undone. Physically, time away from the punishing regime was probably a good thing, and my concern regarding absence was more of a mental one. I was conditioned to the early starts, the regimented discipline; and as if on autopilot, I could now be where I needed to be almost without having to think about it. A week of lying in bed would kill this much quicker than the time it had taken to build, and now, with complete freedom, this became my biggest worry. It was a delicate balance. Time to rest and recover, but not too much relaxation or risk going soft and putting my mental discipline back to where it had no place being.

Friday, 11 August 2006, was my first proper lie-in in months. I finally got up at about 10am but immediately felt out of sorts. While it was nice to get up when it was light for a change, the day seemed to lack momentum without the order and regulation of the dojo. Be careful what you wish for. I felt like a car in first gear that couldn't pull into second. While I'd longed for more time in bed, the reality of the situation was not all it was cracked up to be. I felt sluggish, confused and disorganised. I'd once read that how you start your day is how you finish, and today I'd started badly. This feeling I carried with me all day. I had the freedom to do what I wanted when I wanted, which should have felt much better than it did. I headed off to a Japanese lesson with Hotta Sensei and took my Muay Thai kit just in case. Fairtex was calling, and I had no excuse not to catch up on some Muay Thai, which since April had been playing second fiddle to Aikido. Freedom, though, gave me an excuse, and making excuses didn't feel good. I convinced myself I was too tired and stiff for Muay Thai and headed to Shinjuku instead, where I wandered round the shops aimlessly. I'd also read somewhere that discipline sets you free, and now I felt imprisoned by my own disorganised state. The lack of discipline continued into the weekend. I'd planned to go to Jiu Jitsu, but with no one to care if I bothered to turn up, I convinced myself that I was still too tired and should rest my weary body for another few days before even attempting any form of physical exercise. I went about everyday life and spent a few hours in an Internet cafe next to Meguro Station to catch up with friends and family back home. My precious free time wouldn't last long, and instead of putting it to productive use, I lounged around in Musashi Koyama, watching back-to-back episodes of the TV series *Prison Break*. Perhaps the clue was in the title? I'd felt imprisoned for the last four months, and now, newly released, I was struggling to integrate back into society.

By Sunday I felt relieved to have somewhere to be at a set time. Berlitz was scheduled, and my first lesson started at 9:15am in Sangenjaya. Not having to think about how to fill the day ahead felt good, and surprisingly, the longer I was away from the honbu, the worse both physically and mentally I was feeling. After four lessons, I headed off to Aoyama. Aoyama was an interesting place to walk around, with a variety of shops and a good selection of restaurants. Walking from the station to a cafe I frequented regularly, I bumped into Higa Sensei. Higa spoke good English, and we chatted for a while in the street. He appeared curious to know how my holiday was going and seemed a world away from the image he cultivated in the dojo. I dreaded his classes, mainly because I found them so boring. Left kamae for 30 minutes followed by right kamae for the same was just no fun. I'd nicknamed him 'Mr Precise' because he seemed to obsess over the smallest of details. A degree or millimetre out in Higa's world seemed to make all the difference. There looked to be an accuracy in his Aikido that, as far as I was concerned, would have very little relevance in a real-life combat situation. Even when he spoke, it seemed like he was analysing every word. Was the pitch and tone correct? How could they be improved? Mr Precise seemed intent on finding out. None of us knew much about him away from the honbu dojo. It was rumoured that Kanazawa Sensei was a private detective in his spare time, but we'd presumed that most of the Japanese Sensei were engaged in full-time Aikido. Chatting to Higa Sensei, it surprised me to learn that he was a waiter in a Brazilian restaurant. I couldn't really picture him in this role but imagined that his tables would be perfectly laid and that attention to detail at said establishment would be second to none. He'd no doubt take attentive service to a whole new level! We shook hands and parted company. I had five lessons to teach at Berlitz, and I couldn't afford to be late.

SIGHTSEEING

When I'd first arrived in Tokyo, before Senshusei began, I'd done a lot of the tourist stuff and seen many of the sights. Tokyo Tower, Asakusa with its ancient Buddhist temple and the Meiji Shrine near Harajuku Station had all been ticked off, but not much further afield. It was clear I was getting very good at talking myself out of training, as even with four days of rest under my belt, I was yet to make it to Axis or Fairtex. Maybe it was too much of a busman's holiday for me to get excited about, even though Jiu Jitsu and Muay Thai offered a very different experience than Aikido. What I needed to break the boredom was a little adventure, and in Japan you were never very far from an opportunity to explore and see something new.

Meguro, which was probably best described as a commuter hub outside of central Tokyo, had its very own Parasitological Museum. I'd never imagined there were that many parasites to warrant a full-blown museum or that such a museum would find itself in a residential suburb. In disbelief I wandered past row after row of glass jars housing a variety of strange and somewhat disturbing parasites, all of which, at some point or other, had taken up residence in a human body. On display were over 300 different species, including one almighty tapeworm, which was enough to put anyone off raw fish for life. I also found myself in Odaiba. Described in the tour guides as a high-tech entertainment hub and located on an artificial island in Tokyo Bay, it had its very own Statue of Liberty and VenusFort. The latter was Tokyo's nod to the European Renaissance with domed ceilings, water fountains and spacious plazas all presented in a style that, for a moment, made me feel like I'd left Japan and had been transported to Rome in Italy. Odawara was a longer trip outside of Tokyo to Kanagawa Prefecture and was the home of

Odawara Castle. Walking round the museum, which contained a vast array of antique weaponry and armour, I felt like I'd stumbled onto the set of *Shogun*. I'd watched this TV series as a kid and had been fascinated by the tales of John Blackthorne, a shipwrecked English navigator who integrated into the complex world of feudal Japan. An early episode shocked and possibly scarred me for life. One of Blackthorne's stranded shipmates was put in a cargo net and dunked into a boiling vat of soybean oil and water. Screaming for his life the ordeal continued until Blackthorne acquiesced to the Japanese nobility! My Mum hadn't permitted my watching it, but staying the night at Nansie's house was the perfect opportunity. What Mum and Dad didn't know wouldn't hurt them, and Nansie, along with Sally, enjoyed the programme as much as I did. Was I now living my own version of *Shogun* courtesy of the honbu dojo? Perhaps watching this TV drama at the tender age of ten had sparked an interest in the Land of the Rising Sun that had just never gone away?

I'm pretty sure it was also Nansie who first introduced me to *Clive James on Television*. The programme's offering included funny and bizarre clips from TV shows around the world. Japan was a firm favourite and in particular excerpts from the TV game show *Za Gaman*. *Endurance*, as it was known in the UK, featured Japanese contestants in torturous challenges or as Clive James described it, *'the Japanese game show that puts its contestants through hell'*. Forced to drink a bottle of hot sauce while *wasabi* (Japanese horseradish) was shoved up your nose – made to lie on your back while clutching a block of ice between your feet, before it fell and bashed you in the balls – neither sounded like much fun but both made great viewing. In one episode set in the Egyptian desert, in a handstand position wearing only pants, the contestants had hot sand thrown over their bodies while a magnifying glass projected the sun at their nipples. There was no limit to the methods of torture and in Japan 20 million people regularly tuned in. Was the popularity of *Endurance* a clue to the Japanese psyche and the hardship at the honbu? Perhaps it had influenced my choice of entertainment at the welcome party?

The Japanese word for Japan is *Nihon* or *Nippon*, which, roughly translated, means *sun's origin*. I was exploring a Japanese castle, imagining what life would have been like in the time of the Samurai. I was in search of my Budo roots. I'd read *Hagakure, The Book of the Samurai* by Yamamoto Tsunetomo and had found it enlightening. A window into the Samurai mind, the book outlined an ancient code for living, just as relevant for today. Now I was walking in the steps of the Samurai. My bubble was, however, soon burst. The Japanese had a habit of commercialising everything, and to my surprise in the grounds of this 15th century monument, I found a zoo. Why a historic castle would be the home of a modern-day zoo, I had no idea. Having previously visited Tokyo's version at Ueno, I wasn't a fan of Japanese zoos. I was no expert, but the living conditions of the animals looked far from satisfactory.

I'd had my fill of culture, and with only one day left until I was thrown back into the cut and thrust of the course, I was finally determined to do some training. A dose of Jiu Jitsu at Axis would warm the muscles and let my body know that it was back in business. While Aikido seemed to stretch and strain my body into unnatural postures and positions, I'd found Jiu Jitsu to be much kinder. The moves seemed more fluid, and the leveraging of any joint could be alleviated with a simple tap – and while tapping was also an option in the dojo, it was far too often ignored!

BACK TO THE MADNESS

Friday, 18 August 2006, came around far too quickly. Still contracted to Chida's deal, I was up at 4:20am, which again was a massive shock to the system. Anticipating the enforced early start, I'd not slept well the night before. Thoughts raced through my head as to what the next phase of the course might hold and how my mind and body would cope after the week off. I felt down and depressed, but there was no escape. There was cleaning duty to be done, the morning meeting and the first class at 7am. It was a baptism of fire with Chino Sensei in the house. Thankfully, in the first session of the day, we once again trained with the regular students, so he had to go easy.

After my encounter with Higa Sensei in Aoyama, I was pleased to see him arrive to teach the second class. There was no acknowledgement of our meet, no smile or nod of the head in recognition that we'd conversed as normal human beings outside the honbu. It was back to business with the dreaded kamae class, which was more of a mental challenge than a physical one. It was just so boring, and unfortunately, today, my posture communicated to Mr Precise that I was just that. Pulling up alongside to check the exact angle and positioning of my hands, he told me, *'don't be lazy, or you will regret it later!'* There was obviously no favour to be found in getting close to Higa or any other Sensei. It seemed to make matters worse. The more I'd socialised with Paul Sensei, the more he'd turned up the heat in the 8:30am class. It was them and us, and we'd best not forget it! Chino Sensei was back on the mats for the third class, which was the second Senshusei class of the day and the one we shared with the cops. Chino disliked the cops. This was both good and bad news. The good news was that if there was discipline in the form of a verbal assault to be dished out, it was probably one of the Kidotai who would cop it. The bad news was that, thrown into a collective mix, if Chino wanted to push the cops hard, the Kokusai would be collateral damage and unwilling participants dragged along for the ride. It was still roasting hot, and as Chino showed the finer points of nikajo, I caught the image of Dror out of the corner of my left eye. He was staggering backwards and didn't appear to be in control of his legs. Eventually stopped by the wall, he slumped to the tatami, and from what I could tell without turning around, he looked like he'd passed out. It was hard to stay hydrated and, cloaked in white pyjamas, it was almost impossible to stay cool. Lack of fluids or heat exhaustion was probably to blame, and Chino, in a rare show of emotion, seemed deeply concerned. He mumbled to Graham Sewanin in Japanese, and with that, Dror was dragged off the mats to get some water.

In the last class there was no doubt we were well and truly back to the madness. Murata Sensei explaining the theory behind *taino henko ichi* and *hiriki ichi* (both moves from the kihon dosa) compared them to Boxing and ice cream. I didn't understand what he was going on about and was too tired to care. After a lot of standing around, we finally got to practice some moves. I was in my element as Boxing was on the agenda. For once I knew what I was doing, and the bonus was the opportunity to throw punches at Geoff's head!

AIR CON

The dojo had looked much the same after we'd returned from the summer break, apart from one noticeable difference – air conditioning had been installed and, with the summer heat getting more and more intense, along with Dror's collapse, we had high hopes that at some point, it might actually be turned on. Why go to the expense of installing air con if it was never going to be used? A lot of things I'd seen in Japan made little sense, so if I never got to hear the whir of the system in full and glorious flow, it wouldn't be too much of a surprise. As we finished out the short week, the units looked down from the walls like an evil temptress. *Turn me on, turn me on, turn me on*, was their subliminal cry. Alas, I'd find out in quick time that in Senshusei classes, they'd never be turned on. The blistering heat was all part of the hardship, and if that meant one or two of us ended up fainting, then so be it. The switch to instigate the flow of cool air would only ever be flicked on for ippan students. The only 'con' we got as Senshusei was the conditioning that formed part of the daily regime. Having the air con at all, as far as I could tell, was one big deception. It was one big con!

Kambara was having a hard time. In his early forties, Kambara was the oldest on the course but definitely one of the toughest. He and Inazaki just got on with the job in hand. You never heard them whinge, whine or moan about the hardship they were experiencing. As the elder statesman, Kambara had been prone to ongoing injury since the start. Ronen told me that he'd shown him the metal pins in his knees. The way Ronen described it they sounded more like bolts. A clue that Kambara had more than his fair share of knee problems. To add to his troubles, he was this week's Shinkoku and had been caught taking the Shinkoku diary out of the dojo. There was only one place permitted to write the diary, and that was in the tearoom. The diary leaving the confines of the honbu dojo, even for a moment, was a serious breach of honbu rules, and the Sewanin were determined to set an example. With no consideration for his knee injury, they made Kambara sit in seiza for Saturday's first class. It was a crazy decision, given the guy was already suffering, but Kambara, in true Senshusei spirit, just sucked it up. He was made of tough stuff and served as an example and inspiration to us all.

The week finished, and Dave, Ronen and I headed off to Axis. With only two days of training, we still had some gas in the tank, and Jiu Jitsu was calling. Dave had been training at Axis on a fairly regular basis since he caught the bug when I'd taken him along to watch one session. Today was Ronen's first time, but he wasn't new to ground fighting. I was keen to see what he'd think and how he'd fare. Despite it being his first session at a new gym, Ronen was invited to spar. In the formal classes following the warm-up, we'd practice a series of set techniques. After we did these, it was then free sparring, which meant you rolled with your partner and could utilise any techniques you knew to control, unbalance and submit your opponent. This would be interesting. I'd already seen that Dave was no match for Ronen in the stand-up game. In any confrontation on the feet, Ronen would have had Dave for breakfast. He'd have chewed him up and spat him out. Dave wouldn't stand a chance. Jiu Jitsu was a different ball game altogether, though. I likened it to being thrown in a swimming pool when you couldn't swim. Rolling with a proficient practitioner was like drowning slowly. No matter what you did, you just sank deeper and deeper into trouble. Although Dave was less than proficient, he had another string to his bow! Dave and Ronen squared up, and Ronen suggested, *'let's take it easy, we don't want to get injured'*. Ronen had a plan – tire Dave out and wait for his opportunity. Dave came out like a bat out of hell. He went ballistic and was either on a mission to prove a point or possessed some morbid death wish. Ronen found himself with knees and hands on the mats and Dave, seeing an opportunity, circled to his front. Looping his right arm under Ronen's chin, Dave pulled up sharply, trapping Ronen's neck between his forearm and chest. This was the infamous guillotine choke. Despite taking its name from the apparatus used to dispatch heads so efficiently during the French Revolution, we weren't in France; it wasn't the year 1789, and beheading wasn't on the Jiu Jitsu syllabus. When Ronen didn't tap, Dave took things a step further. Beheading looked to be his intent as, still clamping Ronen's neck, he proceeded to backward roll. I couldn't watch. This was an extremely dangerous move that could cause serious injury. Dave seemed to have no clue what he was doing or the danger he was putting Ronen in. Finally, he let go. *'Fucking idiot'* was Ronen's response. Rightly so, Ronen wasn't happy. Dave had just signed his own death warrant. Back at the honbu dojo, I was sure there would be retribution. It was only a matter of time!

After class, Dave and I travelled back to central Tokyo on the train together, stopping on the way at the Jiu Jitsu shop we frequented from time to time. I needed to buy a new dogi. The owner of the shop, who didn't speak very good English but recognising two of his regulars, gave us a Brazilian ice snack to try. Although it didn't look the best, it tasted quite nice, and fresh from rolling, anything to help cool down was very much appreciated. As we tucked in, the shop owner explained that it was full of guarana, apparently a native plant found in the Amazon basin. He assured us that not only would it give us energy, it would be sure to give us 'wood', too! I was happy with just the energy, but Dave seemed equally happy with the wood. Well, Saturday night was almost here, and Dave was a young guy with an exciting city to explore. Maybe he thought his luck was in! My evening plans were tamer. I'd arranged to meet Nate. We met up in Shibuya and went to a *shabu-shabu* restaurant. Shabu-shabu was a style of Japanese cuisine where you were given a hot pot at your table to cook your meat and vegetables. This brought a whole new meaning to the notion of freshly cooked but was a bit too labour intensive. Still, when in Japan! It was nice to try something different and to find out how Nate was getting on. We continued at Hobgoblin, a British pub next to the station. After a couple of pints, I was sozzled and realised the course had diminished my tolerance to any kind of alcohol. Alcohol was the enemy of early starts, and the last thing I wanted was a *futskayoi*, which was the Japanese term for *hangover*. Translated, it meant *two days drunk* and had been a good reminder to stay off the sauce as much as possible. Two pints were enough to let my hair down and to induce me into a somewhat subdued, relaxed state for the two trains I needed to catch to get home. I eventually arrived back in Musashi Koyama at 9:30pm, absolutely shattered. The last time I'd emptied my bladder was at 2pm after finishing Jiu Jitu and now, approaching 10pm, I'd only just felt the urge to go again. Despite numerous bottles of water throughout the day and two pints of beer at the pub, I'd gone eight hours straight. It was a big clue as to how dangerously dehydrated I'd become!

LINE DANCING

My Mum had sent me to ballroom dancing classes very early on as a child. I vividly remember her telling me, *'it's the only way you'll get a girl!'* I absolutely hated it and was terrified I'd be spotted and that my classmates at school would find out. Eventually they did, and the ridicule was intense, so I'd parked dancing as something I didn't do and firmly resolved never to do it again.

Chida Sensei's deal was almost done, but Wednesday, 23 August 2006, was yet another 7am class with the ippan students before the normal Senshusei day began. Lloyd was on form again. Training with one of the regulars, he'd inadvertently hurt his uke, who was subsequently benched for the rest of the class. Lloyd was fast getting a reputation as the dojo destroyer, and someone you messed with at your own peril. Higa took things too far in the second class. After a shorter-than-usual spell in kamae, he unlocked unwelcome memories from my past. He had us stand opposite one another and move about while maintaining equal distance. First backwards and forwards, then side to side. It seemed to me to be a form of line dancing, and dancing was something I didn't do. The restriction to move in grid-like formation was finally lifted and followed by the joy of freestyle footwork! Just when I thought I couldn't take any more excitement, we were told to grab a bokken and to do the same. The whole coordinated sequence was hilariously funny. Geoff moved side to side, crossing his feet in true Ninja style. But I wouldn't and couldn't. Cross your legs in Thai Boxing, and a clued-up opponent would take you off your feet with a crushing low kick. After all my Muay Thai training, crossing my feet like dancing, was something I didn't do, either. I really didn't get what was going on, but suspected it had something to do with building connection between shite and uke. I had very little interest in building a connection. With fighting, I had only one intention. I wanted to smash my opponent!

Despite the week's break, Senshusei really seemed to be taking its toll on Geoff. He'd well and truly thrown himself in at the deep end in signing up for the course, a decision he was now possibly regretting. It was Geoff and Dave who were on the Sewanin's watch list and in Thursday's zagaku Dave didn't do himself any favours. Called upon to read his reflection and habit we all struggled not to laugh. Dave reflected that he was disappointed not to have been graded to 1st kyu in the Dai Ni test. He botched his pronunciation and finished up with *'ego desu'*. It was close to ijo desu, but not close enough. Graham Sewanin wasn't impressed. After 30 minutes of zagaku the last thing we needed was more seiza, but Graham lined us up. He explained to Dave that ego desu was exactly why he'd only received a 1st kyu grade!

In the class before zagaku Laurance had punished us. I'd played 'Snake' on my old Nokia phone and like the 1982 film *Tron* I'd been transported inside my own game! We ran the tatami in single file. Up and down, up and down. On the green tatami of the dojo it was like mowing the lawn without a mower. Cutting the grass without a machine was a pointless exercise and this was, too. On Laurance's call the Senshusei at the back had to sprint to the front – *'run...run...faster...get to the front!'* Malik was the character in one of the books my Dad had read to me as a child. *'Run, run as fast as you can. You can't catch me, I'm The Gingerbread Man.'* Malik challenged Dror, who was at the back, to catch him. Dror was struggling. Ronen to motivate his fellow countryman shouted words of encouragement. *'Tefos et ha gamad!'* I had no idea what the Hebrew meant, but it seemed to do the trick. Dror sprinted to the front like a man possessed and Malik was left in his wake. I checked with Ronen afterwards. *'What did you say to Dror to make him run so fast?'* His words had brought Dror back to life and I wanted to know what they meant. Ronen smiled; *'catch the midget my friend, catch the midget!'* No wonder Dror had run so fast. It was no wonder, too, why it had been such a painful zagaku. Our legs were completely burnt out!

By the end of the week, Geoff was in bits and said he was having severe stomach problems. I wasn't sure exactly what he meant, but spotting a pair of dogi pants hanging on his locker, which looked to be stained with an unpleasant mix of blood and shit, was a big clue that all was not well. Training in white pants with a bad stomach was a constant worry for us all. The last thing you wanted to do was shit yourself on the mats, but with all the throwing a weak stomach was only a stone's throw away from brown trousers. I'm sure it must have happened on previous courses and didn't want to imagine the humiliation. A morning emptying of the bowels and an Imodium tablet in times of trouble was a ritual I observed. Malik Sewanin had little sympathy for Geoff, and as Geoff's partner it meant he had little sympathy for me, either. After Friday's last class Malik wasn't happy with the speed Geoff, Dave, Dror and me had been moving, so as if five hours of training wasn't enough, we were held back for a set of 100 press-ups. I was too tired to listen and too exhausted to care. I stared right through Malik as he ranted on, then got on with the job in hand. Ronen appeared to have had enough, too. He'd never really got past the mouse comment, and I'm sure he would have taken any opportunity to get back at Malik if they bumped into each other outside the sanctity of the honbu dojo. Malik was living on borrowed time!

LOST IN TRANSLATION

I continued to push on with my Japanese studies, but despite living and working in Japan, not to mention studying a traditional Japanese martial art, I was finding it hard going. My vocabulary was littered with the Japanese words for Aikido techniques, which out on the street possessed very little conversational value. The one opportunity I had to converse with Japanese students was at Berlitz, but this was strictly prohibited. Because I was studying their language, I could sympathise with the students I taught. Japanese was tough for me, and English was tough for them. The only way to get better was to practice, but practice when your pronunciation wasn't great could be the source of immense amusement or even offence.

At Berlitz's Sangenjaya school, I was teaching a student what you should say to your host when you leave a party. Guided by the teaching material, we'd run through the sentence structures and vocabulary and then practiced with a series of role plays.

Student: *'Thank you for having me.'*

Me: *'My pleasure, I hope you had a good time and enjoyed yourself.'*

Student: *'Yes, I did. You have a great cock!'*

Me: *'Excuse me?'*

I could hardly contain myself. It was one of the funniest things I'd heard. Of course, he'd meant to say I was a great cook, but I was happy to take the compliment. I wondered what cock-ups I'd made on my travels around Tokyo. On more than one occasion, my attempts at Japanese had been greeted with smiles and giggles, but I thought this was just an expression of nervous politeness in the face of an embarrassing foreigner. Still, at least I was trying. When in Rome, you learn Italian. When in Japan, it felt only right to at least give Japanese a go.

Back at the honbu, everyone apart from Clyde, Kambara and Inazaki was continuing to butcher the weekly reflection and habit. Dave was by far the worst and, as a result, also the most amusing. We wanted him to be called upon because of the comedy value. The expressions on the Sensei's faces

178

told their own story, and the confused and usually misinterpreted response took the humour to a whole new level. Whatever Dave said was always lost in translation. Trying not to laugh provided an additional level of discomfort to the pain we endured in our legs!

DAY 100

The 100th day of training coincided with the onset of September, which I'd longed for all month. The start of the new month meant the completion of our special arrangement with Chida Sensei and an end to the ridiculously early starts and five-hour training days we'd suffered on Wednesdays and Fridays throughout August. I suspected before the course was over there'd be more of the same. Early morning summer training was in the bag, but early morning winter training was four months away. Any future Chida deal would have to be scrutinised before signing. The summer deal had felt like a bad one, and we'd all be on guard the next time. September also meant a potential turn in the weather. August had been a scorcher, and we'd all sweated buckets. I was certain I was suffering from dehydration and, as the month turned over, appeared to have caught Geoff's dodgy stomach. It was inevitable. As my partner for Dai San, what he had, I was bound to get. I greeted Ronen in the toilets. *'Boker tov, ayef tamid!'* I was now picking up some Hebrew in addition to Japanese. I wished Ronen *'good morning'* and in the same breath confirmed what he'd come to know; I was *'always tired!'* We'd pee together most mornings and today was a special day. While I was counting the days up, Ronen was counting them down. We knew we'd meet in the middle at some point but weren't sure when. *'It's day 100 mate, what've you got?'* He knew already, he always did. *'Chotto matte kudasai.'* Even when I didn't or forgot to ask, he'd give me the number and I knew what it meant. *'One moment please'*, was all it took to confirm today's count as *'123'*. There were 123 days until the end of the course and not quite halfway, if only it were as easy as one…two…three. This would be no easy count; there was still a hell of a long way to go!

Day 100 was a psychological milestone. Dai Ichi was over, Dain Ni was complete, and we were now well on our way with Dai San. I knew there would be more challenges to come, but if I could get through 100 days, I could surely get through the rest. The more techniques we learnt, the more techniques we had to remember. The Sensei knew this and took delight in calling out random ones for us to perform. Romeo Sensei enjoyed this sport. With his accent it was sometimes difficult to work out what he'd said, but there was no opportunity for us to ask him to repeat or clarify, which meant we had to guess, and guessing wasn't something we were very good at. The honbu dojo was next to a busy road, and noises from outside were a constant distraction. With the windows open, our very own version of air conditioning, it was sometimes very difficult to hear. In one particular class, Romeo called out the next technique just as a motorbike sped past. None of us heard what he'd said, so just stood there motionless, as if playing a game of musical statues. Malik Sewanin, who was now back from his trip, started screaming. I mouthed to him that none of us had heard. In response, he screamed out the technique again in a manner that suggested our collective lack of movement was all my fault.

In between classes and after training, the conversations we had as a group were getting stranger. I'd been to see a film called *United 93* at the cinema complex in Roppongi Hills about the September 11th terrorist attacks and one of the hijacked planes. Ronen, Dror and Boaz had all done military service back in Israel, and during cleaning, the conversation turned to how to use grenades. We concluded that if terrorists attacked the honbu dojo then Ronen, Dror and Boaz would sort it out, but if Samurai attacked it, we'd be better off leaving things to Geoff, our own resident Ninja!

MY EVEREST

I was enjoying the Jiu Jitsu training at Axis much more than my time at the honbu. The techniques seemed more practical, and in the sparring we did at the end of every class, I got to test them out for real. Aikido's version of sparring was jiyu waza, which to me felt more like a coordinated dance than anything resembling free fighting. Uke would attack with the same technique over and over again and then went with the flow when shite responded with a variety of techniques. There was little resistance, and if jiyu waza looked messy, it was just as likely to be uke's bad ukemi that got blamed as it was shite's poor technique. As Geoff always had poor ukemi, I had no choice but to crank on my techniques to make him move. I'd convinced myself that this was the bonus of partnering with Geoff. My Aikido had to work for real, as there was no relying on uke. At Axis, if your technique didn't work, your opponent wouldn't tap. In rolling you were at risk from being choked, arm-barred, leg-locked, and a whole host of other nasty techniques, that if not addressed in the right way, could cause serious injury. It was escape, tap or snap! I began to think I'd made a mistake in signing up for Senshusei and wondered how good my Jiu Jitsu could get if I dedicated four hours a day to it. Jiu Jitsu was something I did when I wasn't too tired or bashed up from the course. It wasn't my primary focus but seemed far more in tune with what I'd come to Japan to learn.

The United States had the UFC, and Japan had Pride. These were the ultimate proving grounds where pretty much anything went. The fighters needed to be proficient in Muay Thai, Wrestling and Brazilian Jiu Jitsu to stand a chance. As far as I was aware, no one had competed in the cage or square ring and gotten very far with Aikido. Pride was even more brutal than the UFC. It was legal to soccer kick a downed opponent in the head, a practice that was banned in the UFC for being far too dangerous. In Pride, warriors like Sakuraba, Mirko 'Cro Cop' Filipovic and Fedor 'The Last Emperor' Emelianenko regularly put their lives and reputations on the line to the cheers of adoring fans. MMA was big in Japan, and the MMA gyms stood alongside the dojos that were home to the traditional Budo arts of Judo, Karate, Kendo, and Aikido. I'd trained for a while at Tokyo's Chute Boxe Academy, the fighting team of Wanderlei 'The Axe Murderer' Silva and Mauricio 'Shogun' Rua. I'd loved it, and now I couldn't seem to recall why I'd taken the traditional, less practical path.

I'd heard from previous Senshusei, including the Sewanin themselves, that the course offered much more than training. There was something else, something deeper, and the only way to find out was to complete it. This intrigued me, and just as my thoughts turned to jumping ship, I reminded myself of this. Senshusei was like Mount Everest. It was my Mount Everest. Why do people climb Everest? Is it an enjoyable experience? Does it make sense to put your body, mind and spirit through such an arduous and difficult task? As I've never climbed Everest, I couldn't be certain about the right answer to the first question, but I guessed that for at least some brave men and women who had reached the summit, their reasoning, in part, was simply because it was there. This had been my reason to climb Mount Fuji, Japan's most famous natural landmark. I hadn't fancied the overnight trek, the oxygen-starved legs or reaching the top in freezing cold conditions that chilled me to the bone. If I'd given too much consideration to any of these things, I probably wouldn't have done it. I'd climbed *Fuji-san* because it was there. The Japanese proverb states that *he who climbs Mount Fuji is a wise man, he who climbs twice is a fool*. This proverb dates from a time when women were prohibited from ascending the mountain. The first woman to do it stuck a finger up to the Japanese authorities and reached the summit in the middle of the 19th century. I was no fool and had no intention of climbing it twice! During the recent break while I was sightseeing, Ronen, Dror and Boaz had climbed Fuji-san with Graham Sewanin. I knew from my time that it was an exhausting experience. Perhaps this explained Dror's collapse on his return to the dojo? I'd done it before the course, but they'd done it during. Like me they'd climbed it because it was there but under very different conditions!

Senshusei was also there. Ever since I'd read about the course in *Angry White Pyjamas,* the thought of doing Senshusei for myself had become a relentless itch that needed scratching. Thinking about it, my reason for doing the course wasn't about becoming a better fighter, it wasn't even about getting better at Aikido. The reason for doing it was because once I knew about it, like Everest, its summit had to be conquered. From the books and articles I'd read about Mount Everest, I'd discovered that the answer to my second and third questions was no. On the ascent I'm sure there would be moments of enjoyment, but the physical and mental toll of such a feat of endurance would quickly dissolve into the inescapable reality of the dangerous task at hand. Everest, I suspected, was something you got to enjoy when it was all done and dusted. It was something to be revered when the task was over, when it was safe to look back at even the most dangerous of times through the safety of fond memories.

Senshusei was probably the same, and I wouldn't know what it really meant to me and my life until it was finally over. Training at Axis would never be Everest, but it could and would provide a much more enjoyable experience along the way. The rolling after class was a great way to measure my progress – and something missing at the honbu. Grades and belts didn't mean much to me; what mattered was how good I was and whether I was improving. As a Jiu Jitsu white belt, I'd submitted several blue belts, and in the first Monday class of September, I stopped a much heavier white belt with an arm-bar and then a choke. Talking about me, I heard him say *'sugoi chikara',* to someone in the changing room afterwards, a term I now understood thanks to Chida Sensei. This pat on the back felt good and was a welcome change from the honbu dojo, where praise was rarely forthcoming. If I had good strength, it was because of Senshusei training. Even if my ability to fight wasn't improving because of my time on the course, I was getting stronger and developing a tolerance for even the most merciless of beatings. As I was leaving, Taka Sensei (Axis' version of Kancho) called me back and said that he wanted me to wear a blue belt from the next class onwards. To move up in Jiu Jitsu didn't require a formal grading; it was always at the discretion of the teacher based on his or her assessment of your understanding of the techniques and your ability to apply them. Taka had seen enough to award me my promotion, and I felt proud and happy. Although belts didn't matter to me, I was working hard at Jiu Jitsu despite the constant pressure of the course, and it was nice to have my efforts acknowledged. The recognition boosted my energy levels, and, not done for the day just yet, I fitted in a Muay Thai session at Fairtex, followed by a Japanese class with Hotta Sensei.

Back in Musashi Koyama, I cycled across with my washing to the coin launderette and knocked my sunglasses off in transit. They fell onto the road, which scratched one lens. This put a minor dent in what had otherwise been a great day. I had to remind myself of the Japanese concept of *wabi-sabi*, which is the *acceptance of imperfection*. As somewhat of a perfectionist, I found this view of the world difficult to grasp. Still, everything takes practice!

SIZE DOESN'T MATTER

The first full week of September started on shower duty with Ronen. The cleaning was second nature now. We knew what was expected and, in our respective pairs, just got on with things. This time of day was always the calm before the storm, and conversation would always turn to nagging injuries and what we thought the day might bring.

Chino Sensei had been spending more and more time teaching the Senshusei and was more visible around the honbu than Chida Sensei, despite Chida being the Dojocho. I sensed the two had an unspoken rivalry and never saw them speak directly to one another. Ronen and I were very much in the Chino camp, and although we dreaded his classes, they were what we'd come to Japan to experience. None of the other Sensei had what he'd got. The T-1000 was incredible to watch. *'Zzzoooooooottt!'* – the sound Chino Sensei made, when his hydraulics kicked in as he demonstrated a technique, always got my attention. It was that *Boyz N The Hood* moment at the 'lowrider' meet. *'We gotta problem here?'* – Ice Cube as 'Doughboy' stepped up in defence of his half-brother before rolling off in his Chevy Impala. A lowrider car had a lowered body which sprung up on its suspension in order to drive. Chino was the dojo's lowrider, and no one dared have a problem with him!

Chino Sensei seemed to favour Thursdays, and in Thursday's second class, he arrived on the mats with what seemed like a point to prove. Perhaps he'd had a bad start to the day, a poor night's sleep followed by a crowded and uncomfortable train ride to Ochiai? Whatever the reason, it was straight into hajime geiko to a count that got faster and faster. As he paced the dojo, I noticed that even when I was in an extended position, with my front leg bent at the knee and back leg straight, I was still taller than him. It showed that size didn't matter. I'd read somewhere that Bruce Lee had once said that a good big one would always beat a good small one. With Aikido, I was a bigger one, but not in Chino's league. Despite his inferior size, his Aikido would always beat mine, but I wondered what would happen if the fight went to the ground. Would his hydraulic system still work if he found himself flat on his back with 80 kilograms of English beef sat on top? It was a thought that would never become a reality, but it was an interesting one at that. As my mind wandered, I completely forgot the technique I was supposed to be doing. *'Chigau!'* Chino shouted right next to me, which sent a seismic shock through my body. His cry told me I'd messed up and reminded me it was always wise to pay attention in his classes. It was foolish to switch off, and he wasn't done with us yet. Hajime geiko moved to jiyu waza. We performed in pairs, throwing each other at least 20 times before changing over. By the end of the class, there was a line of sweat where we'd all been standing. Chino had made his mark, and it was a class none of us would ever forget. Chino Sensei didn't pull any punches. If you were wrong you were wrong, and he wasn't afraid to tell you. This was very different from what I'd experienced at the Shudokan where a 'praise sandwich' was on the menu of every class. *That's great... try this to make your technique better...that bit is brilliant by the way!'* – I'd been taught this method of instruction as a member of the 'SWAT'. I'd not joined the US law enforcement unit – 'Special Weapons And Tactics' – but instead, Sensei Ken's version. The 'Special Winning Attitude Team' wore black dogi to distinguish themselves and helped out with the teaching. While I understood the rationale, it sometimes took a while to get to the point. Chino's directness while terrifying, was also very refreshing!

In Friday's first class, Romeo Sensei had gone ballistic. We practiced ukemi back and forth until everyone was dizzy and then got into pairs to work on techniques. Matt had injured his knee and Geoff his neck, so I was paired with Dave. Dave had already proven he could be dangerous in his attempt to decapitate Ronen, and now it was my turn in the hot seat. Dave gripped my wrist with such force that his nails, which he never seemed to cut, broke my skin. With my heart pumping, the blood flowed and dripped all down my dogi. With Chino Sensei rumoured to be up next, I'd now need to fit a quick change into the 30-minute break. My hand was still bleeding as we marched out to face a second dose of Chino Sensei in the same week. I was expecting the worst, but much to my surprise, the worst never came. Chino Sensei was unpredictable, and you never knew what to expect. Yesterday's Chino had been replaced by a much calmer version, and during the class, he marched us off the tatami and into Kancho's office. Kancho's office was off limits to Senshusei and off limits to pretty much anyone else at the honbu, for that matter. Finding the office too hot, we moved to the kitchen across the corridor, where Chino showed us pictures in an old book of Kancho Gozo Shioda performing eri mochi techniques. Matt and Geoff were still in mitori geiko and had been forgotten in the dojo. Eventually, and probably after much debate about what they should do, Geoff knocked on the door of the kitchen to ask if they could come in. There were definitely two sides to Chino Sensei, and in the space of one week, we'd seen them both! Ronen had missed the fun and games. He was on a train to Narita and then a plane to Hong Kong. His visa was about to expire, and it was time to renew. He'd missed an interesting day, but I'd have been more than happy to be in his place.

Size also didn't matter when it came to Geoff. Matt had taken to psyching himself up on the train into Ochiai each morning. He'd watch Pride fights on his iPod and in particular, the pride of Russia, Fedor. We'd often review and dissect bouts in the tearoom, and, on one particular occasion, our viewing caught Geoff's interest. Although Geoff was big, he was no heavyweight; Fedor on the other hand was. *'I could beat Fedor!'* – we knew Geoff had Ninja skills, but his statement was ridiculous. Matt couldn't believe what he'd heard; he'd watched enough Pride to know what damage Fedor could do. In astonishment, he asked Geoff, *'are you mad?'* Geoff was adamant; *'if Fedor punched me, I'd lower my forehead and break his hand!'* I had some experience of head-butting the heavy bag at Master Lec's to build up neck strength, but even I wouldn't have been stupid enough to consider such a feat. Matt wasn't finished. *'Do you mean to tell me that if Fedor Emelianenko, the Pride heavyweight champion, punched you, you'd break his hand with your head?'* Ronen who observed the scene play out, was beside himself. *'Of course'*, confirmed Geoff, with a confidence that if the opportunity ever arose, would surely get him killed!

SICK NOTE

Although I'd had my fair share of injuries, I'd so far avoided any real sickness, the type that back home would have seen me laid up in bed for a week taking medicine and sucking throat sweets, accompanied by the background hum of daytime TV. On Saturday I'd gone toe to toe with Neville. I'd split his lip with iriminage and in return he'd clotheslined me, nearly crushing my windpipe. My throat had felt ropey afterwards, but with the promise of my Jiu Jitsu blue belt, I'd still trained at Axis. In keeping with tradition, having been awarded my new belt, I was told to crouch on all fours in the turtle position. Everyone in the class then removed their belts and filed past, taking it in turns to whip me across the back. It brought back memories of the Senshusei welcome party, but this time without the clothes pegs and fake chillies. My throat felt like I'd swallowed a packet of razor blades, but with the determination expected of a Senshusei, I'd still gone on to do three rounds on the pads at Fairtex, which had only made matters worse.

Filing into the honbu dojo on Tuesday morning to face another week, I was in bits. I felt terrible, and despite the pain of mitori geiko, it was the lesser of two evils compared to a full day of training. If you were really sick, there was a possibility the Sewanin could send you home. This seemed the more sensible option. For one, it would ensure a speedier recovery, and for two, it would quarantine the germs and stop them spreading around everyone else. I decided I'd try my luck. When I arrived the Sewanin were nowhere to be seen, but eventually Malik arrived. My preference had been Graham, but unable to locate him, I explained to Malik how bad I felt. He seemed sympathetic, but this didn't stop him telling me to get changed into my dogi and start my cleaning duties. On my hands and knees scrubbing the floor of the women's toilets, I was at my lowest point to date. The course was hard enough when you were healthy, and now, feeling as sick as a dog, I had no idea how I'd make it through the next five minutes, let alone the rest of the day. My fate would be sealed in the morning meeting, but before that the toilet rolls needed changing and the sanitary bin emptying. Lined up in the tearoom in front of the Sewanin, I formally declared myself as sick. Graham told me to fill in a form requesting mitori geiko and that he would speak to Murray Sensei when he arrived to see if I could go home. My fate had been passed up the food chain, and with Murray Sensei being responsible for the Kokusai, I didn't fancy my chances of a compassionate discharge. The form had too much white space, and the rule at the honbu dojo was that you had to fill it all. I couldn't simply state I was sick in one or two sentences with a brief description of my symptoms; I had to fill a whole page of A4. This seemed like a ridiculous rule. Why pack a page full of words when a few would do? Someone would have to read my waffling drivel; someone who I was sure would have better things to do. I did my best to elaborate on my condition, but found I was repeating myself, writing the same explanation in a slightly different way over and over again. I was sure Murray Sensei wouldn't read it, but honbu rules were honbu rules, no matter how nonsensical they seemed. Murray Sensei arrived but was too busy to come and see me in person. Instead, he sent Malik with the message that I could leave the dojo only to see a doctor. I needed to get a note from a doctor, which I then had to bring back to the honbu for review. Malik Sewanin advised that Murray Sensei had also said that if I was sitting at home, I might as well be sitting in the dojo in mitori geiko! This wasn't music to my ears. It seemed crazy that Murray Sensei could make any comparison between recuperating at home and sitting in my dogi in seiza for four hours. Also, he'd got it wrong. I wouldn't be sitting at home; I'd be lying flat on my back, fast asleep.

Officially signed off to seek medical attention, I got changed out of my dogi, bowed out of the honbu and caught the train home. I'd managed to get a doctor's appointment for 2pm, so with a few hours to spare, I went to bed. There was method in my madness. A doctor's appointment at the end of the training day meant no training that day. Despite the instruction to take a doctor's note back to the honbu the same day, this was now impossible, as by the time I'd get there Murray Sensei and the Sewanin would have already left. Dr Gabriel, who through my frequent visits was getting to know me quite well, confirmed I had the flu and wrote me a sick note to that effect. Despite him offering, I had to stop him detailing on the note that under no circumstances should I do any Aikido training for the next few days. It would have looked far too suspicious and like I'd dictated what to write. I headed back to Musashi Koyama and went back to bed. I just lay there, feeling too sick to get up and even too ill to be bothered to watch TV. As the prescribed tablets kicked in, I perked up a bit and booted up my laptop to find that Matt had sent me an email after class to tell me I'd missed nothing today and to get better soon. I was awake on and off throughout the night, and somewhere between consciousness and slumber, I decided that I wouldn't go to the honbu in the morning as nothing good could come of it. I concluded that if I still felt ill, neither training nor mitori geiko would serve me well, and either option would delay me getting better and potentially increase the severity of my illness. When my alarm went off at 5:20am, I ignored it and went back to sleep. Not reporting at the honbu dojo was against the rules. No matter what, you had to report for training in person, even if the outcome was that you were immediately sent home. I wasn't a kid and now had a diagnosis from a doctor to support how dreadful I felt. I didn't need Murray Sensei or the Sewanin to tell me this and couldn't face the three trains I'd need to catch. In my semi-conscious state, I decided to stay away. When I woke up properly just before 7am, the potential consequences of this decision now became a very worrying reality. Even if I'd wanted to, it was now too late to get to the dojo on time to start my cleaning duties. Whatever I did, I'd be late, and I convinced myself that being late was almost as bad as not turning up at all. If I was late, I'd be at the honbu and in physical form, open to all manner of punishment. If I wasn't there at all, they couldn't do anything to me, and any punishment would be delayed until I was back on my feet and better able to take it.

The honbu dojo had a phone, but not just any phone. The pink telephone that sat on one of the cabinets outside the tearoom and opposite the door to the office hardly ever rang. When it did ring, it was for an important reason and this meant it had to be answered in as fewer rings as possible. The Senshusei early start meant that responsibility for answering the phone often fell to us, but it was also possible that a passing Sewanin or Sensei could take it upon themselves to pick up. If I was not going to the dojo, I had no choice but to make the call. Timing was everything, and my timing had to be perfect. Phone too early and I could disturb one of the office staff; phone too late and it could be one of the Sewanin or a Sensei who answered. I had to do my best to catch one of the Senshusei, bowing into the honbu or starting the cleaning roster. Although I'd ultimately need to speak with one of the Sewanin or Murray Sensei directly, I favoured easing myself into this difficult conversation, by first getting the lie of the land from one of my own. I made the call at 7:15am, and Malik Sewanin answered almost immediately. I explained the situation, and that I was too ill to come to the honbu. On first response he seemed to understand and told me to *'rest and take lots of medicine'*, but then in his next breath asked me where I lived. I was 45 minutes and three trains away, but for the rest of the day I was in a state of high alert in case he turned up, which thankfully he didn't!

By day three I was still not 100 percent, but as the tablets were working their magic, I decided I probably should put in an appearance. Arriving at the honbu dojo, I didn't know what to expect. I'd been away for only 48 hours, but it felt like a lifetime. There was no sign of the Sewanin, so I got changed into my dogi. Coming out of the locker room, I bumped into Malik, who asked how I was and told me I shouldn't train today. In the morning meeting I formally requested mitori geiko and, after it was over, asked Graham if I should sit in seiza. To my horror he responded *'yes!'* Matt had also requested mitori geiko. His knee was still bad, but he now had an ingrowing toenail on both feet on each of his big toes. Sometimes the smallest things can cause the biggest pain, and Matt was in agony, shuffling around on his heels to remove the pressure off his primary digits. He told us he'd operated on both toes the night before. Gritting his teeth to take the pain, he'd used the point of a kitchen knife to dig them out. His room had resembled a murder scene. With pools of blood on the floor and a blood-stained knife in hand, he'd have made a terrifying sight if any of his roommates had made the mistake of wandering in. His home surgery had all the hallmarks of Senshusei mentality, and we were all in hysterics as he recounted his story. Murray Sensei, as judge and jury, decided he wanted to quiz Matt before passing sentence. *'Can you walk or is it just pain?'* Matt could walk, albeit with huge discomfort and responded, *'it hurts a lot, especially when I walk, osu!'* With that, Matt had sealed his own fate. Pain was of no consequence, and he'd inadvertently said he could walk. Any hopes he had of mitori geiko were dashed. Pain was the close friend of all Senshusei, and Matt, still hobbling, was thrown into the thick of it.

For my first class back, Paul Sensei was in charge. As friends outside the dojo, I once again hoped he might take pity on my situation, but yet again he was to disappoint. I sat motionless in seiza for an hour without putting my hands down. After about 10 minutes I felt my legs fall to sleep, and after 45 minutes the pain had become so intense, I thought I would faint. In the hope of some temporary relief, I periodically tensed my thigh muscles to raise my body up to take some pressure off my knees. This allowed a little blood to flow from my body to the tips of my toes, and dropping my weight back down, I felt pins and needles all the way to my feet. It was a strange sensation – a kind of pleasure and pain all mixed into one, with pain being all I was left with once the small amount of pleasure faded away. I was determined to get through the first class with a strong seiza. I'd been missing for two days and was worried that I could have lost some respect of my fellow Senshusei. Sucking up the seiza was a way to claw back credibility, which seemed to work, given the pats on the back and praise received, as I staggered to my feet and off the mats at the end of the class. My absence meant a special Shinkoku, and there was an additional special Shinkoku to request mitori geiko instead of the normal day's training. To make matters worse, this was to be done in front of Chino Sensei, but after all was said and done, the Sewanin concurred I'd done a good job. Chino strolled onto the tatami to take the second class, and after the formal bowing to open proceedings, I took my place in the corner. After about five minutes, Chino called Graham Sewanin over to ask why I was sat in seiza. He told Graham that I could sit on a chair, and with a look of surprise on his face, Graham said, 'Sensei has shown compassion for you'. It was his rather formal way of saying it was my lucky day. It was a very welcome reprieve from an even longer detail of seiza than I'd struggled through earlier on. Like a prisoner on death row with hopes of last-minute clemency, Chino Sensei had come to my rescue. In the last class, Chino's kindness seemed to have caught on as Kanazawa Sensei told me I could practice walking up and down the dojo, stopping in kamae every few steps. Despite not being convinced of the benefit of this practice, I wasn't about to argue. Anything was better than seiza! The weekly zagaku which followed didn't trouble me one bit. Having done an hour of seiza in the first class of the day, zagaku felt like a breeze. I watched as my fellow Senshusei grimaced and winced in pain. I didn't move and felt a real sense of achievement in not putting my hands down even once. Maybe I'd finally found something in seiza after all this time and it had taken mitori geiko to root it out. As if to burst my bubble, in my closing special Shinkoku, Noriki Sensei, holding the door for Kancho, asked on Inoue Kancho's behalf what was wrong with me. To keep things simple for all parties, I replied, *'fever!'* Noriki translated, and Kancho, seemingly unamused, grunted, turned his back on me and headed back into his office!

BACK IN THE GAME

I'd had my fill of mitori geiko and was sick of sitting on the sidelines. I felt the odd one out and although being on the bench had given my body time to recover, it had knocked me for six psychologically. I'd felt a distance creep in between me and the rest of the Senshusei, and getting back in the game was the only way to get things back to normal. Going to bed on Thursday night, I felt excited about getting up and training on Friday morning. When Friday morning arrived, I still had a raging sore throat, but thankfully with my fever all but gone, my energy levels were getting back to normal. Although my flu had dissipated, my stomach seemed to have taken a turn for the worse. Back at the honbu, it was business as usual. Dror and I went about our morning ritual with me in trap one and him in trap two. It was probably the drugs I'd been taking to combat my illness that had impacted on my stomach and were also making me feel somewhat spaced out.

With Chino and Oyamada Sensei rumoured to be on the teaching schedule, I was unlikely to get a warm welcome back. The cops were absent from the second class. Apparently, they were somewhere else learning to shoot. Perhaps they'd concluded that unarmed combat was just too difficult and had decided to rely on their right to bear arms instead? Despite being one of the safest countries I'd ever visited, in Japan law enforcement still carried firearms. Come to think about it, I'd still not figured out why Japan even needed a Riot Police! After 10 minutes of training, Chino Sensei led us off the mats and once again into Kancho's office. It was my third visit and Ronen's first. *'It looks like a porn movie set from the seventies'*, he told me out of earshot of Chino. I didn't disagree; Hugh Hefner's man cave minus the *Playboy* bunnies! To my surprise Chino Sensei explained the difference between his and Chida Sensei's Aikido. It was confirmation of what I'd always understood to be the case. Chino and Chida were at odds, and we were all about to find out what that meant when it came to their Aikido. Chino Sensei explained that Chida's way was *'not to unbalance uke so much'*, whereas Kancho Gozo Shioda's and, by default, Chino's way was always to *'extend further to unbalance uke more'*. As Gozo Shioda was the founder of Yoshinkan, I wondered if this was Chino Sensei's way of having a dig at the Dojocho. There appeared to be little love lost between them, and I'd still not seen them talk. Chida, when he did take the class, never really seemed as if he could be bothered to teach us anything, and here Chino was opening up about one secret to the strength of his Aikido. Whether or not it was a dig at Chida Sensei, it seemed that way.

In Oyamada's class I took on board Malik Sewanin's tip of not tensing so much as uke. It seemed to pay off; as Geoff was getting more and more tired, the more I relaxed, and the less resistance I put up. As his energy drained, he made more mistakes. He really cocked up one technique, and after four or five attempts, Malik had to come over and show him how to do it. At the end of the class his reward was yet another round of usagi tobi. Working with Geoff made life more difficult, but despite this it felt good to be back with the team, and I was pleased to have survived the day.

SELF-DEFENCE

As the days came and went, my sore throat got better and my time in mitori geiko was pushed further to the back of my mind. Dai San was proving long and tiresome, with very few highlights to break the daily monotonous grind. Fortunately, Malik Sewanin was always on hand to motivate his troops and, in doing so, provided some welcome humour that I suspect he never intended. Dave who regularly bore the brunt of his screams, was told to *'stop shaking'* and *'don't mess with me today!'* Dave was partial to strong coffee and the caffeine did him no favours. Always prone to shaking, after two or three cups he became the victim of his very own earthquake!

Sotai dosa was something we now seemed to practice every day, and I really didn't get it. I understood the rationale behind the kihon dosa and the importance of practicing its six basic movements which formed the foundations for all the applied techniques. Sotai dosa, though, took things a step too far. Essentially a version of the kihon dosa performed with your partner holding your wrists, it seemed like a performance with very little point. Trying to do this with Geoff and make it look smooth and graceful was impossible. Geoff was just too big and uncoordinated. Because his Aikido looked bad, it made mine look bad, and I was relieved when I heard he would have to temporarily return to Canada to renew his visa. Paired with Clyde and with the weather getting cooler, things were looking up. It was much better training with Clyde. As he was smaller and lighter, it took less effort to move him than Geoff's awkward frame. With Clyde I seemed to have more energy and even got through a double Oyamada class relatively unscathed. We knew we'd be doing self-defence as part of the Dai San syllabus, but none of us really knew what that meant, despite Takagi Sensei providing an earlier taste. If the Aikido we were learning really worked, why did we need anything else? For me, martial arts had always been about self-defence, and if something didn't work in a real situation, it had no place being learnt. On Thursday, 21 September 2006, we got our first proper introduction to what self-defence at the honbu dojo might be all about. After Dave's attempt at beheading I'd warned him in the tearoom ahead of the morning meeting. Raising each fist, I brandished my weapons. *'Left hand pain, right hand goodnight!'* I didn't want any repeat of the Axis incident where Dave had lost his head, and as a result, Ronen nearly had, too. If Dave tried anything today, he could have one or both. If Dave came for war, I was ready. I was like Tony Montana in *Scarface* – *'Dave, do you wanna play rough? Say hello to my little friends!'*

On the mats Murray Sensei was in charge and challenged us to stop each other standing up. Not for the first time, I was confused. Why was uke on the floor? Had uke been attacked? Why were we being asked to stop uke getting up? I lay down on the mats first, and despite Clyde's best efforts to keep me down, I got to my feet every time. I was sure my Jiu Jitsu experience was paying off, and as an avid watcher of all things UFC and Pride, my time in front of the screen seemed to be paying off, too. We switched roles, and as Clyde attempted to clamber to his feet, I took him down and applied a rear naked choke courtesy of Axis Jiu Jitsu. *What better way to keep someone on their back than to choke them unconscious?* I thought to myself. This felt like proper self-defence to me, and I was enjoying every minute. Before I got too carried away, Clyde tapped my arm, signalling his acceptance of my submission. In the scramble, he'd somehow cut his lip, so Graham Sewanin temporarily stepped in. Lying on his back, Graham tried to get to his feet. Self-defence to my mind meant any shite and uke relationship went right out of the window. This wasn't Aikido anymore; this was war. I pushed Graham down, climbed on his back and applied the same choke I'd done on Clyde. With no Jiu Jitsu experience, I wasn't sure Graham knew the etiquette of tapping, so I released the choke early just in case. An unconscious Sewanin wasn't a good idea, and – as I'd already learnt the hard way – tap too late and while the brain might still function, the body didn't always respond. This had previously made for a scary experience, as I slipped into darkness with no ability to let my partner know I'd had enough. Death would have followed swiftly were it not for the fact that he recognised the signs. My body flopped, and I started to gurgle. My partner released the choke, and in a matter of seconds, I was awake again. In applying my Jiu Jitsu skills on Graham, my excitement had got the better of me. I suspected I'd already be in trouble for trying such a move on one of the Sewanin, but whatever the punishment, if it came, it would be worth the experience. Self-defence had added a new dimension to the course, and it was one I liked. I looked forward to Geoff's return!

THE MISSING KEY

Despite our best attempts, none of us had found the missing key to improve our Aikido. Chino Sensei had highlighted the importance of unbalancing uke, but when that failed, we all resorted to brute force. The benefit of brute force only worked for so long. With hajime geiko and the endless repetition of techniques, our energy levels were too depleted to put strength into much for any length of time. The missing key turned up in another form, much to Ronen's surprise. In the middle of Laurance Sensei's class, Graham Sewanin spotted a locker key lying on the tatami. There were strict rules governing the use of locker keys. They had to be formally requested from the office each morning and then deposited back as soon as we were changed into our dogi and ready to start cleaning. We'd been rushed by the Sewanin. Robert from *Fight! Japan* was back to film more of his documentary and the Sewanin wanted us to look our best. With minutes until we were due in seiza, we'd been told to change into fresh dogi. It was frantic in the locker room. A storm of dogi and belts flew about in all directions. In a similar scenario to Lloyd's peanut, Ronen, in the hysteria, had forgotten to return his key and left it tucked inside his dogi. We'd practiced ukemi back and forth and the more flips we did the more dislodged Ronen's key had become. With all the aerial acrobatics, it was only a matter of time. Ronen's key had fallen out, and his flouting of dojo rules set the tone for the rest of the class. Laurance Sensei decided it would be a good idea to get the Sewanin to practice jiyu waza with each of us. This had all the makings of a bad idea. They probably had a few grievances they were keen to settle, and we most definitely did. Choking Graham had felt good, and now there was a further opportunity for us all to have a pop at the Sewanin as payback for the shouting, screaming and excessive punishment.

Robert hit record as I was called out opposite Malik Sewanin to perform *shomen uchi jiyu waza*. I purposefully went lighter than I did with Geoff out of respect for my honbu superior and because I didn't want to antagonise an already fragile relationship. I was well aware that Malik could make my life a misery. He was already making a good job of it, and I wanted no more than my current quota. We changed roles. As uke it was now my turn to attack Malik and, as shite, for him to throw me. Despite me going easy on him, he turned up the heat.

On each attack he threw me as hard as he could, and as I went in for my last strike, he smacked me across the side of the mouth with the blade of his right hand, bruising my jaw. I was mad and Laurance, sensing my anger, shouted *'yamae'* (stop), which called time on my next attack, where there would have been no holding back. Malik's conduct was out of order, and Laurance seemed to agree. *'Remember, you're not Chino Sensei!'* Laurance shouted at Malik in earshot of us all. Take a liberty with one Senshusei, and you took a liberty with us all. I only hoped Lloyd would get called up next to face Malik. Lloyd took no prisoners, and I was sure he would return fire in restoration of my honour! No such luck. Malik got his pick and called out Clyde. He knew he could dominate Clyde, and what followed was a brutal display that sent Clyde flying all over the place. As Laurance called time on this fiasco, Malik glanced over in his direction and shouted, *'is that it?'* I didn't get what was going on in Malik Sewanin's head. I knew him being hard on us made for a richer experience, but now he'd crossed the line by cracking me across the jaw and humiliating Clyde. At the end of the class, Malik called us over to the corner of the dojo. As we sat in seiza, he brought up the key incident and said as punishment we'd all have to do one circuit of usagi tobi.

Fair enough. Ronen had made a mistake, and we were all being punished for it. I didn't blame Ronen. His mistake today would be mine or someone else's tomorrow. There was no animosity towards him, just a desire to get on with the punishment, so we could leave for the day. But Malik wasn't finished. Turning in my direction and looking me straight in the eye, he said aggressively, *'Simon, your shomen uchi strike was shit!'* I was in shock at the harshness of his words and his use of profanity. *Well, don't hold back,* I thought to myself, and with that Malik told me I'd be doing an extra round of bunny hops. I was raging and had to summon all my strength and willpower not to square up to him right there and then. For a moment I was back at boarding school, face to face with one of the bullies responsible for tormenting my earlier years, but now I was equipped with the skills to settle the score. It wasn't worth it. I hadn't come this far on the course to be kicked off it for knocking out one of the Sewanin. I sucked it up and did my two rounds double-quick with no emotion, all the while making sure I showed no visible signs of pain. This seemed to rile Malik further, and he gave me an extra round for my trouble. Malik still wasn't finished. He summoned me over for another word, knowing that even a moment longer in seiza after three rounds of usagi tobi would be complete and utter agony. He called me out again on my shomen uchi strike. I had to restrain myself from telling him I was going easy and responded the only way I could. *'Osu!'* He still wasn't done. *'I don't know what it is with you, but if it happens again, I'll show you what I can do with shomen uchi!'* This was a challenge I was ready to accept. His shomen uchi strike against my Muay Thai and Brazilian Jiu Jitsu. The only problem I'd have was making a decision on whether to knock his block off or rip him limb from limb. Shomen uchi wouldn't save him. Nothing would save him! *'Osu!'* I responded yet again. I sensed he wanted a reaction, and I was determined not to give him one. I felt I'd won a moral victory.

Everyone had witnessed Malik's behaviour, and after class, Ronen was the first to say he was proud of me. I'd remained calm and collected despite huge provocation. Perhaps this was part of the missing key to what Aikido was really all about? In the tearoom I overheard Kambara and Inazaki discussing the incident in their native tongue and asked them to explain in English. They said they thought Malik was jealous, as my jiyu waza was better than his. I wasn't so sure but was grateful for their support. Even Laurance Sensei told Clyde that it was nice to see a bully get beaten up. I thought I'd been going easy but watching the footage back at a later date on the *Fight! Japan* episode, my technique did seem strong. Robert providing commentary had called it right – *'Simon practices with his teacher. There is seemingly no love lost between these two!'* This was an understatement. By remaining calm, perhaps I'd discovered yet another key to Aikido? Did true Aikido strength result from not using strength? Perhaps relaxation was the key? Unintentionally, I'd given Malik Sewanin what we all thought he deserved. Whether or not I'd meant it didn't matter. I was glad Malik had finally got a taste of his own medicine.

After class I had a debrief with Matt outside FamilyMart. We dined on DARS chocolate and *meronpan* (melon bread) washed down with Aquarius and Pocari Sweat. The latter was a strange name for a sports drink, but I guess it made sense. Having sweated all morning in the dojo, perhaps it was the best way to rehydrate? The sugar rush was intense and was topped off with a double caffeine hit thanks to Kirin Fire and Suntory BOSS. Cold coffee in a can was always a winner and apparently, according to the advertisements, US actor Tommy Lee Jones drank it. If it was good enough for Tommy, it was good enough for me! Fed and watered and with a pressing need to vent my anger, I headed off to Fairtex to hit the bags and do a few rounds on the pads. It felt good to release my rage, but after all the bunny hops, my legs were fried. The fact that Laurance Sensei was also a colleague at Berlitz had its advantages. It gave me the opportunity to grab his ear away from the honbu dojo and talk outside of the Sensei-Senshusei relationship. That evening I asked him, *'what would happen if I disposed of one of the Sewanin?'* Even though I was deadly serious, I think he thought I was kidding and, shaking his head, walked off with a smile on his face!

KNOW YOUR PLACE

We didn't need reminding of our place at the honbu. Our cleaning duties, including crawling around on the floor of the Sensei's locker room to pick up pubes with our fingers, was daily confirmation that we were the lowest form of life. We knew our place, but the Sewanin must have thought we'd forgotten. In Tuesday morning's meeting following the previous week's incident, Graham Sewanin gave a speech on ego and about knowing your place in the dojo. Malik Sewanin was also present but chose not to speak. It was the first time I'd seen him since we'd bumped heads, and I half wondered if Graham's message had hidden meaning. Was it really directed at Malik, but dressed up as meant for us? Malik eventually broke his silence to criticise our self-defence techniques. He told us that some of us were trying to be grappling champions, and that this wasn't on. Malik and Graham's messages seemed well-rehearsed. Although neither made direct eye contact, I couldn't help feeling that both Sewanin were speaking directly to me. I was the one who had gone head to head with Malik, and now Graham was reminding me to know my place. I was the one that applied a choke on Graham, and now Malik was reminding me that Jiu Jitsu was not something I should use in the dojo. The Sewanin had closed ranks. While they'd communicated their feedback to us all, it felt very personal indeed. After the day's training, it appeared Graham had more to get off his chest. He called us into the tearoom to deliver yet another speech. Graham was angry as Kambara had told the Sewanin to give Tachiki a chair. Chivalry wasn't dead, and seeing the female cop struggling in mitori geiko with a bad foot, Kambara had attempted to jump rank. Also, Inazaki had told Vic to tidy away some scrolls Noriki Sensei had been working on in the corridor outside Kancho's office. Graham Sewanin was usually so calm. It was funny seeing him get angry and, in the process, turn a bright shade of red. In case we were in any doubt, he closed his sermon with a strict reminder. *'Know your place in the dojo!'*

With Tuesday over, I'd mistakenly thought the issue with Malik Sewanin had been put to bed. It turned out, however, that I was wrong! On Wednesday morning I seriously considered walking out of the honbu dojo and never coming back. Paul Sensei drilled us on jiyu waza in the first class, and despite sticking to the basics and avoiding doing anything too fancy, all I could hear was Malik shouting in my ear. *'Zanshin, Simon...zanshin, zanshin, zanshin!'* *Zanshin* was an important concept in Aikido and other Japanese martial arts that I'd struggled to get my head around. Zanshin was both physical and mental. To display zanshin, after throwing someone, my body posture had to be directed towards my fallen opponent, and despite the throw being complete, my mind had to remain in a state of awareness. I had to remain connected to uke in both the physical and mental sense. It made sense, I guess, as uke's job was to get back to their feet and attack me again. If I was facing in the opposite direction or had switched off from the task in hand, then I wouldn't see it coming. As far as I was aware, my posture had been good, and my mind was very much in the moment. It hadn't wandered off to a more comfortable place or drifted back to thoughts of slumber earlier that morning, before I was routinely dragged out of bed by the requirement to be up at 5:20am. Why was Malik shouting? Things were feeling even more personal than they had yesterday. Like a prisoner who unwittingly catches the attention of a prison guard, I was now caught in Malik's sights, with no opportunity of escape. What he screamed or shouted really didn't matter. What mattered was that I'd caught his attention for all the wrong reasons, and with five months left to go, every day now had the potential to be miserable. I was caught between a rock and a hard place. Ignoring him might feel like the right thing to do, but if I didn't put up any resistance, what was to stop him carrying on? Fight back, which had gotten me into this mess in the first place, and matters were sure to get worse. For the moment I decided to grin and bear it. Maybe in time he'd get bored with me and find a new victim.

After Paul Sensei's class, Malik called me, along with Dror and Kambara, over to the far corner of the dojo and told us that if we didn't like the course we could leave. In my mind, the course wasn't something you ever liked; it was something you did. There was little enjoyment in the ascent of Everest, and I hoped I'd find satisfaction of some sort or another once it was done. There was an unanswered question at the back of my mind. *Why am I here?* I'd put my faith in discovering the answer once the course was over and trusted that I'd get a positive one to make the 11 months of hardship seem worthwhile. Malik continued, *'Kambara, your osu is too weak! Simon, you have no zanshin, and the toilets were dirty this morning!'* I wondered if things could get any worse. I was physically exhausted, mentally tired and now had the worst Sewanin on my back. I hoped there was some light at the end of the tunnel, and in the second class, a tiny chink shone through. Geoff was back from Canada. Visa secured; he was now free to stay in Japan for at least the next few months. His misfortune of having to leave the country, ironically so he could stay longer, had been my gain. I'd got to train with Clyde and found out that training with Clyde was a much easier and far more enjoyable experience. Murata Sensei took the second class, which usually meant a fair bit of standing around. His classes were always an opportunity to rest, but despite this, on his first day back, Geoff broke his little toe. It wasn't clear how he'd done it, and it wasn't long before rumours of a faked injury were circulating around the tearoom. The Sewanin believed him, and Geoff was back in mitori geiko for the foreseeable future. Despite my already difficult week, I could raise a smile knowing that Clyde and I would be paired together for as long as it took Geoff to recover. I didn't quite get it. A big toe was key to balance and posture in Aikido, but a little toe? Matt had trained with the discomfort of two ingrowing toenails he'd dug out with a blade, which served up so much pain that he had to hobble around the dojo on his heels. While I was definitely out of favour, Geoff for some reason, remained in. I wondered if it was the Canadian connection. Murray Sensei was also from Canada. Did Geoff have friends in high places that were looking out for his well-being? There was no point pondering. Geoff's benching was good for me, at least in the short run. On the negative side, the further he fell behind on the techniques, the more difficult he'd be to train with when he eventually got back on his foot!

SIT ON YOUR PAIN

As Thursday rolled in, the Sewanin seemed to be full of less than helpful advice. The message of the week had so far been to *'know your place'*, and now, ahead of another zagaku, we were set to receive more. In the morning meeting, we were told that under no circumstances would they tolerate us putting our hands down today. Dave looked horrified. He was a frequent hands-putter-down; it was the only way he could get through the pain. He wasn't alone. All of us had difficult zagaku days that made relieving some pressure critical to our survival. The Sewanin were clear with their instructions. *'Sit on your pain!'* There was to be no wriggling, no fidgeting and definitely no putting hands down.

Geoff disappeared off to hospital in the first class. His toe had taken a turn for the worse, and it was time to seek a professional opinion. Chino Sensei was in the building for the second class and put us through our paces on *kihon dosa renzoku* for just over an hour. I got the point of kihon dosa, failed to understand the reasoning behind sotai dosa, and the purpose behind kihon dosa renzoku was also a mystery to me. Kihon dosa renzoku was a slightly more complicated version of kihon dosa that was usually performed as a group. We knew we'd be performing at the upcoming Enbu and that kihon dosa renzoku was what the Senshusei usually did. From what I'd seen so far, it reminded me very much of synchronised swimming! Lined up in strict formation, we performed kihon dosa renzoku to the count. The challenge was remaining in sync, as any mistake would immediately be visible. As Chino drilled us, you could feel the tension in the air. We were all terrified of Chino Sensei, and this, coupled with the Sewanin's over eagerness to impress, made for a very uncomfortable environment. After Malik Sewanin's roasting yesterday, Kambara was once again on the ropes. He probably wished he'd taken up Malik's invitation to leave the course, as this time his oppressor was Chino. Chino Sensei told Kambara in no uncertain terms that his kihon dosa *'lacked spirit'*. There was also an undercurrent to his message that seemed to tell Kambara to shape up or ship out! Kambara's suffering continued in zagaku, when Chino provided condescending feedback on his reflection. There was no reprieve for him, and I observed that the Japanese really enjoyed kicking a man while he was down. They did it in Pride with soccer kicks, and now in the dojo, Kambara was getting kicked in the head by the severest of tongue-lashings. Temporarily, I was out of the spotlight. Thanks in part to Geoff's absence, we all got through zagaku without putting our hands down. For once we'd listened to the Sewanin and followed instructions.

Geoff was back for Friday's classes and gave an hilarious description of himself – a description that was likely to stick with him much longer than he'd intended. Standing in mitori geiko because of his lower limb injury, Geoff had found himself in a more comfortable position but still wasn't satisfied. After Chino's kindness in giving me a chair, Geoff expected the same but wasn't so lucky. As we stepped out of the dojo after the second class, he told me, *'I felt like a flagpole, stood on one leg for an hour and a half'*. Geoff had compared himself to a flagpole, and I couldn't stop laughing! Chino Sensei still had the bit between his teeth for Kambara. Like a dog with a bone, he'd further humiliated our fellow Senshusei by calling him to the front of the class to perform *shido ho*. Shido ho translated into English as *teaching*. The Sensei were getting us familiar with this now, even though the official teaching phase of the course would be Dai Yon. Kambara lacked confidence in his understanding of the technique he'd been given and also in his delivery. Chino ripped into him yet again! Even my basic level of understanding caught the meaning. Kambara was not up to standard, and Chino wasn't happy.

The week was almost done, and with only Saturday to get through, all of our sights were firmly set on 1pm. It was the last day of September, and by my quick calculations on the way to the honbu, this meant there were now only five months or a more palatable 19 weeks of training left. We were six months deep into Senshusei, and now, past the halfway point, the end was starting to seem like a real possibility. When I arrived at the dojo, I found Malik Sewanin in the locker room. The tension between us seemed to have calmed, and he told me he might have to start missing Saturday training due to other commitments. I faked a look of disappointment while secretly cheering inside. Graham was rarely in on a Saturday, and now with no Malik pending, Saturday would become a no-Sewanin day.

In the second class, Sonoda Sensei put us through a now-all-too-familiar rendition of kihon dosa renzoku before turning his attention to self-defence. He invited Malik Sewanin to get up and teach some techniques, and much to my surprise, Malik selected me as his uke. I wasn't clear why, but I suspected this would be an opportunity for him to exert his dominance and wreak revenge for our jiyu waza session. On the one hand, Graham's instruction to know my place echoed through my ears, but on the other, this was self-defence, and any attacker on the street would be unlikely to have good ukemi. I didn't want Malik to get the upper hand. The thought of this took me back to boarding school and was worse than any punishment the Sewanin could dish out. It was being bullied that had sparked my interest in martial arts, and I would not let myself be on the receiving end again. I was shocked. Malik went easy, and the renewed tension I'd expected never showed up. Perhaps the wounds of battle had healed, and we'd reached a fragile truce, at least for now? I really enjoyed the class, although I wasn't sure Clyde had. Self-defence was my thing and a rare opportunity to mix in a bit of Muay Thai and Jiu Jitsu when the Sensei or Sewanin weren't looking. Clyde was on the receiving end and seemed to take things quite literally on the chin, safe in the knowledge that my intent was not malicious. While we were sweeping up after class Ronen explained that Yoshinkan's self-defence techniques weren't actually that effective. A qualified instructor in Krav Maga, he should know. I didn't disagree and told Ronen, *'I'm not sure why I'm doing it!'*

As the week's Shinkoku, there was still the bowing and scraping ceremony to get through before I could escape for the day. Malik had left early, so there was no Sewanin present to exert an added level of pressure to get things right. I'd been left to fly solo! As the others scurried about, doing a final tidy and check of their cleaning stations, I wrote up the Shinkoku diary in the tearoom before heading off to Jiu Jitsu with Ronen and Clyde. With self-defence at the forefront of my mind, I did well in sparring and submitted a fellow blue belt with a 'can opener', which, in true Dave style, involved cranking his neck. I was pulled up for using an illegal move. I'd clearly been watching too much MMA! Divine retribution was never far away, and my illegal neck crank was rewarded with an injury of my own. Caught in an uncompromising position, I twisted my neck the wrong way and now would nurse an injury inflicted by my extracurricular training – training the honbu explicitly banned. Ice was needed, and I headed home to apply some, hoping it would do the trick. If it didn't, I would have some serious explaining to do on Tuesday!

WHERE ARE THEY?

October had finally arrived. In between the intense heat of summer and freezing cold of winter, the temperature was cooler and made for a pleasant backdrop to the relentless training. In the morning meeting, Malik Sewanin once again brought up the subject of self-defence. *'Remember this week that none of you are Gracie Jiu Jitsu experts, so don't grapple!'* In the first class, Higa Sensei, aka Mr Precise, arrived on the mats and positioned himself perfectly under the shomen. After a perfect bow and a precise call to positions, it was kamae as usual. Today's kamae practice was short-lived and replaced by an exercise that would have sat better in a Murata Sensei class. I'd seen Higa Sensei practice this on his own many times before and had always wondered what the hell he was doing. I was now about to find out. He told us to stand with our feet shoulder width apart with palms turned up to the ceiling. We were to relax and focus our energy on our centre. *What a pointless waste of time*, I thought to myself, only to be interrupted by Higa's explanation. Surprise, surprise, his exercise was supposed to improve internal kamae. I'd been tortured with external kamae and now was disappointed to discover there was an internal version, too!

As usual, the first break was tight on time because of Shinkoku. I went to the toilet near the end as I normally did and came out to find everywhere unusually quiet. There was no one in the tearoom and my mind frantically raced to try to work out where everyone could be. *Where are they?* I thought to myself as a surge of adrenalin raced through my body, a clue I was entering panic mode. I ran to the door of the dojo and to my horror saw everyone, including the Sewanin, lined up in seiza awaiting the Sensei who would be teaching the second class. I was not the Sensei and had no business being late. They had left a space for me, and I took it as quickly as I could. Malik Sewanin turned and glared down the line. I ignored him but was certain his look meant he'd be dishing out some form of punishment later on. In the last class, Takashima Sensei ran us through the finer details of ikajo, nikajo and sankajo. It was a good class, and I enjoyed getting some Aikido secrets directly from Yoshinkan's resident wizard. I thought Malik had forgotten about my tardiness, but at the end of the class, he called me over to the corner of the dojo, alone. I was convinced the time for my punishment had arrived. Being late was inexcusable, and surely the Sewanin wouldn't let the opportunity pass to make an example of me. It turned out I was wrong.

Malik had been watching The Wizard weave his spells with a keen interest and had called me over to try out his nikajo. He struggled to use his second control to drop me to my knee, but I went down anyway. It was easier to play his game than to fight it. I played good uke, even though I was probably doing him an injustice by giving him false confidence in his application of a technique that hadn't fully worked.

On the train home, I picked up a text from Matt, which caused me to forget where I was and burst out laughing. In his philosophical message he summed up how he was feeling about the course. As I read it to myself, Matt's voice played back in my head. *'It reminds me of my Dad driving. When he gets lost, he won't admit it and just carries on. He's too proud! The sensible thing is to stop, turn around and go in the right direction. Think we should have turned around a long time ago mate!'* Matt was probably right. We were very lost. I seemed to have lost sight of my reason for signing up to the course. I was too proud to quit and determined to get to the end, even though turning around was probably the most sensible thing to do.

Malik Sewanin may have brushed my lateness under the carpet, but Graham Sewanin wasn't prepared to do the same. In Wednesday's morning meeting he quizzed me in what was becoming a more frequent angry tone. *'Why didn't you apologise for being late?'* I for one thought I had, and *'osu'* was my only response. Dror also got it in the neck. As the prior week's Shinkoku, he was responsible for making sure all of us were in the right place at the right time, and *'osu'* was his response, too! 'The big O' was in the building, and that meant in the third class, Oyamada Sensei would test our mental resolve once again. The only break from the monotony was towards the end when we practiced throws from various wrist, elbow, chest and shoulder grabs. Clyde and I were struggling to make anything work, and Oyamada wandered over to provide direction. He motioned for me to grab his chest and moved his body sharply with the aim of controlling my mass to throw me over. Nothing happened. My balance wasn't broken. The Sewanin were close by, and in the split second between him applying his technique and nothing happening, I reminded myself to know my place. I flipped in the air like a good uke and slapping the tatami landed on my side at Oyamada's feet. It must have looked odd – a visible manifestation of the time delay I sometimes got on a phone call home. This was the nonsense I couldn't bear. It made no sense to kid yourself that your Aikido worked if it didn't. I understood that as the teacher, Oyamada would want to save face. However, any encouraged deception that his application of a technique had worked when it really hadn't set a dangerous precedent that wasn't helpful to the reputation of Aikido. I knew Aikido worked in the right hands. Chino Sensei would have toppled me, and I'd have had no say in the matter. Ukemi when faced with Chino was there to ensure your survival. In sharp contrast, ukemi in the face of Oyamada had today been used to make him look good.

BATTLEFIELD

The rain started at the end of the week and showed no signs of stopping. Japan was a country of extremes, and the force and volume of water resembled the monsoon showers I'd experienced during my travels in Thailand. The smell in the locker room was damp – wet clothes from the rain and wet dogi soaked in sweat. A dark grey colour enveloped the sky, and the lights in the dojo seemed to dim sympathetically in response. The grey summed up my mood and the mood amongst the Senshusei.

Clyde had injured his hip and successfully requested mitori geiko. With Geoff still out of action, I was being passed from pillar to post, and with no spare Senshusei, I was paired with the Sewanin. Graham Sewanin told us in the morning meeting that self-defence was all about atemi; striking was something I understood. Kru Tony had taught me to punch properly, and now the Sewanin appeared to be giving me the green light to use my striking skills the next time self-defence training was on the cards. I didn't have to wait long. In Friday morning's second class, Chino Sensei brought a smile to my face with the announcement we'd be practicing just that. I was dying to see him demonstrate self-defence techniques, but unfortunately, he didn't oblige. I suspected that his understanding and application of Aikido was self-defence enough, and as an Aikido purist, this is what he would use on any unwitting assailant who was stupid enough to attack him in the street. We'd be doing *kakari geiko*, which translated as *group training*. When it came to self-defence this meant continuous attack. This sounded good to me and I couldn't wait to get started. We lined up in rows of four. One shite who would fend off attacks that would arrive from three uke aggressors. And so, the fiasco began. As bodies lurched left and right to the sound of screams and shouts the scene resembled a medieval battlefield. It was disorganised chaos, and Chino Sensei couldn't disguise his feelings. He grabbed his stomach to ease the pain from laughing so hard! I was in a world of my own, throwing knees, elbows and anything else I knew to incapacitate my opponents. This caught Graham Sewanin's attention, who shouted across the dojo, *'Simon, use Aikido, not Muay Thai!'* Alongside me, Ronen was in just as much trouble. Graham screamed, *'don't use other martial arts!'* Moments after starting, Ronen's line already needed replenishment. He wasn't even waiting for uke to attack! The best defence is usually offence and utilising his Krav

Maga skills, in a flurry of grabs, head-butts, knees and throws, by the time his attackers knew what had hit them it was already too late. The cops looked in a state of shock. None of their previous training had prepared them for a combined British and Israeli assault!

Dave found himself opposite Tsuzuku, one of the smaller cops and probably the best at Aikido. Dave had already proven his ability to inflict injury without knowing what he was doing, and today was another opportunity to showcase his skills. Dave had been training regularly at Axis Jiu Jitsu with me and some of the other Senshusei, and as I was about to witness, a little knowledge could be dangerous. Having thrown Tsuzuku to the ground, Dave jumped on top. To quote Dave's retelling of the story later in the tearoom – *'I pushed him down, jumped on his back and got my hooks in. I don't know what happened!'* In Jiu Jitsu terminology this meant that Dave had clambered onto Tsuzuku's back and locked both of his legs around Tsuzuku's lower body to control his hips and legs. With no experience of Jiu Jitsu or what to do in this situation, Tsuzuku had tried to stand up. In doing so, with Dave still controlling his lower body, he'd twisted his knee. Tsuzuku screamed in pain. A chilling scream which brought everyone to a standstill and the class to an abrupt pause. Tsuzuku's knee was badly contorted, and he was carried out of the dojo and taken directly to hospital. He reappeared a couple of hours later, hobbling into the honbu on crutches. He'd been well and truly 'Daved', and now he would be out of action for at least six weeks. I'd no idea what this meant for his career or his ability to pass the course, but it didn't look good. Ronen, who had never forgotten his brush with Dave at Axis, was the first to criticise him for his dangerous play. We all felt the same and ribbed Dave for his stupidity. Matt, who had already got the measure of him, was especially critical. *'Dave, you're dangerous! No, wait...you're crazy...Crazy Dave!'* And with Matt's pronouncement, we christened Dave with a new name. 'Crazy Dave' was born! Tsuzuku was popular with the cops and the international Senshusei. He was friendly and always seemed to have a smile on his face. In one moment of madness, Crazy Dave had wiped this smile, and the poor guy's future now hung in the balance. Crazy Dave had been tried in the tearoom court of the Senshusei and now felt very guilty indeed!

Malik and Graham Sewanin weren't happy, and rightly so. The incident had happened in Chino Sensei's class, the class that nobody wanted anything bad to happen in. Dave's actions and Tsuzuku's injury would reflect poorly on the Sewanin and the honbu dojo itself. The honbu had a long association with the police ever since the days of Kancho Shioda. This relationship was now potentially compromised, and I imagined Inoue Kancho would have to eat his fair share of humble pie at his next meeting with the police's top brass. Graham Sewanin laid into us. *'No more grappling and no more punching will be tolerated!'* On the mats moving forwards, and specifically with regard to self-defence, we were to use Aikido and Aikido only. This seemed to contradict the message that atemi was the key to self-defence that had been put forward by the same Sewanin earlier in the day. Graham Sewanin looked to have changed his tune, and as a result, we'd need to change ours, too. Self-defence in that moment lost its future appeal. It would now be a lot less interesting, and there was no one to blame but Dave.

It was still raining heavily when I left the honbu dojo. This wasn't the rain I knew back in the UK; this was torrential rain, Japanese style. My clothes were still damp from the morning trip in, and, not wanting to get any wetter, I bought an umbrella from FamilyMart. No sooner had I put it up, than it was ripped inside out by a gust of wind. That seemed to sum up my day. It had started so well but was then taken sharply in an altogether different direction by Dave's reckless behaviour. I headed off to my Japanese class and then caught the train home for a rest. Later that afternoon I popped out to Musashi Koyama's shopping arcade to buy some food, and with the downpour still raging, I decided I'd risk another umbrella. No sooner had I got my second purchase out of the shop than it had blown inside out. I gave any thought of shelter up as a bad job and arrived back at my apartment drenched!

DON'T YANK UKE!

A week into October, Clyde and Geoff were both still injured. Paired with the Sewanin, in reality, meant I spent most of my time with Malik. There was no doubting his extensive knowledge of the intricacies of the Aikido techniques we practiced repeatedly. He'd been Senshusei the year before, and covering everything again, and so soon, meant both he and Graham knew their stuff. This should have made training with Malik Sewanin a breeze. There wasn't the immovability of Geoff or the hesitancy of Clyde, but there was another difficulty that I found even harder to handle. If I went hard with my techniques, he didn't like it and thought I was making a statement. When I went too soft, that was no good, either, as it just wasn't Senshusei. It was like trying to serve two masters with opposing views. No matter what I did, I couldn't get things right! In Murray Sensei's class, Geoff and Clyde were instructed to call out techniques from mitori geiko. This made life even more difficult for me with Malik, as Geoff messed up in naming more of the techniques than he got right. With no clear instruction, it was only a matter of time before Geoff's incompetency infected those on the mats, and one by one, the whole class seemed to fall apart. A good orchestra needs a good conductor, and without one, no matter how good any of us were at playing the flute, trumpet or oboe, we were never likely to be in tune with the string and percussion sections. To pull things back into line, for the final 30 minutes of the class, Murray Sensei prescribed shido ho. If we couldn't perform techniques properly, we might as well teach them!

A day with double Sonoda Sensei was a day that thankfully didn't happen too often, but when it did, it was always full of surprises. In the second class we ran through kihon dosa renzoku, which was a welcome break from working one on one with Malik. In the last class, and our second helping of Sonoda, he decided we needed to improve our flexibility and instructed us all to sit on the tatami to stretch our legs. The course was notorious for making us hold static and uncomfortable positions for extended periods of time, which only tightened my muscles and undid all the flexibility improvements I'd made from my Muay Thai training. Now, sitting down to let the blood flow freely around our lower limbs, where it naturally wanted to go, felt too good to be true. Sonoda was suddenly our favourite Sensei, but as with everything, all good things must come to an end. As we moved from lower body stretches to focus on our upper, Sonoda Sensei told us to sit in seiza. *What, sit in seiza, after we've just stretched out?* I thought to myself. *What kind of madness is this?* It was like doing a warm-up, only to then stop for ten minutes to cool down, before starting the vigorous exercise you'd warmed up to prepare for in the first place. It made no sense. The secondary action defeated the primary purpose, and once again I was left flabbergasted by some of the ancient training methods the honbu still employed. For the remaining time, Sonoda Sensei announced that we'd be practicing our teaching skills – not in our pairs privately, as we usually did, but instead each of us in our pairs taking on the role of Sensei to teach the whole class. As none of us really had any teaching skills and had limited knowledge of what we were teaching, things were about to get interesting. What's more, our teaching style, or lack of it, and knowledge, what there was of it, would be on public display for all to see.

Temporarily paired with Boaz, we volunteered to go up first to teach *shomen uchi ikajo osae ichi*. Boaz as uke would strike me on the top of my head using his right arm like a sword blade. In return, as shite, I would intercept his arm, and gripping his right elbow turn him away from me, to then control him smoothly down to the tatami. It sounded simple enough. As one of the first techniques we'd covered on the course, Boaz and I had already done it a thousand times. With any recipe, though, *too many cooks spoil the broth*, and Sonoda Sensei mixed things up by adding his own sprinkle of special sauce. As shite it was easy for me to teach the whole thing, but Sonoda's added ingredient required that Boaz and I alternate the role of instructor after each individual stage of the technique. This caused massive confusion, and while both of us knew the technique inside out, which is why we'd picked it, neither of us was clear on who should be doing what and when. To make things more comical, Boaz took on the role of television host. *'Ikajo is...grip uke here...now let's take a closer look!'* He sounded more Saturday night TV than serious Sensei, and everyone tried to stop themselves from bursting out in fits of laughter. The highlight was, however, yet to come! Boaz and I had been the appetiser to a main course served up in the form of Matt and Dave. Picking another shomen uchi technique was a safer bet than taking on some of the more complicated techniques that we'd covered as part of Dai San, but they still cocked up the whole thing. Dave seemed to make things up as he went along, and his description of why and how to perform certain elements of *sankajo osae ni* had us all choking on uncontrollable laughter in a doomed effort to keep it in. *'Don't yank uke...stroke him instead!'* Dave's technique involved stroking uke? This was too much for any of us to bear. I felt like I was about to collapse in a fit of giggles, and as I did my best to contain it, tears rolled down my cheeks. I'm sure Dave hadn't meant to be humorous. Given past performances, though, everything Dave did seemed to be unintentionally funny or extremely dangerous, with nothing much in between. Crazy Dave wasn't done yet. *'On the osae...uke's arm will feel hard!'* The sexual innuendo was overpowering. Dave had to be stopped before the whole class erupted into chaos. Sonoda called a halt, and we finished up with a few rounds of self-defence. Sonoda picked me as uke and put my wrist in a gooseneck. It was massively painful. I was impressed! What a day, and no doubt the funniest so far. I felt exhausted – not, for once, from the training, but from all the laughing I'd done!

GOING NUCLEAR

The weekend arrived and, with it, a rare night out that I hadn't made an excuse to duck out of because I was too tired. The venue was an izakaya in Shibuya, and the occasion was Amanda's leaving party. Amanda, a fellow English teacher, was leaving the Aoyama office. It would have been rude not to turn up, so I made the effort. I met Paul and Naoko, two other Berlitz colleagues outside Shibuya Station, and made the short walk with them to meet up with everyone else. I got a dreadful seat opposite this big guy who seemed to be a hanger-on and didn't appear to work for Berlitz. He must

207

have known someone there, someone who had decided to ditch him, and now he was on my watch for the rest of the evening. My social skills had taken a turn for the worse since I started the course. Outside the brotherhood of Senshusei, I had little time for anyone else. I was always too tired for small talk, and no one really got why I was in Japan or what I was going through. I made polite chit-chat. *'Where are you from? What are you doing in Japan?'* It was the standard questioning gaijin rolled out when they met one another for the first time. The conversation only picked up when the big guy let it slip that he trained at Axis Jiu Jitsu. Perhaps we had something in common after all?

Laurance, who was sat at the far end of the table, came over and chatted to me about the course. It was still weird seeing him at Berlitz or at a social gathering, where he wasn't shouting and screaming at me. Out of his dogi he was a nice guy, but I remained wary about his line of questioning and cautious with what I revealed. Laurance always wanted to know what was going on and took tonight as the opportunity to suggest that Malik's days might be numbered. He'd somehow found out about the antics in Iwama, albeit six months late. He wasn't happy about the stripping down to our underwear and said he was going to tell Murray Sensei. While it was no secret that I didn't have the best relationship with Malik Sewanin, I had no desire to see him kicked out of the honbu. His early departure would have dialled down the hardship that we were all experiencing on the course but also reduced what it would mean to complete it. On the ascent to the summit of Everest, Malik was the ice, wind and storms sent to test even the most experienced of climbers. Harsh conditions were character building and would make the course's ultimate completion mean so much more. Also, if they kicked Malik out of the dojo, there would be a witch hunt, no doubt carried out by Graham Sewanin and some of the international Sensei. If Laurance knew what went on at Iwama, this meant there had to be a leak in the Senshusei camp. I didn't imagine Malik or Graham would have been the source of Laurance's information. Nobody liked a grass, and with the leak clearly pointing at one of the Senshusei, even with Malik gone, our lives could potentially be made even more miserable. I'd probably had the most run-ins with Malik, so if anyone had a motivation to see him ejected, it was probably me. In any crime drama I'd ever watched, the investigating officers looked to identify a motive. I had plenty of motive, and if no other culprit came forward voluntarily, the finger would probably be pointed at me. Guilty until proven innocent would be the way of things, and I'd be tarred with the brush of distrust. Even though I was innocent, in the eyes of the Sensei and remaining Sewanin, I'd be the one who grassed, I'd be the guilty party, and

I'd be the one they'd make pay! It was a sticky spot to be in, and Laurance was about to open one hell of a can of worms. Malik was a known quantity. What happened if he went was not. Better the devil you know. I hoped Laurance buried his secret, but only time would tell.

The next morning, I woke up with a bad headache. I really didn't want a hangover, and especially not the Japanese version of *futskayoi*. It was Monday, and two days drunk would see me nursing the excesses of Sunday night at the honbu, something I couldn't afford to happen. I had an urge to immerse myself in Japanese tradition and thought the experience of attending an *ikebana* exhibition might calm my nerves about the whole Laurance-Malik issue. *Flower arranging* wasn't really my thing, but when in Japan and all that. I'd heard of *hanami*, the Japanese custom of *enjoying the transient beauty of flowers*, in particular *sakura* (cherry blossom), and found it had a calming effect on my otherwise chaotic life. Apparently, the Japanese were the best in the world at ikebana, so I decided to go and find out what all the fuss was about. It turned out I was right; it was most definitely not my thing, but my trip had achieved its purpose. It had taken my mind off the honbu for a while and the prospect of the trouble tomorrow might bring. At night I did my best to relax and did the usual jobs around the apartment to prepare for the week ahead. On most of the TV channels there were news reports dedicated to a situation developing in North Korea. Near Japan, North Korea posed a constant threat. The regime had nuclear capability, and the worrying reports coming through every channel were about North Korea's testing of its latest nuclear bomb. I didn't understand all the Japanese so texted Dad back in the UK. He replied to say it was all over British TV, too. North Korea appeared to be going nuclear, and living in Japan, I was right in the firing line! I went to bed early, still nursing a bad headache, and drifted off to sleep, more than a little concerned by what I'd seen on the television. Although North Korea was a much bigger concern, if Laurance told Murray Sensei about Malik at Iwama, things at the honbu would almost certainly go nuclear, too!

HEADLESS CHICKENS

Everything was building up to the 51st All Japan Enbu, which was scheduled to take place on Saturday, 28 October 2006. This meant that for the next few weeks, the Senshusei would run around like headless chickens getting everything prepared, including our own demonstration. The All Japan Enbu was the annual event that showcased the very best of Aikido and the world's best instructors. Practitioners travelled from far and wide to make the trip to

Tokyo, and the influx of international visitors, who would be performing or just attending, usually took an interest in the current year's Senshusei.

We'd been practicing kihon dosa renzoku for the past few weeks, but Tuesday, 10 October 2006, was the first day we realised what a big day the All Japan Enbu would be. The final class of the day ended early. A meeting was scheduled with Ito Sensei, which turned out to be a pointless one. Conducted in Japanese to a predominantly English audience and with no translation, we shouted *'osu'* at natural breaks and to fill in gaps. Only Clyde, Kambara and Inazaki knew what was going on, so our collective *'osu'* was more a display of willingness than an acknowledgement of understanding. With Clyde's post-meeting help, we gathered that Dave and I had been allocated the job of sticking up the team names for the kihon waza competition. We were to share this responsibility with Inazaki and Kambara, which was a relief to me. Anyone sharing anything with Dave previously had come a cropper, and there was safety in numbers, particularly when those numbers were Japanese. From what we'd gathered, the remaining Senshusei would provide security around the perimeter of the mats throughout the day's proceedings. This meant being on public display all day, the requirement to stand to attention all day, and being at the beck and call throughout the day of anyone with more authority, which was everyone. At least organising the competition would allow some freedom of movement and provided a degree of power. The trade was a higher level of responsibility. We couldn't afford to mess things up!

Robert, who'd filmed my altercation with Malik, was back in town to complete the *Fight! Japan* episode about my life in Tokyo. He'd got plenty of footage of me in the honbu and now wanted to capture something of my everyday life. I'd cleared the filming with Peter, my boss at Berlitz, and arrangements had been made to rope in a suitable student. Berlitz were keen to get the publicity and in return agreed to give away a free lesson as an incentive to the willing volunteer who would join me on camera. I'd never met the student before, so to begin with, the lesson felt clunky. With new students there was always a feeling-out process as they got to know me, and I got to understand the difference between what they thought they knew and what they actually knew. Robert only needed a few minutes of footage to edit down to the appropriate length and managed to capture a few scenes with me looking like I knew what I was talking about and the student seeming happy. *If only my life at the honbu could be edited down to the best bits,* I thought to myself on the train home. Still, it was supposedly about the journey. The good and the bad times combined to make the experience what it was and what it needed to be.

Chino called his own meeting on the All Japan Enbu, and as the more senior Sensei, whatever he said would trump Ito. Again, the meeting was conducted in Japanese, but I think it was pitched primarily at the cops, who we now learned would join us in our performance. After a while he escorted the cops out of the dojo and into the privacy of their own room. I didn't know why, but in the confines of the sho dojo, I didn't envy their situation. Trapped in a small cage with a tiger was not a safe place to be! Left at the mercy of Malik and Graham, we practiced the set routine repeatedly. By now we'd all had enough. I hadn't enrolled on the course with this in mind, but for the last few weeks and undoubtedly the next few to come, the kihon dosa renzoku was set to dominate. To add a bit of variety, Malik instructed Geoff, who was still in mitori geiko with his bad toe, to call the count. He made such a poor job of it that Malik took the baton back. As a reward, at the end of the class Geoff was given press-ups by the Sewanin, which was possibly a course first – the first time a Senshusei had been punished whilst in mitori geiko!

GEOFF VERSUS KANCHO

Geoff was in trouble again before the day was out. In zagaku he was called upon to read out his hansei and habit. I'd told him ahead of time that he needed to add the word *shukan* into his statement, which was the word for *habit*. Geoff ignored my advice and reassured me that all would be fine. *It's his funeral,* I thought as I left him in the tearoom. I hoped it wouldn't be, but Geoff thought he knew best. As predicted, during zagaku, Kancho hadn't realised that Geoff had delivered his reflection and habit as one. *'Shukan!'* Kancho screamed at the top of his voice. Geoff decided the best way to combat Kancho's confusion was to add more confusion into the mix. He fought confusion with confusion by repeating his reflection and habit, exactly as he had just done. Had it worked? There was a moment's pause. *'Shukan!'* Kancho screamed for the second time. All eyes were on Geoff. What would he do next? What could he do next? I'd heard of a Mexican standoff, and now the Japanese version was playing out right before my eyes. A Mexican standoff was the right description. We were witnessing a confrontation where neither side had a strategy to achieve outright victory. Geoff in his mind had delivered his habit, and Kancho hadn't heard it. Kancho, on the other hand, having not heard the word for habit in Geoff's garble, was adamant that Geoff had only shared his reflection. Geoff paused. He paused some more and then went right back to first principles. He read out what he'd already said twice before in Japanese, but this time in English. Inoue Kancho looked bemused, everyone was confused, and, unsure of where to go next, Kancho moved on.

Geoff was victorious in battle. He'd stuck to his guns and got one over on Kancho. He'd done this in full view of all the Sensei and both Sewanin. Did Geoff have more guts than we'd given him credit for, or was it stupidity that had won the day? Kancho had probably just heard enough. Geoff's rambling because of his decision not to take my advice had cost us dearly. Zagaku lasted 40 minutes. This was longer than the normal 30 minutes we were still trying to get used to. Kancho, in fact, was the victor. He had the power to say when zagaku finished. Geoff had delayed the end for us all, and I suspected Kancho had talked longer just to even the score!

KILLING IN THE NAME

I'd always been superstitious, and Friday the 13th brought with it an increased level of fear that something bad might happen. To kick things off, Matt and Boaz joined Geoff and Clyde in mitori geiko. The previous day, Laurance Sensei had ordered us to flip over mats stacked high and then to practice our ukemi on the wooden floor at the entrance to the dojo. The duo of Geoff and Clyde had become a quartet overnight. Matt had damaged his hip and Boaz his shoulder. If things carried on the way they seemed to be going, there'd soon be more Senshusei watching than training. With the Enbu on the horizon, it was imperative that everyone got back to fitness as soon as possible. Kihon dosa renzoku was a group exercise, and coordinating with everyone else, the cops included, was no easy task. Repetition was the only way, and there was little hope of anyone slotting in at the last minute without standing out.

Boaz had filled out his mitori geiko form in such a way that the Sewanin were concerned. They took it to the office and consulted those of more senior rank to establish the best way forward. Boaz's narrative seemed to hint at a potential claim against the honbu dojo. I hadn't heard of any previous Senshusei threatening litigation, but from the tone of his statement, Boaz seemed to be suggesting that owing to Laurance Sensei's arguably dangerous class, he'd found himself in his current predicament through no fault of his own. Where there's a blame there's a claim! Injury was part and parcel of the course, and any suggestion that Boaz might be in the mind to sue seemed to go against the whole spirit of Senshusei. The Sewanin, having taken advice, held Boaz in the dojo after the first class was over. No one knew what was said, but Boaz was soon back in the tearoom rewording his form. Boaz probably didn't have much of a case. Before the start of the course we'd all been given a document. Written in both Japanese and English it stated that no medical bills, whatsoever, were covered by the dojo. In addition, if you were injured or died during class your family couldn't sue. There was a high risk of injury due to the intensity of Senshusei training. If we got hurt, we were on our own! I'd planned ahead. In agreement with my Dad, I'd set up an Enduring Power of Attorney. If something happened to me on or off the mats, he had full legal authority to handle all of my affairs. If the honbu killed me or incapacitated me in some way, so that I was no longer compos mentis, I knew I could trust my Dad to take care of things.

In Murata Sensei's class, he related Aikido to music. *This could be interesting,* I thought to myself. He compared Aikido to Boxing, and in his words, *'while Boxing is rock music, Aikido is a soft melody, almost silent music'*. With a mind to take Murata's analogy a step too far, we continued the debate in the tearoom once the class was over. The general consensus was that I was more Rage Against the Machine, while Dave was definitely Right Said Fred! *Killing in the Name* was on my iPod playlist, and as our debate raged on, the lyrics played out in my head. *Fuck you, I won't do what you tell me! Fuck you, I won't do what you tell me! Fuck you, I won't do what you tell me!* Was this the anti-Sewanin anthem I'd been searching for? The lyrics seemed to fit the bill almost too perfectly.

It was a fun end to the day, and before we were released for the weekend, there was a very humorous incident involving Kanazawa Sensei. Kanazawa was an interesting character. For one, he was one of the friendliest of the Sensei; in fact, at times it felt like he was more one of us than them. For two, away from the honbu, he was a private detective. I had images of him following his target in a long trench coat and wide-brimmed hat, a master of disguise and an international man of mystery. If there was an opening for a Japanese James Bond, he'd be in with a shot! On Saturday morning, Kanazawa Sensei turned up to take the first class. There was nothing special about this class, just more kihon dosa renzoku to prepare for the All Japan Enbu. By now I could probably have done this in my sleep. Life in the dojo was getting tedious and any distraction was a welcome one. Any opportunity to lighten the mood was received with open arms. Kanazawa was about to provide just that. After class he wandered into the tearoom with what looked like a magazine tucked under his arm. It was rare for any of the Sensei to come into the tearoom, and when they did, whatever we were doing had to stop. As Kanazawa entered, we jumped to attention, bowed and shouted the customary *'osu!'* We had no idea what he wanted, but he had a smile on his face – a clue that whatever he had to say wasn't bad news. He took the magazine from under his arm and put it down on the table, ushering us all to crowd around and take a look. *Trendy* was the name of the publication, and flicking through the pages to the one he'd marked for us to see, we were all shocked to find a full-page spread featuring Kanazawa Sensei himself. Suited and booted, he looked sharp adorning one of the inside pages of what looked to be a Japanese fashion magazine. As we looked at the page, Kanazawa Sensei looked over our shoulders and beamed with pride. As we digested what he'd revealed, smirks of amusement rippled from one Senshusei to another. While only Kambara and Inazaki could read the Japanese, the product image gave the game away. The product Kanazawa Sensei appeared to be advertising was in fact a cure for baldness!

PICK YOUR SWORD

Halfway through October meant 10 weeks until Christmas, and during the Christmas break from training, I planned to go home – not home to Musashi Koyama, but back home to the UK. I was ambivalent about the whole idea. I wanted to see Mum and Dad and had already missed Dad's 69th birthday at the end of September. Some home comforts would be nice, too, and a break from the endless rice and noodles. On the flip side, I'd become hardened by my time in Japan, and the last thing I wanted was to go soft back in the bosom of my family home, the home I'd grown up in. I'd hoped to catch a flight with British Airways on 23 December to arrive back home for Christmas, but unfortunately everything was fully booked. It was looking like a Boxing Day return, which would mean Christmas in a country that didn't really celebrate Christmas. Before I could make the long flight back, there was work to be done, and life at the honbu went on as normal. It wasn't all work, rest and no play, though. At the weekend, if I had the energy and time, there was a chance for exploration.

The Tsukiji fish market was a place I'd read about and was a recommended tourist attraction for anyone visiting Tokyo. Despite my visit to the Parasitological Museum, I'd acquired a taste for *sushi* and *sashimi*. The two were often confused. Back in the UK, sushi was a term regularly used to describe raw fish, but I'd learnt since my arrival in Japan that sushi was rice accompanied by seafood, vegetables or occasionally fruit. Sashimi was in fact the correct term for raw fish or meat, served up on its own. Tsukiji, the largest wholesale fish and seafood market in the world, was a train journey out of central Tokyo. While London had Billingsgate, it was nowhere near the scale and magnitude of Tsukiji. It was an early start – up at 4am and on the train by 4:35am. Like the Senshusei the market did its business before the sun came up, and I didn't want to miss it. Tsukiji was a hive of activity. All types and varieties of fish were on display, and traders shouted and screamed their orders at one another. Transportation vehicles, which were a cross between a scooter and a car, buzzed around and, on more than one occasion, nearly took me out. It resembled the organised chaos I'd experienced at the start of the course. People rushing here, people rushing there. But within the visible disorganisation was a living, breathing organism where everyone and everything knew their place and reason for being. Being up so early with time to myself was a refreshing change. Whatever I ended up doing after the course was over, if I could maintain the early starts, my productivity compared to the average man or woman would be through the roof.

Back at the honbu dojo and the start of another week, I found myself on bin duty. Tuesday mornings were always difficult, with the change of cleaning roster, and shock immersion back into the discipline and routine I'd done my best to escape on my two-day break. As I walked down the corridor past the pink phone, to my surprise, it rang. There was no one else around, so I did what I had to do and answered it. *'Ohayou gozaimasu, honbu dojo de gozaimasu, Simon Senshusei desu!'* Malik Sewanin was on the other end, and our previous telephone roles had been reversed. This time he was calling in sick and asked me to let Graham Sewanin know. I told Matt who didn't look surprised and explained that yesterday was 'Gaba Day'. Gaba was a rival English-language school to Berlitz with an interesting motto that it regularly used in its marketing campaigns on most of the subway trains across Tokyo. 'Man-to-man' was a confusing brand message. I was reliably informed they taught women, too! Gaba Day was downtime from the regular teaching schedule and involved lots of drinking. Had Malik called in with a hangover? While we waited for the morning meeting to begin, we took the mickey out of Dave. He'd gone out on Saturday night with Laurance Sensei, Graham Sewanin, Matt and Clyde to meet a group of girls that Laurance knew, one of whom Laurance was interested in. The *gokon*, which translated as *mixed meeting* was popular in Japan. A group of single men, a group of single women and a night out with romantic intent. The story went that for some reason Laurance had to leave early. After his departure, Dave had moved in on the girl Laurance liked. Typical Dave, he'd already sent one of the cops to hospital and had now advanced to stealing a Sensei's girlfriend!

In the first class we had Murray Sensei. Boaz was made to sit in seiza with his shoulder injury, and Geoff stood alongside. Both were still in mitori geiko. Geoff had been for an X-ray yesterday to find out that his little toe was still broken. The doctor had told him he'd be out for another three weeks. At this rate Geoff would miss half the course. I was dreading training with him again when he eventually made it back. Ahead of the second class a TV crew had set up in the dojo, and as we ran through kihon dosa renzoku for the umpteenth time, they looked to be filming. I found out later it was the Discovery Channel, a US television network that had made the trip to Tokyo; such was the international interest in the course. I was pretty excited. On the plane out to Japan I'd watched a documentary called *Go Warrior*. Created for the Discovery Channel; filmed in 2003, it featured many of the people I'd now met. Perhaps this was the follow-up, and, another documentary? The last class finished early. There was more All Japan Enbu work to do. The programmes for the event had arrived at the honbu. On close inspection by the office staff, a glaring error had been discovered, much to the annoyance and embarrassment of Inoue Kancho and the rest of the Sensei. The 2006 Enbu was the 51st, but the programmes displayed the number 50. With no time for a reprint, the honbu had got creative and thought on its feet. Stickers with the number 51 had been produced, and for the next 45 minutes, my job was to apply a sticker to each programme, one after another. I wondered who had made this cock-up. Someone's head would have rolled for making such a humongous mistake. I was glad it wasn't me. Sticking stickers turned out to be not that bad. I roped in a few of my fellow Senshusei, and we sat in the tearoom, chatting, while we got on with the job. It definitely beat an extra 45 minutes of Ito Sensei's class. My right knee was acting up, and it felt like a strange lump was developing inside the joint. Any opportunity to rest and take the weight off it, even for a moment, felt great.

Life in the dojo seemed to be getting less brutal but more boring. After Laurance Sensei's class, the one that had taken out both Matt and Boaz, the Sensei seemed keen to keep us fit, healthy and uninjured, at least until the Enbu was over. This meant less hajime geiko but more kihon dosa renzoku, which by now was boring the life out of all of us. Dave kept us entertained between classes and led a debate on what kind of sword would be best in a combat situation. It was like an enhanced game of 'rock-paper-scissors' where we each had to pick our sword and debate its merits against the other selections. Dave picked a fencing foil. I picked a Samurai sword. Confident in my choice of weapon, I told Dave, *'my Samurai sword would chop through your foil'*. Dave wasn't convinced. *'Maybe, but my foil is longer. I could thrust at you and stab you through the chest before your sword could reach me!'* Matt had the last word on the subject. *'Dave, you look more like a sword swallower than a sword fighter!'* Combat humour and debate were regularly on the tearoom agenda and brightened even the most boring of days.

BEYOND THE GRAVE

We'd now been given our places for the kihon dosa renzoku performance at the 51st All Japan Enbu. Takashima Sensei had shown us where to stand and carefully arranged us in height order to make everything look and feel balanced. I was happy with my position. I wasn't on the front row in direct line of sight of the Sensei we'd be performing in front of. Instead, I was tucked safely inside the group, which meant I had someone to watch in all directions, just in case I forgot any of the moves or my timing slipped. Our allocated positions didn't last long. Chida Sensei decided he could do a better job, and as Dojocho his arrangement trumped The Wizard's. Nobody questioned the rearrangement; nobody questioned anything at the honbu dojo if it came from a higher power. To my horror, my new position was in the far right corner, with nowhere to hide at the front. This meant I'd be the one everyone looked to in order to find their respective positions. I'd also have the job of calling the count and setting the pace for everyone else to follow! The news was even worse. Before we could begin our performance at the Enbu, we'd need to get from the warm-up area and onto the tatami, which would be positioned at the centre of the stadium. It wasn't as simple as walking. We were Senshusei, and we'd be marching. This wasn't to be just any march, either; it was a march I would now lead! Unfortunately, marching didn't appear to be something the international Senshusei were very good at. As we practiced marching around the perimeter of the dojo, Geoff commented from the sidelines, so only I could hear. *'You guys look like the Hitler Youth!'* It was inevitable that Geoff, with time on the bench, was slowly falling out of the group. Two days in mitori geiko had left me feeling like an outsider, so I had some sympathy for his situation. None of us really understood why a broken little toe was an impediment to training. Sure, it might have been painful, but pain wasn't a valid reason to take mitori geiko – just ask Matt! I told Malik in the locker room that I thought the Sewanin had given up on Geoff. While he didn't say yes, he didn't say no, and I suspected he was as fed up with Geoff as we were all becoming.

With my injured knee, marching was proving difficult, and I'd taken to applying an ice pack to it every night before I went to sleep. As a result, and on more than one occasion, I'd woken up in the morning with a frozen joint – frozen solid, I couldn't bend it and so couldn't get out of bed. It had forced me to set my alarm to go off earlier to allow time for my knee to thaw out. I didn't know whether freezing any part of the body was good medical practice, but it seemed to work. Cryonics was something I'd read an article about. The practice of freezing a human corpse to resurrect it in future years, when medical science had advanced to cure whatever had killed the person in the first place, seemed to suggest that freezing was a good idea. Han Solo had survived its effects at the hands of Jabba the Hutt in *The Empire Strikes Back*, so how bad could it be? My plan was simple; freeze my knee regularly and often in the hope that it would survive until the end of the course when I could get it fixed properly.

Dave was an accident waiting to happen. For him, leaving the honbu dojo was just as complicated as entering it, but in reverse. Having retrieved your shoes from the shoe cupboard and put them on, it was compulsory to bow to the office even if no one was there. Every bow had to be accompanied by a loud osu, and there was one more of each to do before any departure from the honbu dojo was complete. I left with Dave at the end of Thursday's training. Having successfully made my exit, I was now waiting for him. As Dave turned to face the statute of Kancho Gozo Shioda, he bowed, shouted 'osu', fell backwards off the step and collapsed in a heap at the top of the stairs. It was the funniest thing I'd witnessed in a while. Dave had got his comeuppance. The step opposite Kancho's statue was out of sight of the office, and while the rest of us followed the correct etiquette, Dave would regularly just walk out without turning to bow and osu as he left. The one time he'd done things properly, Gozo Shioda must have been looking down. As Dave faced Kancho's statue properly for the first time, from beyond the grave, the founder of Yoshinkan Aikido had maybe used his kokyu ryoku breath power to blow Dave off the step!

JUST CUT IT OFF!

Comeuppance or karma was never far away. Geoff was winding everyone up by his extended stint in mitori geiko. I was the one who would pay the heaviest price for his absence. With our test for black belt not far away, doing a good job was looking less likely. I'd had very little opportunity to practice with my uke, and given Geoff was awkward at the best of times, we probably needed more practice than most. By the end of the week, I decided it was time to confront Geoff about his toe, which I'd carefully planned to do in full view of everyone during the first break. *'Geoff, why don't you just cut your little toe off and be done with it? I would if it was me!'* I was deadly serious. I'd been watching *Prison Break* back to back, and in the second episode of season one, the lead character Michael Scofield, played by Wentworth Miller, had his little toe cut off. *It wouldn't be too hard for a few of us to recreate this scene,* I'd thought to myself. The Senshusei course felt a lot like prison, and I was sure we could find a quiet spot to ambush Geoff and relieve him of his faulty digit. I was confident one of us could smuggle a pair of gardening shears into the honbu, which would make easy work of the job. If we did it at the end of the day, the wound would probably heal overnight, and Geoff, even if not at first, would eventually be grateful for the favour we'd done him. Geoff looked horrified and changed the subject quickly. On my way out of the tearoom, for my regular pre-class toilet stop, I accidentally caught my little toe on a chair leg. I screamed in pain. I'd bent it right back, and it hurt like hell. Geoff couldn't hide his amusement, and nobody else could, either. Were the tables about to be turned? I sat down to inspect the damage. Luckily, my toe wasn't broken. What a relief. If it had been, I'd be the one getting ambushed, and Geoff would be holding the shears!

As the Enbu grew closer, the tedium of the preparation involved, which often made no sense, was driving me mad. In the middle of Friday's second class, the training stopped, and we were promptly called to attention. Chida and Chino Sensei entered the mats, and much to my surprise, they were together. As usual, we had very little idea what was going on until it was actually happening. Apparently, we were to have a rehearsal for the prize-giving that would take place at the Enbu. To add to the confusion, all the other Sensei filed in, too, carrying a table that was placed under the shomen and then decorated with a collection of trophies that would be given out to those Aikidoka who impressed the judges. We stood to attention and awaited instructions. The discussion was in Japanese and centred on a heated dialogue between Chida and Chino, which seemed to be about what colour flag to raise when those competing entered the arena. Whether the decision was red or white didn't seem that important to me, but the two Sensei argued their point of view with an intensity that showed there was little love lost. I was still firmly in the Chino camp. Chida Sensei might have been the Dojocho, but I had little time for him. He never seemed to want to teach us anything and when he did venture onto the tatami, he'd usually ask questions and then laugh at our answers. I'd also heard that he smoked like a chimney and drank like a fish and that his doctor had apparently told him to stop or die. These weren't habits I looked up to. This whole debacle had dragged on for 90 minutes, and by the end, as far as I could tell, nobody was any further forward in making a decision, and we were none the wiser.

After the boredom of the day, the highlight came after I'd left the honbu. I'd gotten permission for *Fight! Japan* to continue the documentary, this time at Fairtex. In anticipation of the filming, Ryuji, the manager of the Muay Thai gym, had given me a wristband in the colours of the Thai flag to wear for good luck. Unfortunately, the honbu didn't permit such items, so no sooner had I put it on than I'd had to remove it. I hoped Ryuji wouldn't notice as Robert and I arrived at the gym to start the filming. Robert filmed me doing rounds on the pads with Choke. I was exhausted – I always was – and tried not to show it. I mustered an extra bit of effort, and afterwards Robert said I kicked like a donkey. I didn't know how good donkeys were at kicking, but from the tone in which he said it, I took it as a compliment.

SERGEANT MAJOR

I didn't have to wait too long to receive my orders. I knew they were on their way and had been dreading their arrival. The honbu had drafted me to lead out the troops on Enbu day. I was to be the Sergeant Major who would ensure everyone marched onto the mats in time, performed the kihon dosa renzoku in time, and then left in the same orderly time. This would be no easy task, and, although this honour had been unwillingly received, I decided to make the best of it. Malik Sewanin had also got a new job description. Graham had let slip to Ronen that Malik had described himself as *'The Sheriff of this town'*. Presumably the town was the honbu, and we were a band of troublemakers that 'The Sheriff' had seen fit to round-up. Perhaps I'd been wrong in my first assessment? Perhaps it wasn't Pitt and Norton or Riggs and Murtaugh? Perhaps the Sewanin were much more *Toy Story*? Like Woody it was easy to pull Malik's string, although he rarely needed a reason to talk. Like Buzz Lightyear, Graham was more logical and, arguably, the group's protector from the Sheriff's impulsive tendencies!

The weather was turning increasingly cold and for the first time I'd worn my winter coat to the dojo. The intense heat of summer was slowly switching to the icy chill of winter. It was like a climatic version of the changing of the guard that I'd watched as a child at Buckingham Palace, but there was no fanfare and nothing to formally mark the change. The heat vacated, and the cold crept in, and before we knew it, we had a new enemy to deal with. Though the heat posed the constant threat of dehydration, the cold brought with it the very real fear of injury. Cold muscles were muscles that were easily strained or snapped and there was no relying on the daily taiso to prepare the body for strenuous activity. Any standing around during class that had been a welcome break during the summer months was now much less welcome. Once the engine had started on a cold, frosty morning, you had to keep it going!

And so, another week began, and in Tuesday's last class, Murata Sensei appeared on the mats. Normally this would be good news, but too much talking, and not enough action was not what any of us now wanted. He called me out to the front of the class and said that he was going to do something that was bad for the body, so he would only be doing it with me! The promise of doing something bad, and to my body, didn't sound all that appealing. Perhaps I'd offended him, or perhaps he just thought I was the only one who could take what he was about to deliver? I didn't know, but I was about to find out. To my surprise, he asked me to low kick him. Was he kidding? Didn't he realise I was a trained Thai boxer? I liked Murata, and the last thing I wanted to do was drop him with shins that had been conditioned from years of pounding the Thai pads and heavy bag. It wouldn't be a good look for a Sensei to be seen crawling off the tatami, unable to feel one of his lower limbs. It was all right for us to do it after zagaku, but that was different. I had no choice but to kick him but decided the best course of action was not to go full power. As my right shin struck his thigh, he tensed his leg and, in his own words, 'bounced off the energy'. Whatever he did seemed to work. He was left standing, and thankfully my leg returned to its starting position in one piece.

Murata instructed us to get in pairs, so we could practice individually what we'd just learnt. This was music to my ears. One thing I knew how to do was kick, and the low kick was a specialty of the Muay Thai practitioner. I grabbed Matt, and we got to work. Slaaaaaammmmmmmm! My shin drove hard into Matt's thigh, and he dropped to the tatami. His leg was dead, and he couldn't get up. He laughed, and I laughed more. This was Senshusei humour and our unique ability to find pleasure through pain. Watching Matt squirm around on the tatami like a fish washed up on the shore, trying in vain to get back to sea, was hilarious. Matt eventually got back to his feet and tried to return the favour. His attempts were in vain. Years of conditioning offered me protection, and despite his best attempts, I remained on my feet. Murata Sensei, watching out of the corner of his eye, came over. Once again, he asked me to attack him but this time didn't specify how. He instructed me to use my Muay Thai skills to attack him in any way I wanted, and he would use his Aikido to get past, or at the very least, dodge my strikes. I threw combinations of punches and kicks and he couldn't get past. Any attempt to get close to me was pushed back with a well-placed front kick or jab. In Muay Thai you never telegraphed your movements. Wide, swinging motions told your opponent in advance what you were about to do. As Murata and I went toe to toe, I kept my movements short and sharp. Murata was playing in my world, and his Aikido didn't seem to work. Muay Thai had its origins in Krabi Krabong and Muay Boran, both of which had been honed over the centuries on the battlefield. Aikido seemed to work against an aggressor throwing a committed attack, but against Muay Thai, at least on this occasion, it had come up short.

Justice was just around the corner, and as if a reward for questioning the art I was in Japan to learn; I somehow bent my little toe back under my foot. The dojo was cold, and this made feeling your feet difficult. If you couldn't feel your toes, you didn't know where they were until it was too late. I'd bent it good and proper and this time suspected it was broken. Would I now have to cut it off? I was the Sergeant Major for the Enbu and there was a lot of marching still to be done. I decided self-mutilation was not such a good idea after all and resolved that ice and painkillers would have to do instead. I'd just have to suck it up. There was no way I was joining Geoff in mitori geiko. I'd never live it down!

FROM RUSSIA WITH LOVE

The Enbu was nearly upon us, and Aikido practitioners from all over the world descended on the honbu. The All Japan Enbu was the event of the year and an annual pilgrimage made by many. It was a chance to meet old friends and watch the best of the best in action.

Matt was in the spotlight for all the wrong reasons. In a midweek Oyamada Sensei jiyu waza session, Malik Sewanin had shouted words of encouragement for Matt to keep going. *'Matt, this is your breakfast!'* We weren't sure what Malik meant. It was way past breakfast time, but this call to arms provided a good opportunity to rib Matt in the tearoom during the break. It was all done in the usual Senshusei spirit and Matt took it well. I knew that taking the piss was a common thing that happened in the military. In a life or death situation it was a way of calming things down and keeping spirits high. As Senshusei we had our own version, and today it was Matt's turn in the hot seat. Matt was the golden boy and like a pair of socks at Christmas, he was about to be given a present he really didn't want!

To be honest, we all felt sorry for him. A black belt from Russia had chosen him as his uke for the Enbu, although we suspected the Sewanin had brokered the match. This was a high-profile gig, as this would be the first Aikido practitioner from Russia to ever perform at an All Japan Enbu. Our Russian friend clearly wanted to make a good impression, and since his arrival in Tokyo, he had dragged Matt onto the mats to practice his routine during every precious break. This gave Matt very little downtime and no opportunity to rest. When he wasn't suffering in one of the Senshusei classes, like a young Sean Connery, he was being bashed up as uke *From Russia with Love*. Matt told us he'd tried to engage his newfound friend in conversation. I suspected that, much like a kidnapped and tortured soul, Matt had attempted to humanise his existence, hoping he wouldn't get smashed so hard. He'd tried to break the ice and asked the Russian if he liked Japan. The reply was to the point. *'Not so much; I much prefer the motherland.'* End of conversation! Matt was more than a little worried. We'd all already had a brush with Ivan Drago through the words of Malik. *'If he dies, he dies'* played through Matt's head. He didn't want to end up like Apollo Creed!

My toe was still painful, and my heel had finally cracked because of all the hard skin that had built up from sliding around the dojo. No matter how much cream I applied, my heel didn't seem to get any better, and any residue left made manoeuvring on the tatami feel more like ice skating. The Enbu practice wasn't helping. The relentless marching and kihon dosa renzoku were the last things I needed, and every move sent a surge of pain through my lower body. We'd even taken to practicing with our eyes closed as a real test of our ability to move as one unit. Closing my eyes helped with the pain, but it didn't help with synchronisation. At the end of a run-through, we'd open our eyes to find we were all facing in different directions and were a good distance away from where we were actually supposed to be. You'd think that with all the practice, we'd be getting better, but Chino Sensei had a very different view. Not happy with Noriki Sensei leading the count, he called me out by name to take over. This was both good and bad news. On the one hand, it meant that Chino Sensei knew my name. Of course, he knew my name. It was written in katakana in thick black marker pen on my dogi top, bottoms and belt. This had helped during the summer when during difficult hajime geiko sessions I'd sometimes struggled to know where and who I was! Hearing your name on the lips of a Sensei meant you existed. An existence that lasted for at least the brief moment it took to spit it out. I was no longer just one of an anonymous bunch of Senshusei. I was Simon Senshusei and had been personally selected by the main man himself. On the other hand, I was on his radar. Leading the count for kihon dosa renzoku meant there was no place to hide and no room for error. If I cocked it up, I cocked it up for everyone.

The pressure was well and truly on. Chino mustn't have been happy with what he saw and moved on. He decided to make an example of Kambara. Kambara was called up to demonstrate in front of everyone and, not for the first time, was publicly humiliated. Staring straight at Kambara, Chino said that our waza was really bad and that we needed to work on it. We couldn't expect to teach students if we couldn't perform the techniques properly ourselves! Dai Yon would be the instructor phase of the course, and Chino already had his reservations. He told us to break off into groups to practice teaching some of the Dai San techniques. I teamed up with Clyde, Dave and Matt. There would be one timekeeper, one technique caller and two demonstrating, one of whom would teach the technique that had been called.

With five minutes to teach a complete technique the pressure was on. I'd been training myself to know what five minutes felt like. At home, at Berlitz, and on the train, I'd regularly play the five-minute game – counting seconds to determine when five minutes was up – but rarely got my timing right. The Sensei wanted five minutes; no more and ideally no less! Graham Sewanin observed our group but, unable to hide his laughter, didn't stay long. Dave was on form. His unique teaching style, which was meant to be serious, instead left us in fits of laughter – laughter that we couldn't openly show during the class, but laughter that would burst out uncontrollably in the sanctuary of the tearoom. *'Don't do this or your technique will fall to bits...some practitioners of Aikido do this the wrong way, but I do it this way.'* I couldn't imagine Dave ever teaching Aikido. Stand-up comedy, yes, but Aikido, no! Chino, like Graham, had seen enough. He led us into Kancho's office to show us old pictures of Yoshinkan's founder doing *shomen uchi shomen iriminage ni*, one of the techniques we'd be tested on. Once again, he implied that Chida's style wasn't the original Yoshinkan style. Chino encouraged us to stay true to Yoshinkan's origin by closely studying books and pictures of Kancho Gozo Shioda.

THE BIG MAT MOVE

There were no mats at the location of the Enbu, which meant the tatami from the honbu dojo would have to be transported there in advance. When there was a job to be done, there was always an underpaid, overworked team on hand. The lowest of the low would be given the dirtiest and most difficult of jobs. The clue to the big mat move was a video Murata Sensei made us watch. A video of the Senshusei in a prior year moving the mats didn't make great viewing, but it gave us an inkling what would be expected and what we were now on the hook to do. There was a specific way the tatami had to be laid out at the Enbu location, and from one video viewing, we were expected to commit this arrangement to memory to ensure that when the time came, we replicated it exactly. The Enbu would take place on Saturday, 28 October 2006, and true to form, when Friday the 27th rolled in, we still had no clue what the plan was. The Sensei and Sewanin seemed to take pleasure in revealing nothing to the Senshusei until the very last minute. This meant we were always on edge and could never plan. When will the mat move happen? Will it be during or after class? What time will I be able to leave? Do I need to change my teaching schedule at Berlitz? These were all reasonable questions in the real world, but the honbu dojo was often a world away from reality. These questions could never be asked, and if anyone dared, it would likely result in punishment at the hands of the Sewanin. In an environment where things happened on a need-to-know basis, it appeared that despite the Enbu being tomorrow, the Senshusei didn't yet need to know.

The only bonus was that training was easy. In the first class we had Paul Sensei, who usually went hard but today, after a few rounds of kihon dosa renzoku, told us we could stretch. Clearly, he was under orders from up high not to kill anyone, at least not until the Enbu was over. In the second class with Chino Sensei, we didn't practice the demonstration routine once. Instead, it was back to teaching, and it was Lloyd's turn in the spotlight. After Kambara's dismantling we all feared the worse, but Lloyd did a great job explaining a *kotegaeshi* technique and Chino seemed pleased. Kotegaeshi, I knew from past experience, was a Lloyd favourite. He'd obviously enjoyed bending my wrist back on itself and forcing me to flip over my head to avoid breaking my arm. Ahead of the third class, there was general confusion about whether or not it would go ahead. We still had to get the mats to the Enbu location in readiness for tomorrow, and time was marching on. The Sewanin finally confirmed that there would be no third class and that we could all take a break until 1pm. We still didn't know what the schedule was for the rest of the day and headed to Jonathan's for pizza, chips and all-you-can-drink soft drinks. We always murdered the drinks bar. Fresh from training and usually dehydrated, we regularly drank the bar dry.

As a Senshusei it paid to be early, and we were back at the honbu just before 12:45pm. The hell was about to begin. All the mats in the dojo had to be lifted up and carried down the stairs to be loaded onto a van outside for transportation. I was assigned the job of carrying mats from the dojo to the honbu's entrance. I was then to pass each mat to what could best be described as a chain gang of Senshusei positioned at staggered points on the stairs. A position on the stairs was by far the worst job. Carrying mats wasn't easy at the best of times but getting them down the stairs was another level of complication altogether. There was dust everywhere. We might have cleaned the tatami every day, but that was the surface and not underneath. I'd prepared myself well with a face mask, the type the Japanese wore in public when they had colds, and protective gloves. Despite my best efforts, the dust kept getting in my eyes, and it was hard to see where I was going. It wasn't just moving on the agenda, with so much mess we had to clean, too! The mats were eventually all piled downstairs, and the next job was to load them onto the van. There appeared to be a splattering of dog poo on the steps just outside the front of the building, which only I seemed to notice. From time to time some of the others appeared to be treading directly in it. I did my best to steer clear, but with

Sensei and Sewanin everywhere there was no chance of shirking. The mats were finally loaded and thankfully we wouldn't now see them for a while. I couldn't believe how many there were, it had been an endless task. Each mat had been individually numbered to help matters when they returned. Ronen confirmed, *'144 tatami'*. He had a head for figures and knew there were 64 steps up to his room on the fourth floor of a building in Takadanobaba. *'You make me sound like the Rain Man mate!'* Ronen wasn't Dustin Hoffman in the movie *Rain Man* – with Senshusei knees, climbing the stairs every day had etched the number firmly on his mind.

We caught the train to Komazawa-daigaku Station. Malik decided not to join us and instead opted to take his life in his own hands on the back of Sonoda Sensei's motorbike. If he came off the back at speed, all the ukemi in the world wouldn't save him. I've no idea what Sonoda was wearing, but it appeared to be a purple shell suit. The bottoms were tucked into a pair of matching purple socks. As the 'Dynamic Duo' pulled away, it looked like Malik was being kidnapped by the Joker from *Batman*. Graham went on his motorbike, so the trip over with the cops was a chance to relax before we got to the end of our journey, where we'd repeat the exercise we'd just undertaken, but this time in reverse. The mats had arrived before us, and so, too, had Graham Sewanin, who gave me the job of coordinating their unloading and placement in the Komazawa Gymnasium, which would play host to the Enbu. I later discovered that I'd been allocated this task because, in Graham's opinion, I'd made the best notes in one of the planning meetings we'd had. It would be my job tomorrow to lead the Senshusei in our performance of kihon dosa renzoku, but before that could happen, I was now leading the placement of tatami. My notes didn't appear up to scratch. They made little sense, which was probably no surprise, given that more than one Sensei had been involved in their construction. There was more than one version of how the placement of tatami should run. *Too many cooks* really had *spoiled the broth*! We were all working from a handful of different instructions from different Sensei and trying to decipher what we were supposed to be doing from pictures taken in previous years. I was in charge of this huge headache and, like all good leaders, tried to remain calm on the surface, to ensure everyone around me remained calm, too. I was the proverbial swan, serene above the water but paddling like fuck underneath!

Eventually it was finished, with the next task being to hang around until someone decided what to do next. Inoue Kancho eventually arrived. Hopefully, he could now decide what to do next. If he couldn't, then we were all in trouble and would probably have to bed down for the night. We were all starving and relieved when the bento boxes arrived. I had no intention of sitting near Kancho or any of the other Sensei. I was far too hungry! I figured that if I couldn't see that any of them had finished their food early, then I would be free to keep going. Finally, we were released, and I arrived back at Musashi Koyama just after 9pm. After a quick shower, it was straight to bed. I had a feeling that tomorrow was going to be an excruciatingly long day!

ALL JAPAN ENBU

It was Saturday, 28 October 2006, the day we'd been practicing for in the dojo, hour after hour, day after day. I was sick of kihon dosa renzoku. I dreamt about it, I constantly thought about it, and today I was about to do it at the 51st All Japan Enbu in front of the Aikido greats. I woke up feeling nervous, but was glad of the lie-in. A 6:20am rise was an hour later than I normally needed to be up, but the anxiety I usually felt ahead of each day was at an all-time high. We'd been told to meet at 8am in front of the Hachiko statue just outside Shibuya Station. Hachiko was famous across Japan – the statue of a dog that made the journey to meet his master after work at the station and continued to do so for nine years after his master's death. Such loyalty was to be commended, and the Sewanin would now test ours. Malik and Graham were travelling directly to the venue, which meant we were to meet some of the international Sensei instead. Despite their absence, the Sewanin had made their instructions crystal clear. *'Don't be late! Don't be late! Don't be late!'* They'd told us repeatedly. Being late wasn't an option. At 7:55am I had a text from Ronen to say he would be late. His train for some reason had come to a standstill and hadn't moved for five minutes. At 8am, Malik Sewanin called me. *'Simon, is everybody there?'* Ronen wasn't there, and not wanting to drop my buddy in it, my reply was deliberately vague. *'I think so, but we're just about to do a headcount.'* Hachiko was always a busy spot, so my explanation sounded half plausible. Thankfully, Ronen arrived seconds later and blended into the crowd. It was a close call, and we'd both had a lucky escape.

At the stadium we got changed into our dogi and practiced our routine twice. This was the first opportunity we'd had to practice where we'd be performing, and without the visual reference points, we relied on back at the dojo, we all felt disoriented. Kancho would be watching, Chida Sensei would be watching, and, scariest of them all, Chino Sensei would be there, too. I had no place to hide and would be almost eyeball to eyeball at the front of the pack. I tried not to think about it. It was only a demonstration. What was the worst that could happen? Dave, Inazaki, Kambara and I had a job to do. We went back upstairs to manage the lottery draw for the kihon waza competition.

I'd been in the kihon waza competition with Carlos as an ippan student at the 50th on Saturday, 24 September 2005. Despite practicing for hours, being two big guys, we'd struggled to make things flow and were knocked out after the first round. My previous experience wasn't going to help. Today already felt very different! Dave and I acted as runners sticking team names on a big board in the reception area, while Inazaki and Kambara, who both had the language advantage, did the meet and greet as the contestants flooded in. With people everywhere, it was absolute chaos. When we weren't pinning, Dave and I stood to attention, backs straight and heels together. We were Senshusei on show, and the eyes of the world were watching. Dave wasn't one for the rules. Even falling out of the honbu and nearly breaking his ankle hadn't cooled his courage. It wasn't long before he'd had enough of formality and told me to relax just as Malik and Graham Sewanin walked up the stairs on their round of checks. *That's the last time I listen to Dave*, I thought to myself. I cut my thumb on the Sellotape dispenser and was the first person at the event to go on the first-aid list. When it came to the Senshusei, the honbu didn't seem too concerned with health and safety. I'd never seen an injury recorded in the honbu dojo, despite there being plenty of them. For everyone else, it appeared to be a different story. Even a Sellotape injury had to be logged! Plaster intact, Dave, Inazaki, Kambara and I went downstairs for the orientation, which was led by Oyamada Sensei. The rest of the Senshusei were positioned at various points around the stadium. In full view of everyone, they had to stand to attention throughout. There was no relaxing or sitting down. We now had to reluctantly join them with no clue about what we were there to do. Everyone who had a part to play in the day's proceedings was there, sitting in seiza in front of the three tables neatly covered with white tablecloths that had been positioned under the Japanese flag. The orientation was conducted in true Oyamada style. With what seemed like little enthusiasm for the whole thing, he rambled on and on, stopping only to call up two people to demonstrate how to bow to the shomen and then move into kamae. The opening ceremony was followed with the Japanese national anthem. I'd always been a bit funny about observing another nation's national song, particularly one we'd been at war with, but out of respect for the country I'd temporarily made my home, I stood to attention.

Malik Sewanin gathered us together and delivered a speech. *'If the uke of any Sensei is injured or knocked out, you must run on, drag uke away, and take his or her place!'* For the lower-level Sensei this was feasible, but once the big guns rolled out, the ones more likely to do the injuring or knocking out, such an action would be suicide. Chida, no thank you, Chino, not likely, and Takeno Sensei – possibly the most terrifying of them all – not in this lifetime! I'd met Takeno Sensei at the gasshuku I'd attended shortly after arriving in Japan. Another direct student of Kancho Gozo Shioda, I'd watched in awe as he smashed his uke into the tatami. Possibly the biggest of Gozo Shioda's students, he was an imposing figure that you wouldn't want to upset. From time to time, Takeno, Ando, Payet and a number of other Yoshinkan Sensei, who taught out of town, would visit Ochiai for a meeting with Inoue Kancho. Towards the beginning of Dai San, Takeno Sensei, who based himself in Yamanashi Prefecture 80 miles west of Tokyo, had made the trek across. Ronen, as Shinkoku, was sat in the tearoom after training to write up the dojo diary, when Takeno appeared in the doorway. His meeting with Kancho was over and he was on his way out. *'Hello, are you the Senshusei?'* His English was perfect and with Ronen's somewhat shocked *'yeesss'*, Takeno came in and sat down. With a grin like a Cheshire cat, a maniacal laugh and hands like spades, Ronen and Dror were wary. With the diary still to finish, Ronen muttered to Dror in Hebrew. *'Al tashier ohti ito levad'* (don't leave me alone with him). Discovering that Ronen and Dror were Israeli, Takeno smiled and said, *'I know a guy from Israel. He trained in my dojo and I broke his collarbone and caused a concussion!'* Takeno Sensei proceeded to talk about his own Senshusei course, *'one month of shihonage...one month of ikajo...!'* He told Ronen and Dror that the honbu Sensei had told him that the 16th year was one of the best ever. Technique, discipline, but mainly the collective group of people – *'good people and good Aikidoka!'* This was a huge honour and somewhat unexpected. Boosted by this feedback, Dror plucked up the courage to ask – *'what do you remember most about Kancho Gozo Shioda?'* Takeno paused, reflected and, to his captive audience, said that his teacher was a very small man who didn't look threatening at first glance but had springs in his legs! *'When he did a technique on you, he sprung from the tatami with such force that it was very powerful!'* Ronen told me later, *'I felt honoured and scared shitless at the same time. It was like having Darth Vader sat at my lunch table!'*

After what seemed an eternity, it was finally time to line up in preparation for our demonstration. Now I was really nervous! Stood alongside Kambara, I fixed my eyes on Takashima Sensei, who held up a white flag. The flag dropped on his call of *'ii yo'*, which meant we were good to *'go'*. *'Mae ni susume!'* I screamed at the top of my voice, and with that we were on the move. We marched out to the far-left corner of the matted area, made a sharp right and continued into position. Marching on the spot, I brought us to a standstill and ordered us to turn and face the line of Sensei to take the obligatory bow to the shomen. *'Zentai tomare! Hidari muke...shomen ni rei!'* Inoue, Chida, Chino, Takeno, Terada and all the other top Sensei were right in front of us. They clapped before we bowed, which must have meant the marching was all right. The game was finally on, and no sooner was the bow over than we were all running to our set positions on my command of *'ichi ni tsuke!'* This was no easy task in surroundings very different to the honbu, and I was thankful we'd had time to practice twice. I'd been really worried for the past few days about making a mistake. I saw Kambara wobble as I turned for *hiriki no yosei ni,* which calmed me down momentarily; then I wobbled, too! We got through with no major mistakes, but it wasn't the best kihon dosa renzoku we'd ever done. Good kihon dosa was all about extended and projected posture, but the last thing I wanted to do on the day was project too far over my front toes and land flat on my face. It appeared I wasn't alone in my thinking! It had gone well, and as we lined up to take our finishing bow, the Sensei started clapping. I just wanted to stand there and take the applause. The high was immense and reward for all the repetition we'd endured to prepare for this one performance. Ours was one of many demonstrations that day, so my time in the spotlight didn't last too long. *'Migi muke mae susume!'* Reluctantly, I led the march off the mats. Watching a video of our performance later on, I was pleased to see that our collective timing had been almost perfect. No one appeared to have made a mistake, and Geoff's toe had survived the ordeal. All the training had been worthwhile.

Dave and I were due for our first break and went upstairs to get a bento. Murray Sensei spotted us and shouted *'good'* from his vantage point on the stairs, and the Sewanin seemed to have smiles on their faces. It felt good to be appreciated for once, and it felt particularly special for me having been the one to lead us out. Demonstration rolled into demonstration, but there was only one that I wanted to see. Chino Sensei entered the auditorium, followed by Graham Sewanin. Graham looked like a condemned man being marched out to the block by his executioner. Chino was the axe, and decapitation was guaranteed. The only question was how long would Graham last? Graham was up for it and attacked strongly, but every shomen uchi strike was intercepted using an array of techniques by the Aikido master. At one point, Chino glided just out of reach of Graham's incoming strike, which sent the Sewanin crashing to the tatami in a heap. This was true Aikido, not fighting force with force but rather not being there in the first place. Thinking back to how Aikido had been explained to me, Chino was getting off the track. As the techniques flowed from one to another, Graham was getting visibly tired. Tiredness to Chino Sensei was like blood to a shark. Sensing Graham's flagging energy encouraged him to go harder, and the relentless destruction continued. Graham was Senshusei, and Senshusei spirit meant never giving up. There was only one option – to keep going no matter how long the ordeal lasted. Once the shomen uchi jiyu waza was done, Chino Sensei invited Graham to grab his wrists and the merciless beating carried on. An incredible 36 throws after it had begun, Chino Sensei's demonstration ended.

I spent the rest of the day kicking the mats back into place in between each demonstration to remove any gaps that had appeared. Gaps between the tatami had a habit of resulting in broken toes or twisted knees. As the mats were placed on the shiny wooden floor of the gymnasium, gaps were a constant menace. Matt had his date with the 'motherland' and did a good job. Clyde, too, had also been roped in to be uke for a Sensei from the United States. The final demonstrations included Chida Sensei and Takeno Sensei. Ronen and I found ourselves in a precarious position at the edge of the tatami. We held our breath, crossed our fingers and prayed that Takeno didn't kill his uke. Neither of us wanted to be assassinated next. Being publicly murdered would be an embarrassment after all the training we'd done. It would be a slow, painful and crushing death! Thankfully, Takeno's uke was more than up to the job and we were off the hook. The finale was Inoue Kancho, who conducted what could best be described as an impromptu seminar, instead of a formal demonstration. This involved a lot of talking and therefore far too much seiza for his collection of uke and everyone else watching.

After the demonstrations were over, we were allowed to get changed and leave in a huge convoy to make our way back to the honbu. The university students would pack up the mats, and we would await their arrival back at the dojo. Not since the gasshuku had I been so happy to find myself back at base camp. The Enbu had been an experience, but not one I ever wanted to repeat. I was keen to get back to the business of training, and the daily grind looked more appealing than ever. We ducked into McDonald's for a takeaway and packed into the tearoom to tuck in. The mats arrived shortly after, and the chain gang we'd run the day before got into full swing, this time in the opposite direction. I'd never been good at jigsaws and had never understood their appeal. Taking the tatami out of the dojo had been the easy job. Putting them back in the right place would prove a lot more difficult. This wasn't a challenge I relished, so Ronen, Dave, Lloyd and I volunteered to offload the rubbish that had also made its way back from the Enbu. It was a dirty job, but somebody had to do it. On the plus side, it involved a walk down the road, which kept us away from the command centre and the debate that was no doubt raging about how the tatami fitted back together. We finally finished and rolled back into the honbu to find the last mat being carefully put in place. It was perfect timing! Moments later Takashima

Sensei, who had been Commander in Chief of the day, announced that we'd all have to leave by 10:30pm before they closed the gate downstairs. It was like music to my ears. After 48 hours of not knowing what would happen from one moment to the next, we finally had closure.

HALLOWEEN!

Despite it being Halloween, there was nothing to fear when I entered the honbu dojo to start yet another week. It felt good to be back into the routine of daily Senshusei life, and although there was never 100 percent certainty what would or wouldn't happen on any given day, I knew at least I'd be done and dusted by 2pm when I could once again get back to the real world. Sunday had been a full day of teaching at Berlitz, but yesterday I'd ditched any thoughts of Muay Thai or Jiu Jitsu in favour of staying in bed.

In the morning meeting, the Sewanin were in a good mood. They shared direct feedback from the Sensei on our performance, and the consensus from the powers that be was that we were *'the best Senshusei year ever!'* In communicating this the Sewanin were at the same time knocking themselves down. As the prior year's Senshusei, technically they were now playing second fiddle to the 16th international course. However, the best year ever didn't necessarily mean the best Aikido; it could easily have meant the best cleaners, tatami movers or security guards. Whatever it meant didn't matter too much, though; it was formal recognition of all the time, energy and effort we'd put in over the last seven months. Questioning the meaning to any great degree would only detract from this rare but very enjoyable moment, so there seemed little point bothering. Matt was in the firing line. His dance with the visiting Russian had also gone down well, and in his diary he'd now got back with feedback for September, he'd scored straight eights for basic movement, technique and attitude. His golden-boy crown was firmly intact, and as a reward we took the mickey out of him for the rest of the day. The praise from the Sewanin didn't last too long, and it was back to normality. Geoff made his official return from mitori geiko, and that meant training with me. We'd had very little time to get used to one another, and I knew things would only get more difficult. On the bench he'd let himself go and clearly forgotten the importance of personal hygiene. As he stumbled past me in the tearoom, he dragged one of his overgrown toenails right across my foot! This was out of order, and with all his time sat on the sidelines, he had no excuse not to know that his nails needed a good trim. Toenails were weapons and, when applied to human flesh, risked lacerations that could become infected and take ages to heal. The last thing I needed was Geoff inflicting bodily harm on my already battered body, and I told him straight, *'cut them by tomorrow morning, or I won't be training with you!'* How I thought I would enforce this threat if he didn't cut them, I wasn't sure. There was no use whining to the Sewanin, as they wouldn't care. Geoff took my threat seriously; the Freddy Krueger who had turned up on Halloween had thankfully put his blades away – my *Nightmare on Elm Street* was over.

It was hard to blend in with Geoff. The tallest of the Senshusei, he stood out like a sore thumb, and our position on the tatami right in front of the shomen meant that even the smallest of mistakes rarely went unnoticed. In Wednesday's second class, Noriki Sensei called out, *'shomen tsuki hijiate kokyunage ichi'*. I hesitated while I tried to process the Japanese into meaningful English but came up blank. Just out of sight, but well within shouting distance, Malik Sewanin jumped on my hesitancy and screamed at the top of his voice. *'Come on, this is basics!'* It wasn't. Noriki had made a mistake. We'd never been taught this technique, let alone had the opportunity to practice it. As Senshusei, though, someone else's mistake was always our mistake. There was no point protesting, complaining or arguing back. Geoff had tried this many times before, and it usually ended up in tears. Thankfully, he'd learnt from previous experience and on this occasion kept his mouth firmly shut. In the last class of the day, we were all happy to see Murata Sensei. He'd been at the Enbu and spent most of his time sat in a corridor off the main arena, chatting with two other guys. We didn't understand what he was doing or what he was talking about, but that was regularly the case. Today he decided he'd teach us how to hide behind a sword. As far as I could tell I was much wider than the average bokken blade; in fact, I didn't know of anyone who was thinner. It was a human impossibility, but apparently, through the projection of energy, you could create a safe area in front of you. Perhaps hiding behind a sword was possible after all? Dave and I weren't convinced. With the Sewanin banned from Murata's classes, we decided we'd have some fun instead. I swung my bokken at Dave's head, trying to make him flinch, stopping just inches from his dome; he did a good job in maintaining his composure and not moving. But when I switched things up to go for his bollocks instead, I'd never seen him move so fast!

SHINE A LIGHT

The mystical side of Aikido, I really didn't get. For me martial arts had always been about strength, conditioning and speed. Higa Sensei, however, seemed to have a very different opinion as to what made a good martial artist. In one of the strangest classes I'd experienced on the course so far, he instructed us to stand across from one another in kamae. This was something we did every day, but on this occasion, he told us to imagine we had a car light shining from our chests. This car light was to shine forwards and illuminate uke, just as an actual car is designed to illuminate the road ahead on a dark night. Lloyd faced off across from Boaz and told me later on that day that as Malik walked between them, he'd felt a change in energy. The energy he'd felt from Boaz was stopped, having been momentarily intercepted by Malik Sewanin's body. *'I felt energy from my side, but not his anymore'*, he said. I couldn't believe what I was hearing. Lloyd, as far as I'd seen, was a blood-and-guts martial artist like me, but was he now showing a softer, more spiritual side?

Geoff's return was enlightening but for all the wrong reasons. Oyamada Sensei clearly didn't care that Geoff had been out of action for an extended period. In Thursday's class he threw us into 45 minutes of hajime geiko followed by jiyu waza practice. Geoff looked bemused, confused and completely out of his depth. The rest of us had been drilling the techniques that now seemed new to him for weeks on end. They had been forced into our subconscious minds, and we could perform them without thinking. Geoff was trying to make sense of everything in his conscious thoughts and as a result was slow to react. Even once he'd figured out what he should do next, he was just as slow to move. Standing on the sidelines, his strength and fitness had suffered. Back on the tatami, he was lined up at the start of a marathon with an elite group of athletes when really, he should have been way back in the pack with the amateur runners. He appeared emotionally drained and physically exhausted and during hajime geiko looked like he was going to pass out. In stark contrast, I was still on a high from the Enbu. I was pumped up, energised and ready for whatever the course decided to throw at me next. Geoff and I were called out for jiyu waza first. I attacked him relentlessly with shomen uchi. Jiyu waza was just as much about uke's spirit as it was shite's technique. As uke it was my job to strike hard and fast and, having been thrown to the ground, get up as quickly as possible to attack shite again. Oyamada instructed us to switch from shomen uchi to yokomen uchi. Geoff was still a few steps behind and expecting my shomen uchi strike. As the blade of my right hand caught him on the side of the head, he looked at me, paused, and then collapsed to the floor. I was convinced I hadn't hit him that hard, and his reaction had all the telltale signs of him looking for a way out. Oyamada Sensei wasn't impressed and hadn't been fooled, either. He grunted and then motioned to Geoff to get to his feet. Geoff may have been looking for an early exit, but on the course, there was no escape.

TRADING CARDS

When I was a kid, I'd spent hours and a huge amount of money trading cards and stickers. *The A Team* and *The Incredible Hulk* were two I distinctly remembered. I'd get an empty album for next to nothing and then buy packs of cards or stickers, hoping they'd contain the ones I didn't yet have. I was always in search of those final elusive few that would complete my collection. At the start it was easy. Every card filled a gap in the album. As time went on, it became more difficult, and the pile of duplicates would inevitably grow bigger and bigger. The school playground became a trading pit where cards were fought over, swapped and exchanged. The weekly zagaku was feeling like history repeating itself. We were all running out of ideas as to what our reflection or habit could be. Most of the time neither were based on reality. An honest reflection or habit risked public retribution at the hands of Kancho or one of his henchmen, and as very few of us could speak any Japanese at all, keeping things simple and safe was proving to be best practice. Like the trading cards and stickers of my school days, the tearoom had become a trading den for reflections and habits.

After Thursday's last class and before zagaku began, Malik Sewanin marched into the tearoom and announced that Matt would be chosen by Kancho today. Matt looked panicked. He'd not prepared anything and now had a matter of minutes to cobble something together. We were yet to hear Kancho Sensei's response to someone failing to prepare a hansei and shukan, but I didn't imagine it would be pretty. Geoff's experience had been an uncomfortable one for all concerned. He'd incurred Kancho's wrath despite having a habit. *Matt's done for*, I thought to myself. Matt was now really panicking. He'd turned pale and sat on the sofa we rarely sat on, with his head in his hands. *'What the hell am I going to do?'* His question was more of a cry for help and, still feeling responsible for him being in Japan, I felt obliged to come to his rescue. I offered Matt a trade and a lifeline. He could have my reflection and habit. Lloyd also came to the rescue and Matt, feeling more comfortable with what Lloyd was reflecting and claiming for his habit, picked his. As we sat in line, waiting for Matt to butcher in Japanese a reflection and habit he hadn't even written and had only just seen, I'd switched off and was busy focusing on trying not to focus on the pain in my legs. *'Simon Senshusei!'* Kancho had called my name and not Matt's. If I'd have been sat on a chair, I'd have fallen off it in disbelief. I was caught completely by surprise and wasn't prepared. It felt like I'd been dragged into consciousness from a deep sleep – a deep sleep I'd been rudely awakened from with no time to come round. Had Malik set us up? Had he figured out what was going on? Had he somehow found out that the tearoom doubled as a trading pit? I reached into my dogi jacket, praying that the piece of paper I'd nearly given up a few minutes earlier was there. If it wasn't, it was me who was done for. I hoped it was and very much needed it to be. As my fingers came into contact with paper, I breathed a sigh of relief and got on with the job. I'd had a lucky escape and learnt two important lessons. Never trust the Sewanin, and always be prepared even when you don't think you need to be. I spoke about my ukemi not being as good as it should be, how I wanted to improve, and that before I left the dojo each day, I'd made it a habit to check the toilet slippers were lined up neatly. Chida Sensei commented that he thought it was a very good hansei and shukan.

After the stress of the day, and with a national holiday in the form of Culture Day tomorrow, I needed a drink. Dror had turned 24 a few days ago, so it seemed a good excuse for us all to get together for some beers. Culture, the arts and promoting academic endeavour might have been the purpose of the holiday, but it was all wasted on us. After a Japanese class with Hotta Sensei and a few rounds on the pads at Fairtex, I met Dave, Matt and Lloyd in Shinjuku. We headed to Roppongi and had some food at Wendy's before meeting everyone else outside Almond. Half cafe and half shop, Almond was a popular meeting spot, which, very similar to Hachiko in Shibuya, made finding everyone even more difficult. Roppongi was probably my least-favourite part of Tokyo, with its seedy undercurrent. I'd already run into trouble before the course began. In Tokyo, where space was at a premium, buildings played host to bars and restaurants on multiple levels. Taking a lift from the street, you were never quite sure what you'd find on any given floor. When the lift doors opened directly into the establishment, you were committed before you arrived. On one particular night out, I got caught short and, in search of a toilet, took the lift to the third floor of a typical building, where I found an empty nightclub. While emptying my bladder, I heard voices outside and found myself confronted by two muscular and very angry men who weren't too happy with my trespassing. The situation became heated very quickly, and as they started to push me around, a thought fired in my head. *I will soon be Senshusei, what can these guys do to me?* I looked directly at them, told them I was leaving and got back in the lift. Was this Bruce Lee's *fighting without fighting*? I wasn't sure, but it was a strategy I would use again on Brian at Berlitz.

The Japanese loved a good theme bar, and in any part of Tokyo, you didn't have to look too hard to find one. We headed across the road to Geronimo, which could best be described as a North American and Indian-themed pub. It was like stepping onto the set of a spaghetti western with

Native American artefacts adorning the walls and bar area. I'd only intended to stay out for an hour but was still there at 10:30pm. The more I drank, the more relaxed I was becoming, and the more I wanted to drink. It was a dangerous spiral, and after four beers, I was already feeling quite drunk. Dave was on usual form. For some reason he'd got it into his head that both Dror and Boaz's girlfriends were trying to chat him up. He wouldn't stop going on about it, much to the annoyance of everyone. The highlight of the evening was bumping into Michael Stuempel and Roland Thompson ('Stumpy' and 'the Terminator' from *Angry White Pyjamas*). We swapped war stories, compared notes on the course and had a good laugh about the craziness of the whole thing. They seemed pretty relaxed with life and didn't seem to have suffered any permanent damage as a result of their own Senshusei experiences. It gave me a much-needed glimpse that life could and would get back to normal after the course was over and that I'd be a better person for having done it.

On the way home as I climbed the stairs in Meguro Station, I thought to myself, *my body is just a machine and if I put my mind to it, I can do anything.* If I was in any doubt, this revelation was confirmation that the course was changing me and making me stronger. Pain and pleasure were never too far apart, and Friday's cultural experience began with one almighty hangover. My body clock had kicked in as normal at 5:20am; and raising a smile, I turned over and went back to sleep. Eventually I made it out of bed and, after breakfast at Starbucks in Shibuya, caught the train to Ueno and wandered across to the park where there was a temporary exhibition of art from the Hermitage Museum in Russia. It was a trip down memory lane, as I'd visited Russia in my early twenties. This had also been a cultural experience, but not on the same level as the one I was now having in Japan.

THE CROCODILE AND KI

Saturday morning arrived all too soon, and after the previous day's holiday, it was even more difficult to get out of bed. To make matters worse, I'd had a really weird dream where I was being chased by a big green crocodile, and no matter where I went, it just kept pursuing me with its jaws snapping open and shut, as a prelude to what it would no doubt do if it ever caught up. I'd always thought that no matter how strange or unrelated to reality a dream might seem, it was probably trying to tell me something. As I stumbled out of bed bleary-eyed, I wondered if the big green crocodile was a reptilian manifestation of the Senshusei course. No matter where I went, at least until the end of February next year, there was no escaping it, and it felt like the relentless training was doing its best to mercilessly chew me up.

I arrived at the honbu and got changed. My stomach wasn't feeling too good, so naturally I felt worried about training in a white dogi. Any accident would instantly show up, and while in the real world you could excuse yourself and leave the mats if you got caught short, Senshusei offered no such practicality. Although I was suffering, Victoria was in much more pain. Vic was the only female on the course, but that hadn't held her back. She was tough and had so far dealt with things much better than her boyfriend Geoff. Vic didn't moan, whine or complain. She got on with things calmly and quietly. What she lacked in physical stature she made up for in mental strength, and it was this mindset that had impressed the Sensei, Sewanin and her fellow Senshusei. However, a freak injury was never far away, and staggering into the dojo on Saturday morning, she was visibly in pain. A couple of weeks before we'd been practicing *futari dori jiyu waza*. Futari dori was a step up from regular jiyu waza and, translated, meant *two-person attack*. Vic was one of two people attacking me, and as she threw a shomen uchi strike at my head, I'd entered inside her technique and sent her spinning off awkwardly to my side. She'd shown no immediate signs of discomfort and had carried on training, not just on that day but on all the training days since. Vic had some neck pain, but we all had that and didn't think much of it. But yesterday's holiday had given her body a chance to catch up and realise something was wrong. A trip to the chiropractor had confirmed that she'd misaligned her spine. Vic would need ongoing treatment to fix her neck and the rest of her vertebrae. The chiropractor had apparently told her that there was too much to do in one visit! This meant she'd be in mitori geiko for the foreseeable future, and while I hadn't intended to hurt her, and her injury was the result of an awkward fall, it didn't do much to ease my overwhelming feeling of guilt. I'd practiced martial arts for a long time, and thankfully I'd rarely hurt a training partner. In the ring it was a different story. During my Muay Thai career I'd broken one guy's arm with a roundhouse kick but hadn't felt guilty afterwards. When we both stepped into the ring, we'd known the risks, and in the heat of full-contact battle, anything went. War was war, and you did all you could to crush your opponent! This was a very different situation. There were still four months until the end of the course, and I felt dreadful that my throw might put Vic out for a good part of it.

Luckily Kancho was on hand and invited Vic into his office after class to perform a special *Ki* massage. Ki was a concept I'd never quite believed in or fully understood. Probably best described as *the energy that flows through all of our bodies*, it was supposed to have both healing and combative powers. Tai Chi practitioners were experts in it, and I'd seen demonstrations when one minute they'd heal and the next minute hurt. Kancho instructed Vic to sit down and wiggle her toes for an hour. A rather unusual request, but Vic did as she was told. There appeared to be method in the madness, as the wiggling encouraged Ki energy to travel up through her body and, in the process, straighten her spine. How I'm not sure, but it worked, and on another visit to the chiropractor, Vic had it confirmed that Kancho had defied medical science and put her twisted vertebrae back to normal. To say thank you, Vic had cooked Kancho some food. I asked her if she'd spiked it with anything, and Dave suggested that she pop in some crushed-up Viagra to straighten Kancho out, which gave us all a good laugh! I was just relieved she was back to full health. Dave had destroyed one cop in a moment of madness, and his initial remorse now seemed long forgotten. I didn't want Vic's inability to train on my conscience and was very pleased that Kancho, the wizard of wizards, had worked his magic.

BUFFALO SOLDIERS

Training continued, and in the run-up to Christmas, we had lots to pack in to get ready for our shodan test. Naruo Sensei gave us an interesting explanation of zanshin in one of his classes. I'd thought it was a heightened state of awareness in the application of a technique, which was maintained after the technique was over, but Naruo had another and far more worrying explanation altogether. According to Naruo, zanshin should feel the same as cutting your opponent's head off with a sword. Post-decapitation, as the head flew away, zanshin manifested in the ability to spike the defeated opponent's head on the point of your sword! I wasn't sure whether Naruo Sensei had ever decapitated anyone and didn't feel it appropriate to ask. We were all more than a little concerned by his explanation, an explanation we would now never forget.

All the talk of decapitation must have encouraged me to lose my head. On the evening before Bonfire Night, I bought a bottle of Hennessy and watched a film called *Buffalo Soldiers* about a group of US troops stationed in Germany who seemed to spend most of their time drinking, dealing in illicit contraband and getting into trouble. Left unregulated, I was sure the 16th Senshusei could very well wind up down a similar road, and as if to prove my point, one drink led to another and then another. When I got up to go to the toilet, I could hardly stand. Thanks to the amount of Hennessy I'd consumed, Naruo's zanshin, it appeared, had finally caught up with me!

When I woke up on 5 November, it felt like fireworks were going off inside my head. I had a hangover from hell and was very glad it was Sunday. I rarely drank the night before training, and this morning's futskayoi was a potent reminder why!

HE DIDN'T BOW!

My time working in the recruitment industry before the course had taught me the importance of body language. The words we speak have power, but how we look, carry ourselves and all the stuff we don't say can often have more meaning. As the second week of November got underway, and after a rather strange Murata Sensei class on kicking, which saw Dave bruise his shin on a bokken, we were all to be publicly snubbed by Chida. Lined up outside Kancho's office for the closing Shinkoku, we learnt that Kancho was not in the building. The office changed things last minute, which meant Chida Dojocho would respond to Boaz's official thank you for the day's training. As we shuffled into position outside the office door, a couple of metres down from Kancho's office, Chida appeared and looked disgusted that we were in transit and not yet ready for his arrival. Boaz cried out a perfect Shinkoku. We bowed, the Sewanin bowed, but Chida Sensei turned and went back into the office. It was customary for the Sensei receiving Shinkoku to bow in return, but today Chida had taken umbrage, picked up his ball and gone home. This was a disaster, and we all knew what would happen next. Malik Sewanin called us into the tearoom and lectured us on the need to get into line quickly. *'No wonder he doesn't teach you and didn't bow to us'*, he shouted at the top of his voice. Reading between the lines, it felt like Malik was more aggrieved that he and Graham had been snubbed, too, and less concerned that the Senshusei to date had had very little instruction from the Dojocho. I tried to look concerned, but I really didn't care. Yes, we'd made a mistake and should have been lined up and ready, but the last-minute change by the office in response to Kancho's absence had not been our fault. If Chida had taken offence at such a minor thing that was his business. If one of the primary reasons behind the Senshusei course was to send honbu-trained international ambassadors out into the world to promote Yoshinkan Aikido, Chida Sensei as head of the dojo wasn't going about things in a very smart way. After training and four classes teaching English at Mizuho Bank, I'd had enough. The Hennessy bottle looked so tempting when I got home that I had to indulge. A quick nightcap put just enough distance between me and the nonsense of the day.

The following morning, Chida's displeasure seemed to have rubbed off on Malik Sewanin. While having my pre-class pee, Malik burst in and shouted, *'get on the mats now, Simon; this isn't toilet time!'* There wasn't much I could do. In the spirit of the TV series *Mastermind*, and the immortal line, *'I've started so I'll finish'*, I muttered under my breath and did just that. I finished up as fast as I could and ran into the dojo to find everyone doing taiso. As I joined the circle of swirling arms, Malik wasn't finished yet. He screamed at the top of his voice, *'Simon, you're late!'* As if I didn't know that already!

CATCHING AIR

It was good to have Geoff back training, but with six weeks of absence from the weekly seiza class, I had serious doubts about his ability to get through it. Thursdays came around far too quickly, and to heighten the pain of zagaku, the Sensei teaching the preceding class always seemed determined to get as much blood pumping as possible around our soon-to-be static legs. Today this privilege fell to Sonoda Sensei. Sonoda always had the potential to overcomplicate even the simplest of exercises, and this class was to be no exception. We got into two lines, one line facing out from the shomen and the other line on the opposite side of the dojo facing in. We would be called out to perform jiyu waza in front of our peers and awaited Sonoda's command. If we'd been left to perform with the person opposite, things would have been much simpler, but why make a task simple when, with a few minor tweaks, you can make it incomprehensibly complicated?

One of my favourite quotes had always been Leonardo da Vinci's *'simplicity is the ultimate sophistication'*. Sonoda Sensei had the opposite idea and introduced a rotation system on who would be called up that none of us understood or had any ability to question. Geoff finally got into the right position opposite Boaz. Although Geoff had only recently recovered from a broken toe, Boaz showed no mercy and attempted to take his legs out from under him with a particularly venomous throw. This is what our ukemi training was for. The throw might look bad, but with knowledge and experience of the right way to fall, uke could survive perfectly intact. Geoff had some knowledge, but with so much time in mitori geiko he lacked recent practical experience. When performing good ukemi, there was no time to think. To get off a technique safely, your body had to react instinctively. Geoff had clearly forgotten how to breakfall. Instead of landing as he'd been taught, in a very dangerous attempt to avoid breaking his knees, he'd jumped off the ground and over Boaz. How he'd managed this Olympic feat, no one was sure. It was an amazing spectacle, and Geoff had well and truly caught air! Like a skateboarder attempting aerial theatrics, Geoff had elevated his huge frame above and beyond Boaz and somehow landed perfectly, causing no damage to Boaz or himself.

Geoff was understandably nervous about getting back to zagaku and positioned himself in between Matt and me. After 10 minutes he started to crumble. After 15 minutes his noises were getting louder. As his pain intensified, his breathing was becoming more and more laboured and resembled the sound a scuba diver makes when using breathing apparatus. Unfortunately, there was no buddy system available to Geoff. There was nothing Matt or I could do to help him, and Kancho, positioned at the head of the line under the shomen, simply ignored Geoff's pathetic and very noisy plea for mercy. It wasn't long before the sobbing started. Geoff was in bits, and Malik Sewanin was getting concerned. Not, I suspected, for Geoff's welfare but rather for how Geoff's performance would look to Kancho and the rest of the Sensei. We'd done zagaku many times now, and the expectation was that we should be used to it. Malik glared at Vic. As Geoff's girlfriend she was naturally worried, and to avoid making eye contact with the Sewanin, she glared across at me. Her facial expression was urging me to do something, but there was nothing to be done.

After zagaku the Sewanin called us into the tearoom to tell us we would have to pay 12,000 Yen for our shodan test (at the time c.£60). On the application form we all had to complete to take the test, Dave noticed that if you were taking your rokudan (sixth dan) test it would cost a whopping 120,000 yen (at the time c.£600), and from then on until we left the dojo, this was the only thing on his mind. I'd no idea why he was so bothered. Did he really have aspirations to get to rokudan? He'd already told us on more than one occasion that after the course was finished, he would quit Aikido for good! Riskily stepping above and beyond my station, I checked with Malik. *'Does anyone ever fail their rokudan test?'* I was sure there was no way anyone ever did. If you failed your test the fees were reimbursed, and I was certain the honbu dojo wouldn't relish handing back all that money. Malik said nothing, but he hadn't disagreed.

In the locker room prior to departing for the day, I caught wind of a conversation between Graham Sewanin and Neville. Compared to Malik, who was always shouting and screaming, Graham was much quieter. He had a calmness about him, and I was sure there were deeper levels to Graham that none of us had seen. Graham chatted with Neville about Aikido and life. Graham was opening up and said that he'd realised early on that he wasn't naturally talented at Aikido and had been forced to work hard at it to get to where he was now. In a very humble and self-reflective mood, he explained that he was happy he'd had to work hard because *'as soon as you think you're good at something, God can take it away!'* He continued with a specific example, *'if you think you're beautiful, in a flash through a car accident, it can be lost in an instant'.* Graham had revealed his depth of character and a sense of humility we'd not seen from either Sewanin before.

THE MONK AND THE MANIAC

My favourite classes were the ones where we got to mix around. Having an allocated partner was becoming tiresome, and given that this was the longest part of the course and I had Geoff, any break from the normal routine was always very welcome. Before the week was out, Noriki Sensei gave us the opportunity to mix things up a little, and when there was a change of partners to be had, at the top of my list were Matt, Dave and Lloyd. Matt and I had trained together back in the UK, Dave was always good for a laugh and Lloyd could take any level of pain I cared to dish out. Matt was good for technical stuff, Dave to lighten the mood and Lloyd was the perfect choice when I wanted to test out the power of my techniques and how well they'd work in a real situation.

We were practicing shomen iriminage techniques. This was the technique I'd seen Steven Seagal perform in his films, which had sparked my interest in Aikido. It was a hard technique to get off at speed and one of the most brutal techniques we'd learnt so far. Matt and I went at each other with force, and noticed the Sewanin laughing as we smashed each other into the middle of next week. Humour was usually linked to pain at the honbu, and the Sewanin's sadistic chuckles were a shining example. Lloyd was next, and in his company, the level of intensity stepped up a gear. We smashed each other back and forth, doing our best to make our techniques harder and harder. My aim was to bounce Lloyd's head off the tatami, and his ambition appeared to be the same. We'd seen Gozo Shioda do it in the videos we'd watched, and now it was our turn! The harder we tried and the more strength we used, the more difficult it became to apply the throw properly. Aikido was about the application of proper technique, something Lloyd and I had temporarily ditched in favour of brute strength. Before the class was done, I found myself opposite Neville. His style was very different to mine, and he started off performing the technique lightly. I'd always found him more spiritual than physical and as we went about our business, it was very much the monk and the maniac. In the smash-fest Neville had no choice but to up his game and by the end of our time together he'd definitely increased his power. In the tearoom after the class, Lloyd admitted that one of my throws had bounced his head off the tatami. I'd not noticed at the time, as Lloyd hadn't complained. I got the feeling he'd enjoyed the experience, and knowing Lloyd, he probably had. The Sewanin appeared and called us back into the dojo. This usually spelled trouble, and I wondered what we'd done wrong this time. Perhaps their amusement had waned, and the sight of the Senshusei going no holds barred in an attempt to knock one another out would not go unpunished? To my surprise, they were in a complimentary mood and said that they'd both been really impressed with our training and energy over the last few days, and especially today. Malik said it had been a beautiful sight, with the sun shining through the windows as a backdrop to our efforts. He even said that we all had a bit of Chino in us, which put a smile on everyone's faces. It had been a good day and one where I felt very proud to be Senshusei.

This would have been a great way to finish the week, but Saturday was still to get through. The eleventh day of the eleventh month was an important day, and one I always observed to honour and remember members of the armed services who had died in the line of duty. I'd proudly wear my poppy every year, but in Japan there were no poppies and Remembrance Day wasn't observed. Murata Sensei's class finished at 11am, and at the eleventh hour of the eleventh day of the eleventh month, I privately observed the two-minute silence to remember those who'd made the ultimate sacrifice. It was a poignant moment about the futility of war – 65 years earlier, my time in Japan would have been a very different experience.

I was struggling with the onset of a cold, and yesterday's smashing had left me hurting all over. I was ready for the weekend, which couldn't come fast enough. In the tearoom after the final class, during which Takagi Sensei had added to my aches and pains, Geoff was talking to Francis, a former Senshusei and a good friend of the 16th. Browsing through an old Aikido book together, Geoff pointed to a picture of Kancho Gozo Shioda and asked Francis, *'who is this guy then?'* Ronen, who was also in earshot, looked at me and rolled his eyes. I intervened and pointing to the book and Yoshinkan's founder queried, *'you mean this guy?'* Geoff replied, *'yeah, who is he?'* We couldn't believe what we'd heard!

SAME OLD SHIT, DIFFERENT DAY!

The weekend had been a nightmare. My cold had gotten worse, and I'd felt like crap. I'd done very little, but when I had ventured out, everyone seemed to be coughing and sneezing. Illness and injury were still my worst

244

nightmares. In my attempt to get better in time for Tuesday, I'd drained my bottle of Hennessy dry and followed up with a chaser of Night Nurse. This wasn't the best combination, and the medicine bottle advised: *Avoid drinking alcohol with Night Nurse. Drinking alcohol with Night Nurse can make you feel very sleepy, dizzy or confused.* The advice was right. I'd felt very sleepy and had had no trouble dropping off. Waking up, however, was another matter; and with the start of yet another week I was thrown headfirst into a state of confusion. Music had to be the answer and on the train to Ochiai I listened to US rock band, Puddle Of Mudd's *Nobody Told Me*. Somebody had told me that Hennessy and Night Nurse didn't mix. It was clearly written on the bottle, but for some stupid reason, I'd chosen to ignore it. The lyrics pounded through my head and seemed to speak to my present situation.

Nobody told me where to go.
Nobody told me where to run.
Nobody told me where to go.
Nobody told me, nobody told me.
Same old shit, different day, gotta get up, gotta get up.

Never was a truer word sung. 'Same old shit, different day, gotta get up, gotta get up' was the story of my life! Ronen joined me on the train. His knees were messed up and although he lived only a short distance from the honbu, cycling was no longer an option. We had a system for counting the days to the end of the course and now since he'd ditched his bike, a system to meet on the train. In the switch from the JR Yamanote Line at Takadanobaba it was either the front or last carriage on the Tokyo Subway prearranged by text. We didn't speak, we were both too tired. In a world of our own we travelled the last stretch of the journey listening to our favourite music. I bought a Roots black coffee from a vending machine. Hot coffee in a can wasn't something I'd ever tried back home, but in Tokyo it had regularly been my lifesaver ahead of another punishing day. As we walked into the honbu dojo, I told Ronen, *'I've no idea how I'm going to make it through this week'*. The coffee was a start and would hopefully at least get me through the first class. After that there was always the buddy system!

Tuesday passed in a haze, and Wednesday arrived. Wednesday was brutal. The combination of Paul, Oyamada and finally Takashima Sensei played havoc with my left hip, which was now badly swollen. As the weather got colder, the tatami got harder, and with the endless jiyu waza, the experience of being uke and landing repeatedly on my pain spot was excruciating. Instead of relaxing my body into the fall, I'd started to brace myself in anticipation of the pain. Tensing up just made matters worse, and as I left the honbu and headed off to Berlitz, I could hardly walk. I needed to fix things quickly and stopped by Oshman's in Harajuku. I bought another ice bag and some tape. On arrival at work, I filled the bag with ice and used the tape to strap it to my back under my shirt. I had to get the swelling down, and ice was the only way to do it. In the middle of teaching my first class the ice had partially melted and all I could hear was the sound of water swilling around inside the bag as I walked around the classroom. I wondered what my student must have thought. Perhaps he suspected I'd filled a colostomy bag I had deposited discretely under my clothes? I didn't explain. My English was up to it, but his was most definitely not. In the break between classes, I adjusted the bag and applied more tape. While there was ice still in it, I couldn't afford to take it off. I had to get rid of the swelling even if it made for an embarrassing situation. I trusted in the fact that my Japanese students would be far too polite to ask what the strange water sound was as I squelched around the room!

POLICE TEST

The cops were to test for shodan first, and the day of their test arrived. Thursday, 16 November 2006 would be the culmination of all of their hard work and the opportunity to show the Sensei how far they'd come. I was pleased they were up first. It would give us, the international contingent, the opportunity to see how things would work on our test day. The only price we'd have to pay for the privilege was yet another painful session of seiza.

Before that there was Laurance and Oyamada Sensei to get through. In between classes Dave was on hand to lighten the mood. He told us about this thing called 'Bangkok' he'd experienced while at school. I'd trained Muay Thai in Bangkok a number of times, so knew the city well. What Dave was about to say, though, was anyone's guess, and we waited in anticipation for his story to unfold. Bangkok, it turned out bore no relation to Thailand's capital city but was a prank that had done the rounds in his formative years. When the older boys walked past him at school, they'd hit him in the balls. Bangkok, it turned out, was 'bang cock'! Now every time he heard the word Thailand or Bangkok, it sent a shiver down his spine. This explained a lot. In one of our very first conversations, I'd told him about my time in Thailand. Dave had looked nervous, not, as it turns out, from my tales of training, but because he thought I was going to bang him in the balls! I didn't know it then, but in Oyamada's class, I was to be reminded of a prank that had been a staple at my school. During hajime geiko Geoff had been slow at getting started on a particular technique. Behind everyone else's timing, he'd swung me round in his sankajo lock. Absorbed by the distress of taking uke, I was unaware that Matt was on all fours behind me, having the final part of the technique applied. I caught my feet, fell back and landed in a heap on top of him!

We sat down in seiza at midday. Inoue Kancho, Chida, Oyamada and Sonoda Sensei put the cops through their paces. The grading lasted for 90 minutes, and my legs were soon asleep. The pain ebbed and flowed, and I alternated leaning forwards and putting my hands down with sitting back in the proper position. I wanted to concentrate on the test, but the pain had an all-consuming, distracting and debilitating quality to it. While I was physically present, after the test was over, I had very little idea what had gone off and how the cops had done. I heard later that Tachiki had made a poor defence from a wooden *tanto*, which had been thrust in her direction in the self-defence section. She'd been slashed across the ribs, and I shuddered to think what would have happened had it been a real *knife* in a real situation. Any preconception I'd had about the toughness and fighting abilities of the Tokyo Riot Police by now had vanished. I hoped the Japanese crime rate remained low to ensure the future safety of my newfound friends. We didn't have to wait too long to learn that the cops had all passed. This was the last test they'd do. After our shodan we'd be staying on for the final phase of our course, where we'd learn how to teach and take the instructor's exam. The cops wouldn't be joining us, and they'd soon be back on the front line, fighting Tokyo's miniscule crime problem. We'd now be seeing very little of them, unless we got ourselves in trouble while out and about!

Clyde, Ronen, Dror and I headed across to the sento. I was hoping to put on a wash while I washed myself, but both the laundry and sento were shut. Undeterred, we found a seat in the Royal Host and discussed the events of the day. Clyde was usually calm, but today he was probably the most annoyed I'd ever seen him. It turned out he'd had his fill of Malik Sewanin and said that earlier on that day, he'd been close to snapping and smashing him in the face in the middle of the class. I was glad he hadn't, as that would have seen Clyde kicked off the course or worse still. To appease his plight, we made an informal pact to get together and find a way to smash Malik before the course was over. Mess with one Senshusei and you mess with the rest. Where was Lloyd when we needed him?

I caught the train to Tokyu Hands, the huge department store close to Shinjuku Station, and met Danielle, who was over in Japan from the UK to compete in a Karate tournament. Danielle and I had worked together in recruitment back home and had always got on well with a shared passion for the martial arts. As I walked up to her, she looked shocked. We hadn't seen each other since I'd left for Japan, and she immediately noticed how much weight I'd lost. We grabbed a coffee in the restaurant and reminisced about old times and life back in England. It was a welcome break and a chance to have a normal conversation about normal things. At 6pm, I said goodbye, and we went our separate ways. There was still dogi washing and food shopping to be done before I could get my head down for the night.

BILATERAL AGREEMENT

Friday arrived, and once again I successfully dodged Chino Sensei outside the honbu dojo. As I snuck in, he looked to be heading up to FamilyMart. He no doubt liked to browse the magazine rack and purchase drinks and snacks just like everybody else.

Ahead of the Enbu, it had been kihon dosa renzoku all the way, and now, ahead of our black belt test, it was endless jiyu waza that was set to become the Sensei's preferred tool of torture. In Romeo Sensei's class, Neville made use of a move that involved sliding on his knees under uke's oncoming attack. Partnered with Vic, he'd hit this technique four times on the bounce, which was a very difficult thing for her or anyone else to get off safely. Time things wrong, and one of two things could happen. Too early, and you'd land on shite's back with the distinct possibility of injuring shite and yourself. Too late, and through the pressure exerted by shite's body, your legs would be locked in position in the opposite direction to the way your knees were designed to bend. Breaking both knees was one of the worst out of a long list of potential injuries available to a Senshusei. Breaking your neck came first, closely followed by any major trauma to the spine, with the double-knee break bringing up the rear in third place. It was rare, but it did happen. Vic wasn't happy and made her displeasure known in the tearoom.

Yesterday, to support Clyde, Ronen, Dror and I had made a pact, and now it was time for me to make my own special pact with Geoff. We stopped short of signing a formal contract, but the negotiations leading up to our verbal agreement were complex, detailed and seemed to be heading towards a formal written declaration. Like two superpowers debating the terms of a bilateral nuclear disarmament, we finally reached an agreement. The knee slide was off limits. Under no circumstances would either of us utilise this technique on each other, no matter what. Getting over Geoff's hulk required gymnastic ability that I didn't possess, and Geoff, still struggling with a painful toe, probably had more to lose from any breach of terms. Our negotiation ended just in time to set the dojo up for lunch. In a similar format to the one we'd experienced at the start of the course; today's lunch was to celebrate our success at the Enbu. The big guns, including Kancho, Chida and Chino, were all in attendance, and despite the lunch being held for our benefit, it was an uncomfortable and awkward experience. We took our seats and sat bolt upright in our chairs, ready to begin eating after Kancho had started his bento box. Once again, we were stopped abruptly in our stride when Kancho was full. As the chopsticks went down, there was some general chit-chat from the top table followed by an awkward silence. What could have been a fun and enjoyable lunch was anything but. Everybody sat staring at each other, waiting for something, anything, to happen. Kancho eventually got up and left, which was the Sensei's cue to get up and leave, too, and our signal to get cleaning. I found it strange to be invited to a party where there was no opportunity to relax, it was frowned upon to speak, and I'd be expected to clean up before going home. This was the honbu dojo way, and there was no choice but to like it or lump it!

MAULED BY A BEAR

My agreement with Geoff might have saved my knees from irreversible damage, but when I woke up on Saturday morning, my body was still in bits. My left ankle felt weak, my left hip was still badly bruised, and to top it all off, something felt like it was about to pop out of my right knee.

In the first class we had Romeo Sensei, and for some reason, we all performed badly when called up to do a mini mock test. Neville and Vic seemed to forget every technique they'd practiced. Even Malik seemed subdued and out of sorts. He shook his head on the sidelines but had no appetite to shout or scream. Only Matt brought him back to life. Matt was arguably Malik's favourite, and although the feeling wasn't mutual, Matt could do nothing about it or the mickey-taking we gave him as a direct result. Matt's techniques had on more than one occasion been greeted with appreciative cries from Malik Sewanin. *'Beautiful! All day, all night Matt – keep it going!'* But today, even Matt messed up. His mistake caught the attention of Malik who shouted out in disbelief! In the second class, the cops, kitted out in their new, shiny black belts, made a surprise appearance. I had thought our time together was pretty much at an end, but an opportunity to flaunt their new grade in front of us was too good a one to miss. I suspected the Sewanin might be behind their appearance in an attempt to gee-up our flailing attitude and ability. It worked. We got back on our game and, determined to outdo our now more senior grades, trained at an intensity that made Graham and Malik smile. In the last class, we had Murray Sensei, who arrived on the mats looking less than his best. We'd been told at the start of the course that we must at all times present ourselves in the dojo in a clean, tidy dogi. It seemed as if it was one rule for them and one rule for us. We knew there was a stuffed bear in Kancho's office. We presumed it was stuffed – apparently it had been given to Kancho by the Russians. How it had made its way through customs was beyond me. Kancho must have had friends in high places! As Murray Sensei strode out to take his position under the shomen, he looked like he'd been mauled by a bear. Had Kancho's bear come to life? His usual immaculate dogi had been exchanged for one with rips and his hair was a mess. A native of Canada, perhaps he'd taken on the ultimate opponent nature had to offer in a bid to test his Aikido? I suppose anything was possible!

AM I GOING MAD?

The course had already given me my fair share of difficulties and had proven itself to be one huge physical and mental rollercoaster. Like an inmate within the prison system, I was now used to the punishing routine and the quirks of dojo life – quirks I had to be aware of to ensure my long-term survival and ultimate release back into civilisation. During my rest time away from the honbu, I'd begun to contemplate what life on the outside might be like. Was I ready to return to normality? How would I utilise my time when it came flooding back in abundance? Would I miss what I'd initially hated but, through an extended and ongoing period of acclimatisation, was possibly now growing to love? I'd even started to enjoy Oyamada Sensei's classes and had on more than one occasion felt sad at the thought of the course ending. At the start, the end was all I could think about. Now I was starting to savour every day, which had the ironic consequence of speeding time up. Classes that had previously dragged on and on were now going quickly, and, like sand slipping through my fingers, I was trying to grasp at every grain. I wondered if I was going mad, or was this all part of the Senshusei experience? Hate and love were supposedly two sides of the same coin. Perhaps I was transitioning from one to the other?

As if to interrupt my new, surprising relationship with the course, a national holiday arrived to disrupt my flow. Thursday, 23 November, was Labour Thanksgiving Day, a day to give thanks for production and to encourage thinking about the environment and human rights. Away from the honbu, I found myself with the one thing I was now beginning to fear – time on my hands! Wandering through Shibuya Station on my way to meet Clyde at Jiu Jitsu, I witnessed one of the strangest sights I'd seen in Japan to date. Ignored by everyone else going about their daily business, through the bustling crowds staggered an old man well into his seventies, on a pair of crutches. At first there was nothing unusual about him or his appearance until I glanced down at his feet. He was sporting a pair of women's backless pink stilettos! Was he using the crutches to help him balance in his unusual footwear, or had wearing his choice of shoes caused an injury? It was impossible to know, but if I was going mad, I wasn't alone!

PIDDLE PANTS

Toilet timing was an essential part of dojo life. Getting caught short in the middle of a class was not an option. Routine was everything, and after months of practice, I was like a well-oiled machine timing everything, including toilet visits, down to the precise second. In Friday morning's meeting, Malik Sewanin threw us a curve ball. I didn't realise it at the time, but one hell of a curve ball it was about to be. For the best part of eight months, we'd started the morning taiso at 8:15am. We'd be on the mats just in time for the week's Shinkoku to call out each exercise to the count. Now, for some strange reason, Malik had made the decision that taiso should start at 8:10am and not the 8:15am we'd all gotten used to. A small change it might have seemed, but with my routine carefully planned, even a small change could have potentially big consequences.

In the first class, Kanazawa Sensei ran us through yet more jiyu waza. The more I moved about, the more conscious I became that I needed a wee. What started as a drip grew into a trickle, and before long there was a torrent of waves crashing relentlessly against the inside of my bladder. The coffee I'd bought at Musashi Koyama Station from one of the many vending machines had gathered force, and the disruption of losing a precious five minutes was pushing me closer and closer to the possibility of pissing my pants. Wetting yourself came second only to shitting yourself. A white dogi and poo didn't mix, and any indiscretion of this type was impossible to hide. Wee, on the other hand, could be mistaken for sweat, but not the amount I was carrying. I had no choice but to hold it. The pain was intense and with each fall I took at the hands of Geoff; I wondered if this time the floodgates might burst. Thankfully, the first class ran for 60 minutes. If this had happened in the second or third class, by the time I left the dojo for the day I'd have been christened 'piddle pants'. The class finally ended, and I ran to the toilet like a man possessed. I'd recently come to the realisation that hate and love were closely related, and as I emptied my bladder, I experienced firsthand that pain and pleasure were much the same. What had been angry waves with nowhere to go on the inside, now set free, felt like a hot, steamy shower on a cold winter's day!

SICKIE BUG?

If shitting yourself was the number one violation followed by pissing your pants, puking your guts up in the dojo came in third. In Saturday morning's meeting, we learnt that Boaz was ill. To be fair, he didn't look well. He usually bounced around the dojo, but today he dragged himself along as if he had the weight of the world on his shoulders. The colour had drained from his face, and he had a sweat on. As far as I could tell in assessing his situation, it was only a matter of time.

In the first class, Murray Sensei sat us in seiza and gave us a talk on the meaning of Senshusei. He said we were like soldiers and that our job was to do as we were told each and every day. Our job was to follow orders and never to question them. What our superiors told us to do, we had to do. Our job wasn't to think, but to act out the wishes of our commanding officers. I'd always drawn a parallel between honbu life and what I expected life in the military would really be like. Murray Sensei's explanation made sense. He continued. Although the honbu dojo had trained soldiers, what they really wanted were leaders. We'd been drilled into following commands without thinking, but once we graduated from the course, the honbu dojo and the IYAF wanted an army of leaders to take what we'd learnt and to promote the art of Aikido back in our home countries. Murray Sensei urged us to start thinking about this now and, having sown this contradictory seed, finally got on with the business of training. His speech had wasted 15 minutes of the class, which was no bad thing, although the requirement to sit in seiza was always the fly in the ointment. While we got on with the physical side of the class, Boaz, who had now turned an unhealthy shade of grey, was relegated to mitori geiko and made to sit in the corner.

Murray Sensei's class led into Sonoda's and what would probably now be our very last session with the cops. I suspected this might be the case as Inoue Kancho had opened the class, and while most of us didn't understand what he was saying, the smiles and nods from the Kidotai seemed to have significance. Sonoda Sensei then ran us through a complicated rendition of set moves with a wooden tanto, which all of us struggled to follow. The cops didn't seem to care. They'd made it to the end, and while we were yet to test for shodan and still had three months left, they had reached the finish line. Kancho returned at the end of the class to deliver a 10-minute speech, which once again, most of us didn't understand. A Kancho speech meant seiza, and

Geoff, positioned next to me, was in his usual agony. Kancho could have told him the earth had stopped spinning, and the sky was about to fall in, and Geoff wouldn't have cared. All he could feel and focus on was the pulsing pain in his legs and a wish that Kancho would stop speaking.

In the last class, like a breath of fresh air, there was a new Sensei in town. Marshall Sensei from Australia, who had completed the course some years before. He took us through jiyu waza techniques in groups and finished with a detailed explanation of his signature move, *koshinage*. Koshinage was a technique that terrified me. It involved being thrown across shite's lower back and was accompanied by a difficult fall that was easy to get wrong. Unfortunately, paired with Geoff, lower back usually meant his shoulders. It felt like falling out of a tree, and I hoped Marshall Sensei could improve Geoff's technique and ease my pain. Dave, though, wasn't in the mood to ease anyone's pain. In another moment of madness, he threw Matsuki, one of the ippan students, on his head. Luckily there didn't appear to be any permanent damage, but with high falls, hard tatami and the occasional lapse of concentration, a nasty, life-changing injury was never far away. As Matsuki nursed his head, concern for him was momentarily disturbed by a heaving sound which emanated from the corner of the dojo. Boaz had thrown up and failed to follow the rules. Instead of puking in his dogi top, he'd been caught short and sprayed the entire contents of his stomach all over the mats! I did my best to look busy and successfully avoided mopping-up duty. Sick, especially someone else's, wasn't my favourite thing; and if it was caused by a sickness bug, getting close to it wasn't the smartest idea. It transpired that Boaz's condition wasn't in fact a sickie bug. It was instead put down to a dinner he'd been to the night before. Dror had been due to attend, but luckily for him had to miss out because of work. It looked like Boaz had been served up an unhealthy dose of food poisoning and we'd all paid the price.

Saturday night couldn't come quick enough. Seb, who taught me at the Shudokan, was in Tokyo with his girlfriend, Ewa and their friend Andrew. Matt, Dave, Clyde, Ronen and I met at Shinjuku Station's east exit. Marshall and Laurance Sensei arrived with Seb and Ewa, and we headed off to find an izakaya to do some long-overdue catching up. Seb had carried on training for a while at the Shudokan and told me that Sensei Ken wasn't very happy that I'd left to go to Japan without asking his permission. On finishing the course, I'd hoped to conduct some of my international ambassador role back at the Shudokan, but having upset Sensei Ken, and on Seb's advice, I'd now need to rethink my plans. In Japan, Seb and Ewa hadn't trained at the honbu dojo; it was never in the plan. After leaving the Shudokan in Nottingham, they trained for a time with Sensei Paul Stephens in London. Under Takeno Sensei, Stephens Sensei had made an introduction, and Seb, Ewa and Andrew had spent three weeks in Yamanashi with Yoshinkan's very own Darth Vader. Takeno Sensei, along with his principal uke, Nakagawa Sensei had provided an unforgettable experience and looked after their Polish visitors like family. Seb shared a story which made me smile. One day after training, Seb and Andrew were getting changed in the changing room when Takeno walked in. Spotting a tattoo on Seb's arm, Takeno Sensei asked Andrew, *'do you have one?'* *'No Sensei!'* Andrew had nervously replied. With no advance warning, Takeno hit Andrew in the middle of his back with a palm strike which left a red imprint of his hand. *'Now you do!'* Takeno Sensei smiled, laughed and walked out! I said farewell and caught the last train home. With work the next day, I had to call time on a great night. Matt, though, was made of sterner stuff. I found out later that he'd stayed out all night and gone to work and taught classes the next day in the same clothes. He'd met us from work, had a big night out and then gone back to work in the same threads!

As I headed off to work with a very sore head, I recalled a hazy conversation I'd had with Dave. I'd caught a glimpse of his bank card, which had the word 'honour' or 'honourable' on it. I remembered quizzing him about it and being given a very evasive response. There was evidently more to Dave than met the eye. I'd always wondered how he could afford to stay in Japan without ever working. Was Dave one of the gentry? Was he from noble stock? Was Crazy Dave a member of the House of Lords?

YOU DIRTY RAT!

On Monday I'd doubled up on extracurricular training – Axis Jiu Jitsu in the morning and Fairtex Muay Thai in the afternoon. I'd burnt through the cobwebs of yesterday and was in good spirits until I received Ronen's text. Ronen's message said that he'd bumped into Graham Sewanin, and in conversation Graham had told him he thought I was a rat. Graham suspected that I'd been talking to Paul Sensei about the Sewanin and had leaked what had happened at Iwama. I'd been nervous since my conversation with Laurance at the Berlitz party that the finger of suspicion might be pointed at me. I'd expected Murray Sensei to pull me in for a confidential chat, but it was Graham who somehow seemed to have put two and two together and made five. I wasn't the leak, but now it was looking like I was! Ronen told me he'd triggered the buddy system and put Graham straight. I hardly saw Paul and had said nothing about Iwama or anything else for that matter to anyone apart from my fellow Senshusei. Still, rumours had a habit of taking hold. The last thing I wanted anyone, and especially Graham, to think was that I'd been telling tales.

When I arrived at the honbu on Tuesday morning for the start of another week, I was still raging about Graham's accusation. It was a precarious situation. He didn't know that I knew, and I couldn't let him know that I knew for fear of dropping Ronen in it. I wanted to confront Graham head-on, but the only option available to me was to *let sleeping dogs lie*. In the morning meeting, Graham said that he and Malik had been to a party on Saturday night with the cops and had been joined by some of the international and Japanese Sensei. The seating arrangement had been planned, and the cops had positioned the Sewanin next to Kancho Sensei and away from the international Sensei. Graham said that this had been an honour. Kancho always got the best seat in the house, and being seated in such close proximity meant something. Ronen and I had earlier caught up in the locker room on the events of the weekend. As Graham recounted his current version, I reflected on what Ronen had told me that Graham had shared privately with him about what really went down. Graham had told Ronen that he and Malik had been positioned near Kancho because the international Sensei disliked the Sewanin. This, it turned out, had been part of the catalyst for Graham's rat accusation. Rumours of the Iwama incident were indeed circulating from some unknown source, and they hadn't been well received. Both Sewanin felt they were being shunned, but as the principal protagonists, they had no one to blame but themselves. It was a shining example of there being two sides to every story, and I suspected the truth lay somewhere in the middle. Back in the meeting, Graham wasn't done yet. He said that during the meal, one cop had come up to him and Malik to thank them for their help on the course. He said that the Kidotai had seen the Sewanin pushing the Kokusai, and that this had inspired them all to greater effort. Graham explained that he'd said in response, *'you understand Senshusei'*, and the cop in acknowledgement had given him a knowing nod. Reading between the lines, I took Graham's sermon to mean that he still suspected I was the source of the Sewanin's troubles, and that while the cops were now the real deal, we still had one hell of a way to go!

THE COPS GRADUATE

The cops, like a bad smell, were still hanging around. I'd been expecting them to disappear for a while, but they were still present in the odd class, and there had been no formal finish to their time on the course. Wednesday, 29

November 2006, was set for their official graduation and that meant only one class. Romeo Sensei took this, and we pushed ourselves to the limit, knowing that the rest of the day would be spent watching the Kidotai's passing-out parade. Normally, I'd leave at least some gas in the tank after the first class. With two 90-minute classes to get through afterwards, operating on fumes wasn't a good idea. Romeo called out technique after technique in hajime-geiko style. Although I pushed myself hard, I felt that my techniques were getting worse, and with not long until the shodan test, this wasn't where I wanted to be. My despondency turned to despair when I learnt that the graduation ceremony was now being pushed back to 11am, instead of the originally scheduled 10am. To fill in the time we were sent to our cleaning stations. Cleaning duty was about to get a lot harder with the departure of the cops, and it seemed like the Sewanin wanted to give us a head start in keeping the honbu dojo spick and span. I vacuumed the locker room for a second time that day, two hours after I'd previously done it. This was cleaning for cleaning's sake, and the time passed slowly. There was a danger that the graduation ceremony might run over, and any delay to the precious 2pm finish would mess up my teaching schedule at Berlitz.

With the overdose of cleaning finally over, we headed into the dojo to set up. Chairs were put in place, and those that had seen better days, as a makeshift repair, were stuck together with tape. We were also ordered to move the soft mats into the sho dojo. Navigating big, unwieldy mats through a small door in the corner of the main dojo was no easy task, and Malik Sewanin added his own brand of help by pushing us even when, because of spatial restrictions, there was no room to move! The scene reminded me of the 'train pushers' I'd see, during the busiest times on station platforms throughout Tokyo. Rail employees in white gloves pushed commuters into overloaded carriages to fill every last bit of space. I'd never seen anything like this in London, or anywhere else for that matter. When the train arrived and the doors opened, people would literally fall out. That didn't stop the train pushers. If you wanted to get on you had to stand with your back to the open doors, brace yourself, and, be prepared to be shoved in!

The graduation ceremony was one big anticlimax. The international Senshusei sat in seiza while the cops sat comfortably on chairs. This was a glimpse of the future we'd potentially also enjoy. Every now and again, one of the cops jumped up to attention and bowed to Inoue Kancho. None of us really knew what was going on and lived in hope that whatever was happening would end soon. These hopes were well and truly dashed when a quietly spoken woman got up to make a speech. The speech dragged on and on, and just when it looked like it was ending, it dragged on some more.

After more bowing and scraping, it was finally over. As the cops rose easily to their feet, we staggered to ours. With over 25 minutes in seiza, I was less than steady. On legs that were unresponsive due to lack of blood flow, I grabbed hold of Matt to assist my ascent and narrowly missed knocking Chino Sensei over.

There was still more work to be done. Miyakoshi Sensei had started rearranging the chairs in preparation for a lunch we thankfully wouldn't be attending, and like good Senshusei, we ran to help. Miyakoshi seemed quite happy on a solo mission and told us he was fine on his own. We'd been trained to provide assistance even when it wasn't needed, and for the next 10 minutes, we followed him around the dojo like a pack of hungry wolves determined to catch our prey. We tried to grab chairs off him so we could say we'd put them in place. It bordered on harassment and was complete and utter chaos. To the untrained eye, the Senshusei were trying to over-engineer a relatively simple task and causing an unnecessary disturbance. Before we could escape for the day, there was the small task of folding the Sensei's hakama. We set up a production line in the tearoom and ploughed through them all ahead of schedule. Practice hadn't made perfect, but it had definitely improved our performance.

I CAN READ YOUR MIND

The last day of November was finally here. I couldn't believe that with the Christmas break, there were now less than three months left of the course. The day got off to a positive start as Malik Sewanin phoned in sick. Where the Sewanin were concerned, two eyes were better than four, and although I no longer trusted Graham since his accusation, he still marginally won out in the popularity stakes. In the morning meeting, Graham unveiled more of his spiritual self. He complained that someone hadn't bowed to him properly, and the culprit, who now was looking rather sheepish, turned out to be Inazaki. Graham said he could see right through people and could tell whether or not they really wanted to bow to him. I was concerned, because if he possessed such an ability, I had no desire for him to know what I was thinking! If Graham Sewanin could read minds, we were all in trouble, and for all of our sakes, I sincerely hoped he was bluffing. I'd never seen a crystal ball in his possession, or a pack of tarot cards fall out of his bag, but anything was possible. It was rumoured that a dream had been the catalyst for him doing the course. A vision that he'd been a Samurai in a previous life had led him to Japan. Whether there was any truth in the story I couldn't say for certain. I was sure, though, that there was more to Graham than first met the eye!

After a beasting by Paul Sensei in the first class, we were back in Sonoda world. Sonoda Sensei had come up with a way to combine kihon dosa with kihon waza that left us all confused. Dave had taken it upon himself to move before Sonoda told him to. This was a breach of the rules and prompted Sonoda to walk up to Dave and slap him on the shoulder. Dave didn't learn his lesson and made the same mistake later on in the class. I wasn't sure what a shoulder slap escalated to, but luckily for Dave, it turned out to be just a verbal bashing.

For zagaku, I was astonished to see the cops were back. Hadn't they graduated the other day? If I'd have graduated, I might have popped back for a coffee and a chat in the tearoom or to attend one of the ippan classes, but no way on this earth would it cross my mind to come back for the weekly seiza class. That was just sadistic. To my mind the cops either loved pain or had been misinformed about what a return to the honbu would involve! Their continued reappearance was getting tiresome. We couldn't seem to get rid of them. Like a band at the end of a concert coming back for encore after encore, they'd now played to the audience too many times. Once would have been more than enough! Their return came with hidden repercussions. They'd each be sharing their individual feedback on the course. We'd got used to the regular format. Two reflections and two habits with feedback were just about doable. We were now faced with the prospect of 10 cops droning on about what Senshusei had meant to them. As if their individual ramblings weren't enough, a Sensei would respond to each statement. After 30 minutes there was no sign that the ordeal would be over soon. I counted each Japanese Senshusei in turn and willed each to finish. At 45 minutes in, Geoff was convulsing. A strange force looked to have taken over his body, and he twitched and shook in a way I'd not seen him do before. It looked like he was having an epileptic fit. Seeing him locked in his own world of seizure after seizure, I was concerned he wouldn't make it to the end. I was worried he didn't even know where he was! Out of sight of Inoue Kancho, I tapped Geoff on the lower back to show support and to encourage him to stay focused and in the game. We'd had our differences, but in Dai San, we were partners. His pain was my pain, and to get through shodan and the remaining part of this phase of the course, I needed him in one piece. Tachiki, who, like Vic on the international side, was the only female on the Kidotai course, started crying during her speech. She'd found the course extremely tough but had been given *sandan* (third dan) for her efforts. Tachiki didn't compare to Vic in terms of strength, skill and ability. *If Vic doesn't get awarded the same at the end of our course,* I thought to myself, *there'll have been one big miscarriage of justice.* The cops finally finished. They were done and dusted, and it was time for them to leave. Permanently this time. Our course was longer and, given our early start, arguably much harder. We'd gone toe to toe with them and come off better! Geoff, Dave and Lloyd had struggled the most throughout the whole ordeal. Geoff's blood-starved legs couldn't move even when the opportunity to do so presented itself. I helped him up and held him steady while his blood supply took advantage of gravity to surge back into place. This only made matters worse. As Geoff's legs woke up, so did he. Now more conscious of the unpleasant sensation screaming through his veins, he convulsed even more. Like a patient under anaesthetic who wakes up in the middle of their operation, Geoff was in shock. My injured comrade needed professional medical help, but no help came!

ADVENT–URE

The first of December had arrived, and I couldn't wait to open the first window on my Advent calendar. Little things were important, and the opening of the first door signalled the countdown to the Christmas break. Although it was Advent, nothing changed at the honbu dojo. The 'advent-ure' would continue in the same way it had up until now. I'd always loved Christmas, and it was never too early to get into the Christmas spirit. On the train journey in, I scrolled to Christmas carols on my iPod, instead of the overplayed assortment of tracks I used to psyche myself up. *O Come, All Ye Faithful* and *Hark! The Herald Angels Sing* didn't provide the usual surge in adrenalin I needed, but it was tradition, and tradition mattered more today.

Matt and Dave were in a comical mood. Assigning both of them to cleaning duty in the men's toilets was a recipe for disaster. As Matt put it, this was *'British management with Irish labour!'* It was clear who would bear the brunt of the work and Dave, although from the Isle of Man, was born in Dublin! In the first class we had Takagi Sensei and reviewed sankajo. In one technique, Matt, in a bid to maintain his dominance, bounced Dave's head off his knee. Dave was really worried his eye would swell up, and he wasn't the only one in the wars. In the second class, this time under Chino's supervision, Lloyd caught me with an atemi to my right eye. My arm had gone up to block it, but somehow the strike had slipped through. The force knocked me down to the tatami and as I got back to my feet, it was watering so much that I couldn't see through it. Recreating a scene from the film *Gladiator*, I promised Lloyd, *'I will have my vengeance, in this class or the next!'* I did just that and in the last class of the day I smashed him as hard as I could into the tatami as revenge for his earlier indiscretion.

There was no work at night, so I decided a break from the norm was in order. I caught the train to Roppongi Hills, had a quick gingerbread latte at Starbucks to celebrate the start of the Christmas season, and then settled down to watch *Flag of our Fathers* at the cinema. The film directed by Clint Eastwood was about the Battle of Iwo Jima, a major conflict of the Second World War, which saw US Marines capture the island of Iwo Jima from the Imperial Japanese Army. It was a key victory for the Allies and the first to take place on Japanese soil. It was a surreal and uncomfortable watch while in Japan, and as the lights went up at the end of the film, I realised I was one of only a few Westerners in the audience. Very few gaijin lived in Musashi Koyama, so I was used to standing out, but this experience felt very different.

The first of the month ended, but the second saw a new and welcome first for the Senshusei. We saw Inoue Kancho in and around the honbu dojo all the time and most days for Shinkoku. We suffered in his presence during zagaku and did his daily bidding by keeping the dojo clean and tidy. Despite our efforts and despite being the head of Yoshinkan Aikido, which used the Senshusei course to create international ambassadors, he'd never once taught us. I'd always thought this strange. Kancho had never taken any of our classes and Chida Sensei as Dojocho had taken only a few. I wanted to feel Kancho's technique and got the opportunity halfway through the class. He taught us *taino henko ichi* and *ni* (the first and second moves from the kihon dosa) and then applied the principles to kihon waza in the form of *sokumen iriminage*, which was the technique I'd used to misalign Vic's spine! As usual, I was finding it difficult to make anything work on Geoff, and Kancho came over and asked me to grab his wrist. I did as I was told and felt a surge of energy through my arm and body. His movement was perfectly timed, and he broke my balance with ease, sending me crashing to the tatami. Inoue Kancho was in his seventies, and I was impressed. At half his age and twice his size, he'd still thrown me with minimal effort.

We'd all noticed them and discussed them in the tearoom several times. Kancho's feet were like nothing any of us had seen before. At the point, where his big toe joined his foot, there was a bit that stuck out. Was it bone? Was it muscle? We weren't quite sure, but there was definitely something unique about his feet. From the sitting position of seiza they almost looked webbed. Amphibious feet with a Yoshinkan twist and the envy of any swimmer. Were Kancho's feet the source of his power? I wanted feet like Kancho's – they connected to the tatami like receptors of energy. Perhaps an energy that formed a deeper connection to the earth and Mother Nature that the limits of my human mind couldn't contemplate? In a class back in June, had Murata Sensei given us a clue to Kancho's power? *'Keep your heels always to the floor to maintain energy flow. Your feet are like the four legs of an animal. The ball and heel like two feet. Think of them as having roots in the ground!'* Kancho had more roots than anyone and I was grateful to have had the opportunity to feel his technique. Kancho had given me another glimpse of the real Aikido I was still struggling to find. It was a shame that at this late stage of the course he'd only taught us once, but at least he'd got around to it in the end!

It wasn't until later that I found out we'd been scheduled for a Kanazawa Sensei class instead. Kanazawa had bumped into Kancho as he arrived at the honbu and suggested that he might like to teach the Senshusei. This sounded like a breach of honbu hierarchy, but I was very glad that Kanazawa had taken the risk. I wondered if Kancho or Chida planned to reward him with a round of usagi tobi, but observing my place in the pecking order, I'd never find out!

JAPANESE FOR BUSY PEOPLE

When time and energy permitted, I studied Japanese. If a student didn't show up at Berlitz, I'd get my Japanese books out and work on my grammar, vocabulary and practice writing kanji. On the train I'd pull out one of the many notebooks I had containing scribbled phrases I'd picked up or shuffle through flashcards with images of everyday items with the word in Japanese on the back. I'd practice what I learnt, in the tearoom before the morning meeting, much to the amusement of Inazaki and Kambara. *'David-san wa...*(insert a word I'd learnt)...*desu ne.'* After Dave's destruction of Tsuzuku, *'David-san wa baka desu ne'*, was a term I practiced often. It translated as *'David is crazy isn't he'*. My timing was always perfect – 15 seconds before the Sewanin walked in – I'd deliver my line. It became a daily ritual that never gave Dave time to respond!

Hotta Sensei was my official guide. I'd regularly show up at her house in a dishevelled state once training was over for a working break before it was time to head off to Berlitz. I'd worked through the first two books in the *JAPANESE FOR BUSY PEOPLE* series and would now put what I'd learnt on the line by taking the Japanese-Language Proficiency Test, or JLPT for short. I'd be taking the basic level of the test, which was jointly administered by Japan Educational Exchanges and Services and the Japan Foundation. Test day was Sunday, 3 December 2006. I met Paul Sensei at Shibuya Station, and we caught the train together along the Keio Inokashira Line to

261

arrive at the test centre just in time. Paul was also an avid student of Japanese and, like me, had decided to solidify all of his hard work with a formal qualification. The test ran in three parts, writing and vocabulary, listening and reading, rounded off with grammar. As we took our seats in what looked like a school classroom, things got serious. The test staff were on high alert and stopped in front of everyone to compare the physical face before them with the photograph that had been submitted as part of the registration process. I suspected that professional test takers had previously been caught taking the exam for those who weren't prepared to put in the considerable effort needed to pass – those without the diligence and discipline to learn, who needed the certificate for whatever reason. I'd lost some weight since my picture was taken, but it was definitely me. Thankfully, the examiner agreed!

The invigilators were a scary looking bunch, but having faced off against Chino, Chida and the rest of the honbu gang I was more than prepared. If there were any problems, pens would be put down and Paul and I could get to work. Looking threatening was one thing, but being able to back it up, quite another. The test was tough, and the pressure was on. If there was one thing I was used to, though, it was pressure, and with Paul Sensei in the room it felt like I was back at the honbu where everything was always intense. To the hum of scribbling we got through part one, moved on to listen to garbled Japanese played through speakers at the front, and finally, with head in hands, navigated the complexities of Japanese grammar. It was a tour de force! It seemed to go well, and I hoped I'd passed, but I wouldn't find out for a while. On Monday, after a morning at Jiu Jitsu, I headed off to Hotta Sensei's house to begin the third book in the series. Like the course, it was time to push on. There was always more to learn and even more to do!

PUBLIC ENEMY NUMBER ONE

Some of the ippan students had taken their shodan test over the weekend alongside a few of the Sensei who were testing for more senior grades. Matsuki had tested for his black belt and ragged his uke around so aggressively while performing shihonage that he'd knocked him out cold. On first hearing this sounded impressive – until we found out that Matsuki's uke had been an old man with glasses. Rumour had it that the old man's head had hit the tatami with such force that as his lights went out; his glasses had bounced a good distance up in the air. If there was anyone more dangerous than Crazy Dave, it was Matsuki. A violinist by day but a wrecking ball in the dojo, he was best avoided. Kanazawa Sensei was drafted in as replacement uke as the old man was carried off the mats in a semi-conscious state. Undeterred, Matsuki had gone to work on Kanazawa, trying to knock him out, too! I'd have paid money to see this. Matsuki was a force to be reckoned with, and Kanazawa must have had to muster up all of his private detective skills to escape by the skin of his teeth. A *yondan* (fourth dan) being given a hard time by a 1st kyu was unheard of and illustrated the whole problem with the shite and uke relationship. If shite went hard, uke had little choice but to take it. When it came to the Sensei, we also learned that Romeo Sensei had narrowly failed his yondan and that Marshall Sensei had got his *godan* (fifth dan). It had been a busy weekend, and it was all set to be a busy week.

Boaz was back to full health, but he was about to feel sick again for a completely different reason. It came to light that he'd queried directly with Murray Sensei why morning taiso had been moved to start five minutes earlier. Sure, the time change had led to me nearly wetting myself and momentarily had been a bit of an inconvenience. Going above the Sewanin's heads, however, was a stupid move and one that could very likely see Boaz lose his. There was no jumping honbu hierarchy, not unless you had a death wish. The Senshusei weren't permitted to query anything directly with the Sensei. Communication at all times had to pass through the Sewanin. Over the weekend Murray Sensei must have communicated his displeasure. Malik and Graham had got it in the neck. Boaz had jumped rank, and as payback, the Sewanin were about to jump all over him! Graham stormed into the morning meeting, visibly pumped up with the first order of business directed at Boaz. *'Why did you speak directly to Sensei about the timing of taiso?'* You could have cut the atmosphere with a knife. A deathly silence cascaded through the tearoom, and all eyes fell on the offending Senshusei. Graham glared, Malik glared, and we glared, too! Boaz looked down. He had no answer. Compared to Graham, Malik was surprisingly calm. It was Graham who was fuming and showing a side of himself we hadn't seen very often. He ordered us into the dojo and made us clean. As we brushed the tatami, once again he referred to his psychic abilities. *'I can look right through you and some of you have no Aikido in your technique!'* He was referring to our brushing. I, for one, still wasn't convinced that the daily dose of cleaning served to better our Aikido. As far as I was concerned, it was one big con to get us to do the jobs that nobody else wanted. Scrubbing the toilet floor, picking up pubes and taking out the rubbish hadn't improved my kamae, strengthened my posture or helped me remember any of the techniques. With the cleaning done, it was time to run the lines. We ran back and forth from one side of the dojo to the other as punishment for Boaz's crime. Graham was now even more pumped up and screamed at the top of his voice, *'no talking! The only place you're allowed to talk is in the tearoom. There should be no talking when getting changed, no talking while cleaning, no talking in class, and Boaz, no talking directly to Sensei!'* This was how things went down. If one of us messed up, we'd all share in the punishment. They used a similar tactic in the military and encouraged new recruits to police one another's behaviour. It might be a badge of honour to disobey the wishes of a superior officer, but when this cost the team, any solo disruptive action was quickly stamped out. Boaz was public enemy number one, and he knew it. In the tearoom before the first class, he made a formal apology to everyone, which was unanimously accepted. Boaz had learnt his lesson, and the rest of us had learnt it, too!

GOOD COP / BAD COP

Although the cops had left, a police state was still being enforced by the Sewanin, but Graham and Malik appeared to be switching roles. On Wednesday, Graham called in sick. Perhaps yesterday's rage had worn him out, and he now needed a duvet day to recover? Whatever the reason, I was glad he was absent and happy that Malik, who was becoming increasingly more pleasant to be around, was present instead. Was good cop going bad and bad cop turning good? On the face of it, it seemed that way. I found myself warming to Malik and enjoying his company. Although I knew he was there to do a job, he'd pushed us too far in the past. Perhaps Malik had come to the realisation that the course would end soon and that an overdue vendetta was potentially heading his way? We'd made a promise to Clyde, and Lloyd, our silent assassin, had more than one reason to seek revenge. Like a man nearing the end of his days, it seemed Malik Sewanin was endeavouring to make peace with his maker to ensure his ascent to the afterlife. If the 16th Senshusei turned on Malik, he'd need allies, and now was the time to make them.

Malik mentioned in the morning meeting that unless we had a work commitment, we'd need to be available for *osoji*, which would take place on 17 December. Osoji was a Japanese tradition and my worst nightmare. It translated as *big cleanup*, where the population tidied, cleaned and polished to ensure they entered the next year in the best surroundings. There was a problem. In fact, there was more than one problem. First, 17 December was a Sunday, and the last thing I needed was an extra day at the honbu. Second, I'd already signed up for my first Jiu Jitsu tournament where I'd be representing Axis. Third, so I could attend the Jiu Jitsu tournament, I'd already booked a day's holiday from my normal teaching schedule at Berlitz.

I was stuck between a rock and more than one hard place. What a mess! I was certain that fighting in a Jiu Jitsu tournament wasn't an acceptable excuse to miss the big cleanup and thought about my dilemma all morning, playing out different scenarios in my head. I couldn't wait to consult Ronen and Matt and convened an emergency meeting in the men's toilets to ensure we'd be out of earshot of Malik or anyone else who might be listening. I tabled the idea of asking Graham on his return to the dojo if I could do the tournament, but both strongly advised against this course of action. Honesty wasn't always the best policy, and while my preference was always to play with a straight bat, Graham had been too unpredictable in recent weeks. Ronen and Matt's advice made sense. I felt like the king in chess, forced into a position by the opposing pieces so that only one move was possible. With no alternative, I rang Peter at Berlitz and told him I now really needed to work on the 17th, then phoned Axis to pull out of the Jiu Jitsu competition. It was a stalemate. I'd successfully avoided osoji, but at the expense of the tournament. I hadn't won, and I hadn't lost. Instead, I'd found myself somewhere in the middle.

OVERDOSE

Graham was still ill on Thursday, and I was about to join him. With each successive day, the dojo was getting colder, and the seasonal coughs, colds and worse still had started to do the rounds. I was a regular at FamilyMart and had taken to downing a staple Japanese vitamin drink that promised protection from all manner of ailments. Sold in small glass bottles, C1000 Vitamin Lemon professed to contain 1,000 milligrams of vitamin C. With the recommended daily allowance of vitamin C for an adult male set in the region of 100 milligrams, with my three bottles of C1000, I was exceeding this by a multiple of 30. This was without taking into account everything else I was eating and drinking! There was no way I should get sick, but my head was pounding, and my skin was clammy. I was getting ill, and no amount of overdosing on vitamin C, it seemed, could save me.

If I'd overdosed on vitamins, I'd most definitely overdosed on zagaku. No matter how much of it I consumed, it never got any easier. There had been very bad sessions and slightly better ones, but sadly, there was no general improvement in my overall ability to get through it in one piece. I'd tried everything to make it a more comfortable experience, but nothing had worked. It was something to grin and bear, and deep in its clutches, the only option was to hope that time passed quickly. Today's zagaku was much quieter than normal. With no cops, fewer of the Sensei had bothered to show up, and on both counts, it meant we were all now closer to the shomen and far too close to Kancho. There was nowhere to hide and no possibility of blending in. In today's session, we'd be on stage with no exit left or right. Dave was called upon and botched his pronunciation. It was so bad that I could barely make out any of the words he said. The less clear he was, the less likely Kancho was to understand. If Kancho didn't get it, there was an increased risk that things would drag on longer! The monotony was broken only by Geoff, who, towards the end, let out a huge fart. The offending noise was such a shock to everyone that Dror and Vic momentarily forgot where they were and burst out laughing. I was sure punishment would now be on the cards, but Malik Sewanin either didn't hear or chose to ignore it. There was criticism from Malik afterwards, but it was about something else altogether. Once Kancho had departed, Malik Sewanin called us over to tell us we needed to stop moving our heads around so much. I'd not been conscious of any head movement, only weight shifting from leg to leg in a bid to make the blood flow easier. When he'd gestured for us to join him, I'd still yet to make it to my feet, which had both turned a worrying shade of blue. Any longer in seiza, and I could have lost both of my limbs. If my feet had died beneath me, there was no chance of them coming back. I'd have been destined to walk the earth on stumps and as a slightly shorter version of my current self. Matt and Ronen hauled me upright, and I listened in with one arm over each of their shoulders. Dave commented that my predicament resembled a scene from a war movie, and he wasn't far off.

We finished our final cleaning duties, and Ronen, Clyde, Matt and I headed off to Iidabashi for food at Tokyo Tom Yam. The last time Matt and I had visited this eatery we'd yet to start the course. How naive we were back then. In enlisting, we'd had no real idea of what we were doing or how bad things could get. Dazzled by the glory of war, we'd spent very little time considering the horrors of each individual battle. After eating, we made our way across to Kudanshita. At Sakuraya & Co., Ltd, the dogi shop near the station, we ordered our black belts. It felt like we were tempting fate. We hadn't tested yet and, given our recent performances, seemed very unlikely to pass shodan. Still, there was a lead time on the belts, and Chida Sensei had finally confirmed the test date as Tuesday, 19 December 2006. We felt like we'd already earned the right to put Senshusei on our belts. We weren't yet at the finish line, but as we got closer to the end, the prospect of making it was becoming a reality. There were numerous choices of coloured thread for the embroidery. Gold was a popular choice, but as Chino Sensei had red, I decided on red, too. If red was good enough for Chino, it was good enough for me! There was also a choice on the type of belt and what to have written on it. I settled on a silk and cotton mix with my name embroidered in katakana on one end and at the other, Yoshinkan Senshusei in kanji. The shop also sold a variety of Japanese swords. The *katana* was the weapon of choice of the Samurai and the thing I suspected Naruo Sensei wielded on his days off. I now felt this was something I should have in my possession as a symbol of my time in Japan and my experience on the course. There'd be an opportunity to pick one up after Senshusei was over, and this would give me enough time to work out how I was going to get it through customs on my return home. I felt exhausted, and it was time to head back to Musashi Koyama. I went straight to bed having popped two Beechams cold and flu tablets. I was careful not to overdose on these and stuck to the recommended amount. I wanted to wake up in the morning. I wanted to complete the course!

THE JACKET AND THE GEEK

I woke up on Friday feeling much better than expected. Either the tablets had done the trick, or the C1000 had finally kicked in. Either way, I didn't care, I was just glad to feel well again. I took the same journey every day, and as all Tokyo's commuters no doubt did, I became very familiar with my surroundings. I'd regularly see the same two guys get off the train at Ochiai. One was always dressed smartly in a tweed jacket, and the other, geekier-looking man resembled a stereotypical student. While 'the jacket' carried a briefcase, 'the geek' sported a rucksack. They appeared to know one another, and I wondered how. They were different in every way, and in Japanese society, where everyone had a place in a strict social hierarchy, it was a mystery to me why they were always together. To pass the time and satisfy my curiosity, I invented the story that the geek was a stalker who was obsessed with the jacket. He wanted to be him, and the best way the geek knew to realise his dream was to follow the jacket around. The jacket, on the other hand, wanted nothing to do with the geek, but in a country where superficial harmony was always required, he was too polite to say so. To distance himself, the jacket strode ahead. The lead position was one of seniority, and the jacket was making his status known to onlookers like me. The jacket hoped the geek would get bored and find another jacket to follow. Until such time, not wanting to offend, distance to communicate superior stature was his only option.

This morning while crossing the road outside the station, the jacket had seized his chance to get away. The geek, blocked by a surge of traffic, was left behind, and the jacket carried on walking, even though the pair had been speaking before. Undaunted, the geek ran after the jacket and eventually caught up. It was a curious observation and perhaps more evidence that the course was having a detrimental impact not just on my physical well-being but also on my mental health. As the scenario played out, it drew interesting parallels with the honbu. The Sensei were the jacket and the Senshusei the geek. We tried to catch up and wanted to be like them, but they always managed to evade us. The only difference was that the Sensei via the Sewanin weren't backwards in putting us in our place. The honbu dojo was some distance from polite society despite its unwavering advocacy of the rules of hierarchy.

Back in reality, Matt and I were on duty in the men's toilets. In the warm-up Dave was pulled up by Malik Sewanin and told that in the break, he needed to clean the entrance to the office building that housed the honbu. There was mud on the steps, and Kancho had noticed. Poor old Dave – he'd cleaned the steps first thing but had no control over who came in later and whether their shoes were dirty. It was history repeating itself. Last week Dave had been assigned to the men's toilets. After the morning cleaning duty was over, he'd been reprimanded by Malik. Someone had taken a dump between the morning meeting and the start of the first class and had forgotten to flush. When Malik did a spot-check, he'd lifted the seat and found the offending item bobbing up and down. In a similar scenario today, Dave had been called upon to explain. On both occasions, 'osu' was Dave's response. It was regularly his response!

BELT UP

Dave remained on Malik Sewanin's watch list for the rest of the day. How Dave had resisted the temptation to tell Malik to belt up, I'd no idea. Malik was pushing Dave's buttons, and everyone, including Dave, had a breaking point. In Friday's first class, Marshall Sensei took his final guest session before heading back to Australia. We practiced self-defence, which started off well but ended badly, at least for me. *Juji nage* was one of my least-favourite throws. In a nutshell, shite crossed uke's arms over one another and projected forwards. With one elbow trapped inside the other, uke had no choice but to fall – or risk snapping one or both arms. Vic threw me and forgot to let go of one of mine. This meant I couldn't soften my landing by slapping the tatami with an outstretched arm. Instead, I banged my already sore hip, and a shot of pain surged through my body. As I staggered to my feet, there wasn't much I could say or do. It was on with the show, and while I never suspected Vic had hurt me intentionally, I guessed we were now even. I'd temporarily misaligned her spine, and she'd now finished off my hip in return. In the last class, I partnered with Dave. We practiced *katate mochi yonkajo osae ichi*, which wasn't an easy technique to pull off. Although inflicting pain was never supposed to be the aim in Aikido, the only way any of us could make this technique work was by causing uke as much of it as possible. Malik Sewanin was breathing down Dave's neck. I'd been told in the past I had a high pain threshold, and Dave was struggling to apply the technique properly. Malik told Dave that he was worried about him not passing shodan. This was anything but motivating, and Dave's face was a picture of rage. I told him to calm down, but for the rest of the day, you could tell he was upset.

The whole black belt situation was to get a lot worse before the two-day break. In Saturday's morning meeting, Malik outlined the procedure for getting black belts. This was a problem as Ronen, Clyde, Matt and I had already ordered ours from Sakuraya. Whoops! We'd taken matters into our own hands and would now pay the price unless we could somehow make good of a bad situation. With different messages from different Sensei on when and how we'd be able to source our shiny new black belts, all built around the presumption that each of us would actually pass, the four of us had already ordered ours. In anticipation of the situation we now found ourselves in, Matt had been unofficially voted in by Ronen, Clyde and me to tell Malik that we'd gotten ahead of ourselves. *'Why have you lot gone off on your own and ordered your black belts? You had no business doing that!'* Malik had a point, and Matt didn't really have a response. *'Erm, erm, osu!'* Matt squirmed uncomfortably. The presumption that we would pass our shodan test had annoyed Malik, and I feared the worst for the test itself. Would our wishful thinking now go against us? Might Chida Sensei now fail us to prove a point? My fears were only curtailed when Malik told us we'd need to order our black belts through the official channels. The belts were to be funded out of the coffee-club money. This was news to me, and I wasn't alone in not knowing that we had a coffee club. Where did the club meet? How was it funded? Were biscuits available to accompany the drinks? Now wasn't the time to find out, and it was best to get off the topic as quickly as possible. We added our names to the list that would be given to Noriki Sensei next week and left things at that.

CHRISTMAS SPIRIT

I wasn't sure if Japan did Christmas or not. Tokyo as an international city adopted the tradition of Christmas decorations, with the retail outlets taking advantage of the commercial opportunity the holiday season presented.

Whether there was any more substance to the celebration of Christmas in Japan wasn't immediately clear. I'd heard that Christmas would stop almost just as it had begun, and that the physical manifestation of this was that by Boxing Day, all the decorations would have disappeared. I'd always enjoyed the lead-up back home, usually more than the day itself, and while the Christmas decorations remained up in Tokyo, I was determined to get into the spirit. The only thing I didn't enjoy was writing Christmas cards. I'd bought some in Meguro but as yet had failed to find the time or motivation to write them.

On Sunday evening I found myself in Omotesando. One of the main thoroughfares through Tokyo, it was always a hive of activity. As night drew in, it glimmered with lights from a vast array of shops, some selling products I knew and instantly recognised with others selling items that were less familiar to Western eyes. After a quick Starbucks, I noticed that there was a carol concert starting at a church nearby that looked to have links with the British Embassy. I wandered in and took a seat towards the back. With the sound of the traditional carols I always enjoyed, I was momentarily transported back to my childhood and the safety and sanctity of a family Christmas with Mum, Dad and Sally. The professional choir did the heavy lifting with the vast array of waifs and strays, who, much like me, seemed to have wandered in off the street to escape the cold, contributing when and where we felt like it. It was fantastic and a great way to finish the week. With only a fortnight until Christmas, I'd finally found some spirit. The concert did the trick as on Monday evening, possibly as a distraction from my pre-week jitters, I finally got round to writing my cards!

WHAT DO I SAY?

As I arrived at the honbu dojo on Tuesday morning, the pink phone was ringing. Dave ran out of the locker room on a mission to get it and ran into me removing my shoes. *'What do I say, what do I say?'* Dave asked in a panic. *'Honbu dojo de gozaimasu......'*, was my response, but Dave, never the linguist, went with his own special version of the correct Japanese. *'Honbu dojo David ohayou gozaimasu...!'* Well, I guess he was halfway there. The caller promptly hung up, which increased Dave's anxiety. Had he offended them, or had they just not understood? When the phone rang again, I answered it to find Malik Sewanin on the other end. He wasn't coming in. He didn't give a reason, and I didn't ask. This meant that Graham was the only Sewanin in the building and, until Malik's return, was the only Sewanin we had to worry about keeping happy.

In the first class, under Kanazawa Sensei's command, we mixed things up a bit. I found myself in a group with Graham and decided that, to show respect and to curry favour, it was a good idea to formally thank him for training with me at the end of the class. Dave and Lloyd took my lead but made the mistake of bowing with brooms in hand. Graham shouted at them for being too slow and, so as not to leave me out, even though my bow had been performed unencumbered by a sweeping device, screamed across the dojo. *'You're also too slow, Simon!'* I couldn't believe it. He clearly still suspected I was a rat and was determined to use any opportunity to get back at me.

It seemed I was also on Ito Sensei's radar for all the wrong reasons. Ito was laughing at Geoff and me again. We weren't trying to be funny, and while our comic abilities were purely accidental, they caused him much amusement. I would have loved to hit him with Joe Pesci's line from *Goodfellas*, but there was little chance he'd understand. Geoff and I had no choice but to grin and bear it and did our best to put any smirks that showed up on Ito's face firmly to the backs of our minds. In the mood to ridicule, Ito Sensei called us out in front of the whole class to demonstrate shomen uchi ikajo osae ichi. He pointed out that my ukemi was incorrect and took delight in explaining that my backside was in the wrong position relative to Geoff. Earlier on he'd also called us out to demonstrate *suwari ryote mochi kotegaeshi ni*. I'd completely messed this up, partly because it was overcomplicated and partly because the technique, as far as I was concerned, was complete and utter nonsense. With no potential real-world application, I just couldn't be bothered. I didn't imagine I'd ever find myself in a position where, while kneeling, an assailant attacked me by grabbing both of my wrists. The only time I ever knelt was when I was forced to adopt the seiza position, and I had no plans to ever voluntarily put myself in such discomfort when the Senshusei course was over. After my ukemi mishap, Ito took this earlier mistake as an opportunity to poke more fun. Switching from shomen uchi ikajo osae ichi back to suwari ryote mochi kotegaeshi ni, he announced that once again we'd be practicing *'Simon's favourite technique!'* The megaphone man was winding me up. Embarrassing me in front of my peers wasn't a cool move.

TENSION

Malik Sewanin was back on Wednesday. He looked well, and there was no apparent reason for his absence. It was actually good to see him, as the more exposure I'd been having to Graham, the more I was favouring Malik. While his actions and comments annoyed me at times, he brought a tension to Senshusei which enhanced the whole experience. As we got closer and closer to the day of the test, having this tension was important, and I was glad to see him back in the dojo. Malik's presence, I knew, would up my game and help bring out the best in me. I needed all the motivation I could muster. I felt exhausted, and my right knee was bothering me. The only saving grace was that I'd avoided the illness that was plaguing Matt, Geoff and Vic. The physical exertion of training was causing them to cough and sneeze all over the place. Thank goodness for C1000, which was costing me a fortune every day but now seemed to be doing the trick.

In the first break and after Shinkoku, Neville and Geoff were arguing in the tearoom. Apparently, Geoff had shoved Neville while lining up, so Neville in retaliation had pushed back into Geoff. It looked to be getting out of control, but luckily Ronen was on hand to intervene. The tension was rising as we all got more stressed about testing for shodan. The good news for today was that Oyamada Sensei was in Russia. Although I'd been enjoying his classes more recently, they were still monotonous. I joked with Matt about how disappointed the Russians must have been to have gone to the hassle of flying out a honbu instructor to their country only to have him call out ichi, ni, ichi, ni while they ran through their waza. I was sure there wouldn't be much teaching, which made the trip a pointless and very expensive exercise!

After yesterday's actions, Ito Sensei was still in my bad books, and my heart sank when I saw him arrive to teach the last class. For the first 15 minutes, he gave us time to practice anything we wanted. I was up for practicing my skills at relaxing in the tearoom but didn't think that was quite what he had in mind. After drilling some of our weaker techniques, we were put through our third mock test of the morning. Takagi had done one, Takashima had done one, and now it was Ito's turn to put us through our paces. In the jiyu waza, we were told to incorporate the technique that Geoff and I had abolished through our bilateral agreement. A week before the test, being forced to bring this into our repertoire seemed ridiculous, not to mention dangerous. We had no choice, and getting over Geoff as he slid in to take my knees from under me felt like jumping over a small car!

At night I was determined to relax, and through some of my English teaching contacts, I'd secured a ticket to a football match, which was being played at Sendagaya. Aside from the World Cup, I'd never been that keen on football, but a new and different experience was always welcome as an antidote to the monotony of daily dojo life. The FIFA Championship match was between Brazil and Egypt and turned out to be a good game. The only downside was a group of screaming kids who sat behind me, which was an unwelcome reminder of the summer camp I'd endured back in August.

TIME STOOD STILL

Matt was Shinkoku, and that meant he had to orchestrate the taiso. As the weather was getting colder, some of the Sensei were allowing time at the start of the class, as opposed to just the start of the day, to get our bodies ready for battle. In Thursday's last class, Kanazawa Sensei did just that. Matt began. *'Ichi, ni, san, shi, go.........!'* He stopped in the middle of the count having only made it to five. It was really strange and felt like time had stood still. We watched and waited to see if Matt would resume his count, our motionless forms temporarily frozen. After what seemed like an uncomfortably long time, he continued, *'...roku, shichi, hachi!'* He'd finally made it to eight. I asked him afterwards what had happened. Matt explained that he thought he'd made a mistake in his numbering even though he could now count to eight in Japanese in his sleep. It was a routine we practiced every day, and while he didn't always lead the taiso, he'd heard the count more times than any of us cared to remember. A surge of fear had shot up his spine, and he'd paused to collect his thoughts and analyse his previous sequence for error. We were all paranoid about messing up, particularly now the shodan test was almost upon us, and Matt's cock-up was a prime example of how we all felt. Hesitation was nobody's friend, and in the black belt exam, there would be no time to think. We'd have to respond to the commands given instinctively. There'd be no opportunity to dawdle, delay or second-guess. It was our subconscious minds and not our conscious ones that would need to be ready to run the show. The nerves were catching. Geoff drew a complete blank with one of the techniques Kanazawa called out. Malik Sewanin, not for the first time, stood behind us with his head in his hands!

In zagaku at 1pm, Neville and Boaz were called upon to share. Neville talked about how he and Vic hadn't been getting on and Boaz about how people thought he was arrogant, but that he didn't know why. Boaz's reflection went on for ages and quite possibly could have rivalled Sonoda Sensei in the explanation stakes. When Boaz was finally done, Kancho whispered *'mijikai'* to Sonoda, who was now – and somewhat ironically – invited to respond. Despite my still-limited knowledge of Japanese vocabulary, this was one word that, when combined with Kancho's expression, I understood. Even Kancho's legs must have been getting tired, as he instructed Sonoda Sensei to *'keep it short'*. Sonoda disregarded Kancho's orders and outdid Boaz with the length of his response. It

273

was all too much for Inazaki, who at one point fell asleep. The giveaway was that while in his unconscious state one of his hands had slipped down towards his knee. Instinctively he'd reacted to steady his balance and woke himself up!

BROKEN DOWN

Friday's stress levels were always high. Chino Sensei was usually around, and Chino didn't suffer fools. When I arrived at the honbu dojo, a rumour was circling amongst the Senshusei that Chino wouldn't be in today. The rumour was that Chino Sensei was ill! I was in shock. I couldn't imagine Chino ill. Was this even possible? While Chino was visibly a man, in my mind he was more machine. While machines didn't get ill, they could break down. That must have been it. Chino Sensei had broken down and was in for repairs that would no doubt see him return stronger and even more dangerous. With our very evident human qualities, we hadn't broken down as such, but we were all broken in our own individual ways. Graham Sewanin seemed to sense our collective dilapidated physical and mental state and brought a brown paper bag to the morning meeting, which contained what he described as *'lucky nuts'*. He was leaving for Canada early next week, so he would miss our shodan test, and his parting gift was a bag of nuts. We suspected that Graham had mystical qualities. He'd already claimed he could read our minds and now insisted that we eat his lucky nuts just before the test. Jack had his beans, and Graham had his nuts. Perhaps a 'giant' performance awaited us if we took his advice? Perhaps the lucky nuts were infused with the spirit and energy we'd need to get through? Perhaps if we ate his nuts, Graham would be with us on test day in more than just spirit? We decided to keep them safe, just in case!

It was Geoff's birthday. As his training partner for Dai San, and partly to quash any ill feeling that may have developed between us during the last few months, I gave him a Terry's Chocolate Orange I'd managed to pick up in Musashi Koyama. This was a rare find and a taste of home that I was hoping to sample myself. Still, it was his birthday, and with a bigger payoff in mind in the form of a good test, I reluctantly handed it over. I also went one step further and promised Geoff that I'd be nice to him for the whole day, no matter what. In the first class we had Naruo and did a mock test, which felt like the real thing. Naruo, Malik and Graham walked around, each with a clipboard, pen and paper in hand, marking us on every technique and making notes on areas we needed to improve. In our grading pairs, we only did two techniques each, and Geoff messed both of mine up with poor ukemi. There was nothing I could say. I'd made a promise to be nice to him all day, even if he had made me look stupid.

Ito Sensei was up next and thankfully appeared to have turned his unwanted attention away from me. To continue what was becoming a recurring theme, he ran his own version of a mock test and gave us the opportunity to ask questions about any technique we were unsure about, once his test was over. As Chida Sensei's principal uke and student, his response to Vic's question didn't surprise. *'Sensei, how do you apply sankajo properly?'* She asked. *'What are you talking about?'* Ito responded. A response straight out of the Chida playbook. In his summing up of our performance, Ito caused a wave of laughter to ripple through the group. He described Dave as *'weak'* and Matt as *'strong'*. This was too much for Clyde, whose ripple turned into a torrent as he burst out laughing!

I made a big mistake ahead of the last class. I not only drank a lot of coffee; I'd become partial to chocolate-coated coffee beans. Post-Ito and pre-Noriki Sensei, I'd polished off a whole packet of Wonda beans and felt completely off my head. I was spaced out and, when the class was over, had very little recollection of any aspect of the test that Noriki had just put us through. Perhaps Wonda coffee beans were the secret ingredient I needed to get through next week's shodan test with no fear? Perhaps Wonda beans would be a better choice than Graham's nuts? One thing was for sure, they looked more appetising!

BONENKAI

Back in the UK, I was always up for a drinking party, a chance to get together with friends, relax and have some fun. I was about to find out, though, that in Japan, and especially when the honbu dojo was involved, things would be very different. Ahead of the shodan test, we'd be entertaining Inoue Kancho and the rest of the Sensei at an izakaya in Takadanobaba. A *bonenkai* was a traditional Japanese party that took place between co-workers towards the end of the year, with the literal translation of the word being *forget-the-year party*. This sounded like exactly what I needed. There were plenty of things I wanted to forget from the year just gone, and plying myself with alcohol was one way to do it! The Senshusei were in agreement. On the face of it, the bonenkai seemed like a good idea. The Sewanin had been keen to put us straight. *'The bonenkai is not for you!'* Malik and Graham had told us in no uncertain terms before we'd left the honbu yesterday, and now on Saturday, 16 December 2006, any illusion that tonight's party might be fun had almost vanished. Our job as Senshusei was to meet and greet the Sensei in the street and escort them to the party. They would arrive at different times and from different directions, which would mean one big headache!

Before the bonenkai was upon us, there was the small matter of three classes to get through. In the first class, Dave asked Matt not to show him his *irimiski* strike, as it scared him too much. A *palm strike to the face* never seemed fair in jiyu waza, but irimiski was a legitimate technique. Dave told Matt that he would rather not know it was coming, which was exactly how I felt about the bonenkai. But the bonenkai was coming, and in only a few hours, we'd be suited and booted in and around Takadanobaba. Like secret police assigned to close protection duty, we'd be escorting important guests safely and securely to the party destination.

There was just enough time for me to return home after class, get changed and then get back to Takadanobaba to meet the others at 5:30pm. Back at Musashi Koyama, I had some food and then, exhausted, from the week's training and in anticipation of the night's longevity, fell fast asleep for half an hour. My alarm clock woke me up, and now, with only an hour before I had to leave, I was horrified to find that my suit jacket and trousers, which I'd been storing at the back of the wardrobe, were covered in mould! My apartment was more hostel than hotel, and I had noticed a damp smell every now and again but had no idea where it was coming from. Now I knew. The back of the wardrobe was thick with mould, and since the start of the course, this mould had been slowly acquainting itself with my suit. I only had one suit, and there was no time to go shopping. I got a wet rag and in desperation began scrubbing the white residue in an attempt to reveal the navy-blue cloth that I knew was underneath. It was tough to shift, but I had no choice. Senshusei were never late. My suit, now wet through from all the scrubbing, would have to dry on my back in transit to the meeting point. What a nightmare, and what a stink. Mould and damp weren't the most pleasant of smells, but it now would accompany me for the rest of the evening. I just hoped the odour, disguised by all the other smells the izakaya would have to offer, would go unnoticed.

I just made it to Takadanobaba by 5:30pm. Everyone was waiting outside the tobacco shop just outside the station. Nobody mentioned my suit or the musty smell in the air, so I didn't, either. We headed off to the izakaya and drew our fair share of stares from Japanese commuters heading home. Inazaki and Kambara blended in, but the rest of us didn't. We voted Ronen in charge. With his military background and a demeanour that wouldn't have seen him out of place in a specialist bodyguard unit, he was the obvious choice to make commander of operations. Ronen split us into groups and stationed us in pairs at various exits and intersections to meet and greet the Sensei who would arrive soon. As we awaited the honbu's head honcho and the other Sensei we were there to protect, the only things missing were a sidearm and headset. Geoff had brought along the only form of communication. Armed with a torch, he began giving signals to Matt, who had positioned himself outside the railway station. As neither knew Morse code, the whole exercise was pointless. The intermittent flashing served only to attract more unwanted attention. Ronen perfectly summed up what we all thought. *'What kind of Ninja brings a flashlight to a mission without knowing how to use it?'*

None of us knew in advance, but the Sensei saw the whole thing as one big game. They didn't want to be met; they didn't want to be intercepted and escorted to the venue. What they wanted to do was to evade detection, to make it to the izakaya unaccompanied and then to complain to the Sewanin that we'd missed them. It was a joke and childish behaviour. I saw the sense in being punished for a mistake I'd made but being reprimanded because the very people I was trying to serve didn't want serving was completely ridiculous! The game was on, and it was a game the Senshusei intended to win. I intercepted Naruo, Higa, Takagi and finally Kancho, who was being escorted by Takashima and Laurance. The big fish had been caught, and this signalled a return to the izakaya to get the bonenkai started, or so we thought. No sooner had we dropped Kancho off than we were sent back out onto the street. Gozo Shioda's son, Shioda Junior, had yet to arrive and his tardiness had all the characteristics of a power play in the offing. Inoue Kancho was the head of Yoshinkan Aikido, but Shioda Junior was the founder's son. Everything in Japan had meaning, and honbu politics were rife inside and outside the dojo. I suspected arriving late was a slur on Kancho's position, carefully planned and orchestrated by the man who thought himself the rightful heir to the throne. It all reminded me of my favourite film *Gladiator*. In a scene near the start, Caesar, the Roman Emperor Marcus Aurelius, lies dying. On his deathbed he requests that his General, Maximus Decimus Meridius, take on one more duty, in place of his son Commodus. *'I want you to become the Protector of Rome after I die…Commodus cannot rule, he must not rule. You are the son I should have had!'* Back out in the street, we bumped into Dror, who had located Shioda Junior. Shioda Junior was an unknown quantity and didn't have the best reputation with the Senshusei. He'd not taught the Kokusai and had been known to brutalise the cops. Kancho Gozo Shioda was Caesar, Inoue Kancho was Maximus, and now that Commodus had arrived in the form of Shioda Junior, the party could finally start.

In Japan there was usually more than one party, and this first one turned out to be a nightmare. I found myself between Sonoda Sensei to my left, Noriki Sensei to my right, and opposite Paul and Murray Sensei. It was a Sensei sandwich of uncomfortable proportions, and I was the meat in the middle! The tables in the izakaya were low to the floor and were the perfect height to sit in the seiza position. In recognition that a comfortable dining experience and an extended seiza rarely went hand in hand, each table had a pit underneath to accommodate bent legs in a relaxed seated position, once any formalities were over. During Inoue Kancho's welcome address, and with my legs comfortably tucked under the table, I realised that I was the only one not sat in seiza. There was nothing I could do. Any movement on my part would have given my mistake away, and for once I didn't care how long Kancho talked. Once Kancho was done and dinner was served, the first thing Murray Sensei did was complain to me that the venue was too noisy and cramped. He also wasn't happy that we were in a corner of the main restaurant and not in a private room. This was a real conversation killer and made me feel even more uncomfortable. I'd had nothing to do with booking the venue or organising the event. The conversation was stilted, and it didn't help when Malik Sewanin shouted over to me, *'Simon, entertain Noriki Sensei!'* I didn't know what he expected me to do. A song, a dance, or perhaps something else? Noriki had taught many a class I'd been in, but we didn't know each other, and there was the language barrier to contend with in addition to the formality and etiquette associated with the fact that he was a Sensei and I was the lowest form of life. I wasn't sure what topics of conversation were acceptable and what were off limits. Ronen would tell me later, *'you should have offered him a lap dance mate, he might be Dojocho one day!'* I was completely out of my depth in more ways than one. I knew Sonoda Sensei a little better, and his English was pretty good, so in my attempt at polite chit-chat, I enquired where he was from. Sonoda paused, turned in my direction, and with a look of disgust on his face said, *'you already know, you've been to my house!'* I politely explained that I hadn't been to his house, only to a seminar before the course began, which took place in a dojo in the middle of nowhere with no house in sight.

It was impossible to relax at all. There was the difficult conversation and the constant requirement to be on alert. The drinking ritual we'd learnt at the welcome party was again in full flow. It was like a drinking game gone wrong and without the fun. The more I poured, the more I was expected to drink; and the more I drank, the more difficult pouring became! Struggling to get any kind of interesting dialogue going, I decided a different type of work was preferable. I stood up and began taking orders for drinks. This was a good move, as I couldn't stay in one spot for too long, which left only enough time to exchange polite pleasantries. Time passed slowly, but eventually it was time for Kancho to leave.

This was no simple exercise. Being Kancho, he couldn't just put on his coat and head for the door. Expecting his departure, the Senshusei had one final duty to perform. We were ordered outside, and as Kancho exited the building, we bowed to him in the street.

Ronen, Vic, Boaz and I went ahead to the venue that would play host to the second party. Graham Sewanin followed close behind and appeared determined to further his decline in the popularity stakes. Malik was climbing, and Graham was slipping, and the role reversal looked set to continue. *'You guys need to learn how to be Senshusei!'* Graham muttered under his breath, but loud enough so we could all hear, as he handed out plastic bags for people to put their shoes in when they arrived. Taking the hint, I offered to take over the plastic bag distribution, but Graham bluntly refused. There was no winning! The second party proved more relaxed. As we were busy serving drinks, there'd been no time to eat at the first, and now at the second, there was more food and an opportunity to tuck in. To make things more interesting, everyone had to cook his or her own food, and with the majority lacking in culinary skills, there was smoke everywhere. Naruo Sensei was struggling and had been forced to position himself in the corner of the room. Too many bodies and too many flames had created a sauna-like environment, and, red-faced, he looked like he might spontaneously combust. The drinks flowed, especially the dangerous combination of whisky and Coke. I got chatting to Malik Sewanin, who confessed that he'd done things he regretted. I appreciated his honesty but couldn't disagree. He said that what he had done, he had done for us. I was starting to understand what it meant to be Senshusei, helped on by the copious amounts of alcohol I was consuming. I appreciated Malik sharing his own reflection with me. There was no Kancho to invite me to comment, so I nodded instead. It was a surreal moment. We'd almost come to blows a few times, but now I was seeing things from his side. I'd witnessed some of the year Malik and Graham had endured at the hands of their Sewanin. They'd been through a tough time, and for me to be worthy of being Senshusei, enduring was something I had to do, too. At 10:45pm the second party came to a formal close. Graham Sewanin got up to leave and imparted some words of encouragement for Tuesday's test and reminded us to eat his lucky nuts. I left soon after to catch the last train home. It had been one hell of a day in more ways than one!

Sunday morning was a struggle. The whisky and Cokes were still doing the rounds in my body, and unfortunately, I was due at Berlitz for a 10am class. I dragged myself out of bed and into the shower. I arrived at Sangenjaya and waited politely behind a woman on the ground floor to catch the lift to the sixth. She pressed the button and after a few moments the lift arrived and the doors opened, but the woman didn't move. I peered round at her from the side and noticed her eyes were shut. As impossible as it seemed, she appeared to have fallen asleep while still in an upright position. I said *'dozo'* (go ahead) and motioned for her to move. Momentarily shocked into consciousness, she walked in, turned and faced the doors, and then shut her eyes again. I thought I was tired, but this lady was taking things to a whole new level. Despite feeling exhausted, anything was better than osoji, which would take place at the honbu dojo today. I didn't dare imagine how those amongst my fellow Senshusei who had stayed out too late, drank too much, and were now busy scrubbing, might be feeling today. That extra hour or two or that final drink might have seemed like a good idea at the time but was something I was sure they now regretted. At 1:45pm I took the train to Meguro, which would then be a shorter hop back to Musashi Koyama later in the day. After lunch and as much orange juice as I could stomach, I taught five classes at the Berlitz school near the station. I heard from Ronen that osoji hadn't been that bad. The dojo had been overrun with eager and enthusiastic ippan students. Takashima Sensei had bossed them around and given the Senshusei an easy ride.

At night it was time for a treat. Domino's pizza and a film. Thin crust and pepperoni with *Gallipoli*, starring Mel Gibson, were just what the doctor ordered. It was another war film, and another dramatic depiction of a brutal battle. It summed up my mood, and with my need for food, I dug in. Monday was a day of rest, and with the shodan test set for the following day, I shaved my head ceremoniously. Tuesday would be the biggest test on the course to date, and I was determined to be ready!

SHODAN TEST

The big day, Tuesday, 19 December 2020, had finally arrived. All the hard work and preparation would culminate in the day's events, and I felt a combination of excitement and nervousness wrapped up into one. The day started like any other. The cleaning duties had to be done, and the honbu dojo had to look its best. As Shinkoku, I got the stepladder out to attend to the shomen. *'I don't like heights'*, I muttered to myself as I climbed to the top to collect the two plants that needed watering every day. I squeezed past Clyde, who was cleaning the hallway, and into the men's toilets, where Dror and Boaz were cracking on with their own respective cleaning duties under what seemed to be the supervision of Ronen. Watering the plants in the sink next to the urinals was always a difficult task. Too little water, and the plants would die; too much, and there was a chance a drip could land on a Sensei's head as he or she opened the first class. A quick dust of the shelf, and the plants were put carefully back in place by 7:20am. Cleaning the shomen was a solo enterprise and a chance for me to contemplate the day ahead. As I finished up, I heard footsteps down the corridor, and Ronen bowed in. *'Simon, what do you use to spray the toilet...the yellow spray?'* Ronen was in fact on toilet duty with Dror but had made the risky trip away from his station to check on specifics. Boaz was now in the tearoom, vacuum in hand, which was one of the better areas to be assigned. After the watering was done, it was time to sweep the entrance hall, where the procession of daily visitors would deposit their shoes and enter the honbu barefoot. Then it was on to the arduous task of cleaning the two large mirrors in the dojo that we were forbidden to look in yet had to keep spotlessly clean with a daily dose of polish, applied and removed with the previous day's newspaper.

Now just before 8am and time for the morning meeting, Malik Sewanin, flying solo as Graham was back in Canada, meant business. *'Hai!'* He shouted, taking position at the head of the table. *'Osu, ohayou gozaimasu, osu!'* We screamed in response. Malik continued with roll call and then asked for disclosure of any injuries. Clyde, Boaz and Geoff declared their specific ailments, and it was then onto feedback from the bonenkai, which was surprisingly all very good. Apparently, several Sensei had shared with the Sewanin how impressed they were with the level of Senshusei this year. This was exactly what we needed to hear – positive feedback to begin the most important day, or as Malik, referencing the film *Terminator 2*, described it, *'judgment day'*. It was nearly time to do battle, and with an infectious determination and sense of pride in the room, it was clear we were ready! Malik told us, *'today you'll meet Aikido God, Chida Sensei'*, and reminded us we had before us *'a once-in-a-lifetime opportunity'*. We'd already met Chida, though not as many times as we'd hoped, but today would be in a very different capacity. Chida Sensei as the Almighty brought even more significance to our day of judgment! Malik continued. *'It's been a long road, and the end is nigh. You have seven weeks left. Today is a major milestone, so I want you to give everything you've got. Show us how good you are, and I know you are good. Ganbatte kudasai!'* In his final two words, he was clear. *'Please do your best!'* It was a rallying cry to his troops. Malik's words had raised our spirits, and like an army lined up ahead of a battle, we were pumped up and ready for war!

We filed into the dojo, and while the others swept the mats, as Shinkoku I adjusted the time of the wall clock and tidied the array of wooden weapons that sat just inside the door. We ran the zokin lines, and the dojo looked as polished and well presented as it ever had. After taiso – hopefully our last one as white belts – we lined up in seiza. For a big test you needed to feel fast and flexible, but for some reason Higa Sensei in the first class reverted to right kamae for 10 minutes, followed by left kamae for the same. In a few hours I would be required to throw Geoff around, and as I stood facing the shomen in motionless contemplation, my blood began to boil. I felt my body begin to stiffen, and even Malik said after the class was over that if it had gone on any longer, he would have questioned Higa on what he thought he was doing. Thankfully, he didn't have to, and kamae was replaced with kihon waza and jiyu waza practice. The blood began to flow, and the repetition of moves we would no doubt be repeating later on generated a feeling of confidence. I was determined to get an early Christmas present in the form of a black belt and didn't dare contemplate what the alternative might be. I had plan A but no plan B. I had to pass, and more than that I wanted to do the best job I possibly could.

To be Shinkoku again on the day of the test felt quite an honour. I'd had the privilege and also the terror of leading the Senshusei out at the 51st All Japan Enbu, and now for shodan, I was in pole position once more. My morning Shinkoku was a special one for test day and also included a thank you for Saturday's party. In Japan things worked differently, and although we'd been the grunts at the bonenkai, accosting Sensei in the street and serving drinks all night, it was still our duty to thank our superiors for the experience. We lined up expecting Inoue Kancho, but Kancho didn't show, so Shinkoku was changed at the last minute to Ito Sensei. Ito appeared to be on good form, and as we held our final bow, he said, *'thank you very much'* in perfect English. At 10am we had the shortest class we'd ever had. A brief stint of 20 minutes with Murata Sensei to run through kihon dosa, ukemi and jiyu waza. Murata was the perfect choice for our last class as white belts. While some of his teaching was off the wall, he always had a calming and relaxing way about him. From 10:20am until 11am, we were free to run through whatever techniques we wanted in order to add some final polish. Geoff and I teamed up with Matt and Dave and ran a series of mini mock tests. The time passed quickly, and thankfully, none of us made any huge pre-test mistakes. We left the mats at 11am to get changed into our test dogi. A clean dogi would make a good impression, and with all the grabbing, sweating and bleeding, many of my white dogi had seen much better days. Back in the dojo at 11:25am, we waited patiently in seiza for Noriki Sensei to run through final instructions. Luckily, he didn't keep us too long, and Geoff and I learnt that we'd be up first on one half of the tatami with Matt and Dave on the other. It felt fitting that I was testing alongside Matt. We'd started our Aikido journey together, and facing today's challenge in each other's company held particular significance.

The test began at midday and it wasn't long before Geoff and I were called to our spots. My legs were like jelly, in part from the adrenalin surging through my body and also from the lack of blood supply, which was an ever-present problem whenever even a short period of seiza was required. Chida, Sonoda and Ito Sensei were conducting the test under the watchful eye of Inoue Kancho, who had the option of his own special chair positioned behind a table covered in a white tablecloth underneath the shomen. He had the best seat in the house, and I wondered how many tests he'd presided over and whom he'd graded from that vantage point. It appeared, though, that Kancho wanted in on the action as he was up on his feet as the test began with clipboard in hand. The test started with kamae and sotai dosa and progressed to five kihon waza techniques picked from what was now an extensive list of ones we'd learnt. The finale was shomen uchi and yokomen uchi jiyu waza, and Geoff and I pushed hard to show the spirit we knew Inoue Kancho would expect to see. It seemed to go quite well, and the clunkiness that usually accompanied Geoff and me working together felt more fluid than ever before. We made a couple of mistakes, but nothing that I thought would seriously jeopardise our chances of passing. On *shomen uchi shomen iriminage ichi,* Geoff struck me when it was me who was supposed to strike him. We turned to Kancho and bowed, and with a cry of *'moichido onegaishimasu'*, we formally requested *'permission to do the technique again please'*. On *ushiro ryote mochi ikajo osae ni,* Geoff pulled instead of pushed, but I was determined this time not to have to do the technique again, so I dragged him with me.

As we sat down in seiza, Matt and Dave glanced over. They looked happy and relieved, and I assumed things had probably gone quite well for them, too. With blood still pumping around our legs after a hectic jiyu waza, we settled into seiza to watch the others test. Neville and Vic, Dror and Kambara, Ronen and Inazaki, Lloyd and Boaz and, of course, Clyde and Malik. I wasn't sure how much Geoff saw of the others. He was quickly a world away from reality in a prison of lower-leg pain. I was struggling, too, but made a conscious effort to watch everyone else. They all did well, and it was clear that all of the drilling and repetition had been worth it. Tsuzuku, the cop that Dave had injured, also tested. He'd missed so much of the course, through no fault of his own, that he'd fallen behind his comrades. He'd been the one to watch at the start of the course, but now he looked a shadow of his former self. Slightly overweight and lacking the energy and fire he'd once possessed; it was sad to see.

After the test, we waited in the dojo for Chida to come back in with the results. Minutes seemed like hours as we waited for the Dojocho to seal our fate one way or another. When he finally graced us with his presence, we were relieved to learn that we'd all passed. We were now officially shodan, but the learning wasn't over. Chida Sensei gave detailed feedback on all of us individually and told me I had a habit of looking down too much and needed to raise my eyeline. After years of Muay Thai, I'd trained myself to keep my chin down for fear of being knocked out and wasn't about to change this habit anytime soon. I took it in the spirit it was intended and gave the obligatory *'osu!'* We were all told that in jiyu waza, we should invite uke more. I didn't really understand what this meant or how to go about doing it, but it didn't really matter. We'd started as an unlucky 13, but today our luck was in, as we'd passed our shodan test together.

After the closing Shinkoku, this time in front of Inoue Kancho himself, we had a final talk from Malik in the tearoom. *'Remember, today, tomorrow, for the next two months, you're always Senshusei. Don't let this change you!'* It was good advice. The tendency for a shodan grade to go to someone's head was something I'd seen before. The course was far from over, and tomorrow would be just another day. With this in mind, we headed to the Royal Host for food and drinks, and then it was off to work. On the train I watched the video Ronen's dad, who was in Japan to support his son, had taken on my video camera. I was my own worst critic. Some techniques hadn't gone as well as I'd hoped, but there was nothing I could do about it now. On the way to Berlitz, I popped into Tower Records in Shibuya and bought *Kanji in Context*, a book that would help take my kanji to the next level. It had been a special day, and I just felt like spending some money to mark the occasion. As I stepped into Berlitz, there was a spring in my step. Although none of my students would know it, today had been a landmark moment in my life. I was shodan – and not just any shodan. I'd passed my test in the home of Yoshinkan Aikido in front of the world's greats. I was proud, happy – but very, very tired!

In Wednesday morning's meeting, Malik told us to take off our belts and gave us each a black belt donated by one of the Sensei to wear until ours were ready. Chida Sensei was required to formally approve the change in colour, and thankfully, he'd not made us wait too long. Training the day after the test in a white belt just wouldn't have felt right, and although the belt I'd wear today wasn't mine, it would do for now. Clyde took off his white belt, carefully folded it and kissed it goodbye. We'd sweated and bled in our white belts, and in some ways, like saying farewell to a good friend, we were sad to see them go. The traditional origin of the black belt was a white belt that had been worn for such a length of time that it turned black. We didn't have time to wait for this to happen and were glad to fast-track. Clyde got Graham Sewanin's hand-me-down, and Boaz got Paul Sensei's. The rest of us made do with what was left, and as I couldn't read the kanji, I had no idea whom my belt belonged to. I hoped it was Chino Sensei's. I'd have two to choose from soon – the one the honbu had purchased for me with the coffee-club money and the one I'd ordered in Kudanshita. Matt's allocated belt was too small and looked ridiculous. Fortunately, Malik had a size four to replace the three Matt had originally put on, and the fit was much better. Geoff asked Malik if we could use our white belts to replace the cardboard that sat between the mats and the wooden surround, which held the tatami in place. It was a nice idea, but I had no intention of leaving my white belt in the dojo as a museum piece. Keeping it would be an everlasting reminder of everything I'd been through. Malik quashed Geoff's idea politely with *'let's leave it for now'*.

Malik seemed genuinely happy and proud of our achievement and formally acknowledged our performance yesterday. *'Senshusei shodan otsukaresama deshita! It looks amazing to see you all in your shodan colours. Some of you are already shodan, but now you're Senshusei shodan, and there's a difference; you've paid your dues. No matter where you go or what you do, you did the Senshusei course at the honbu dojo and no one can take that away from you, so it's a proud moment and you should feel proud. So, remember, shodan; sho means beginning, it doesn't mean end. It doesn't mean that you're a master, it means that you are now a beginner, a beginner in starting Aikido.'* He also advised, *'make sure you don't change'* and *'stay humble as a warrior'*. They were wise words, and although it felt great to be wearing a black belt, I didn't feel any different inside. Malik Sewanin brought the meeting to a close, and we lined up in the corridor outside the tearoom, waiting to go into the dojo for the first Senshusei class of the day. We had Paul, Ito and finally Takashima Sensei. They all seemed to treat us a little differently, and the intensity was kept to a minimum. They turned out to be superb technical classes, but after the mental drain of yesterday, I struggled to take anything in.

HUMILITY

As I arrived at the honbu dojo on Thursday morning, Malik Sewanin's words were still bouncing around my head. We had a long way to go until the end of the course, and the Christmas break was about to disrupt our momentum.

In the second class, we had Sonoda Sensei who ran us through *tanto soho*, a set of movements with a wooden knife we'd practiced a few times before and all found extremely boring. It was complicated, and Sonoda made several mistakes, which led to an increased level of confusion about what we were actually supposed to be doing. Towards the end of the class, he demonstrated the full set of 10 techniques with Malik Sewanin and once again got some of them wrong. As he bowed out of the class, Sonoda Sensei turned to us and said that he was trying to do his best as a teacher and to get better. Sonoda, as one of the most senior Sensei at the honbu dojo, was publicly acknowledging his personal Aikido journey and his determination to improve. This really hit home and echoed the message that Malik had tried to get across to us yesterday. I had a newfound respect for Sonoda Sensei. He'd taught us very little in the class, but his legacy once it had finished was a valuable lifelong lesson in humility.

BABY BLACK BELTS

Friday, 22 December, was the last training day of 2006. Back home at this time of year, I'd have started the festivities with too much drink and far too many mince pies. Instead of winding down, as most people did in the final week before Christmas, we had been winding up. We'd passed our shodan test, been given temporary black belts to wear and received an important lesson in humility from Sonoda Sensei.

In the first class, we had Romeo Sensei, who taught us defence from knife attacks, which was great. Romeo, with his background in Filipino fighting arts, was the real deal and knew how to use a blade and defend himself from one. We were all ears, and the time passed quickly. In the second class, Chino Sensei made us review basic techniques and stopped us frequently to highlight our mistakes. At one point he got me up and asked me to grab his wrist. Though he was half my size, I was always amazed by his strength and in fear for my life. Trying to anticipate his move, I went with the flow. The last thing you ever wanted to do with Chino Sensei was move in one direction while he projected you in another. This was a one-way ticket to a broken wrist, elbow, arm, or even worse. Luckily, today, like a goalkeeper anticipating the placement of a penalty kick, I'd gone the right way. I'd half expected him to acknowledge our new shodan status and had hoped he would. Throughout the class, though, Chino seemed oblivious to our group promotion, which was clearly marked out by our shiny new belts. It wasn't until the end of the class that we got our second lesson in humility in as many days. In contrast to Sonoda Sensei, this wasn't Chino Sensei opening up to us. With a smile on his face but with serious intent he told us, *'you are baby black belts'*. By default, he was the only adult, and he urged us to continually practice the basics in the hope of getting better. If any of us had an inflated ego about achieving our new grade, Chino Sensei in one statement had well and truly burst our bubble. He was right. We might now share the same colour belt, but we were way below his level.

In the last few minutes of the final class of 2006 with Noriki Sensei, and ahead of my final Shinkoku, I thought I'd snapped Dave's elbow in half in the middle of a self-defence technique. Dave's elbow hadn't snapped and as we positioned ourselves outside the office, it looked to be still intact. As it bent it had made a horrible sound, but if Lloyd was the man of steel, luckily Dave was his opposite number. Dave was more 'rubberman' than *Superman*.

After class I headed off for a Japanese class with Hotta Sensei and then with no work caught the train to Akihabara. In the home of anything and everything electronic, I bought a Christmas present for Dad. A video camera for him and, as a little treat for me, a Sony PlayStation Portable. I got the war game *Medal of Honor* to go with it and stayed up until 11:30pm locked in battle!

END-OF-YEAR PARTY

It always felt strange arriving at the honbu dojo when there was no training scheduled for the day. Saturday, 23 December 2006, felt even more strange as this would be my last day at the dojo this year. Today would be a different experience altogether and was set to start with rice making. We all arrived at 9am. The dress code was suits and thankfully mine was now fully aired and no longer gave off the stench of mould.

Clyde had been placed in charge of proceedings, and, as he was the linguist amongst us, this was an inspired decision. We got changed into our dogi and carried various bits of kit downstairs. Kit we'd be using to make rice the traditional way. I usually made rice in a packet with the aid of a microwave or purchased it ready-made from the food shop in Musashi Koyama. I'd also purchased a rice cooker for when I had the time and could be bothered, but none of this prepared me for how we'd be making it today. By 10:15am all the equipment was ready and in place in the courtyard outside, and with time to spare, we headed up to Jonathan's for breakfast. I downed coffee like it was going out of fashion and wolfed down a club sandwich and chips. It was more like brunch, and it was my attempt to warm up and wake up. Fed and watered, we headed back to the honbu and lingered around in the courtyard, waiting for the guests we were told would arrive. We'd worn our coats over our dogi to head out to breakfast, but these were now back in our lockers. Dojo etiquette required that we had to look the part, but a thin dogi on a cold day was not the best option for keeping warm. My teeth were already chattering when the first guests arrived. None of us knew who anyone was, and, so as not to offend, we made a point of bowing to anyone old. The older you were, the more important you seemed to be; and in the absence of any other strategy, this would have to do. Japan would be a great place to retire!

Mochi making was a traditional part of Japanese end-of-year and New Year celebrations. Mochi or *short-grain glutinous rice*, was sticky, elastic and chewy and used for a variety of purposes, both sweet and savoury. I was partial to mochi buns with red-bean filling and would regularly stop off to buy these at the supermarket. Today would be my induction on how to make this sticky staple the traditional Japanese way. *Mochitsuki* was the name for the *traditional mochi-pounding ceremony* that we'd be put to task on to entertain the guests. This would involve beating the mochi in a big wooden barrel with a wooden mallet of sledgehammer proportions. This would require a technique that none of us had been trained for or had the opportunity to practice in advance. Working in pairs, one of us would beat the rice mix with the mallet while the other risked the future functionality of his or her hands by turning the mixture in between blows. This needed skilful timing, as any mistake would cause broken digits and prevent anyone incapacitated from finishing the course. None of us were keen on the turning; the beating looked the safer choice and also the better option for keeping warm. We had a little while to organise ourselves as Inoue Kancho would be the first to drop the hammer. The ceremonial strike over, the baton was passed to the Senshusei to do the lion's share of the work, and for the next three hours, we took it in turns to beat and turn, beat and turn, all to the delighted chant of the onlooking crowd. It was absolutely freezing, and while waiting to jump on the tools, we gravitated towards a fire that had been lit, which was our best hope of keeping warm. As Senshusei we couldn't relax and always had to look busy, so frequent changes to beat the rice after a short stop by the fire seemed the best solution.

At about 3pm, we started tidying up outside and carried everything back upstairs. The dojo was being prepared by a handful of university students who trained at the honbu. With the setup for this evening's end-of-year party safely in their hands, Ito Sensei asked Ronen and me to get dressed back into our suits, ready to formally welcome guests. It was the buddy system security team in action, and yet again we had no clue who anyone was or what we should say to them. The party wouldn't officially start until 4pm, and while Ronen and I got on with the pleasantries, the rest of the Senshusei wandered about, trying to look busy. The party followed a similar pattern to the one we'd experienced for the opening ceremony. The Sensei sat in seiza behind a long table that was positioned in front of the shomen, and our job, as usual, was to serve them drinks. All the honbu heads were there. The names I'd read about in *Angry White Pyjamas* who had inspired me to travel halfway across the world were lined up in front of me. It was an amazing moment and despite the continual hardships the course presented, I felt grateful for the experience. Chino Sensei was there but disappeared soon after proceedings began. Our job was to attend to each and every Sensei, and losing one wasn't good form. Where was Chino? Had he left already? We had to find him, and fast. A party was sent out to search the dojo high and low. It wasn't the easiest of missions, as certain places were off limits, including Kancho's office. After a little while, a rumour began to circulate that Chino had been found and didn't want to be disturbed. While all the other Sensei enjoyed the food, drink and festivities, Chino Sensei sat alone in the kitchen watching old VHS videos of Kancho Gozo Shioda, his hero and mentor. Chino Sensei was on a different level, and his commitment to grow and develop his Aikido, if ever in doubt, was confirmed in this moment. This was the stuff of legend and a story I was sure I'd be telling for many years to come.

The Senshusei had been the cabaret act at the opening ceremony, but today we were off the hook, although Vic and Boaz had voluntarily offered their services. Vic and Romeo Sensei performed a Kali (stick fighting) demonstration, followed by Boaz doing Salsa. Both were really good and lightened up what was soon to revert back to a formal occasion with a speech from Inoue Kancho. A makeshift bar had been set up in the corner of the dojo, and I volunteered to help Takashima Sensei and Matt, who were busy serving drinks. This was when the fun began. I now had direct access to all the booze and started helping myself to whisky and anything else that took my fancy. The drunker I got, the more entertaining the evening got. Matt followed my lead and, in a miscalculation of etiquette, addressed Takashima Sensei as 'mate'. The Wizard either didn't hear Matt's indiscretion or was far too drunk himself to care. Matt and I were legless and struggling to stand up straight, not due to our usual blood-starved legs after a zagaku session but, this time, as a result of intoxication. We were temporarily called away from bar duty to perform Shinkoku. As Inoue Kancho was in the building, we had to formally thank him for the party he'd just presided over. I was in no state to perform and, given the complexity of the Japanese involved, Kambara stepped into the breach. As we bowed, all of us, now quite drunk, found it hard not to laugh, and to hide our giggles, we mustered up the loudest 'osu' we'd ever done. We held our bow as Kancho acknowledged our enthusiasm and disappeared back into the office. As we came back to a vertical position, Dave, always the joker, slapped me on the backside and scuttled off, laughing to himself before I had time to react and slap him back!

Everyone looked to have had too much to drink, and with the departure of Inoue Kancho, the guests left one by one. Like a pub landlord at closing time we tidied up around the stragglers hoping they'd take the hint. As we cleaned and tidied, we glimpsed what looked like the partner list for Dai Yon, which must have been misplaced by one of the Sensei. I found out I'd be finishing the course with Matt, which was great news. I'd hoped we'd get paired at some point, and after five months with Geoff – less his stint in mitori geiko, which made it more like four – training with Matt would be a breeze. What started as a formal event now descended into a free-for-all. We took some photos in front of the shomen, and while I was having my photo taken with Ronen and Laurance, Chida Sensei came up and asked if he could have his photo taken with me. I was in shock. Here was Aikido God, as Malik had described him, wanting his image captured for all eternity with me. I was in even more shock when he addressed me as *'Simon'*. It turned out he knew my name after all!

We left the honbu at around 8pm and, with the night still young, headed off to the HUB in Takadanobaba. I'd had more than enough already, and after one beer, I was ready for the off. As the train pulled into Musashi Koyama Station, and I made the short walk home, I reflected on the last nine months. What a journey, what an experience; and now, as a reward for my efforts, I had a full two weeks off!

TOKYO TINSEL

I was heading home for Christmas, but confusion over the date of the shodan test and when the course would come to its conclusion for 2006 had meant the only flight I could now get was on Boxing Day. I'd left things late, and now, on Christmas Eve, when I should have been surrounded by tinsel, I was sat alone in a Tokyo Internet cafe trying to book a seat. After navigating the booking page and confirming my return to the UK, I headed to Harajuku to do some last-minute Christmas shopping.

It was Sunday, but the shops in Tokyo always seemed to be open. In Japan, shopping was an interesting and noisy experience. There was no such thing as a quiet browse – the staff simply wouldn't allow it. *'Irasshaimase! Irasshaimase! Irasshaimase!'* It never stopped, from the moment you walked in, until the moment you left. *'Welcome! Come on in! Welcome!'* It echoed from assistant to assistant as you made your way around the store. It always reminded me of *Mr Benn*, the TV show I'd watched as a kid. With its distinctive theme tune and repetitive plot, it had made captivating viewing. The narration had always stuck in my head. In every episode, in search of entertainment, Mr Benn went for a walk which *'took him to a special costume shop. A shop that adventures could start from!'* The shop was always empty, that is until, *'as if by magic the shopkeeper appeared'*. I'd always remembered it. Mr Benn lived at number 52, and so did I! I'd found the retail staff's attention unnerving when I'd first arrived in Tokyo. I'd been into Timberland, to buy a pair of boots for my ascent up Mount Fuji – I nearly ran out, I was in so much shock – I thought there was a fire! I finally bought the boots and was followed out into the street by the manager who was clutching the bag. As the sea of shoppers engulfed us, he bowed to me, handed over my purchase, and thanked me for my custom. I'd never experienced anything like it before.

Retail therapy satisfied and ears ringing, I revisited the church. I'd never been particularly religious, but Christmas was different, and the service culminated in a beautiful rendition of *Silent Night* by candlelight. *Silent Night* was the carol reportedly sung in the trenches during the First World War on Christmas Eve, 1914. It led to a truce in the fighting, and as I sang the words; I thought of the young lads spending Christmas on the front line far from home. It was a humbling experience. I was far from home, but in two days I'd be back in the UK and with my family. *Silent Night* was a fitting end to an emotional week.

Christmas Day was a day of packing and preparation. After a long and much-needed lie-in, I got up and filled my suitcase. There was no Christmas dinner on the menu and no prospect of turkey, stuffing and all the trimmings. Lunch at a burger bar at Azabu Juban was followed by a movie at Roppongi Hills. *My Date with Drew* was a fly-on-the-wall documentary about a guy who films his quest to date the actress Drew Barrymore. It was light entertainment and helped the day pass. Christmas Day wasn't a holiday in Japan, and as far as I could tell, it was business as usual. For me, Christmas wouldn't start until I'd landed back in the UK. To remind myself it was Christmas Day, I rented *Noel* from the DVD shop in Musashi Koyama. It had a good Christmas message, and by 9pm, I was asleep. Tomorrow would be a busy day, and I couldn't afford to miss my flight.

Boxing Day was back to Senshusei timing, as I was up at 4:30am to do the last of my packing. I caught the train to Ueno and jumped on the Skyliner to Narita. At airport security I was stopped and searched. The woman who inspected my bag seemed very interested in the ice packs I was taking home to continue my treatment and asked me if I was a footballer. When I told her I was in Japan studying Aikido she seemed very impressed and waved me on. My luck got even better at check-in, where I was upgraded to business class and a seat on my own with a window to one side and the aisle to the other. This was the best of both worlds. I could watch the take-off and also get out to the toilet as and when I needed. After 12 hours I landed back at Heathrow. After a long delay waiting for my bag to appear on the conveyor belt, I walked into arrivals. Mum, Dad and Sally were waiting to greet me, and if I was in any doubt that they were pleased to see me, the welcome balloon my Mum was holding gave the game away! On the car journey back to Stafford I was too tired to talk and drifted in and out of sleep. The return jet lag from Tokyo back to London was much worse than the outbound version. Once at home I had a shower, opened a few presents and then dined on cold turkey, washed down with red wine. By 9pm I was done and headed up to bed.

BACK HOME

Being back home felt strange. Suddenly what I did, and when I did it, was up to me. There was no schedule or duties to perform and nobody shouting at me to get things done. While I was glad to see my family, I was worried that the time away from the honbu would break my routine and with it my resilience. Discipline was a fragile commodity – hard to build but easy to tear down. I needed to be careful to stay in the zone and ready for my return to Tokyo. It wasn't only my surroundings I was worried about; for the next two weeks, my diet would be different, too. I'd been living on rice and vegetables with the occasional European delicacy served up with a Japanese twist by the Royal Host, Jonathan's and, every now and again, Shakey's pizza restaurant, for a special occasion! My body clock was all over the place, and I found myself exhausted in the middle of the day and wide awake at night. I missed the cut and thrust of Senshusei life, and like a prisoner released back into society after serving time, I felt lost, confused and lonely.

Senshusei was a hard thing to understand. Malik Sewanin had alluded to this on more than one occasion; and not quite at the end, I was yet to discover its true meaning. My family knew I was in Japan on some crazy course, but that was all they really knew. Senshusei had already changed me, and now, thrown back into everyday life, I was beginning to sit up and take notice of how different I'd become. My feet were in a dreadful state, and Mum booked an appointment with Frank Peach, a chiropodist in town. I pulled off my socks, and Frank set to work on my feet. I was there for over an hour while he scraped and filed. With each layer of skin he removed, I realised what punishment I'd put myself through, but this was just my feet, never mind the rest of my body.

I'd missed Christmas, so I was determined to enjoy New Year. I would be spending New Year's Eve with Mum and Dad but had scheduled a trip to Nottingham on Saturday, 30 December, for a night out with my mate Justin. 'Juzza' and I headed into West Bridgford, an increasingly popular suburb just outside the city with a vast array of restaurants and drinking establishments. After dinner at Pizza Express, we toured a few bars and caught up with some friends, including 'Gazza', whom I'd not seen for the best part of two years. As we chatted, I realised how different our lives were now. Juzza and Gazza had regular jobs and stable relationships, while my life was a world away in Japan. Both had put on weight since I'd last seen them, while I'd become a lean, mean fighting machine. I wondered what I would do after Senshusei and how I'd transition back to the normality of everyday life. Will hadn't been able to join us. He was about to become a father, and his daughter arrived in the middle of the night. I had a text from him in the early hours of New Year's Eve to tell me that Alaramia had arrived safely at 3:15am and that mother, baby and father were all doing well. Will had been the one to get me into Aikido, and, not able to get back to sleep, I reflected how our lives had moved in such different directions since he'd first introduced me to the Shudokan and Sensei Ken.

I didn't see 2007 arrive. The jet lag was still tormenting me, and I'd fallen asleep at Mum and Dad's well before midnight. I'd missed the fireworks on TV but consoled myself with the knowledge that a different type of fireworks would start again soon back at the honbu. Until then, the quiet life was what I needed, with plenty of rest to heal my battered body. I spent the rest of my time visiting friends, going out for coffee with Mum and Dad and watching TV. As I packed my suitcase on Friday, 5 January 2007, I went up and down on an emotional rollercoaster of excitement and depression. On the one hand, it gutted me to leave my parents, but on the other, I was missing Tokyo and ready to make my return. Sally turned up for what would be our last supper and after dinner I asked Dad to ceremoniously cut my hair. I'd done this myself the night before the shodan test, and now that I was going back to Japan, it was time to do it again. On Saturday, 6 January 2007, Dad drove me back to Heathrow accompanied by Mum. I felt very sad to leave them both. Mum was putting on a brave face, and as I hugged her outside the security gate, she started to cry. Dad had tears in his eyes, too, which made saying goodbye even more difficult. I turned and waved before I disappeared out of sight beyond the security gate. I was especially worried about Mum and called her from the departure lounge to check she was all right. I always missed my parents and, now, on the motorway, she was still upset. As I boarded my flight the time for sentiment was over. I flicked a switch in my head. I was now back in Senshusei mode and ready to get back to Japan.

TOUCH DOWN

I touched down in Tokyo at 11am on Sunday, 7 January 2007. After a turbulent descent and a bumpy landing, I made my way through immigration. The inspector at customs greeted me in a familiar way. *'Shinkoku mono?'* I knew a very different type of Shinkoku. It was the same vocabulary, but with a very different meaning. The immigration officer was asking if I had *'something to declare?'* I didn't and communicated this back in Japanese, finishing with a loud *'osu'*. It was old habits kicking in! I was back in Musashi Koyama by 2pm and fell straight to sleep. The day was a write-off, and after a short walk to the shopping arcade, I was back in bed. I had limited time to get rid of the jet lag, with only one full day to acclimatise in preparation for the fourth and final phase of the course.

There was no better way to get back into the swing of things than a session at Axis. Jiu Jitsu was an opportunity to blow away the cobwebs and to reassure me that my body was still capable of tough training. It was good to see Clyde again, who, sharing my thinking, had made it to the session, too. Thoughts of the UK had now been firmly pushed to the back of my mind. I was prepared for tomorrow. There would be no easing myself in and no gradual turning up of the dial to the level of intensity I'd experienced for the shodan test. Tomorrow would go off at full tilt, and an early night was the best way to be ready!

PART FOUR: DAI YON
(9 January to 28 February 2007)

BACK TO EARTH...

Tuesday, 9 January 2007, was back to earth with a bump. All the excitement that had led up to the shodan test and the end-of-year party was gone. It was back to the daily slog! Still a victim of jet lag, I woke up at 3:15am and couldn't get back to sleep. When it was time to get up shortly after 5am, all I wanted to do was get back under the covers and block out the day ahead. This wasn't an option, and I had the added chore of doing my morning press-ups and sit-ups, which was a New Year's resolution that I'd started on 1 January. This now added to the morning burden and pressure on time and would continue until the 31st. I caught the earlier train out of Musashi Koyama at 6:05am and found myself in the carriage almost alone. The trains got busier the closer I got to Ochiai, and the faces became more miserable. Another working day for Japan's overworked population was underway.

It was good to see my fellow Senshusei, and we exchanged stories of the Christmas period along with greetings of *'Happy New Year'* in English and the mouthful that was the Japanese version, *'Akemashite Omedetou Gozaimasu'*. As I'd suspected, there was little easing us back into the routine. Higa Sensei threw us straight into a review of Dai Ichi kihon waza, which now seemed like a distant memory. This was followed by Murata Sensei, who wheeled a TV into the dojo. Murata was unpredictable at the best of times, but was he really treating us to a post-Christmas movie? Unfortunately, this wasn't the case; we'd instead be watching the *Kagami Biraki* Enbu from two years ago. Another Enbu? I couldn't believe it. I hoped this wasn't all we had to look forward to for the next few weeks. More repetition upon repetition, which had nearly driven me round the bend ahead of the All Japan Enbu last year.

In the tearoom a rumour circulated that we would be taught by Chida Sensei in the last class. I wondered if, now we were black belts, if we were finally worthy of his full attention – a step up from his occasional guest appearance. Chida was definitely on the schedule, but as we lined up in seiza opposite the shomen to await his arrival, another rumour did the rounds. Apparently Chida had forgotten he was down to teach us and wouldn't be turning up. We'd be having Ito Sensei instead. We did some new techniques that we'd be tested for as part of Dai Yon, Enbu practice and finally shido ho. I was ordered up to demonstrate in front of the class. This was twice in one day as I'd been called up in the first class to demonstrate kamae, as part of Mr Precise's mission to get back to basics.

To round off a hellish day, there was no hot water, so it was a cold shower instead! I also dropped my fake Rolex on the floor of the locker room, and a stone from the face fell out. Like me, my 'Bangkok special' was in a sorry state. It was time to get rid of it, and I dumped it in a bin in Takadanobaba. It wasn't just the honbu I'd dived into head-first; it was back to Berlitz, too. After a quick stop in Shibuya to buy a new diary, I reluctantly headed off to work. After six lessons with only one break, I was exhausted and could hardly stay awake. My two-week vacation back in the UK, while enjoyable, had taken the edge off my endurance and ability to suck it up. It would be a difficult week!

MOTHER FUCKER!

I didn't know it when I stepped into the honbu, but Wednesday was to be the worst day on the course to date. In the first class, we had Romeo Sensei, who took us right back to the start of the course, and the trip down memory lane wasn't a pleasant one. He drilled us on seiza, standing, seiza, standing, over and over again. By now we were all well versed in getting to our feet and had already more than enough practice on our knees thanks to zagaku. It was like day one all over again. I suspected it was the honbu's way of reminding us that, as Chino put it, we might be black belts now, but we were only baby ones!

We were fully in Enbu mode, and Romeo wound up his session with a run-through, which Oyamada Sensei continued in the second class after his predictable rendition of sotai dosa. While we were permitted to go at our own pace, and it wasn't hajime geiko, the Enbu demonstration had to be done at speed. At one point I asked Geoff to practice his nikajo pin on my stiff arms just so I could lie down for a bit. I needed any excuse to catch my breath! It wasn't just my stamina that had been affected by the two-week break; my

296

visit to the chiropodist had weakened the resilience of my feet. With the morning's sliding and scraping, both of my feet had started to flake, and the sole of my right foot had spilt. Any attempt to tape up my feet was a waste of time. After a few minutes, any tape secured in the tearoom worked loose and risked littering the mats. Oyamada Sensei finished 10 minutes early at 11:20am. His tea and biscuits must have been calling from the office, but whatever the reason, we were glad it was over. I'd enjoyed his classes towards the end of last year but now questioned the sanity of my previous thoughts.

Vic had escaped the monotony. Vic and Geoff had spent the Christmas break in Hawaii, and in a freak accident, she'd broken her forearm in a collision with a surfboard. With all the training, it was a wonder the surfboard hadn't come off worse. But she'd taken the full force of the impact and now would be in mitori geiko for the foreseeable future. In the last class, Takashima was joined by Chida Sensei. Chida had at last graced us with his presence. He offered some advice on how best to perform the Enbu, but after he'd failed to turn up yesterday, I wasn't all ears. To finish the class, The Wizard made us watch an old video tape from 20 years back when a member of the Japanese royal family had visited the dojo for the Kagami Biraki celebration. It was great to see an 18-year-old Chino doing his stuff and Chida at 34 years old, the same age as me. It was funny to watch Shioda Junior wriggling around in seiza. I'd no doubt he'd been brought up with regular practice in this position and it was reassuring to see him succumb to the pain. There appeared to be no love lost between Takashima and Shioda Junior. In the final few minutes of the video, Takashima seemed to take delight in Shioda Junior's obvious mistakes while doing jiyu waza with Chino as his uke. This contrasted starkly with what happened when the roles were reversed. The Wizard rewound the tape so we could watch Chino in action for a second time. Neither Takashima Sensei nor any of us wanted to miss a thing! We returned to the dojo to bow out, and Geoff summed up the mood in the camp in two words. *'Mother fucker!'* Geoff whispered this proclamation as he dropped into his least-favourite position, when Ronen, the first Shinkoku of 2007, gave the command.

POINTLESS EXERCISE

Every Sensei had a view of how the Enbu demonstration should be performed. Even Graham Sewanin got in on the act, advising that to make our movements more coordinated, we should practice doing other activities together. I wondered what these other activities might be, and we didn't have to wait long to find out. The suggested 'other activities' were sweeping and rearranging the chairs in the tearoom!

It was Thursday and the first zagaku of the year. Three days in, all of our knees were already shot to pieces, and we took up our lines in the dojo with a heightened level of trepidation. The only plus was that none of the Senshusei would be required to share. Instead Kancho invited each Sensei to speak, to offer us advice for the final phase of the course. They all spoke in Japanese, which meant only three people could fully understand what was being said, namely Inazaki, Kambara and Clyde. The advice might have been useful, but because of the language barrier, it was a completely pointless exercise. The only thing I'd partially understood was Chida Sensei's advice to have fun. Given the relentless Enbu practice, which was now dominating every class, any prospect of fun appeared a long way off.

Despite time away from the asylum, given the discussion in the tearoom after class, the madness had been quick to set back in. Conversation turned to how best to kill Chino Sensei. None of us were brave enough or actually wanted to carry out such an act, but it made for an interesting debate. Any weapon that fired projectiles was quickly removed as an option, and our choice limited to those that would require contact at close quarters. I chose an axe, and Geoff chose a chainsaw. Geoff thought he'd picked the better solution until I asked the question. *'But what if you can't get it started?'* Geoff looked to the ceiling as if playing out the scenario in his head, then agreed that an axe was a much better bet!

IN THE WARS

By Friday I was already in the wars. My body was as stiff as a board, the sole of my right foot was cracked and the scab on my left knee, which was doing its best to heal, broke every time I bent it. Malik was back, having taken yesterday off to sort out some visa problems, and I was actually pleased to see him. In the first class we had Naruo Sensei and surprise, surprise we did Enbu practice again. Towards the end of the class Naruo called over to Takagi Sensei, who was teaching the ippan students, to ask her what she thought. *'Hijishime to kotegaeshi warui'*, she yelled back. *'Elbow lock and wrist throw bad.'* *Well, don't pull any punches,* I thought to myself. Takagi wasn't long out of Senshusei herself and some constructive criticism wouldn't have gone a miss!

After debating yesterday how best to kill Chino Sensei, today's tearoom discussion took a more worrying turn. How best to kill yourself was the topic of conversation, which reflected the less-than-positive mood we were all in. I suggested a bottle of whisky and as much morphine as I could get my hands on, whereas Dror opted for blowing his brains out, which we all agreed would be far too messy! In the second class, we had Chino and to continue a recurring theme we did Enbu practice again. He seemed in good spirits and encouraged his band of baby black belts to check the angle of our techniques and criticised our seiza as being too weak. The Sewanin didn't need to be told twice and under licence from Chino dragged us back into the dojo five minutes early ahead of the next class to practice. We really were going back to basics, but if Chino Sensei thought our seiza was weak, there must have been merit in making it better. I was prepared to give him the benefit of the doubt and made every effort to sit still and sit up straight. Geoff was really struggling, so Graham put a piece of paper on his head and told him that if it fell off, we would all be doing five rounds of usagi tobi. Punishing us all for the mistake of one was a strategy that worked, and Geoff held his composure and position to save us all from a less-than-desirable fate.

In the final class, Noriki Sensei, sensing our lack of enthusiasm, moved quickly to jiyu waza practice. Vic was in mitori geiko, and with the injury to her upper body, this meant seiza. Approaching four hours in this position with only short breaks to recover was too much for anyone, and she started to cry. Graham Sewanin took pity and told her to stand up but was challenged by Malik after class. Malik complained, *'on our course, we wouldn't have been allowed to stand up!'* He had a point. From what I'd seen of their course, Malik and Graham had suffered. Still, this was this year, and a glimpse of the old Malik potentially making a reappearance wasn't good news. Boaz pulled me to one side in the locker room to ask me whether I was interested in being a Sewanin next year. He said his brother was planning to do the course and that he could only trust Matt, Inazaki or me to look after him. I took it as a compliment, but I had no intention of being a Sewanin. It was a stupid and misplaced request. If I returned as Sewanin, I'd be more likely to put the hammer down on Boaz's brother for being Boaz's brother rather than grant him safe passage. Nobody wanted to be Sewanin. It looked far too much like doing Senshusei all over again!

KAGAMI BIRAKI

The Kagami Biraki Enbu was set for Sunday, 14 January 2007. An extra day at the honbu was always unwelcome and after the relentless practice of yesterday I needed a break. Inazaki was in bits and stumbled into the dojo hardly able to walk, his knees were so bad. He never complained and was always in good humour, but today he had the weight of the world on his shoulders. There was nothing any of us could do to help him or ease his pain. The course was a personal journey with inevitable ups and downs, and today it was Inazaki's turn to face the down.

Kagami Biraki was a traditional Japanese ceremony steeped in history. It marked a significant change in life and was synonymous with the start of a new year. Translated as *opening the mirror*, the story goes that it got its name because mochi was given as an offering on the same stand used for placing a mirror. I'd also heard it translated as *breaking the mochi* and sometimes *breaking the mirror*. Breaking the mirror made more sense to me. Looking into a mirror was an exercise in self-reflection, and with the mirror smashed, there would no longer be an opportunity to look back, only forwards. The ceremony was over 300 years old and, legend had it, involved the *Shogun* or *ruler* of a particular region breaking open a cask of *sake* (Japanese rice wine). This sounded like a good option, particularly if we got to drink it afterwards! I couldn't help it, but whenever I heard Kagami Biraki mentioned I imagined smashing the two large mirrors in the dojo that we'd all spent far too long cleaning. The only downside would be seven years of bad luck times two, making 14 in total!

At 8:15am we were in the tearoom and awaiting further instructions. The instructions were confused and came from different sources, which saw us in the first hour run around like headless chickens with the Sewanin barking orders. Nobody knew what they were supposed to be doing, but amidst all the confusion, we set up the dojo and, with time to spare, did a final run-through of our demonstration. By 10:55am we were in seiza, ready to begin. With so many people to fit in I found myself on the front row, so had little opportunity to move my legs to keep the blood flowing. After the opening speech and a variety of additional formality, the Senshusei were scheduled to be up third. Paul and some of the other Sensei went first in a demonstration of kihon dosa. I was relieved to see even Paul make a mistake, at one point turning the wrong way. If a Sensei had made an error, psychologically this gave us licence, although I was sure the Sewanin would never see it that way. My feet were numb after less than 15 minutes. If I couldn't feel them and stood up, there was a very good chance that I'd break my ankle, which, having come this far, I wasn't prepared to do. I tried to move, but in full view of everyone and completely sandwiched in, there was no option. On the call to stand, we jumped up and plodded to our start positions. During the first five techniques, I could barely feel my feet. I didn't hear any cracking of bones, and I didn't fall over, so I presumed somehow that I'd avoided any serious injury. The five tachi waza rolled into the five suwari waza techniques that Geoff and I had to get through. Although for Dai Yon, I expected to be officially paired with Matt, Geoff and I were yet to formally part company.

Next, we got to watch the senior Sensei perform, which culminated in jiyu waza. Murray Sensei destroyed Malik Sewanin, and due to the brutality of the display, I suspected there was an underlying issue that Murray Sensei had addressed publicly. Was it Iwama? Had Laurance Sensei or Graham told him? Did Murray Sensei think I was a rat, too? Poor old Malik, he was in the bad books for some reason and had now paid the price! By comparison, Chino Sensei took it easy on Graham. Watching from the sidelines, I couldn't work out whether Chino was going lighter or if it just appeared that way because of Murray Sensei's aggression. Chida Sensei then gave one of the best demonstrations of Aikido I'd ever seen, throwing Laurance Sensei around effortlessly. I couldn't argue with the fact that he was indeed the Aikido God, but still resented the lack of attention he'd given the Senshusei. There was a final sting in the tail before Kagami Biraki was over. Kancho got up and rattled on for ages about how much fun Aikido was. In sadistic fashion, he formally acknowledged how much pain we must all be in sat in seiza and that he should probably speak more quickly, then proceeded with his narrative for another 15 minutes!

At the end I couldn't stand up and Murray Sensei, having burned up his aggression on Malik and in a rare show of kindness, came to my rescue. The moment was short-lived as the bark of the Sewanin's orders rang through my ears. The Senshusei were called into action to put the tables out ready for the food and drink. The Sensei and guests sat down to eat, and we served the drinks. When it was our turn to eat, Chino Sensei came over to Matt and me and told us not to sit in seiza on the wooden floor and to move onto the mats, which were *'much better'*. He poured us a beer and engaged us in brief conversation, telling us he wasn't drinking as he had to go to work in Yokohama. He seemed concerned for our well-being, and as his parting shot, he encouraged us to *'eat lots'*. It was a nice gesture from our favourite Sensei.

I found it impossible not to get drunk at honbu parties. Chino was a better man than me in his abstinence because by the formal close I was most definitely the worse for wear. Malik advised that there would be no final Shinkoku and that we could leave when we wanted. This was an open invitation to drink more and by the time we rolled out of the dojo and onto the street Dave was the most inebriated of us all. He asked one of the older men who had been a guest of Kancho if he could borrow his walking stick to do *hiriki no yosei ichi*, the third move of the kihon dosa, with the stick acting as a stand-in bokken. Halted in his tracks by Murata Sensei's arrival, Dave calmed down. Murata pinched one of Dave's cigarettes and, puffing on clouds of smoke, flipped the bird behind Kancho Gozo Shioda's son as he left. Not Yasuhisa Shioda, whom we knew as Shioda Junior, but as Murata described him, *'the other one'*. Until that moment, I hadn't been aware that Gozo Shioda had another son. Murata provided clarification and suggested that the 'other one' had only turned up to try to get money out of the honbu.

I never understood why Dave smoked. Senshusei was hard enough without the grip of smoke on your lungs. I'd also previously told him. *'When I smell smoke on a guy, it shows me weakness and makes me want to smash him more!'* Dragging Dave with us, we headed off to the HUB in Takadanobaba, which was becoming our regular haunt, for a few more beers to wash down the fish and chips you had to eat with chopsticks. It hadn't been a bad day after all, but the alcohol always helped. Inazaki had started the day by entering the dojo with some nasty-looking wounds, and in his honour, as I kicked back in Musashi Koyama, I watched *Exit Wounds* on DVD, starring none other than Steven Seagal.

MISMATCH?

Monday came and went in a haze, and it was back to business with the second week of Dai Yon. Be careful what you read or find lying about in the dojo. In the middle of Tuesday's first class, Murray Sensei interrupted Mr Precise to announce the new pairings for the last phase of the course. As I heard my name, I fully expected Matt's to be called next, so I was shocked when I was matched with Ronen. Matt was instead paired with Clyde, and Boaz got the Sewanin, which raised a few smiles. Ronen and I always had a laugh and got on well, so I was happy with the allocation. Despite being good friends and invoking the buddy system on a regular basis we had yet to train together for any length of time. Now this Israeli-British match-up would give us the opportunity to test each other out. If there had been a mismatch, it was in our attempt to predict the future, and I wondered if Chida Sensei had gotten wind and changed things around on purpose. Perhaps to ease us uncomfortably in, Higa had us stroking the tops and bottoms of each other's hands to strengthen our kamae. I thought this was a complete waste of time, not to mention a little awkward; and from the looks of everyone else, we all seemed in agreement.

At night I headed off to Berlitz for what turned out to be a very morbid evening. Some students were late. The JR Yamanote Line had been shut, as someone had jumped in front of a moving train at Ebisu Station. Suicide was a common occurrence in Tokyo. Overwork and work-related depression led some, usually men, to end it all. It was a sad end to what I guessed was a sad and oppressed life with little family time and with corporate loyalty taking precedence. I'd read in *The Guardian* that in the previous year, there had been 32,000 suicides in the country. This statistic became even more frightening when I calculated it was nearly 100 every day or one every 15 minutes. I'd heard that you could spot a jumper as they'd first take off their shoes and leave them neatly at the side of the platform. Even facing imminent and certain death the right etiquette had to be followed. In one of my last classes, I was teaching a student to use 'unless' and encouraged her to make up a sentence to show her understanding of the word. What she came up with sent a chill down my spine. *'I will go to work tomorrow, unless I die.'* While grammatically correct, it was a very morbid way to think.

SPANDAU BALLET

The constant conflicting communication at the honbu dojo made life difficult, particularly for us. Graham Sewanin was on the warpath and throwing the Shinkoku diary down on the tearoom table in Wednesday's morning meeting he demanded to know why there was no entry for the day of the shodan test. As Shinkoku it was my job to document what happened on the day, and Graham wanted to know why, instead of words and paragraphs, he'd found a line drawn through a blank page. What could I say, what could I do? Malik Sewanin had told me to cross it out, and like a good Senshusei, I'd done as I was told. There was no point trying to justify what wasn't my fault and, given that Graham already thought I was a rat, no gain to be had by saying Malik had instructed me to do it. The words to Spandau Ballet's hit *Communication* played through my head.

Communication let me down.
But I'm left her.
Communication let me down.
But I'm left here, I'm left here, I, I, I.

In reality, communication hadn't let me down. Communication had let the Sewanin down, and I was collateral damage. My response was short and to the point. *'Osu!'* Graham Sewanin seemed to have got out of bed on the wrong side and laid into Boaz and Dror. Boaz was reprimanded for not getting a skin condition he'd been carrying on his hand seen to, and Dror was criticised for, well, nobody was quite sure. Graham accused Dror of flouting dojo rules and doing whatever he liked for the whole course. It was a catch-all comment which seemed more than a little unfair!

Takagi Sensei had been getting on my nerves ever since her comment about our bad techniques in Naruo Sensei's class. To continue what had already started as a bad day she produced a stopwatch from inside her dogi and timed us doing kihon waza techniques for most of the first class. Takagi said she thought we were slow at the Enbu and that she knew some university students who could perform techniques faster than us. That may well have been true, but university students didn't train anywhere near our intensity and weren't carrying the array of niggling injuries we all were. Also, we'd been sat in seiza for what seemed like an eternity before being asked to jump to our feet, and I hadn't been able to feel my feet for the first half of the demonstration. We played her game, but I couldn't have cared less how quickly we got through the techniques. Put any of the university students up against a Senshusei, and there would only be one outcome. If we were too tired to be bothered, we could just leave them all to Lloyd!

In the last break the Sewanin called us to the far end of the dojo and made us sit in seiza for 15 minutes. They had a go at us about our lack of energy and had gotten the idea in their heads that because we were now black belts, we were no longer trying. This wasn't the case, but the euphoria of how last year had ended and the motivational words that had sent us away for the Christmas break had now gravitated to constant criticism. They were the source of the problem, and the more they berated us, the less energetic we felt!

TOXIC

The relationship with the Sewanin was like a relationship with a narcissistic girlfriend or boyfriend who continually pushed your buttons. We couldn't escape them and couldn't argue back. Whatever they dished out, we had no choice but to take. I'd expected the relationship with them would get better during the final stage of the course and as we'd passed shodan, but it was getting more and more toxic. To be fair to Malik, he'd gotten much better, and it was good to have him around. It was Graham who was least happy and seemed to have the most issues with what we were doing and how we were doing it. Malik must have sensed I was getting sick of the whole thing. As I got changed in the locker room ahead of Thursday morning's cleaning duty, he called me over to have a word. Much to my surprise, and with no advance warning, he said that he thought I was the only one out of the 13 of us on the course that really was Senshusei, and that I should *'keep working at it'*. He didn't give an explanation, and I didn't agree with what he'd said, but it gave me the boost I needed. Clyde and Matt had already started cleaning the shower room well within earshot of the locker room, and I prayed that they hadn't heard. I'd teased Matt on more than one occasion for being the Sewanin's favourite, and now he had the perfect ammunition to get back at me. With my dogi on, I tentatively walked round to the shower area. They mentioned nothing, so I guessed they hadn't heard.

My knees were feeling sore, so I was relieved when Naruo Sensei opted for kihon dosa with a sword. This was a much easier option than most of the things we normally did, and while boring, easy was the only thing I wanted today. Boaz had left his ankle support by the side of the mats, and Graham, spotting it, asked him outright, *'is this the dojo or the locker room?'* There were some visitors milling around, who looked to be Aikido enthusiasts from overseas. They filed into the dojo to watch the last class, and Kanazawa Sensei decided to put on an impromptu show. It was time for a mini Enbu, which combined kihon dosa renzoku from the 51st All Japan Enbu with the techniques from Kagami Biraki. We weren't performing seals and revisiting both demonstrations rolled into one was a step too far. With time until the end of the class for jiyu waza, Kanazawa asked for volunteers. As Senshusei we were supposed to be first to respond, but no one did, which summed up the apathy that had bred through our ranks. Eventually I put up my hand, only because no one else did. As my reward, I was invited to be Graham Sewanin's uke. This wasn't going to go well. Graham had been in a foul mood all week, and now, if he saw fit, he had the opportunity to make an example of me, Chino style. With the visitors on the edge of their seats, I feared Graham was about to step up the action to please his audience. He didn't disappoint and threw me around good and proper. He had no knowledge of the bilateral agreement I'd made with Geoff and slid under my knees on more than one occasion. He had serious intent, and it was only by the skin of my teeth that I managed to survive his techniques. I was exhausted, and the visitors seemed impressed. I'd rarely tangled with Graham, and I didn't intend to again.

In zagaku, Ronen was called upon to share. He reflected on having a new uke who was really strong and that he was struggling to do the techniques. I didn't know how to take this. Was he complimenting my strength or suggesting I was being awkward? It wasn't clear, and I clarified with him afterwards. *'You try doing sankajo on a flagpole that doesn't bend!'* Referencing Geoff's earlier description of himself, Ronen had made his point. Before the day was done, Dave got his belt back from Naruo Sensei. Dave had been allocated Naruo's belt while our black belts were being made and had left it out of his locker on Sunday evening in a state of intoxication. An ippan student who could read the kanji had handed it to Naruo, who was surprised to receive a belt back he had only just lent from someone other than the Sewanin or one of the Senshusei. Ouch! Dave's error was a very good reason for him to go on the wagon. The Sewanin didn't appear to know, and Dave hoped he'd got away with it.

The torment continued on Friday. In Chino Sensei's class, confused by his commands, we'd all been making mistakes. Once the class was over, Malik and Graham called us into the corner of the dojo to give us press-ups. They had a go at Ronen for making the most mistakes and also at Neville for his back heel coming up. Without his back heel glued to the tatami – the mark of a Senshusei – Neville had broken protocol. For good measure we all got a round of bunny hops, and Inazaki, who was now constantly in pain, got another round for not acknowledging Malik. In the last class, we had Chida Sensei. It was a rare appearance and one he used to communicate some of the finer points of kihon dosa. The class went well apart from the fact that one of my toes started bleeding. As I moved around the tatami, I left a trail of blood that would now require Senshusei, zokin and elbow grease to clean up!

KAN GEIKO

We'd survived early morning summer training and on Saturday, 20 January 2007, *kan geiko*, which translated as *early morning winter training*, was to begin. In anticipation I'd had an early night, but that didn't help matters much when my alarm clock went off at 4:15am. I'd often debated as a kid whether it was better to be too hot or too cold. It was the kind of conversation I'd have with Mum, Dad and Sally to pass the time on a long car journey. I'd never been sure which was the better option, but this morning, many years on, I was finding out. It was freezing in the apartment, and my body just didn't want to move. Only a hot shower greased the wheels of action and helped me to manoeuvre once again like a normal human being. Anyone seeing me walk towards them in the dark would have thought an old man was on his way, not a 34-year-old in what should have been the prime of his life.

The train from Meguro was full of drunks who'd missed the last train the previous night. The rabble, now taking the first opportunity to get home, included two guys and a girl who got on at Shibuya. They seemed intent on bothering me, and I got the feeling they were talking about me in Japanese. As I headed for the door at Takadanobaba, one of the guys plucked up the courage to address me directly and shouted in English, *'what's up homie?'* I chuckled to myself as I walked to catch the connecting train to Ochiai. He'd had a lucky escape. If I'd really wanted to, I could have bounced him on his head! I arrived at the honbu at 5:50am and got changed quickly. After cleaning was done, we joined the ippan students for the first winter class under the direction of Inoue Kancho. We assumed the deal we'd made with Chida Sensei ahead of shochu geiko would still hold, but there was no guarantee, and we'd have to wait until the end of the day to be sure the deal was still on. If we lined up for the start of the 11:30am class, we'd know something had gone wrong, but as Inoue Kancho got underway, we hoped for the best. Kancho kicked things off by teaching a strange breathing exercise that nobody seemed to get before moving onto shihonage. I partnered with one of the regulars. Despite being a black belt, he was getting tired as I was getting started. That was the difference with Senshusei!

In the break, Graham Sewanin had a word about our reluctance to volunteer to uke in Kanazawa Sensei's class. Although I'd stepped up to the plate, according to Graham I'd done this too late and without the right intent, so I was still in trouble. He told us that especially for the international Sensei, which was the category Kanazawa somehow belonged to, we'd need to move quicker next time. In the first Senshusei class of the day, Romeo Sensei asked for an uke. We all jumped up like a bunch of teenage girls at a boy band concert, only to be waved off by Romeo, who picked Malik instead. Murata Sensei was up next, and we learnt that his would be the last class of the day, which meant that Chida's word was still his bond. We'd be finishing at 11am, and with any luck, after closing Shinkoku and a quick clean round, we'd be out of the door by 11:30am. We knew Chida had honoured his side of the bargain, but what was less clear was what we'd need to give in return. We'd made good on shochu geiko by turning up early to train with the ippan students in the 7am class on Wednesdays and Fridays throughout August, and I suspected it would be a similar story in February. The possibility of two five-hour days per week next month didn't bear thinking about, and like someone taking out a loan, I focused on the lump sum of cash and not the monthly repayments plus interest that would eventually trigger. With kan geiko in full flow, there was no prospect of a proper weekend and a much-needed lie-in. Chida Sensei taught Sunday's class, and Matt and I trained together. We were in the mood for war and smashed each other, having agreed that UFC rules applied.

Dror was in trouble with the Sewanin. As Shinkoku he'd forgotten to order more toilet cleaner, and on inspection of the men's toilets, Inazaki and Kambara had been hauled over the coals as Malik had spotted there weren't enough toilet rolls in each cubicle. Poor Dror was in even more trouble, having also forgotten to order these. As Shinkoku, Dror was feeling the pressure. Before leaving for the day I spotted him in the tearoom and to get his attention shouted, *'heads up!'* I was going to suggest that he purchased some toilet rolls to bring in tomorrow while the dojo rolls were on back order. He wasn't in the mood, and before I could get my words out, he responded with, *'shut up, Simon!'* I was only trying to help. *'Fine'*, I said, *'you're on your own then'*, and left him to stew in his own juice. Tensions were running high, and friendships were fraying. The constant pressure from the Sewanin was grating on everyone, and it didn't look like things would get better anytime soon. I felt bad about how I'd left things with Dror and bought 10 toilet rolls as a peace offering and took them in on Monday. I'd never bought toilet rolls to extend as an olive branch before. A card or flowers usually sufficed, so this was a whole new experience! Ronen had the same idea, and Dror, to save his own skin, arrived with his own bag of rolls. We'd gone from deficit to surplus in as little as 24 hours and had pulled together as a team. Dror apologised for his outburst, and all was well again. Bad blood between any of the Senshusei, even for a short period, had the ability to infect the group. We needed a united front to handle the Sewanin, and I was glad we were back on track.

Our black belts had finally arrived courtesy of the dojo coffee club, and we handed our borrowed belts back in the morning meeting. My belt from Sakuraya had also arrived, but I couldn't legally wear it until Noriki Sensei's batch had been distributed. Sonoda Sensei took the class, and to continue yesterday's theme, I grabbed Dave. Where Dave was concerned, it wasn't just UFC rules that applied, Pride rules and soccer kicks did, too! After class I headed off to Axis with Clyde, Matt and two of the regular students who wanted to come and watch. One of our guests mentioned to Takagi Sensei that she was going to Jiu Jitsu with Clyde. Takagi wasn't happy and told the regular that Clyde should instead focus more on his Aikido. I know we weren't supposed to train in other martial arts while on the course, but her comment enraged me. If Murata Sensei had been the one to find out, he'd probably have been keen to come along. While Murata was open, Takagi was well and truly shut!

The early starts during kan geiko meant time went slowly, and due to sheer exhaustion, it was difficult to concentrate and be mentally present in any given moment. We used Graham Sewanin's birthday on Wednesday as an opportunity to sweeten him up. Presented with a card and a cake, he seemed to appreciate the thought, but I didn't imagine he'd be easily susceptible to bribery. Takagi Sensei continued to wind everyone up with her negative comments and, having taken uke for one of Dave's techniques turned to him and, in full earshot of those in close proximity, said, *'I can't believe you got a black belt for that!'* Upset one Senshusei, and upset us all. Dave looked visibly shaken, and, as he was one of the youngest on the course, I felt she'd taken a shot below the belt. I manoeuvred myself to pair with her next with the full intention of smashing her into next week, but, thinking better of it, at the last minute, I slammed on the brakes. She didn't speak to me, and I said nothing to her. I glared instead and hoped she got the message. If she didn't, we could always send in Lloyd!

After a laundry visit, sento and meal at the Royal Host, I took my clean dogi back to the dojo and had a very strange feeling. Without my brothers and sister in arms, the place was eerily quiet. There was an emptiness that I knew would exist when the course finished. For the first time while enclosed by the walls of the honbu, I felt a sense of peaceful contemplation wash over me that no zagaku class had ever been able to provide. In that moment I realised how much I would miss the whole experience and everyone involved when it was all over. Senshusei was a once-in-a-lifetime opportunity, and one I resolved to try to relish while I still had it in my grasp. On the train home, I listened to Dire Straits and their track *Brothers in Arms*, which made me feel quite emotional. I didn't know it then, but this song would become my Senshusei anthem that would remind me of the course for years to come.

IT HURTS LIKE CRAP!

I made a big mistake on Thursday. The monotony of kan geiko was getting to everyone, and we were always on the lookout for opportunities to add some variety to the day. Just before zagaku I challenged Lloyd to block my right roundhouse kick to the side of his head. I told him when it was coming and threw my shin at full pelt with every intention of pulling it if he failed to block. Who was I kidding? Lloyd made the block, and he did so in good time by bringing his right arm across his body to intercept my shin. I tried not to show it, but my shin hurt like hell. I settled down into seiza in preparation for Inoue Kancho's arrival. It turned out to be one of the worst seiza classes I'd experienced, and I couldn't work out why. I took comfort that Dror was also struggling and looked like he would pass out. After zagaku was over, I pulled up my trouser legs to discover the cause of my pain. On my right shin was an egg-shaped swelling, one of the worst I'd probably seen in all my years of Muay Thai – the type that would have prompted Master Lec to temporarily stop the class and run over with a bottle of Thai oil. *'Don't worry lad. Pain kills pain...pain is your best friend!'* Pain wasn't my best friend and it was an excruciating few minutes as Master Lec ironed out the lump with his fist. My honbu bump was a timely reminder that Lloyd was made of steel, a lesson I

309

should have learnt in Dai Ichi when we'd first faced off from one another right at the start of the course.

After another far too early start, in Friday morning's first Senshusei class, Romeo Sensei instructed us in the art of applying sankajo. Laurance Sensei, who was in the building and clearly at a loose end, joined us and partnered with me. It was a rare occurrence to get to grips with one of the Sensei, and I decided it was payback time. My shin was still hurting, and it was time to delve into the hurt locker and dish out the pain for a change. Laurance had struggled to get his sankajo to work on me, and I was determined not to have the same problem in reverse. As I applied it on him, he swung round sharply to try to take the pressure off his arm and grimaced in pain. I asked him how it felt and was happy with his response. *'It hurts like crap!'* It put a smile on my face that lasted into the final class of the day with Chino Sensei. I was pleased that my technique had worked and respected Laurance Sensei for ditching any ego and admitting it to me and anyone else in earshot. My high didn't last long. I was struggling with a cold that I suspected I'd caught from Clyde. Clyde had hurt his back in the first class so had been sent off to the chiropractor and then home until Monday. I finished the day sniffling in Chino's class. Our graduation ceremony, we learnt, would involve yet another Enbu, and under Chino's watchful eye, we started preparing our routine. His class was slightly less pressured than usual as Malik Sewanin was away at a job interview. I'd have loved to be a fly on the wall and wondered what the job was. I guessed it was teaching English, even though a prison guard would have been a much more suitable vocation! Clyde's injury was *the straw that broke the camel's back.* He'd been in the wars for a while and everything hurt. Although he'd sucked it up and carried on, there's a limit to how long anyone can continue without doing serious and permanent damage. Clyde had been nervous that something was badly wrong for a while – something with a very visible side effect that a few of us had noticed. When he sat on the floor, legs out straight, his left leg was five centimetres longer than his right. When he ran, he hobbled, when he sat, he leaned. Clyde was lopsided and hopefully the chiropractor would put things right. Rest was prescribed, but there was little chance of that with over a month left to run. Laurance Sensei's wrist may have hurt, but Clyde with an injury of this magnitude, was really in the crap!

HAN'S ISLAND

Why kan geiko was so popular, I couldn't quite fathom. As Senshusei we had no choice to be there, but the ippan students always had the option to stay in bed. When I woke up on Saturday morning, I was feeling rough. My head was pounding, and my nose was running, but thankfully, as yet, I'd avoided a sore throat. Oyamada Sensei strolled out for the first class and looked about as happy as I did to be stood in a freezing dojo at 7am. I trained with Carlos, who by now had become a close friend of the Senshusei. I'd always wondered why he hadn't signed up for the course. He was definitely Senshusei material and would have taken us out of the unlucky number stakes as the 14th Kokusai, in the 16th year of the international course.

The mats were crowded, and practicing hijishime was proving difficult. The technique was finished with a pivot of shite's hips and a swing of the back leg, and with every square inch of tatami covered in bodies, people were banging into one another left, right and centre. It resembled a battlefield and reminded me of the famous scene from Bruce Lee's *Enter the Dragon*. Towards the end of the film, Han's island descends into chaos, and all that can be seen is a mass of white-clad warriors going at it, hammer and tongs. It was in these classes I was glad to be Senshusei. Apart from Carlos, Matsuki and a few others, I had little time for the ippan students. We'd had liberties taken before – a regular with a point to prove and an inflated opinion of themselves would usually later regret their actions – but as a group they never seemed to learn. On Sunday morning a liberty was taken again. The old guy who'd stamped on Inazaki's foot during shochu geiko hurt Vic's arm. She was back training, but only just, and the injury she'd sustained from her battle with a surfboard was causing a lot of discomfort. As the regular applied his elbow lock, she winced in pain and started crying. Amidst the sea of bodies, I'd clocked what had happened and made a mental note to let Lloyd know in the break. There was still one more day of kan geiko to go and all we needed to do to guarantee revenge was get Lloyd fired up and in position. He'd only need a moment to go to work. The silent assassin, if given an opportunity in tomorrow's class, on behalf of Vic and the rest of us, would settle the score!

PHOTOCALL

Monday, 29 January 2007, was the last day of kan geiko. The 10 days of early starts had taken their toll, and I'd spent most of the night alternating between sleep and fits of coughing. Desperately tired, I had no option but to struggle on and make the early morning trek across Tokyo, a journey I could now probably do in my sleep – and regularly did! Before class there was a photocall opportunity. The official international Senshusei picture was taken in the dojo in front of the shomen. I stood at the back between Dave and Matt. From the intense training, the three of us were as skinny as hell but attempted to puff out our chests to look bigger for the camera. War faces were attempted, too. We were Senshusei shodan and had to look scary! From the tourists I'd seen on my international travels, I'd concluded that the Japanese were snap-happy. The official photographer, however, took only two pictures. One with Inoue Kancho and one with Chida Dojocho. *I hope nobody blinked*, I thought to myself, *the dojo must be on a budget*. It was more likely, though, that as Senshusei we were expected to get things right first time, even posing for a photograph. Chida Sensei stuck around for a while afterwards, and we all had pictures of him throwing us. It wasn't yet 7am and a bit early to be thrown by the Aikido God, but there was one opportunity, and none of us wanted to miss it. Chida seemed to enjoy himself and was determined to give us as much airtime as possible. We lined up to watch Geoff get launched. Chida threw him with ease, and Geoff made a smooth landing. His ukemi was now much improved compared to when he'd started.

Inoue Kancho took the last class of kan geiko and started as he'd begun 10 days earlier. The breathing exercise nobody understood was followed by kotegeashi, which was a technique I always enjoyed. Geoff, Ronen, Matt and I had agreed before class to train with each other and to get in the same group as the guy who'd hurt Vic yesterday. Geoff, as Vic's boyfriend would lead the ambush and to avoid early detection Lloyd was stood down. We must have achieved our mission as partway through the class Vic's assailant complained about his wrist being sore. Mess with one Senshusei and mess with us all. We continued to smash him as hard as we could until the class was over and hoped he'd got the message! The class finished 15 minutes early at 7:45am, just enough time for Inoue Kancho to hand out certificates. I now realised why the ippan students kept coming every day, something I'd not clocked during shochu geiko. To get your certificate and photocall with Kancho, you had to complete the full 10 days.

Clyde was back after his enforced break and inadvertently missed Shinkoku. After the class, he'd stood chatting with Naruo Sensei in the dojo and forgotten to line up with the rest of us outside Kancho's office. Nobody had noticed at the time, and his indiscretion only came to light later. The Sewanin weren't happy, and given their reaction, it felt like the world had ended. The matter needed putting right, but how? After much debate and in contrast to what normally happened in similar circumstances, they chose the simplest way forward. Clyde sought out Kancho and apologised. It was Clyde's birthday, so he was due a pass. Kancho accepted his apology, and the matter was put to bed. As I headed into the locker room to get changed, I spotted one of the children who'd just finished the winter training being sick in the tearoom. The tearoom was sacred territory and the closest thing the Senshusei had to a home away from home. During shochu and kan geiko, we'd been pushed out by an influx of regular students who had claimed it as their own. It was one thing for the regulars to relax in there, but puking was a step too far. I grabbed a bucket and slung it under the kid's chin and then ran to call Miyakoshi Sensei from the office to come and sort him out. The smell was horrendous and burnt my nostrils on every inhale. It was so bad I was nearly sick myself! I couldn't wait to have a shower and rushed into the locker room and got in the queue. Delayed by sick duty, the changing area was already busy. If it wasn't cold enough already, having finally secured my shower slot, Kanazawa Sensei decided it would be a good idea to pour cold water over the top. This was a trick he regularly pulled, but until now I'd been one step ahead. Taking advantage of my late entry and using his best private detective skills, he crept up and poured a bucket of ice-cold water over my head. *'Ahhhhhhhhh!'* I screamed at the top of my voice. I was in shock, and for a second, due to my inability to breathe, thought I was having a heart attack. A rumbling of laughter came from the neighbouring shower cubicles, and Kanazawa ran off, giggling!

As we left the honbu, there was news from the office. A decision had been made on what we'd be doing at the Graduation Enbu. I found out I'd be demonstrating self-defence and not tanto soho. Despite the early start, the puking and being frozen half to death, the morning ended on a high. We headed over to the Royal Host for breakfast to celebrate Clyde's birthday. I couldn't stay long as I had a date with the doctor. Still feeling rough when I woke up, I'd booked yet another appointment at the Tokyo British Clinic in Ebisu, where Dr Gabriel greeted me like an old friend. I found out I had a bad case of bronchitis. He prescribed some antibiotics and sent me on my way. For the first time, he hadn't told me to try to rest and relax. Now all too familiar with the course and its participants, Dr Gabriel knew he was wasting his breath!

PARANOIA

As a Senshusei, you were always paranoid – paranoid you hadn't done something, paranoid you shouldn't have done something. Paranoia followed you around like a bad smell. On Tuesday morning I woke up at 4:20am. The last 10 days had adjusted my routine, and despite the chance of an extra hour in bed, my body clock cruelly stole it away. I was constantly coughing and remembered my Mum had once told me that antibiotics took at least 24 hours to kick in. She'd also told me it was the last one that usually did the trick, so on both counts, I knew it would be a tough day! The honbu seemed eerily quiet when I arrived just before 7am, and a feeling of paranoia surged through my body. Was kan geiko still on? Was everyone lined up in the dojo in seiza, waiting for Kancho's arrival? Was I unforgivably late? My heart raced, and I began to panic, a feeling that only subsided when Dave arrived shortly after me. There was safety in numbers, but if I was late, there was a good chance Dave had made the same mistake, too. We took off our shoes and crept up the steps into the corridor and then tiptoed to the dojo entrance and peered in. Thankfully, the mass gathering that accompanied kan geiko was absent, and only a few of the ippan students were lined up for the 7am class. Winter training had ended, and we were in the clear!

In the morning meeting, I told the Sewanin I had bronchitis and handed over a note from my doctor. I also told them I wanted to train, as to my mind anything was better than mitori geiko. They were fine with this and asked me what medicine I was taking. This was the type of request I'd have expected in an environment where health and safety were a priority, but given I'd seen very little evidence of either during the last 10 months, it seemed a strange question. I told them I was on antibiotics, but that they were yet to kick in. Graham responded, *'you're not training with me!'* Today the Senshusei would be teaching. As we approached the start of the final month of the course and what would be our final test to become an instructor, Inazaki and Kambara were selected when the 8:30am class began. They did a good job, and I got up to uke for Inazaki a couple of times. Ronen commented that my ukemi had got better and that the antibiotics must now be working. In the next class, we had Murata Sensei, whose instruction included half an hour of free practice where Ronen, Geoff, Dror, Inazaki, Kambara and I worked on our self-defence routine. This was the demonstration we'd be performing at the Graduation Enbu, and as we were enjoying ourselves so much, Murata ran over the finish time by 10 minutes. In the last class, Ito Sensei brought us back to earth with a 45-minute rendition of kihon dosa renzoku with bokken. It was then a return to the demonstration, and as we got back into our groups, I pondered how much of the course would ultimately have been dedicated to Enbu practice. One month? Two months? It was probably more like three!

GETTING OLD

Unless you were born in March, there was a good chance you'd be spending your birthday at the honbu. When I woke up on Wednesday, 31 January 2007, I wished myself a happy 35th birthday and then got on with the day ahead. A batch of cards had drip-fed through the post since the end of last week, but there was no time to open them. In the morning meeting, I handed out biscuits for the Sensei and Sewanin. It was more usual to receive gifts on your birthday, but as Senshusei the roles were reversed. I folded Oyamada Sensei's hakama, which he'd worn in the 7am class, and when I took it back into the office, only Miyakoshi Sensei thanked me for the biscuits and took the time to wish me a happy birthday. In the first class it was Clyde and Boaz's turn to teach. Like Inazaki and Kambara, who had stepped up yesterday, they did a good job and raised one or two smiles. Oyamada Sensei arrived for the last class, and as we ran through sotai dosa for the umpteenth time he came over to wish me happy birthday. At the time I was holding an extended position which was proving painful, so I took this golden opportunity to stand up straight and bow. Oyamada said it was unusual that I'd given a present, as it was my birthday. I didn't disagree!

After class we all headed across to Takadanobaba for food at a Thai restaurant. Geoff paid for me, which was very nice of him. The others presented me with a card, and Matt handed over two UFC DVDs. I browsed through the messages in the card. It was full of the usual banter we threw around the tearoom on a daily basis. Even Malik Sewanin had signed it. *Simon – you're getting old, you look old + certainly your Aikido looks old (joke!) Have a good one – Malik Sewanin.* He was right; I was getting old and, thanks to the course, was probably now looking a lot older, too. I'd been careful not to schedule any Berlitz classes for later in the day and instead caught the train to Osaki to meet Alex. One of my sister's friends from school, Alex now lived and worked in Japan. After a Starbucks with her, I headed home. That night I felt quite depressed. There's nothing like a birthday to make you question what you're doing with your life and where you might go next. I knew this was something I'd need to confront when the course was over, but for now it was a decision I didn't want to make. It didn't feel much fun being 35; I'd always thought I'd be married with a couple of kids by this age. Back home many of my friends were married or well on the way. Messing about in Japan, I was falling behind!

DAY 200

Pinch punch, first of the (last) *month*, and with that I entered the final four weeks of the course. It was also day 200. I'd made 199 entries in my official diary, which meant today would be the 200th training day as a Senshusei. It was another huge milestone. Day 100 had been a big one, but 200 held much more significance. We were well beyond halfway now and approaching the end.

At the end of each month, we had to hand in a monthly report on what we were thinking and how we were feeling. This was in addition to submitting our diaries and more of a summary of how we thought the previous month had gone. It was less about the technicalities of the techniques and more about our state of mind. For the brave it was an opportunity to elaborate. I always favoured keeping things simple, but Lloyd, in the lead-in to the final month, had a few things to get off his chest. An extract from his submission read, *suwari waza is tearing through my body. I often feel I am doing pointless training now, and my attitude is in retaliation to this. I have given in a lot to pain and allowed repetition to suck the life out of me.* It was prize-winning prose and beautifully summed up how we were all feeling. I wondered if Lloyd had a future as an author and was proud of his honesty in a document that would probably make its way to the Dojocho. Only Lloyd had the guts to sum up the mood in the camp, and on this occasion, his pen appeared mightier than his sword. The life had well and truly been sucked out of me, and now, so close but still so far; I wondered if I'd make it to the end. I'd seen clips of marathon runners who at mile 25 had seen their legs turn to jelly. To be so close to the end, but unable to finish, would be a cruel twist of fate!

There was some good news today. I'd almost forgotten about it, so I was pleased to find out I'd passed the JLPT exam I'd taken at the start of December. I was getting more and more immersed in Japanese culture, and this was the first step in being able to communicate properly. I couldn't wait to tell Hotta Sensei. All of her efforts hadn't been wasted after all!

YOU'RE GETTING WHACKED

Like all aspiring mafioso, I was ready to get my 'button'. I wanted to become a 'made man' and formally accepted into the Yoshinkan Aikido family. However, like for Joe Pesci in *Goodfellas*, the end might have been in sight, but there was still the finish line to cross. Tommy DeVito (Joe Pesci) having taunted Henry Hill had worked his way up through the ranks of the mafia, abided (at least to a point) its code of conduct and now hoped the books would open for him to become a fully-fledged member. Dressed for the ceremony that would see him inducted into the crime family that he longed to join, Tommy walked into an empty room. Bang! Tommy was shot in the back of the head. Brutally 'whacked', his dreams of entry to the exclusive club were over. A similar story played out in *Donnie Brasco*, another of my favourite gangster films. 'Lefty' Ruggiero, realising he's been betrayed by his most trusted friend and now summoned to his death, puts his personal possessions in a drawer before leaving his house, knowing full well he'll never see them again.

On the train from Takadanobaba to Ochiai, the last stretch of my journey each morning, I'd unconsciously take off my watch, turn off my phone and iPod, and place them all for safekeeping in a secret compartment in my bag. It was a morning ritual I'd observed every day on the course. It saved time when I got into the dojo, as in the dojo, time to do anything for myself was a luxury I didn't have. As I did this on Friday morning, as the end of the course loomed, I was conscious I was recreating Ruggiero's steps, and I hoped there wouldn't be any last-minute surprises like Tommy's that would prevent me from graduating. Like a prisoner with only weeks until his release date, it was time to keep my head down and my nose clean. If I messed up, it was unlikely the honbu would extend my stay. If I messed up, it was much more likely that, like Tommy and Ruggiero, I'd be whacked, and I didn't want to get whacked! The end was in sight, and I was determined that nobody and nothing would get in my way.

As I climbed the steps of the entrance to the honbu, I couldn't wait to find Lloyd. I'd finally got round to opening my birthday cards, and the one from my Auntie Joan, I just had to show him. Sandwiched between *Dear Simon* and *Love from Auntie Joan xxx*, she'd shared her views on the current state of the UK and her own special take on Australian history. *I hear you are about to live in Australia. I suppose this country* (England) *is going to pot. The Australians did have the right idea, even though they descended from criminals sent over there!* It had everyone in stitches, including Lloyd. He took it well, and we carried on with the day. I'm glad I hadn't upset him; it would have made walking into an empty tearoom all the more nerve-racking!

IMPOSSIBLE SIGHT

On my journey in on Saturday morning, I saw what I could best describe as an impossible sight on the platform at Meguro Station. I knew the Japanese were overworked and that office workers in particular could lead an unnaturally short and miserable life if they didn't take steps to protect their physical and mental well-being. The 'salaryman' was the epitome of all that was wrong with Japanese employment law – overworked, probably underpaid if you worked out the hourly rate, and at the constant mercy of the boss. At the station it looked like one such salaryman had either met his maker or was enduring a bout of seiza worthy of recognition by Guinness World Records. The gentleman in question, suited and booted, knelt fast asleep on the platform. I suspected that he'd been there all night, probably having missed the last train home. He'd probably started out in a perfect position worthy of even Kancho's praise, but in the small hours, things must have taken a turn for the worse. As he was slumped forwards, I couldn't see his face, which was very close to making contact with the concrete. There were no visible signs of life. Nobody stopped to check on his condition and instead went about their business just like any other day. With my limited knowledge of Japanese, I didn't intervene either and hoped this lack of action wouldn't be something I'd later regret. I was certain he was dead. It had been a cold night, and surely it was impossible to endure seiza for what must have been getting on for an eight-hour stretch. As I boarded my second train headed for Takadanobaba, I concluded that he'd either frozen to death or the pain in his legs had fast-tracked him to the afterlife. Either way, it was a sorry sight and a shocking display of the harshness of everyday life.

At the honbu, I didn't feel great. I had a dodgy stomach, so I took a tablet, which seemed to calm things down. The dojo was freezing and in the first class we had Murray Sensei, who split us into two groups. One group practiced tanto soho and my group ran through the self-defence routine we'd been working hard to put together. Murray Sensei didn't pull any punches when he said he didn't like any of our stuff, so it would be back to the drawing board to devise a new routine! After a main course of Murata, where he shared his latest insights on life and the Budo arts, we lined up in seiza for the final class. As Sonoda Sensei walked out onto the mats, Lloyd, who was positioned next to me, summed up what I was also thinking, as he muttered under his breath. *'Fuck!'* We were back in the land of confusion. As I left the honbu to begin a weekend that was long overdue, I calculated that we'd been 19 straight days without a break. Kan geiko had killed us and we'd now face the prospect of honouring Chida's deal!

IMMUNE

By now I felt pretty much immune to pain. Frequent injuries and aches and pains were a normal part of my everyday existence. My knees, in particular, were in bits and required constant icing. It was a continual battle of damage limitation. I knew that prevention was better than cure, but with no way to prevent the continual wear and tear on my body, cure was the only option I had. Sunday morning's lie-in felt amazing, and I didn't get up until 8am. As my bed was a traditional Japanese *futon*, essentially a *mattress on the floor*, getting to my feet today, as always, required a lot more effort than getting out of a normal bed, the type I'd once again gotten used to over the Christmas

318

period. No rest for the wicked, and with a full day of teaching ahead of me, I trudged off to Berlitz.

One of my students rolled into his class with a terrible cold and was wearing a white face mask, the type my dentist wore back home. During the 2002 SARS (Severe Acute Respiratory Syndrome) outbreak, face masks had become increasingly popular, and I was never sure if people wore them to protect others or to protect themselves. It was somewhat surreal teaching him when, in response to my questions, I couldn't see his mouth move. I wasn't too worried about catching his germs. It wasn't only pain that I was immune to; still taking my daily dose of antibiotics to combat bronchitis, I was confident I was immune to anything he was carrying, too. I felt invincible, which wasn't a bad way to feel even at this late stage of the course, but there was a problematic side effect. I realised that my stomach problems were probably being caused by the antibiotics. I'd been plagued with a dodgy stomach on and off for most of the previous week, and with no let-up in my discomfort, I pulled out of meeting Ronen after work at Shamaim. There was only one potential cure. I rented *Miami Vice* on DVD and began my journey to the bottom of another Hennessy bottle. I passed out just before 11pm. Whoops! At 2am, I woke up with a really bad stomach ache, which lasted for the rest of the night. When I woke up on Monday morning, I still had it, but, conditioned by the course, I pushed on. I trained with Matt at Axis and then had food with him in Shinjuku afterwards. By the evening my stomach was even worse. Instead of resting and taking it easy, I'd been to Jiu Jitsu and followed up with a huge lunch. It seemed I wasn't as immune as I'd first thought. Tomorrow now looked like it would be a very difficult day!

STAR WARS

On Tuesday morning Matt and I were called up to teach the first class. Although I was paired with Ronen for Dai Yon, the partner allocations seemed much more flexible than the previous phase of the course. I guessed the presumption was that you needed to be less in tune with someone to teach with them, compared to shodan where harmony was a key component of a successful test. Matt taught for the first 30 minutes, and I picked up the latter part of the class, focusing on *shomen uchi yonkajo osae ni*. Yonkajo was the most complex of the four controls, and I figured that teaching this would earn me extra brownie points. It turned out I was wrong. Murray Sensei said I talked too much and that there was room for improvement. I'd also likened the yonkajo hand positioning to how you held a sword. Murray Sensei described this as *'hogwash'* and said there was nothing to prove the connection. Matt was also in the firing line. Murray Sensei, in a sarcastic mood asked him, *'have you seen Star Wars recently?'* Matt looked bemused. *'Osu! No, Sensei. Osu!'* Murray Sensei delivered his punchline. *'Why do you keep saying Wookiee, instead of uke, then?'* It was the funniest thing I'd heard in a while, and we all struggled to contain ourselves. Even Matt found it hilarious and, with the image of Chewbacca firmly in his head, did his best to take Murray Sensei's comment on board as serious feedback.

In the final two classes, we worked on our self-defence demonstration again. Our first repertoire had been pulled to bits, and we were struggling to come up with something new. For me, self-defence had to look real and had to be 100 percent practical, but anything we tried to introduce into our routine which didn't resemble traditional Aikido was instantly quashed. It would have been far easier if the Sensei had given us a tried-and-tested routine to perform, instead of granting us poetic licence, only to then criticise everything we came up with.

INTIMATE WITH UKE

Our teaching and the feedback which followed was getting more and more amusing. I'd started to really enjoy the first classes and found myself looking forward to them. The intensity and brutality we'd come to associate with our first outing of the day had now switched to stand-up comedy. The comedy element was never intended; it just seemed to happen. Ronen and Dror taught Wednesday's class, and Dror had us in stitches. He could be forgiven, as English wasn't his first language, but even he realised his error as the schoolboy sniggering rippled through the group. Explaining some of the principles of sokumen iriminage he told us, *'remember that when you do ushiro sokumen, just turn and come all over uke!'* Most of the techniques we'd drilled since the start of the course required us to get up close and personal, but the suggestion we get this intimate with uke seemed a little inappropriate! We were still chuckling as we lined up for Shinkoku. If there was a prize for the best comedy moment of the course, Dror was in with a chance of winning, possibly only rivalled by Dave.

In the next class we had Oyamada Sensei, who actually taught us for once. We focused on ikajo techniques and learnt quite a lot. Takashima Sensei strolled into the dojo for the last class, armed with paper and pens. The Wizard had something up his sleeve, and none of us had any idea what to expect. He told us to write down a plan for our Enbu. I suggested we perform ukemi in a demonstration like the Red Arrows. Instead of jet planes narrowly missing each other in flight, it would be Senshusei risking life and limb as a human version of the world's premier aerobatic display team!

IT'S MY PARTY...

Thursday, 8 February, brought with it something I never thought I'd live to see. Neville declared he was injured. He was out with a knee injury and would be in mitori geiko for the rest of the day. Neville had been consistent since the start of the course, and while the rest of us endured our own personal ups and downs, he'd weathered every storm extremely well. The fact that Neville was now on the bench was a clue we were all close to breaking. If he was injured, there wasn't much hope for the rest of us, but the struggle had to go on. Graham had important advice to share on how best to arrange our Enbu. An Aikido purist, he cautioned against losing martial tradition and said it was important to stay true to serious Budo. This was the same Graham who, later on in the day, would suggest we incorporate an old man with a walking stick sketch into our self-defence routine!

In the first class, with Murray Sensei, we practiced the Enbu and tried in vain to piece together something that would appease all parties. Murray Sensei seemed to be under the impression that it was the Senshusei who wanted to change things since we'd last performed in front of him, when in actual fact it was he who'd been the catalyst. If we weren't totally confused already, we most definitely were now! Short on space, someone landed on Vic's ankle, and she started to cry. Malik Sewanin displayed his usual level of sympathy by screaming at her, '*pull yourself together!*' With time running out until the Enbu, in Murata Sensei's class, the last thing we needed was what he had in mind. We spent the majority of the class balancing a jo, bokken and tanto on our fingers to see which was easier. The jo, being the longest weapon, proved the most difficult, followed closely by the sword. What benefit there was in knowing a knife was the easiest was beyond me. Still armed to the teeth, Murata called an end to the class. As the weapons hadn't been put away, we had to line up and bow out with them. Ronen rolled his eyes and gave a look that was a picture. Hailing from Nottingham, in my opinion, with swords and knives stuffed in our belts and staffs in hand, we looked more like Robin Hood's band of Merry Men than Yoshinkan Senshusei. Or maybe, as Ronen put it, '*a bunch of Teenage Mutant Ninja Turtles*', lined up in front of Master Splinter! In the last class, Kanazawa Sensei ran through the Enbu again. Geoff gave Malik Sewanin a dirty look and was threatened with a round of bunny hops. Having made his point up close and personal, Malik wandered off muttering to himself, presumably about Geoff, but under his breath, it was difficult to hear. We didn't realise it in that moment, but this was the start of a new habit.

Zagaku was, as usual, an extremely unpleasant and painful experience. Dror reflected how the course would soon end and that now, each class was even more precious. Although I'd recently had my own bout of sentimentality, all I could think to myself was *what a load of bollocks!* It was Dave's birthday, and he was in tears. The pain had really got to him, and it was his turn to cry. Lesley Gore's famous song played on repeat in my head.

It's my party, and I'll cry if I want to.
Cry if I want to, cry if I want to.
You would cry too if it happened to you.

Some party! Yet again it had happened to Dave and he had no reason to celebrate. After zagaku we stood outside Kancho's office for what felt like 15 minutes. Standing to attention on blood-starved legs wasn't easy, and at the far end of the line, order was temporarily broken when Boaz staggered forwards to regain his balance. He'd fallen asleep standing up. As he tried to compose himself, he'd almost crashed headfirst through Kancho's door!

ACTING ABILITY

By Friday we were getting desperate. Despite Graham Sewanin urging us to stay true to Budo, the only thing that had stuck was his suggestion to incorporate an old man with a walking stick into our Enbu routine. We were clutching at straws for ideas, and this one seemed to make sense. We built a story around Graham's idea and cast Geoff as a drunk who would pick the old man's pocket. Given his more senior years, Kambara was naturally cast in the lead role. Dave would have probably made the best drunk. On pretty much every night out, he'd been the worse for wear, but it wasn't comedy we needed. Geoff was the biggest Senshusei, so for dramatic effect, it made sense to cast him as the assailant. He'd be the one to hassle the old man, and his size would magnify the audience's perception of the power of Kambara's technique. We thought we'd nailed it, but Boaz had other ideas. In the second break he pulled me to one side to suggest we change things up. The Senshusei had agreed on a strategy, and now one of us was suggesting we change the plan. This was no time to call a meeting to resolve the matter, and I told Boaz to forget it.

Chino Sensei would serve as judge and jury, as we'd be demonstrating what we'd come up with in front of him. As we ran through our demonstration from start to finish, he stood emotionless. No one had a clue what he thought, but we didn't have to wait too long to find out. He gave it the thumbs up and, Chino, having polished some of our techniques, even suggested we ham up the acting some more. As part of the routine, I attacked Ronen with a knife. After he threw me, I ran back to my start position and almost knocked Chino Sensei over. *'Sumimasen'* was the one Japanese word I didn't have to consciously think about before saying. As I brushed past the honbu's deadliest Sensei, a half-hearted apology was all I could mutter. I'd just missed and breathed a sigh of relief. Chino wasn't amused and called me out to demonstrate the finer points of the shihonage pin Ronen had just applied on me. He almost broke my elbow, and as the pain shot up my arm, I wondered if Chino had any acting ability himself. In addition to his T-1000 credentials, he'd always reminded me of a miniature version of Jaws, Richard Kiel's character in *The Spy Who Loved Me*. One thing was for sure, Chino Sensei would make a great James Bond villain!

CUT IT OUT!

Murray Sensei had yet to see what we'd come up with. He'd been our strongest critic, but now that Chino Sensei seemed happy, we were confident that Murray Sensei would be happy, too. On Saturday morning he took a front-row seat for his own personal premiere. As soon as Murray Sensei caught sight of Geoff acting drunk and Kambara with his walking stick, he stopped us in our tracks. *'Cut it out!'* His order was clear. Even before the old man had his chance to make easy work of Geoff, the scene had been edited out and was now on the cutting room floor. What a nightmare! We'd had input from everyone and come up with what we thought would work. Murray Sensei didn't seem to care. He told us in no uncertain terms that when it came to the Kokusai, he trumped everyone at the honbu dojo. I was sure Chino Sensei held a better hand, as did Kancho, but this was no time to argue. It was back to the drawing board, and time was running out!

Sonoda Sensei's turn came next. He asked to see our demonstration, and, having had no time to make any changes; we ran through the original script. He seemed concerned on timing and asked Malik Sewanin if it was long enough. Malik reassured him it was definitely long enough! During Sonoda Sensei's private screening, Dave made a mistake, and Malik screamed at him before wandering off, muttering under his breath. This time I caught part of his rant. *'He's really pissing me off'* was how we'd all felt about Dave at one point or another! This was Malik's second display of his new habit of wandering and muttering that we'd first seen earlier in the week. I wondered if he was all right. Talking to oneself was usually regarded as the first sign of madness!

Instead of the normal last class with the ippan students, Murray Sensei gave us the option to work on the Enbu. We voted to take advantage. After his instruction to ditch the old man, Murray Sensei had told us, *'no more changes'*, but then he changed my knife attack on Ronen. With the Enbu happening tomorrow, it was like a Boxing trainer changing the pre-fight strategy as his fighter climbed into the ring. There was no sense to it and all of us were now totally confused. I needed some divine inspiration and stopped off at HMV in Shibuya on the way home. As I walked in, a display showcasing the *Rocky Balboa* CD soundtrack greeted me. I had no choice but to buy a copy. It was the inspiration I needed!

GRADUATION ENBU

We hadn't graduated yet, but Sunday, 11 February 2007, was the day of the Graduation Enbu. A lot of things appeared back to front in Japan, so pulling the cart before the horse today was of little consequence. I was at the honbu by 10am and in my dogi, standing at attention in the tearoom alongside everyone else, at 10:30am. Malik Sewanin dished out duties, and we filed into the dojo to clean. Matt and I had been given responsibility for ironing the white cloth for Kancho's table. I'd never been great at ironing and was terrified of burning a hole through it. Takagi Sensei, in anticipation of what might happen, had taken the precaution of furnishing us with the smallest iron I'd ever seen. The cleaning and ironing finished, we had about an hour to kill, so we sat in the tearoom, chatting. I took the iron back to the kitchen and knocked on the door. *'Shitsurei shimasu, osu!'* I opened the door to find all the international Sensei in a meeting. They turned and stared at me. Nobody said anything. It was an uncomfortable moment. I explained I was bringing the iron back and Naruo Sensei got up to take it off me. As I handed it over, he burnt his hand on the bottom. *'Shitsurei shimasu, osu!'* I turned and left as quick as my legs would carry me.

The Enbu started at 1pm. Sitting in seiza for the opening speeches would, as usual, make getting to starting positions a game of chance. Murray Sensei took his place in front of the microphone under the shomen. *'This year we have 13 students from six different countries.'* Takashima Sensei translated into Japanese for the benefit of Kancho and other dignitaries in attendance. Murray Sensei continued. *'The Kokusai course began 16 years ago with the intention of bringing students from all over the world to Japan to learn the main fundamental aspects of Yoshinkan Aikido.'* Takashima Sensei translated.

Scene-setting over, our Enbu started with a demonstration of cleaning. Running up and down the mats with zokin in hand was one thing we were good at, and this strange sight drew a rumble of laughter from the audience. Geoff, Dave and Inazaki did this part, which offered an early break from seiza and a chance to stretch their legs. Neville, who was still in mitori geiko, had been given the job of narrator, and in monotone fashion, he introduced the next act. *'Breakfalls are essential. Senshusei learn to train their body and mind for great leaps forward.'* Takashima Sensei translated. It was a clever play on words. *'Ukemi seiretsu...ichi ni tsuke!'* I screamed at the top of my voice and, on very wobbly legs, ran to position. The Red Arrows were in town, and the final flypast saw Boaz forward somersault over five Senshusei lined up and crouched in turtle position. A similar stunt had seen Boaz injure his shoulder earlier on in the course, but this time to the gasps and applause of the crowd he timed a perfect landing. Neville continued his spiel. *'To learn how to move smoothly, turn quickly and develop good posture, Senshusei put in many hours training basic movements. Here we can see a combination of these basic movements linked to their techniques.'* Takashima translated. The dance was on, and the set sequence I'd luckily avoided played out. Vic, Dave, Boaz and Lloyd had got the job with Ronen calling commands. The sequence continued with a mix up of pairs and four more Senshusei joining the party. This time I called commands. Amid it all, Boaz threw Dror into the crowd and almost took Takagi Sensei's head off. Luckily, she had the foresight to lean back out of the way and avoided a serious injury.

Finally, it was time for the moment we'd discussed, debated and laboured over for so long. With things changing right up until the last minute, it was anyone's guess how things would go. There was no old man, no drunk, just six Senshusei going hard at it. After Inazaki had dealt with Kambara, it was my turn to attack Ronen. *'I'm going to cut you up!'* I screamed at the top of my voice. This was a bit of improvisation I'd used that sounded aggressive, and I knew would be lost in translation by most. My battle cry had been toned down, and the profanity removed, but it still sounded threatening enough to mean business. As I stabbed at Ronen's stomach, with a quick turn of his hips, he applied shihonage to evade my attack. Geoff downed Dror, and the sequence ran one more time in reverse. The finale saw Ronen try to take Inazaki's head off with a stick. Ronen and I had been particularly pumped up and as if an Oscar was in the offing, we'd done our best to put on a show. But the show wasn't over yet.

Vic and Dave were up to display their jiyu waza skills, and Vic, despite her injury, was on top form. As Dave went in for a katate mochi grab, she pole-axed him Chino style. Dave's head smashed uncomfortably into the tatami in full view of Kancho, and for a moment I thought Dave was done. *'Ooohhhhhh...aaahhhhhh'*, could be heard from the audience, but Dave, undeterred, got to his feet, only for Vic to throw him this time across her back with koshinage. Dave once again was dumped on his head! He did well to survive and looked visibly shaken by the end. Boaz and Lloyd and then Clyde and Matt followed, but Vic had stolen the show. It seemed like Chino Sensei had a younger sister with some serious intent! The Graduation Enbu was over, and we filed out of the dojo past Murray Sensei. He raised a smile, a clue that after everything, he'd been happy with our performance in the end.

TWO WEEKS

There were now only two weeks left – the last few hundred metres of what had been one hell of a marathon. Tuesday, 13 February, also happened to be Malik Sewanin's birthday, and in keeping with tradition we wrote him a card. Lloyd's birthday wish was the funniest. Referencing Malik's own words, it had a simple message – *sort your birthday out!* When asked to disclose any injuries in the morning meeting, Dave piped up that he had scars all over his body. We could only presume that these had been inflicted on the course, but the way he said it and this being Dave, no one was sure!

It was back to teaching practice, and Vic took the first class with a focus on shomen iriminage. It seemed she'd taken a leaf out of Dror's teaching manual, as she instructed us to *'enter uke'*. This caused the usual rumbling of laughter that all of us struggled to hold in. The innuendo wasn't intentional, but the pressured situation of being at the front of the class in teaching mode brought out the stupidest statements. Takagi Sensei hijacked the last half of the first class with feedback from the Enbu. She didn't mention being nearly decapitated by a flying Dror but provided some insight into why the old man scene had been cut. Apparently one of her relatives had a bad leg and walked with a cane. Seeing Kambara in character limping had upset her. While I could see Takagi's point the 13 of us had suffered with sore knees, aching legs and a whole host of injuries for the last 11 months. Despite our collective plight she'd shown no sympathy!

Ahead of the last class with Murata Sensei, Kanazawa Sensei was spotted running across the dojo with a jo stuffed down the back of his dogi top. It was his way of demonstrating good posture and was the start of more comical things to come. Murata's class incorporated the strangest exercise we'd done to date. He instructed us to adopt a horse stance and put our hands out either side, palms facing forwards. Our job was to turn up our energy volume, and projecting through our palms, to become human loudspeakers. It was bizarre, and I didn't understand what I was doing. Dave was beside himself and couldn't stop laughing. After class, still giggling, he told us a story about his maths teacher who had one eye. Dave explained that he and his classmates used to kill themselves laughing whenever, in their textbooks, they came across question '1i'. It was another example of his crazy sense of humour, and why he deserved the name Crazy Dave!

CHINO STAYCATION

On the train to Ochiai on Wednesday morning, I reflected on the oddest of dreams I'd had during the night. Strange dreams weren't unusual in my sleep-deprived state, but what was unusual about this one was that it was the second time I'd had it. I'd dreamt that Chino Sensei was staying at my family home back in the UK. Mum and Dad were looking after him, but for some reason, I was nowhere to be seen. Was there meaning to this dream? Was there something I should read into it? What was it trying to tell me? I wasn't sure, but its second outing made it even more significant. I knew that Chino, like many other Yoshinkan Sensei, regularly travelled the world to spread Yoshinkan Aikido. Was my dream a glimpse into the future where I'd entertain this Aikido master on his very own Chino staycation in my hometown of Stafford? Was the message more complex, and did I have aspirations to become Chino myself, so much so that in the eyes of my parents I'd become him? Or perhaps I just craved the adulation that all Yoshinkan Sensei seemed to enjoy? In my 35 years on this planet, their status was the closest thing I'd seen to God on earth. My head began to hurt as I ruminated on the answer and in search of relief my mind turned to self-defence. The challenges we'd had in putting together the Enbu demonstration had highlighted a blatant contradiction in my mind as to what the Yoshinkan preached. I'd never considered it before, but in my heightened state of awareness, I now saw things clearly. We'd been told that Aikido was everything and that its principles could be applied to any situation. If Aikido could be found in any martial art, why then, in self-defence, could we only perform Aikido techniques?

In Oyamada's class I was concerned about Malik Sewanin. Despite us getting off to a bad start, I'd warmed to him and realised his intentions were mostly good. He'd been an important part of my Senshusei experience, and without him giving his time, energy and effort the course wouldn't have been the same. I'd noticed him muttering to himself before, but today things took a more worrying turn. While running through techniques we could clearly hear him talking to himself. Although some of his words I could make out, some were unclear. Had the spirit of a past Aikido master possessed Malik Sewanin? As Matt questioned after class – *'was he speaking in tongues?'*

FOOD CHAIN

Thursday was always the worst day. It had always been the worst day since zagaku had been introduced near the start of the course. Now there were only two left – two more opportunities to try out our Japanese and communicate a reflection and habit to an audience that couldn't understand our butchery of their language. I was shattered as I rolled into the honbu dojo. I'd worked late at Berlitz and having been sent across to Otemachi instead of teaching at my regular school in Sangenjaya, the going had been unusually tough. Sonoda Sensei taught the second class and had us performing kihon waza to his commands of *'proper side'* and *'other side'*. We knew where this had come from. Ronen gave me a knowing look. Google Translate was back in business! What Sonoda wanted us to do depended on whether we started in right or left kamae and whether we were doing an ichi or ni technique. It was classic confusion. Even Malik Sewanin came up to me halfway through to let me know what he was thinking. *'Clear as mud'*, he whispered in my ear.

The honbu operated under a strict hierarchy. There was no doubt that Kancho was the head, but the pecking order below was far more complicated. Sensei was the generic term for teacher, but hiding behind this badge were different titles that identified different levels. I still hadn't got my head round it all, and Sensei was the safest bet. Chida Sensei was Dojocho, Chino and Sonoda were *Shihan*, Oyamada and Ito were *Kyoshi*, and Takashima and Murata were *Jokyo*. Shihan meant *expert or senior instructor* and was a badge often given to a teacher of teachers. Kyoshi was similar but more of an *assistant expert* than an expert in the holder's own right. Jokyo appeared to be of lesser status. It was all very complicated, and while we had to reference the correct and proper titles in our official diaries alongside a record of each class, as far as we were concerned, Sensei covered all bases.

In the Yoshinkan kingdom, Kancho was the lion and the Sewanin the antelope. The Senshusei, in case we were in any doubt, were whatever the antelope ate. Everyone vied for position and recognition that came from experience and age. The older you were and the longer you stuck around, the more likely you'd climb the next rung of the ladder, and to maintain order and balance, this often involved waiting to step into dead men's shoes. There was only one Kancho, and Kancho didn't retire. For Chida Dojocho to reach the upper echelon, he'd have to wait for Inoue Kancho to depart this life. It was very much like the mafia without the extortion, prostitution and gun running. To get 'upped' you had to be a good earner, and a slot had to become available. In the mafia slots would free up all the time. In an environment where getting whacked was a very real hazard of the job, promotion could be quicker. As far as I knew, no senior Sensei had ever been bundled into the back of a car, fitted with a pair of concrete boots and given a one-way ticket to swim with the fishes. Promotion to the top was slow and could take a lifetime, if it was ever achieved at all. From what I'd seen from my time at Berlitz, the honbu hierarchy also mirrored corporate life. In the business world, the struggle to climb the greasy pole would see people quite literally work themselves to death. The Japanese had their own word for it. *Karoshi* was an honourable way to go and meant *death from overwork.* Today Noriki *Shidoin* had been promoted to Jokyo. As far as we knew, no one had died of natural causes or more sinister means and his step up was purely on merit. He was one step closer to the top of the food chain, but to inherit the throne he'd need to serve the present king and the succession thereafter, until time or fate delivered his turn.

In zagaku Geoff and Malik, in what was a strange turn of events, were called upon by Inoue Kancho to share a reflection and habit. The Sewanin had never been called up before, but in the food chain they were only antelope. Geoff stumbled through his Japanese pronunciation while Malik seemed surprised to have been invited to share. It was clear he had nothing prepared. He spoke in English, instead of the mandatory Japanese, and was reprimanded by Sonoda and Kancho in turn. I felt sorry for Malik. He'd been caught out, and it was a cruel trick to have played. I had a feeling there was more to it and suspected a possible link to his treatment by Murray Sensei at Kagami Biraki. Maintaining honour was a fundamental principle of the Budo arts, and in being caught out, it seemed Malik Sewanin was having his purposefully and publicly undermined. There was nothing he could do. We had to take his crap, and he had to take theirs. In the law of the jungle the biggest teeth triumphed, and while Malik had bigger teeth than us, he couldn't rival a Shihan or Kancho in the predatory stakes. He left quickly after zagaku without checking up on our cleaning. It was a poignant reminder that everyone had their place!

GRADUATION PARTY

We'd had the Graduation Enbu before we'd graduated, so it seemed only right to also have a party in celebration of graduation ahead of our official passing out parade. The cart was before the horse again, so we jumped on and went for a ride! Friday had been pretty easy, and at night I'd been out late to an Italian restaurant. The price of pleasure was always pain and any moment of enjoyment appeared to have a cost. The penance I would pay turned up on the morning of Saturday, 17 February 2007, the day of the graduation party. As we neared the final week of the course, I felt my body was shutting down. My physical form sensed the end was nigh, and it was only my mental state that was driving me on. My body was preparing to fall over the finish line, while my mind wanted a sprint finish! It would be a long day and I knew I'd need all of my determination and resilience to get through.

In the first class Murray Sensei drilled us in futari dori, something we'd not done since November when we'd been given only the briefest of introductions. Facing one attacker was difficult enough, which made two even more challenging. I teamed up with Ronen and Neville, who attacked me in turn. It was hilarious. Three headless chickens running in all directions, not knowing what was going on. As the scene developed, it was impossible to tell who was shite and who were uke. Murray Sensei agreed and called time on the spectacle. I'd failed to defend myself with any success. The only thing I'd managed to do in a bid to get away was to smash my ankle on the wall of the dojo and it hurt like hell. In the break Murray Sensei came into the tearoom and asked us why we hadn't planned a second party for tonight. He was right, nothing formal had been arranged. An informal trek across to the HUB was the only plan for post-party action. The reason that nothing had been arranged was because Murray Sensei had previously told us not to bother with a second party. True to form, and as we'd experienced in the lead-up to the Graduation Enbu, he was trying to change things at the last minute. *'Osu, osu, osu!'* We responded in unison and then all privately agreed that we would just go to the HUB.

Murata was up next and again, true to form, took us on an Aikido journey that was always very different to the rest of the Sensei. He encouraged us to use sonar! I had no idea what he meant, but it seemed to be an instruction to connect with each other and the surrounding environment using invisible waves of energy. We'd previously used our palms as loudspeakers, and this seemed to be the next step on our journey to enlightenment. After failing miserably to connect with anything, Murata momentarily stopped the class and told us to gather around in a circle. He had an important message to relay. *'I feel confused inside my head, but when I talk, I feel better!'* It sounded like a statement you'd hear a patient say to his or her psychiatrist. It sounded like a cry for help. If Murata Sensei was confused, we most definitely were! Matt and I had joked since the start of the course about the strange classes we'd experienced. *Pick it, pack it, fire it up, come along...and take a hit from the bong!* The line from Cypress Hill's track, *Hits from the Bong*, was on both of our playlists in audible honour of Murata Sensei's classes. To understand them, we'd questioned whether we might need to take a hit from the bong ourselves! Eddie Bravo, the founder of 10th Planet Jiu Jitsu, was an open advocate of smoking a bit of the *skunky, funky, smelly green shit*, to get his creative juices flowing, perhaps we needed to do the same? *Inhale, exhale, just got an ounce in the mail.* I'm sure weed was more than readily available in Tokyo if you knew where to look. We never did partake, even though it might have helped us to understand Murata's classes a little better!

I arrived in Higashi Nakano at 4:15pm with Matt and Ronen in tow. We'd met up along the way. The graduation party was taking place at Pao Caravan Sarai, an Afghan restaurant known to the honbu that had been selected as a suitable venue to entertain Kancho and the rest of the Sensei. We'd been on a recce in preparation and discovered that the restaurant had a raised level that would be a suitable place to seat Yoshinkan's head. Raising Kancho above everyone else would tick the etiquette box, and this area was also far enough away from the toilets so as not to cause offence. It was pouring with rain, and reluctantly, we stationed ourselves outside the establishment to provide a 360-degree view. This time we were determined to intercept all the Sensei and make sure they were escorted properly. None of them were getting through, no matter how hard they tried! My suit was in a better state than it had been for the bonenkai, but as it got wetter and wetter, the musty stench of mould returned. I had the smallest umbrella which barely covered my shoulders, so was grateful when Murray Sensei let me borrow his posh one. News circulated that Higa Sensei had arrived and was making himself comfortable in the restaurant, awaiting everyone else. How had this happened? How had we missed him? What did this mean? Nobody knew. The one thing we knew, though, was that Higa would now take great delight in telling the other Sensei he'd made it through the line, especially if they hadn't. It looked bad on us and at this late stage of the course we didn't want to look bad. Had Mr Precise received tuition from the honbu's very own private detective? Escape and evasion were necessary skills, and Kanazawa Sensei would be the perfect teacher. We learnt later that Higa Sensei had spotted four of us together and, taking advantage of the weather, covered his face with his umbrella to successfully slip through. It made a mockery of the whole thing. Here we all were, getting soaked in order to meet our superiors who did everything in their power not to be met!

The dinner went well, and this time I got a good seat next to Dave and Ronen and opposite Clyde and Takashima Sensei; the conversation flowed.

For some unknown reason, Dave had been selected to be master of ceremonies, and he surprised us all by doing a reasonable job, until he got drunk. Dave was a natural entertainer, and Kancho seemed to be having a good time, which was all that really mattered. A singer and Mongolian dancer provided some risqué entertainment that everyone seemed to enjoy, but according to Dave, the dancer wasn't genuine. How he knew wasn't clear, and it wasn't safe to ask in polite company. Dave had been involved in the organisation, and I asked him where he'd found her. *'The honbu told us to book her. She's a friend of Kancho!'* All was now clear. No wonder Kancho looked so happy! Chida Sensei arrived late and gave a speech, saying he was sorry he hadn't taught us much. He didn't give a reason. It was a shame, as we'd all missed a golden opportunity to spend any extended amount of time under the tuition of Yoshinkan's Aikido God. Chida would pay the ultimate price. Instead of mini Chidas let loose on the world, the honbu would be sending out mini Chinos instead! Like a child brought up by his or her stepfather, we'd lost connection with our biological father, and it was now too late to build bridges. It was left to Murray Sensei to close proceedings. In his speech he said that we'd been a great year and hadn't given the teaching staff too many problems. He explained that he'd been at the honbu for a long time and met many different people who had travelled from all over the world to do the course. Whether they continued Aikido or not, all had gone on to do special things with their lives. It was a genuine speech from the heart and one which moved us all. The evening had been fun with Dave in charge and, as a thank you, he received a double yonkajo from two Aikido greats. Seeing Crazy Dave in the clutches of Inoue Kancho and Chida Dojocho, was a special moment!

The night went smoothly until Kancho announced he was ready to leave. Everybody's shoes had been removed at the door and carefully stored by the Senshusei. Panic set in when we realised that Kancho's shoes were missing. It turned out that the collection and safekeeping of the one pair of shoes we really didn't want to lose had been Boaz's responsibility. As the tension mounted, things escalated; annoyed that Boaz had cocked up the simplest of tasks, Vic went at him. After her destruction of Dave at the Graduation Enbu, Boaz was on dodgy ground. It had been a great evening, and like a punch-up at a wedding, it would have been a shame to finish on a sour note. We searched the venue high and low, and eventually the missing shoes were found. Vic and Boaz stood down and Inoue Kancho left past a line of wet and weary Senshusei who had stepped outside in the rain to formally bid him goodnight. The HUB in Takadanobaba was closed for a private party, so for the second party we found a bar nearby and spent the rest of the night mixing beer and whisky with Laurance and Romeo Sensei. As usual, my head was spinning. A combination of tiredness and the intoxicating effect of the alcohol signalled it was probably time to go home!

ON THE MOVE

I was already making plans for the end of the course. Musashi Koyama had been good, but coming to the end of my rental term, if I was going to stay in Japan, I needed to find somewhere else to live. Matt was going to stick around, along with Clyde who seemed to have made his home in Tokyo. There was good reason to extend my stay and enjoy all that Tokyo had to offer without the requirement to be at the honbu dojo every day. I wanted to be in the thick of it and within easy reach of Axis Jiu Jitsu, where I planned to spend a lot of my time. Shibuya would be perfect and was an area I knew well. As luck would have it, I'd spotted an apartment up for grabs a few hundred metres from the station. Over the weekend and in between teaching shifts, I had a look. It seemed to fit the bill, and I called the agent on Monday to inform her I'd take it. Once the course was finished, I'd now be staying in Japan for at least another three months. I'd miss Musashi Koyama with its quiet streets and shopping mall, but all good things come to an end. It would soon be time for a new start in more ways than one!

NO-SHOW

After Chida Sensei's speech at the party, I had hoped we'd see him on the mats a few times in what remained of the course. He'd seemed genuinely sorry that he'd not taught us much, and although he'd really left it too late, there was still a week to make amends. In Tuesday morning's meeting, Graham Sewanin thanked us for organising the party and told us that Chida would teach the third class today. After Laurance and Ito Sensei, we lined up in eager anticipation to await the Dojocho. I knew once I'd escaped the course and continued my Aikido training elsewhere, people would ask me what it was like to learn from Chida. At the moment I didn't really have an answer, but today was my opportunity to fill in this blank. Chida Sensei was a no-show. I couldn't believe it. Our biological father, the one that had missed every important event until now, but faithfully promised to turn up today, had let us down again. Miyakoshi Sensei arrived instead, and with no explanation for Chida's absence, we carried on as normal. We debated Chida's no-show in the tearoom after class. Had we offended him? Were we not worthy of his time? Were honbu politics we didn't understand at play that had seen Chino as our regular instructor and not Chida? Nobody had the answer, not even the Sewanin. When asked back home what it was like training under the Aikido God, I'd have to change the subject! It's possible he was just forgetful, a trait that had one major upside. Chida's deal had died a death. Despite an early finish during kan geiko, the Wednesday and Friday early starts that had been enforced in August hadn't been triggered in February.

Just when we thought all was lost, in Wednesday's second class, Chida Sensei arrived in front of the shomen. We'd been at the honbu for nearly 11 months, and this would be one of the very few classes he'd be teaching from start to finish. I suppose it was better late than never, but we all still felt like his abandoned children. The class was great, and we focused on the basics of kamae and kihon dosa. This was true Yoshinkan; always back to basics. There were very few people as good at the basics as Chida Sensei. We'd been taught on the course that if we struggled with jiyu waza, we should go back to kihon waza. If we had problems with kihon waza, it was back to kihon dosa. If our kihon dosa sucked, we'd need to get a grip on our kamae. Finally, if our kamae was pants, we'd be back in seiza, which was a place nobody wanted to revisit! I'd learnt that Aikido wasn't the flashy moves I'd seen Steven Seagal use to great effect in his movies. Real Aikido was about the basics. Posture and centre line were the foundations of everything else.

After the last class of the day with Miyakoshi Sensei, Matt and I were chatting in the locker room, when Dave rolled in. As we got changed, Dave made an announcement. I couldn't decide if he'd planned it or if it was on the spur of the moment. *'I can't believe both of you were black belts before the course started!'* Dave clearly had a death wish. Ronen described the scene later. *'It was like two sharks circling Nemo the clownfish...deciding whether to kill the little fishy or let him go!'* Stopping short of putting Dave's head through the nearest locker, we told him that this was a personal insult and that when we got back to the UK, we'd have to tell Sensei Ken. If Dave ever made the trip up to Nottingham, he'd meet the daddy shark and be in a whole world of trouble!

THE LAST ZAGAKU

The weekly zagaku had been at the core of our Senshusei experience. It had been a thorn in all of our sides from the start and, I'm sure, had directly contributed to the vast array of injuries that had plagued us throughout. I couldn't speak for the previous 15 international courses, but I'd heard that the weekly zagaku was new for the 16th. Other years had done plenty of seiza, but we had a diarised, regimented and all-too-frequent appointment none of us wanted to keep. I guess every year was different and each course unique. Instructors came and went, and different things were tried and tested. Zagaku had been our experiment, and if the experiment had been to cause pain and discomfort, it had passed its clinical trials. I wondered if zagaku would now be on the schedule for future Senshusei generations to come, once the guinea pigs had long departed.

Thursday, 22 February 2007, was the last zagaku. Dave had earlier lightened the mood during Noriki Sensei's class. As we practiced *shumatsu dosa ichi*, the third move from kihon dosa, I'd heard him ask Vic, *'do I look straight?'* I assumed he was talking about his body positioning but couldn't be certain! We lined up opposite one another and sank into seiza to await Inoue Kancho and the senior Sensei. We'd done this too many times to remember, but today I felt especially nervous. However, it turned out I didn't need to be. Like the antibiotics I'd taken for my bronchitis and in line with my Mum's advice, it was always the last tablet. The final zagaku felt painless. I wasn't sure if all the previous sessions had prepared me for this final one or whether the emotions we were all feeling had sent a surge of adrenalin through my body that provided the relief. All the Sensei gave us advice for the future and wished us well. I had goosebumps and a tear in my eye, this time not from the pain, but from the realisation that this was it, and that every class edged closer to the last we'd ever have as Senshusei. I felt like a racing driver speeding to the finish line who realises that in his urgency to get to the end, he's missed much of the race. I wanted to slam on the brakes and go back. At the very least, I wanted one last lap. When Graham Sewanin spoke, he was visibly moved and at one point looked like he would break down in tears. In that moment I realised that the year had mattered to him, and while he might not have always shown it, particularly near the end, he and Malik were also brothers in arms. They were Senshusei and had dedicated an extra year of their lives to make us Senshusei, too. I tried to retain the moment, as it slipped through my fingers, and I smiled as I remembered an email Matt had sent us all earlier in the week.

Hi Guys
I was thinking about how I'm going to describe zagaku to everyone back at home and came up with this outline. Let me know what you think.
Start – everyone sits in seiza.
1) A Senshusei reads a reflection and a habit in Japanese. The Japanese Sensei don't understand due to the Senshusei's limited grasp of Japanese.
2) The Senshusei repeats his reflection and habit in English. The other Senshusei understand but realise that the Senshusei has written a load of

bullshit that he thinks Kancho wants to hear. This is especially true of the habit, which usually involves straightening pictures or picking up hairs.
3) A Sensei gives his thoughts on the reflection and habit in Japanese. The Senshusei don't understand.
4) The Sensei repeats his thoughts in English. The Senshusei still don't understand or if they do understand realise that the Sensei is probably saying something that he thinks Kancho wants to hear.
5) Kancho speaks. The Senshusei don't understand.
6) Kancho draws on the blackboard and writes a phrase in English. The Senshusei understand but by now they have been sat in seiza for 30 minutes and their knees are fucking killing.
7) Kancho leaves, everyone bows, Chida Sensei walks on people's legs. Repeat 48 fucking times!!!
Matt

Kancho's blackboard was infamous. It had helped us understand what he was going on about, but although we'd willed him to scribble fast, he'd always taken his time. We'd probably not done 48 zagaku sessions as Matt suggested but factoring in all the additional seiza we'd endured, it sure felt like it! Thrust back into the present by the sound of Inoue Kancho winding up, we bowed for the last time, Kancho left, and zagaku was for ever over. Murata Sensei jumped up and as he ran out of the dojo shouted in English, *'last one'* and then flipped the bird at us for good measure. It was a special moment and one I knew I'd never forget.

THE FINAL TEST

Friday, 23 February 2007, was the day of the final test. Today we'd be teaching in front of Inoue Kancho and the other senior Sensei, instead of the other way round. In the first class we had Romeo Sensei, who gave us backdrops and, once warmed up, time to stretch and practice what we wanted ahead of the test. To graduate as an instructor from the Yoshinkan honbu dojo required more than just the demonstration of techniques. There was the Kokusai 16 Ki Senshusei Course Proficiency Examination also to get through, and ahead of today, we'd all hit the books to make sure we were ready. *Total Aikido – The Master Course* and *Dynamic Aikido*, both by Kancho Gozo Shioda, had been studied in preparation. At 11am we started the second class, where, for the first time, the most physical thing we'd be doing was frantically writing our answers in pencil to a series of questions that would now be unveiled. There were 13 or 14 'directions' from which we had to select five. Some, even after 11 months, were way beyond me, but luckily, I found five that I could have a good stab at.

1) Describe the history of Aikido.

2) Describe the things you should be conscious of during the teaching of Aikido.

3) Describe the importance of kamae.

4) What is the fundamental objective of kihon dosa?

5) Describe kokyu ho.

It wasn't going to be easy and as I began my scrawl, I couldn't believe some of the stuff I was writing! The history bit wasn't too difficult. Aikido had its origins in Daito-ryu Aikijujutsu, which was founded in Japan around 850 AD. I charted the origin through to Gozo Shioda and the opening of the first Yoshinkan Aikido dojo in 1955. Yoshinkan was *a place to study and cultivate the spirit*, and I'd done my best to cultivate mine since the start of the course. The second question was a little more challenging. I led with safety, advising that Aikido was a *dangerous martial art* and *the instructor must ensure the training environment is safe*. I elaborated further, recommending that *any hard or sharp objects should be removed that a student might land on*. Perhaps tongue in cheek, I continued with, *the instructor should create a positive environment for learning, and training should be enjoyable and varied*. My experience had been quite different to what I now willed my future instructor-self to deliver. Not all of our classes had been enjoyable and there had been a distinct lack of variety especially in the lead-up to the 51st All Japan Enbu where we'd practiced kihon dosa renzoku to death. In response to the third question, kamae was easy to describe. We'd drilled it enough and at the hands of Mr Precise stood in it until our legs ached and our bodies seized up. Rigor mortis usually set in a few hours after death, but I was convinced I'd experienced it while still alive. I must have learnt something from Murata Sensei as I wrote that *in kamae we extend our feeling forwards towards our opponent* and that kamae was the *foundation of Aikido*. Kihon dosa too had been practiced relentlessly and to answer question four I used poetic licence to draw a comparison with kamae. *If Aikido is compared to a house, kamae would be the foundations and kihon dosa the bricks. Kihon dosa is literally the bricks of our Aikido house.* It seemed to make sense, and I imagined the person marking my script nodding his or her head in approval. I saved the most difficult question until last. I'd never properly understood kokyu ho. We'd practiced kokyu ho techniques to develop our kokyu ryoku power, but it was all a bit confusing. I articulated that kokyu ho was *having correct rhythm, timing and balance synchronised with our opponent so we can control them effortlessly. Ueshiba Sensei talked about being at one with the universe; an interpretation of this is kokyu ho. When you can read and feel uke's movement, you become at one with them.* I even surprised and impressed myself with this last answer. After 11 months something had definitely sunk in. Even though I didn't fully understand what I was writing, I was sure whoever marked my test would get it and be more than a little impressed! There was also an essay that had to be written. This was probably the trickiest part of the examination and required us to *choose any topic of your choice and describe its relationship to the series and practices of Aikido.* Looking back, I have no record of what I wrote or what subject I picked. I suspect I linked Aikido to business but can't be certain.

We'd flexed our brains, and now it was finally time for the test proper. I didn't feel as nervous as I had ahead of shodan and resolved that as this was my last test at the honbu, I would try to enjoy it. Kambara, Inazaki, Dave and Vic were up first and, on Noriki Sensei's command, bowed, adopted their positions and slid forwards into right followed by left kamae. In the stance we'd adopted a thousand times, Kancho, Chida, Chino, Sonoda and Oyamada Sensei made their inspections, clipboards in hand. Next each movement of the kihon dosa was run through independently as the examining Sensei inspected some more, followed by kihon waza on Sonoda Sensei's command. Finally, it was shido ho and, once the teaching was done, the usual round of jiyu waza. After Geoff, Dror, Clyde and Matt, it was time for Neville, Lloyd, Ronen and me to enter the spotlight. Neville and Lloyd ran to the wrong start positions, an error quickly rectified at Kancho's instruction, and I resembled a wounded soldier returning from battle. With my black ankle support and white tape around my left wrist and right big toe, I was a visible representation of what it meant to be Senshusei. Like a bride on her wedding day in readiness for a new chapter of life, I had something old (my Muay Thai anklet) something new (my black belt) and something borrowed (the white tape). The only thing I didn't have was something blue, but three out of four wasn't bad! I had to teach *katate mochi sokumen iriminage ichi* and self-defence from a rear collar grab. Sokumen had never been my strongest technique, and as I repeated the technique out loud to confirm I'd got the message, I frantically scrambled to find the place in my brain where I could play back what I needed to do. In class I'd heard this technique called out too many times to mention but thrown into the pressure of the test environment, I was terrified of drawing a blank. Ronen and I bowed to one another. *'In Aikido there are two types of iriminage. Shomen iriminage in which I enter uke from the front and sokumen iriminage in which I enter across uke's body.'* The innuendo was evident again, but at least I was off. Also, my preamble had given me just enough time to work out what I was supposed to be doing. I demonstrated the technique in full, from both the left and right sides, and then broke the technique down step by step. It was a surreal situation, teaching Kancho, Chida, Chino, Sonoda and Oyamada a technique they'd taught me, as if they were learning it for the very first time! *'From this position uke grabs my wrist and pulls. From here I move my right leg forwards, making a T shape against uke's foot.'* Ronen did a good job as uke. Sokumen wasn't an easy technique to do slowly, especially for the recipient. I proceeded to highlight some of the common mistakes. I knew these all too well, having made them enough times. Making the 'T' shape and using my hips to throw uke were things at the start of the course I'd struggled to do. Now, in illustrious company, I was publicly showing I'd put them right! There was one final full demonstration of the technique, and then I passed the baton to Ronen.

Ronen got *shomen uchi sankajo osae ni.* English was his second language and Ronen now needed to navigate not only the English but also all the Japanese terminology that the watching Sensei would understand. None of us really knew how much English the Sensei really understood. I was convinced that the more Japanese words we could throw into our teaching narrative, the better. Since the start of the teaching phase of the course, I'd made sure to always include words like zanshin for good measure, and everyone else had followed suit. Next it was self-defence. This would be interesting. By this stage of the course both of our upper bodies had seized up. There would be minimal grace, plenty of pace and a good helping of up in your face! Ronen and I lacked the fluidity of Boaz. This would be like two 18 wheelers colliding head on! *'I will now demonstrate self-defence techniques where uke grabs my collar from behind and pulls strongly.'* It wasn't the most realistic of situations, but it was the one I'd been given. Old habits die hard, and my technique involved a right cross to Ronen's chin. Ronen returned the favour in defending my choke and wrist grab from behind by smashing me hard into the tatami. Today's buddy system was brutal. It was a smash-fest of epic proportions! After a round of jiyu waza each, we were well and truly done. I'd defended shomen uchi and Ronen *shomen tsuki,* an attack I was used to delivering in the form of a *punch to the stomach.* Boaz was the last to test and after a solo performance of kamae and kihon dosa paired up with Graham Sewanin for everything else. Graham snuck in a couple of knee breakers, the technique he'd used on me in our previous outing. If anyone was best able to get off them, Boaz was the man. On both occasions, he flew over the top of Graham with no trouble at all.

Noriki Sensei called an end to proceedings, and Chida, Chino, Sonoda and Oyamada lined up to bow to Inoue Kancho. Kancho took his place to bow to the shomen and then turned and bowed to us. The honbu's head then got to his feet and walked to the entrance of the dojo. In what was now an uncomfortable seiza, along with the Sensei, we shuffled to face the door and bowed to Kancho one more time. After a final bow to Chida, Chino, Sonoda and Oyamada it was all over. The last test of the course was finished, and all that remained now was for the examiners to deliberate and Chida Dojocho to deliver the official results. When Chida reappeared, he said that the shido ho had been bad but that a few of ours, including mine, had not been as bad as the rest. It was a kind of reverse compliment. You weren't very good, but you weren't as hopeless as everyone else! He continued with individual feedback for everyone and shared three specific points with me.

1) In kamae, my shoulders should be squarer.

2) In teaching sokumen iriminage I should project my hips and weight forwards more after engaging uke.

3) In jiyu waza I need to improve my *sasoi* (invitation to uke), tai sabaki and make my movements bigger.

Kambara, Inazaki and Neville were awarded nidan, which was one step up from the shodan they'd received at the end of last year. Neville got all his weight over his front knee when doing taino henko ichi, which caught Chida's eye and had been the principal catalyst for his promotion.

As I left the honbu, I was a mixed bag of emotions. The test hadn't gone as well as I'd hoped, but I'd passed, and that was what counted. I was glad it was over but sad that in three days the course would be finished. As I headed off to my Japanese class amid a bustling Tokyo, I reflected on what life would soon be like.

IT AIN'T OVER 'TIL…

As the proverb goes, *it ain't over 'til the fat lady sings*. I had no idea who the fat lady was or why things never finished until she'd stretched her vocal cords one last time. What I knew, though, was that although the final test was over, the course had yet to sing its final tune. It felt somewhat of an injustice to turn up for training on Saturday morning. I'd thought at least for a moment that we might have been given the day off but quickly remembered that this was Senshusei! Who were we to think we deserved a break? We'd be pushing on until the end and be glad of the experience. The written test results were in for everyone apart from Ronen. He'd been called into the office to rewrite his exam as nobody could read it! Doctors were supposed to have bad handwriting, so perhaps this was a sign of things to come? Not the medical type but a future mad scientist, he'd been made to do it again! I'd passed with 92 points out of an available 100. My weakest score was 17 on the history of Aikido, with 20 awarded for my response to the second question. As the final test had been the instructor's exam, scoring full marks on things to be conscious of during the teaching of Aikido was definitely the way to go. Nobody failed, and we'd find out later that, having rewritten his test, Ronen had passed, too. I wasn't sure whether failing the written test meant you'd be stripped of the physical test you'd passed the day before, but luckily none of us had to find out.

On Saturday afternoon I headed across to Shibuya and had a closer look at the apartment I'd soon be renting. Compared to Musashi Koyama, it was much newer – and without the lining of mould I'd discovered ahead of December's bonenkai. Saying it was compact was an understatement. There was just enough space for a single bed and desk, but there appeared to be a distinct lack of wardrobes. I could barely fit in the bathroom or stand up straight. Still, small was supposed to be beautiful, and the closer to the action I got, the less my budget for accommodation would stretch. The 2 rooms I'd had at Musashi Koyama, in the words of the Spice Girls, were now to *become 1*. I spent the rest of the weekend in a blur of work, Jiu Jitsu and visiting the immigration office. Now I'd sorted out my accommodation, I had to make sure I could legally stay. I smiled sweetly at the immigration assistant and said all the right things to secure the stamp in my passport that would keep me in the country.

Back at the honbu on Tuesday, the highlight of the morning was Dave dropping his locker key down the back of the sofa in the tearoom. He couldn't get it out so had no choice but to alert Graham Sewanin of his plight. For the next 10 minutes they went to work like two guys down on their luck and in search of cash. With no luck, Graham opened the bottom up to finally reveal Dave's missing key. Today would be special. As it was the final full day of teaching, we'd be doing each of the three classes for the very last time. Tomorrow was graduation day, so in nostalgic lament, we lined up for the last 8:30am class, the last 10am class, and the last midday class. Murata Sensei had a guest for the final class of the day. David Fryberger was in town. A friend of Laurance Sensei, Fryberger Sensei was a graduate of the third international course – the year before Robert Twigger had found his way to the honbu. David was in Tokyo for his godan test and, I'd also heard, trained in Brazilian Jiu Jitsu. He took the first half of Murata's class and I liked his technique. I made a mental note to try and get him across to Axis when the course was over. As we shuffled off the tatami ahead of the day's final Shinkoku, Graham told Geoff that there would now be a first class tomorrow morning. Nobody could believe it, and we all felt angry. It would be our last day and one where we'd be passing out officially from one of the toughest martial arts courses in the world. Why bother with one class to get all hot and sweaty before the ceremony – what could they teach us now?

I trundled off to work at Aoyama, bumped into Laurance and, still annoyed, seized my opportunity. *'Why are we having a class on the last day?'* He paused in quiet contemplation. I read this as him deciding whether he was clear to tell me or not. After a few moments, he looked me directly in the eyes and smiled. *'Takagi Sensei requested it!' Ahhhhhhhhh!* I could have screamed. *Wait until I tell the others,* I thought to myself; *they're not going to believe it.* I figured we could always go on strike, but a dojo sit-in when we were set to leave made no sense. I also wanted to go out on a positive note and to finish in the spirit of Senshusei. There was no other choice. We'd just have to suck it up!

BOWING OUT

Wednesday, 28 February 2007, was our last day, and despite yesterday's dress rehearsal, today everything we'd be doing really would be our last time. Kancho had his own toilet, which no one else at the honbu dojo could use, not even the other Sensei. I'd cleaned it many times and always finished by folding the end of the toilet paper into the obligatory sankaku. For my last cleaning assignment, I found myself once again in the throne room and had to use all of my willpower to resist the temptation to relieve myself. Graham and Malik Sewanin seemed subdued and, in the morning meeting, told us to do our best as if it were just any other day. Oyamada Sensei had taught the 7am class, which was always attended by a handful of ippan students with nothing better to do at that time of the morning. As he left the mats, I collected his hakama and folded it on the tearoom table. I'd finally mastered the art of hakama origami, and after a couple of minutes, I knocked on the office door to return the folded item to its rightful owner. As I handed it over, out of the blue Oyamada enquired, *'how do you feel?'* Without thinking, my honesty getting the better of me, I instinctively responded with, *'tired'*!

Takagi Sensei, apparently still with a point to prove, ordered us to make a circle to prepare for backdrops. Backs to the tatami with legs in the air, and then up to our feet using outstretched arms for momentum – we repeated the exercise 150 times. When our solo drills were over, we remained in the circle and this time linked arms, which made the whole exercise much tougher. The stronger had to drag up the weaker, who turned out to be Geoff and Dror on this occasion; and with no arms free to help our ascent, it was an exhausting experience. We had to rely on pure technique as we cracked out another 150 to Takagi's count. Next it was back to day one of the course, with seiza practice followed by kihon dosa. My techniques felt strong, maybe because I knew that now I really only had one last class to survive. To finish we did jiyu waza, which seemed a fitting way to end our time on the hallowed green tatami. Both Ronen and I had been struggling with a cold and sore throat and, despite our initial reluctance to partake in this last class, agreed afterwards that we both felt better for it. We'd done it and hadn't lynched Takagi Sensei in the process.

We set up the dojo ready for the graduation ceremony, aligning chairs with pinpoint precision in front of the shomen, and then got changed into our suits. We had 10 minutes to do this, as under Ito Sensei's instruction, we had to be back in the dojo at 10am, ready for the ceremony to begin. There was no time to shower, and the act of putting on a shirt over my sweaty body was not a pleasant one. We'd all be stinking later apart from Matt, who'd opted for a 'scouse shower' with a wash of his pits in the sink. Malik Sewanin, feeling our pain, popped his head around the locker room door and told us we could have a few more minutes to take a shower. I didn't need telling twice and ditched the suit momentarily to wash away the sweat from 300 ukemi.

Back on the tatami, and to avoid any embarrassing mistakes, we did a quick rehearsal on where we'd be sitting and what to do once our name was called, and then we took our positions for the real thing. Back straight and perched on the edge of my seat, all the memories of the last 11 months flashed before my eyes. The ups, the downs, the happy times, the sad times, not to mention the moments of madness, had all mixed to provide my unique Senshusei experience. We collected our instructor certificates from Inoue Kancho and heard a speech, only three of us could understand, from a lady who was the head of the IYAF. A former Olympian, she'd apparently won a bronze medal in gymnastics at the 1964 Tokyo games. The ceremony was the shortest one I'd ever experienced and, with the luxury of a chair, had also been the most comfortable. As we marched out of the dojo, all the Sensei clapped, which was a very special moment.

Our final Shinkoku was set to be long and complicated. With so much formality to get through, we drafted in Kambara to replace Neville. At the end we all called out an extra-loud *'osu!'* Matt had wound Dave up so much with the usual mickey-taking which had been a staple part of the course that at the lunch in the dojo that followed, Dave sat as far away as possible. It was another formal affair, sitting bolt upright in our seats with one eye on Kancho at all times. Conversation was at best stilted and at worst downright uncomfortable. Kancho finished up, and it was time for the IYAF lady to leave. We all ran into the entrance hall to bow to her in unison and wish her well on her way. We were now free to collect our certificates in the tearoom. There were three in total – one for doing the course, our shodan certificate and, last but not least, our instructor qualification. Graham and Malik Sewanin came in to say their goodbyes and were visibly choked. Malik, in words reminiscent of Sonoda Sensei, said that he was sorry for any mistakes he'd made and that he had always tried to do his best. He said he remembered us all at the beginning, like babies that were yet to walk. We'd worked hard and achieved our black belts, albeit baby ones! He then addressed us individually and had kind words for everyone. Dave had matured, Dror had got stronger, and, smiling, Malik Sewanin turned to Ronen. *'If I ever go to war, I want you by my side!'* We all laughed. In that moment I swept any ill feeling or animosity towards either Sewanin under the carpet. I could have hugged them both, but remembering where I was, formally thanked them on behalf of the 16th international Senshusei for all that they'd done. We emptied our lockers, cleared the tearoom shelves and, as this year's Senshusei, bowed out of the honbu dojo for the very last time!

BITTERSWEET

Ronen and I caught the train to Shibuya together. We were both exhausted from the physical exertion of Takagi's class but more so from the emotion of the day. As the train sped across Tokyo, Ronen fell asleep first, and I followed suit. We said a temporary goodbye, and I continued to Musashi Koyama via Meguro. It was a journey I'd done a thousand times before, but today, instead of the elation of another day in the bag, I felt sad. Saying goodbye to the Sewanin had really got to me. In so many ways they'd been a thorn in our sides and relentless tormentors for 11 long months, but in the final moments of our time together, I'd seen in their emotions that their intentions had always been good. By Malik's own admission, he'd made mistakes. They were learning how to be Sewanin as we learnt how to be Senshusei. We were on the same path but at different stages of the journey.

We'd both been finding our feet in very different ways. I crashed through the door at Musashi Koyama, dumped my bag on the floor and fell into bed. After a much-needed rest I woke up, wrote the last entry in my diary and ceremoniously shaved my head. I also shaved my goatee beard with a razor but soon regretted my decision. My skin burnt and itched like crazy, and the pain of Senshusei was replaced with a very different pain altogether. Perhaps it was a cleansing ritual to mark the end of the course, the rite of passage I'd gone through and the start of a new journey yet to begin?

To celebrate the completion of the Senshusei course and our newfound freedom, we'd all agreed to meet for old times' sake at the Hachiko statue. At 7pm I emerged from Shibuya Station to greet my Senshusei brothers and sister. We crossed the famous Shibuya crossing I'd first marvelled at in *Lost in Translation* and headed up to Elephant, a Thai restaurant I'd frequented many times before. We dined like kings on the set food and drink menu and, with nothing to get up for tomorrow, the booze flowed. Partway through the evening, Lloyd had a phone call from his girlfriend in Australia. The restaurant was noisy, and the line was poor, so he left the party to find an Internet cafe. He'd had bad news from home. His brother was ill, and he needed to phone home urgently. The rest of us carried on and, in a drunken haze, eventually left Elephant and wandered up to the HUB. Matt and I moved from beer to double whiskies, and in the move to spirits, the die was cast for a very messy night. My head was going, and I had little recollection of how the rest of the night played out. In one way it was celebratory drinks, but in another, I was drowning my sorrows. I would miss Senshusei and all it stood for, but even more, I would miss seeing everyone. I knew that the collective force that had brought us together had ended and that in a few days, we'd all be moving on with our lives; heading in different directions and in pursuit of different things. I was aware that we spent some time in Club Asia, a nightclub on Shibuya's entertainment strip. It was dark, dingy and quiet, but it was only the company that mattered. My last memory was waking up in McDonald's with Matt, Clyde and Inazaki at about 6:30am feeling dreadful. In true Tokyo tradition, I'd missed my last train home and sought refuge in the burger bar, which played temporary home to a diverse range of Japanese society until the first trains ran again. Chatting with Inazaki, who seemed to have the best memory of the night, I learnt that we'd been to two nightclubs, and two McDonald's. I could only remember one of each!

I got the train back to Musashi Koyama, feeling sick and exhausted. The mix of drinks I'd polished off combined with very little sleep had destroyed me. What the course had failed to do, the night out had achieved. I was

345

completely wiped out! After drifting in and out of sleep for most of the day, I finally woke up properly at about 5pm and checked my phone. I had a message from Clyde saying that Lloyd's brother had tragically died. Some of the Senshusei who'd made it home earlier had met Lloyd at the honbu dojo to offer their condolences and say goodbye. Those of us who were worse for wear, including Matt and me, hadn't received the message in time. I felt sick to my stomach, and my heart went out to Lloyd. He'd been my first allocated partner for Dai Ichi, and we'd formed a close bond. Lloyd was tough, one of the toughest on the course, but nothing could have prepared him for this. Life had delivered a cruel and crushing blow. At the moment he should have been celebrating his achievement with us, he'd received the worst news from home.

I forced myself out of bed and staggered to the convenience store a short walk from my apartment. I bought a selection of food and drink in the vain attempt to cure my hangover. The green tea ice cream that I'd become partial to, though, was a step too far, and it triggered a bout of vomiting like I'd never experienced before. I was sick to my core, so much so that my kidneys ached. Drinking to excess had been a bad idea. Although injured, I was physically fit. It was like putting diesel in a performance car and expecting it to run. I'd chugged along to the shop, but as the internal mixture swirled around my body, I'd broken down on the way home and only just made it back in time.

The first day of freedom I'd imagined for so long, in reality, felt very different. Like so many things in life, it was bittersweet. In the midst of celebration had emerged tragedy. I couldn't stop thinking about Lloyd, my Senshusei brother, and his family. I already missed the training, I already missed the honbu, I already missed my fellow Senshusei. I even missed the sound of Malik Sewanin's screams pushing me to be a better version of myself. I missed the relentless discipline, and as I lay in recovery, I realised that the biggest challenge now would be to discipline myself!

AFTERMATH

I stayed in Japan for a few more months and moved into the new apartment in Shibuya. I spent my time training at Axis Jiu Jitsu and teaching English at Berlitz, but without the daily routine of the course something was missing. I went back to the dojo for some of the 7am classes to train with the ippan students, but it wasn't the same. The intensity was missing, and even with Chino Sensei on the mats, I couldn't find the energy and enthusiasm I'd had on the course.

I invited David Fryberger to join me at Axis Jiu Jitsu and Laurance Sensei came along for the ride. Laurance wanted to know what all the fuss was about and, free from the constraints of the course, it was fine to take him. We rolled, and he tapped five times. It was a baptism of fire. Laurance drowned quickly in a sea of chokes, arm-bars and triangles. He took it well! I asked him at the end of the class, *'how do you think Chida Sensei would do, if he tried Jiu Jitsu?'* Laurance paused to think, and then told me that Chida would do just fine – his understanding of Aikido and body mechanics would prevail. *'Chida Sensei would find a way to win!'* Laurance did his best to convince me but I didn't buy it. In the church of Jiu Jitsu, Aikido God was an altar boy. Just as I had done on the Senshusei course – to survive and thrive in the world of Jiu Jitsu – he'd need to pay his dues!

Japan had been a stop-off point on my way to Australia, which had become more permanent than I'd ever expected. I'd applied for and secured a visa back in the UK to permanently emigrate to the Land Down Under and soon found myself in Melbourne. I trained for a time with Thambu Sensei, whom I'd previously met in the UK, Australia and Japan. At his head dojo in Melbourne, I had the opportunity to meet up with Marshall Sensei again. They welcomed me with open arms, but I found my training and attendance slipping. With the freedom to do what I wanted, my discipline had waned. My interest in Jiu Jitsu was stronger. Keen to further the skills I'd developed at Axis, I started to train under Professor Ben Hall at the Carlson Gracie Jiu-Jitsu Academy in Prahran. In a similar vein to Senshusei, I removed the blue belt I'd received from Taka Sensei in Tokyo to start out in white. I worked hard and eventually received a second blue belt from Professor Ben. I took the trip up to Brisbane and met up with Lloyd and his girlfriend. It was great to see him again, and we caught up on news and reminisced about the course. I sensed he missed it, too. I'd lost my way in life. There'd been a very specific reason to be in Japan. The different culture and way of life had been a strong enough pull to keep me away from family and friends back in the UK. Another English-speaking country, Australia felt in many ways similar to England, but it was this familiarity that left me feeling alone and craving home.

On my return to the UK, to be best man at Juzza's wedding, I stopped off in Hong Kong. My Dad flew out to meet me and we spent an amazing time together. I'd visited Hong Kong before but being with Dad made this trip all the more special. We did all the usual tourist stuff. On the Star Ferry across the harbour, I felt like Bruce Lee on his way to Han's island. On the Avenue of Stars, we paid tribute at the statue of Hong Kong's most famous son and watched A Symphony of Lights. The light and sound show was incredible and like nothing I'd seen before. Although it was six months since I'd finished the course, I was still in Senshusei mode. As we walked around the streets of Hong Kong in blistering heat, I'd failed to factor in a refreshment break despite my Dad's pleas for water. At the bottom of The Peak, while awaiting The Peak Tram, Dad collapsed – I caught him, and others came to our rescue. The incident terrified me and for the rest of our trip I wrapped him in kid gloves. You only get one Dad and my Senshusei mentality had nearly killed mine! By the time we reached the summit, he'd thankfully made a full recovery, and we both enjoyed the beautiful views.

Family and friends were my priority, and despite Australia being a beautiful country, I'd had enough of life as an expat, and it was time to leave. Back in the UK permanently, I trained once again at the Shudokan under Sensei Ken but didn't stay long. In search of pure Yoshinkan Aikido, I made the journey each week to train in Stafford. I had the privilege to meet and take instruction from Crawford Sensei, the head instructor of Goryukai Aikido Yoshinkan. Crawford Sensei had trained under Kancho Gozo Shioda and most of the senior honbu instructors. Meeting him was a sort of homecoming, and, in my opinion, alongside Chino Sensei, he epitomised the true spirit and power of Yoshinkan's founder. He told me a story that I've never forgotten. *'In 1974 the honbu dojo sent their own instructor, Yu Sensei, to England. He was a fearsome teacher and it wasn't unusual to suffer injuries. It was suck it up or leave. When selected to uke for him, other students would whisper, one lump or two?'* As uke was thrown with such force, the observing students would guess how many times he or she would bounce off the mats! Taking uke for Crawford Sensei provided the same terror and delight that I'd experienced in Japan, and for a time, I'd found a home.

Ronen visited me in 2009. It was great to see him again. We met Neville in Stafford and, three Senshusei reunited, got back on the mats. The monk, the maniac and my Israeli brother, went at it again. I made a return trip to Tokyo in 2010, with Savery Sensei, along with Miranda Sensei who travelled, from time to time over to the UK, from Sacramento. I trained with both in Stafford and before returning to Japan, I was promoted to nidan by Miranda Sensei. It was nice to make the next grade, but the feeling didn't compare to shodan. I took uke at the All Japan Enbu, but going back was to prove disappointing. What was once, is rarely set to be for ever. The honbu dojo where I'd spilled blood, sweat and tears was sadly no more. Shortly after the end of the 16th international course, a power struggle had taken place, which had seen a number of the senior Sensei disperse and the Ochiai dojo eventually close. The new honbu in Takadanobaba was a much smaller dojo without the heritage, history and feeling of Ochiai. It was a chance to train under Chino Sensei once more, and I was pleased he remembered me from the course. I was still one of his baby black belts! Even if it turned out that Chino Sensei didn't have any acting ability, he was a dab hand at karaoke. At a dojo party, I watched in disbelief as he performed in front of an audience which included Kancho (Yasuhisa) Shioda, Ando and Payet Sensei. Chino had a pretty good singing voice and at all times maintained a position of perfect kamae – it was a sight to behold! While at the dojo I met several Senshusei. Maybe I was biased, but the 20th course's schedule didn't seem as tough as the one the 16th had endured, and the Senshusei seemed far too relaxed. There was no Graham and no Malik, and Chino Sensei could only spread himself so thin. Everything I'd taken for granted during my 11 months was sadly missing. Venturing out of Tokyo, I visited Ando Sensei at his dojo in Urayasu; the location of my very first Enbu, where I'd watched while nursing a very bad head! In Kyoto, 280 miles in the opposite direction, I located Payet Sensei at his Mugenjuku dojo and had the privilege of training under him, too. Ando and Payet Sensei impressed me – both had been direct students of Kancho Gozo Shioda and their dedication to Aikido was plain to see.

In the spirit of the 2003 film, *The Last Samurai*, the original title of this book was *The Last Senshusei*. My year wasn't the last, and the course continues to this day. It was, however, the final chapter in a history and legacy that ended in March 2007. I feel privileged to have had my special year in the hallowed walls of Kancho Gozo Shioda's Ochiai dojo, instructed by many of the Aikido greats, all under one roof. They say too much of something is a bad thing, and in 2011, shortly after my return trip to Tokyo, I decided to hang up my hakama. My injuries refused to heal, and the intensity of the course had done irreversible damage to my knees. After every session with Savery and Crawford Sensei, I'd stagger back to my car and wouldn't be able to move properly for the next 48 hours. Like an addict, I was still hooked on the highest high, but the comedown was too costly to bear. The course had won the physical war but had given me a much more valuable prize. An untimely end to my time on the tatami was a bitter pill to swallow, made more palatable by a mental strength that would last a lifetime!

FAST FORWARD

Pack your things, leave somehow.
Blackbird song, is over now.
Don't be scared, I'm still here.
No more time, for crying dear.
From *Blackbird Song* – Lee DeWyze

Since the end of the course, life has changed considerably. I'm now in my late forties and happily married with two young boys. Charles and Maximus tried Aikido for a while but are still in search of what makes them tick. I live in hope that at least one of them will follow their Daddy into the martial arts, but as long as they're happy and healthy, it really doesn't matter. Matt and his wife Caitlin, whom he met in Japan, flew over from the United States to attend my wedding. It was great to see him again, and he thanked me for persuading him to join me in Japan and introducing him to Jiu Jitsu. He's well on his way to black belt and would now kick my ass! Maybe my letter did change his life after all – and for the better. I also invited Ronen and his wife to my wedding. Unfortunately, they were unable to make it, Ronen having just started his PhD and with a 16-month-old baby at home. He still has the invitation and I hope to meet him in England again soon. Marriage and children changed me and changed me for the better. I have regular flashbacks to my Senshusei life, like the time my youngest flooded the bathroom. *'Daddy, the shower is leaking!'* Maxi wasn't kidding; there was water all over the floor. On my hands and knees picking hair out of the plughole, for a moment, I was back in the Sensei's locker room!

The course left a gap that I struggled to fill. For a time, I was lost; very lost! Senshusei taught me to open my mind to new possibilities and I read a book called *The Secret*. The Law of Attraction wasn't something I'd heard of before. The concept that what you think about comes about made sense. O-Sensei emphasised the power of the universe in his teaching and it was something I wanted to explore. The Landmark Forum and Tony Robbins influenced my thinking and direction of travel. Their messages contained concepts I was familiar with and had learnt on the mats. Sensei Michal was right, Aikido really is life. The best option is usually to step off the track and let the negativity fly past! I'm convinced that opening my mind led me to Samantha, my beautiful wife, and my fantastic boys. I have a new kamae now; a new centre and focus. They are my true north, my guiding light and my reason for living. Don't get me wrong, it's not all plain sailing. Family life can be a lot like Senshusei. Tremendous ups, horrendous downs and plenty of shouting and screaming! Still, where's the fun in calm waters? It's all worth it.

On my return from Japan, inspired by the UFC and Pride, I'd gotten more serious about MMA. In Nottingham I found a gym called Bushido, which was the home of Dan Hardy and Team Rough House. It was a spit-and-sawdust place with a good group of guys who wanted to go at it. As it was in a tough part of town, when I left my car outside, I never knew if it would be there when I returned. I did Boxing with Ricardo, who taught me his 'fuck you' left hook, continued my Jiu Jitsu with Lee and joined the 'Squad'. Saturday mornings were a fight-fest and culminated with 10 rounds of 'sprawl and brawl', which saw me crawl out of the gym and spend the rest of the day recovering on the sofa. I had two amateur MMA fights at SENI, the International Combat and Strength Sports Show in London, but while Dan was the real deal, I was just playing. MMA had come too late for me, and I had to accept it. At SENI, I attended a seminar with Royce Gracie. The winner of UFC 1 and a living legend, he demonstrated his rear naked choke on me. It came on fast and I almost went out! I wondered how many people he'd inspired to get into the sport and marvelled at how big MMA had grown in under two decades. In 2017 I picked up a copy of Dan's book, *Part Reptile: UFC, MMA and Me,* and read it on holiday. In chapter 2 he talked about his path to MMA and reflected on how his time in China had given him a psychological breakthrough – the belief that through consistent effort, he could achieve anything. Wow, his words sent a shiver up my spine. This had also been my experience in Japan!

I no longer train in Muay Thai. I went back to Master Lec but, with a heavy heart, have now hung up my gloves, too. Muay Thai is a contact sport and no matter how good your evasive skills, it's impossible not to get tagged at least some of the time. Back in the day, as part of my conditioning routine to build a stronger neck and chin, I'd swing the heavy bag away from me and head-butt it on its return. When I started Muay Thai, nobody worried about the potential damage to the brain from an accumulation of punches. In one session I caught an elbow to the forehead. As my heart was pounding, my head exploded, firing blood across the room. It looked worse than it really was but had exposed my skull. A visit to the hospital and a line of stitches later, I looked like a laced-up boot. There must have been a run on A&E, as with no flesh-coloured thread, they gave me black. I still bear the scar today – a visible reminder to keep my hands up! Back then, Dementia wasn't a condition that was well publicised and understood. Nowadays, kids are no longer allowed to head a football, and several high-profile footballers have developed brain injuries in later life. I've had more gym wars than I care to remember, and a leather ball doesn't come quite as keen as a leather glove. As the body gets older, it's less able to recover. It was time to call it a day. I had a good innings, and in a sport where in Thailand you retire in your twenties, I lived to a grand old age! While getting punched in the face makes you feel alive, its cumulative effects in the long run can prove costly. I hope I haven't stored up trouble for my later years, but you never know.

Older and wiser and in search of self-defence, I made the switch to Krav Maga, where I started this book. One day I might be the old man with the cane, and I wanted to be ready. I trained under David Stevens, one hell of a tough guy and a senior instructor in the UK under the IKMF (International Krav Maga Federation). I stepped into Ronen's shoes for a while and found that my blend of striking, locking, throwing and ground-fighting skills were well suited to this highly effective fighting system. Again, the knocks added up, and now, only a couple of years off my 50th birthday, I solely train in Jiu Jitsu at Gracie Barra Nottingham under Professor Victor Estima. Jiu Jitsu is kinder than Aikido on my body but is no less deadly. In 2018 I graded to blue belt under Professor Victor. A blue belt from Japan, Australia and the UK must be some sort of record, but for me a belt is just a thing to keep your dogi from flapping open. Training in the martial arts has nothing to do with belts and has very little to do with fighting. In *Enter the Dragon*, Bruce Lee is asked, *'what's your style?'* He responds, *'my style? You can call it the art of fighting without fighting!'* In Jiu Jitsu the moves make perfect sense and enable a smaller person to control a much larger opponent. There's no seiza, and the positions seem much more in tune with natural body mechanics. At Gracie Barra Nottingham, I've found what I lost at the end of the Senshusei course – a new band of brothers and sisters who make even the toughest of sessions enjoyable. Although I've embarked on another long journey, it's one I hope to enjoy to the end of my days.

Training in the martial arts has given me more than I probably know. The negative experience of being bullied at school set me on a path of self-discovery – a path I'll never leave. It's a journey with no finish line, and one that I hope will never end. I went back to my boarding school to give a talk.

It was an emotional return to where my story really began. Through adult eyes, although it looked the same, it felt very different. Standing in the Memorial Hall in front of my audience, I was distracted – a ghost from the past, a distant moment in time – for a spilt second, I was the 13-year-old boy who'd sneaked in to watch Adrian train. What would I tell my younger self? If only I could speak to him now.

I was very sad to hear of the passing of Inoue Kancho in December 2017. He was a direct student of Kancho Gozo Shioda and became Kancho himself in 2002. Inoue Kancho resigned from the Yoshinkan in March 2007 and, having received *kudan* (ninth dan) from his teacher in 1992, was awarded *judan* (10th dan) by the International Budo Federation in April 2009. An inspiration to many and a legend in his lifetime, he will be sorely missed. I'll always remember zagaku, his blackboard and the power of his technique.

FINAL REFLECTION

And I'm grindin' 'til I'm tired.
'Cause they said: 'You ain't grindin' 'til you tired'.
So, I'm grindin' with my eyes wide.
Lookin' to find a way through the day, a light for the night.
From *My Life* – The Game ft. Lil Wayne

I am still standing in line. The line may have changed over the years, but it's synonymous with life. I'm standing in line, ready to act, ready to move, ready to face life's next adventure. I was 34 years old when I started the course, 35 when I completed it, and now, as I finish this book, I've just turned 48. It took me nearly two years to write it. I started in September 2018 and wrote the introduction. I picked things up again in March 2020 and made the book's completion my primary focus. It was tough to get it done, but nothing compared to Senshusei itself. On the course I put myself through hell. There were 223 days of training – days where I found myself on the tatami practicing or performing the art of Aikido. The 223 included the summer gasshuku, the 51st All Japan Enbu, Kagami Biraki and when I turned up far too early for shochu and kan geiko. There were other days – days when I didn't train but where Senshusei responsibilities took hold. I'll remember them all and especially the ones that involved blood, sweat and tears!

There has been a lot of water under many bridges since the course ended, and the reflection from this water has been a mirror to who I am and who I want to be. Am I a better person for taking the course? Yes, I think I am. Stripped down to a natural instinct to survive, the challenge in hand reveals things about oneself that the majority never get the opportunity to find out. Senshusei broke me down. It laid my foundations bare to uncover what was there and what wasn't, and then rebuilt me back into a better human being – a person with more courage, the determination to keep going and an attitude to never give in. I firmly believe that it's our responsibility to forge ourselves in the fire of life. Not to take the easy road, but instead the one that captivates our interest and excites us into action!

Throughout this book I've compared my experience on the course to what I imagine life in the military to be like. It only takes a small amount of discomfort and a consistent lack of sleep to reveal someone's true personality. The beasting in basic training has a serious purpose. It removes any ego and uncovers any baggage that an individual might be carrying that could have a negative effect in a real-life combat situation. While Senshusei was never a life-or-death situation, albeit at times it felt like it was, the result of our hardship was much the same. In the modern world, it's easy to get too comfortable. Being too comfortable breeds complacency, but life isn't like that. Life is quite literally a series of inhales and exhales, a continual cycle of ups and downs. Who we really are comes to light when we're scared, beaten down or under pressure. Most of the time, we do our best to hide our vulnerability from the world outside, which only adds to our fear – the fear of not being enough, the fear of not being ready or the fear of not being able to live up to who we say we are. Once we truly know who we are at our lowest ebb, fully exposed and with nowhere to hide, we're liberated. Senshusei took away my ego and laid bare before my own eyes who I really am.

I still search out the extreme. As a family we regularly holiday together in a beautiful part of Gran Canaria. The Maspalomas dunes are simply stunning. On most days I'd embark on a 90-minute run to take in their beauty. In the spirit of Senshusei, in the intense heat, I'd sweat profusely but never drink water. A 'Well Man' health check last year shocked me into sanity. The doctor told me in no uncertain terms. *'You've got to stop or you're going to kill yourself!'* Since then I've taken things a little easier. It's a strange, somewhat cruel dichotomy. The young have increased physicality but often poor mental strength, whereas with age our physical capability weakens as our mental strength grows – sometimes to a level that we ignore our body to the detriment of our health!

It's 13 years since I completed the 16th international Senshusei course in Tokyo, Japan, with Matt, Ronen, Lloyd, Geoff, Dave, Clyde, Boaz, Dror, Neville, Kambara, Inazaki and Vic. One year has passed for each of us who started and finished our journey together. We've rarely been in touch, and this book has already been an opportunity to reconnect. On completion of the first draft I reached out to everyone to let them know I'd written it and also contacted Malik and Graham. Despite the passage of time it was like the last time we met. The response was incredible and the chance to reminisce and reflect on an amazing experience. Senshusei is a brotherhood and a bond that can never be broken. Writing this book has been therapy and a deeply moving experience. My gift to a fantastic group of people I've missed and a legacy that will last for ever!

The three quotes at the beginning of this book form part of my final reflection. They all have significant meaning and were very carefully chosen.

'Do not pray for an easy life, pray for the strength to endure a difficult one.'

Bruce Lee inspired me to start martial arts. His quote speaks to me on many levels. Life at times can be tough, and we had best be prepared. Through adversity we grow. Relish whatever lands in your path and learn from the experience.

'Perseverance in any profession will most probably meet its reward.'

If I'm ever asked whom I would most like to meet, either living or dead, my answer is always Admiral Lord Horatio Nelson. I was first introduced to the stories of this great man by my Dad. I wondered who the statue at the top of the column in Trafalgar Square in London really was and made it my mission to find out. 'Britannia's God of War' spent his life in search of one thing. It wasn't money or status that drove him, but the pursuit of glory. Naturally weak in stature and health, he wasn't who you'd imagine your typical seafaring hero to be, but through grit, determination and ultimately perseverance, he rose to the pinnacle of his chosen profession. None of us on the course walked into the honbu dojo on day one as the finished article. It was only persistent hard work, through both good and bad days, which got us to the end and led to our ultimate reward. The reward for me wasn't the black belt, and it wasn't the instructor's licence. The glory for me was found in what I learnt and the people I met.

'Live your life while you have it. Life is a splendid gift.
There is nothing small in it. Far the greatest things
grow by God's law out of the smallest.
But to live your life, you must discipline it.'

'The Lady with the Lamp' rose from humble beginnings to shine a light on the nursing profession. Florence Nightingale's quote has religious overtones. Senshusei was a spiritual experience, and through digging deep and working hard on the smallest of movements and in doing the simplest of things, I discovered something special. To get anywhere in life requires commitment to a course of action and the discipline to carry it through, especially when the going gets tough. As far as we know, we only have one life, and the time to live it is always now – not tomorrow, not next week, and not next year. Don't wait, don't procrastinate; instead, seize every opportunity as if it were your last, and enjoy this splendid gift we've all been given. None of us knows when it might be taken away.

And finally, what is probably the motto of the course and a mantra for life is summed up in one proverb.

Nana korobi ya oki.

Fall down seven times, get up eight. It doesn't matter what happens; it's what you do in response that counts.

I AM SENSHUSEI

With determination and discipline, I'll take the fight.
Despite pain and hardship, I'll continue with might.
Today is mine to do my will.
Today is mine for the very thrill.
Of challenge, journey and the ultimate goal.
To strengthen, grow and nurture my soul.

On my return to the UK, I went back into recruitment. In September 2008, just after I left a secure job to start my own business with two of my colleagues, Lehman Brothers collapsed. This kick-started the financial crisis, and as I found out, when markets collapsed recruitment was the last thing on an organisation's mind. Martin, Danielle and I were committed. The recruitment industry was on its knees, and there were no jobs for us to go back to. Danielle – the same Danielle who visited me in Tokyo – was worried and said that she was thinking of getting a bar job. She asked my advice, and without thinking, my Senshusei experience kicked in. I told her, *'there's no plan B; we can't lose focus, we have to keep going!'* I'm proud to say that's exactly what we did. Senshusei was about focus and taught me that if you push hard enough you can achieve anything!

The financial contagion was bad, but the current challenge facing the world is much, much worse. As the COVID-19 pandemic tightens its grip, it has impacted the way we live, the way we interact and what we believe the future might hold. The world is at war with an invisible enemy that doesn't discriminate in who it takes. People are scared, life is disrupted, and in enforced isolation is where demons gain strength. Although isolated and distanced we're more connected as a community than ever before. It's ironic that enforced separation is what it's taken to bring us closer. If there's one positive to come out of this pandemic it's a move towards real, not just superficial, connection. This is the biggest test of all of our lives, where courage, a commitment to keep going and the resilience to never give up are needed more than ever. As the proverb states, *obstacles do not block the path, they are the path.* Under the rules of lockdown, I've enjoyed my permitted daily run. Through restricted freedom, I've seen the world as a playground of possibility more vividly than ever before. I'm not usually one for poetry, but the words above came to me at 6pm on Monday, 23 March 2020. In the midst of lockdown, they arrived, and I frantically scribbled them down. They summarise what I think it means to be Senshusei.

I love Yoshinkan Aikido – I love what it stands for and the people it helps to create. I have huge respect for every Sensei, Sewanin and practitioner of Aikido throughout the world, whatever his or her style. While all of us are individuals in our own unique ways, Aikido connects us, and is a force for good. With hindsight, I wish I'd stayed longer in Japan. Ronen, Matt and I were all asked to be Sewanin, but we all declined. We didn't hate Aikido and we didn't hate the honbu dojo; we just needed a break. Senshusei was extreme discipline – and in the moment we were asked – we'd all had enough of the daily grind and taking orders. We'd been programmed to be machines; for 11 months we took it on the chin, but all of us had a wild spirit inside that, while temporarily subdued, was waiting to get out! I've often wondered if we had PTSD (Post-Traumatic Stress Disorder). I'm not a doctor and I'm not sure – I Googled it and although we'd not returned from a war zone – some of the symptoms rang true. *Negative thoughts* about myself, a sense of *detachment* and *hopelessness about the future*, were all things I definitely felt. While I can't speak for everyone, some of my fellow Senshusei, consciously or unconsciously, *distanced* themselves *from some of the memories.* But no matter what – despite the hardship and despite the discipline, I am absolutely certain – Senshusei was the defining moment of my life.

Malik Sewanin told me once that one day I'd understand. During the cut and thrust of the course, I had no idea what he meant, but as I've grown older, I think I've finally got it. Senshusei has nothing to do with the martial arts. It has nothing to do with fighting. Senshusei is an attitude, an energy, a spirit to push on no matter what and to never give up. It's the discipline, determination and drive to succeed against all the odds. The course taught me Aikido, and in the process to take one hell of a beating. But what it really gave me above all else was a way to tackle life, a way to see possibility in even the darkest of times and the ability to try one more time when all appears lost. There is always an option, always a way through; and in the most testing of times we learn the most. Senshusei gave me a mindset, a DNA implanted without my knowing that is with me today, every day, for the rest of my life.

Possibly the best and most succinct explanation of the true purpose and meaning of Aikido – a post in the Yoshinkan Aikido Fellowship Facebook group, by Paul Stephens Sensei, caught my attention. *'I have found that Aikido is really useful in maintaining a neutral reaction to aggression. Violent people expect to see one of two reactions from you; fear or competing aggression. If you show either, then they control the interaction. If you can just maintain maai (space / distance) and keep a neutral open demeanour, most aggressors will realise that their display has not provoked the reaction that they expected, and they will back off. It also means that you can see clearly what is in front of you and sense when a real attack is coming amongst the macho posturing.'* Reading this was a lightbulb moment that encapsulated what I now know but was struggling to articulate. It's a sentiment shared by my fellow Senshusei in the next chapter, and in the final chapter, it's what Yoshinkan Aikido's founder always knew. I believe the real strength of Aikido is its ability to harmonise with and ultimately diffuse physical aggression or emotional confrontation.

I hope that, having read this book, some of its messages have had a positive impact on you, and as a result, you find an ability to explore new opportunities and push on harder when the going gets tough. I am eternally grateful for the opportunity I had and to the people mentioned throughout. You all played a special part in what was a truly enriching and life-changing experience. As I like to say, *'whatever life brings, whichever wind blows, roll with the punches and dodge the throws!'*

In the final stages of editing this book I lost my Dad. He'd been ill for a long time and I'd watched him fade. *'To live in the hearts we leave behind is not to die.'* Matt on hearing the news sent me these powerful words by Thomas Campbell. Dad was an amazing man who always put his family first. While it's hard to lose someone you love so much, I take comfort from the fact he lived a good life. I knew Dad didn't have much longer and was rushing to finish this book. Dad left us suddenly and peacefully. Sadly, although he'll now never get to read my book – I can't be sure – but I believe he helped me finish it. I'd lost some of my training notes and, despite searching high and low, I'd been unable to find them. On a trip back to the family home to spend time with my Mum, between Dad's passing and his funeral, I noticed a box at the end of my bed. On the box Dad had written 'SIMON' in black marker pen. Curious, I opened it, and, to my astonishment, inside I found my missing notes. Thank you for everything Dad – from the closing scene from *Gladiator* and my last written words to you – *'I will see you again, but not yet, not yet'*. I dedicate this book to my wonderful Dad. The man who gave me life, loved me always and showed me what it means to me a man.

Ijo desu!

WHERE ARE THEY NOW?

We all got a bit older; we all got a little wiser. Noriki got upped when Chino Sensei left the new honbu dojo and stepped down as Dojocho. Yoshinkan politics still play out in Japan, and Noriki Sensei is one step closer to the top job. He still has time to become Kancho if the cards fall into place.

I reached out to Matt first to tell him I'd written a book. It was great to reconnect. We'd not spoken since my wedding back in 2012 and he was excited that the story of our year would be told for all to read. He found my letter – I was shocked he still had it – but as you'll read shortly, it had more of an impact on the direction of his life than I could have ever imagined when writing it.

The surprise of deciding to tell this story is how it's brought the 16th international Senshusei back together and what an emotional experience it's been. I reached out to everyone and asked three questions.

1) What are you doing now?

2) What impact did Senshusei have on your life?

3) What is your strongest memory / the story or thing that happened that stands out the most?

Some responded instantly and others had to be chased. Ronen was there immediately. He always was on the course and he still is now. Since I let him know about the book, we've talked almost every day. It's good to have my buddy back and he's helped me fine-tune, remember and add important details to my story. I hadn't intended to write this chapter but giving the principal players, during an amazing year, the chance to tell their stories is something I had to do. Looking back is not always the best idea, but the thoughts and feelings they shared had to be told. Although I thought the book was finished, clearly it wasn't. While the pre-order went on sale, in the background, I got to work.

Up until now *Suck It Up Or Go Home* has been my story, but my decision to write it was much more than that. As I told Ronen in one of our many chats, *'the book is for all of us to remember the good, the bad and the ugly. I wrote it but I could only write it because of what we all did.'* Writing the book is not about me gaining anything or taking anything from others. This book is about legacy and capturing a time that had a massive influence on all of our lives, before it fades into forgotten memory. None of us will ever have this time again. For some, Senshusei meant less than it did to others. For others, I know that Senshusei meant the world and changed their outlook on life for ever. The majority of us no longer practice Aikido, but what we learnt on the course still takes centre stage. It reinforces what Malik Sewanin told me and my own belief that the course wasn't really about martial arts. Its teaching ran much, much deeper. If this chapter has taught me anything it's what a wonderful bunch of people I spent a magical 11 months with. It's also reinforced what I already knew; the power of Aikido to connect – one of the principal wishes of Yoshinkan's founder. Did the Senshusei course work? It depends what you mean by work. From the answers to my questions, it worked on a personal level, but from the honbu's perspective and its desire to promote Yoshinkan Aikido to the four corners of the globe, in our year, in the main it failed.

What follows comes directly from Matt, Ronen, Lloyd, Geoff, Dave, Clyde, Boaz, Dror, Neville, Kambara, Inazaki and Vic. I also reached out to Graham and Malik and have had back-and-forth dialogue with both – I share their updates, too. At times I've summarised or risk writing another book, but where possible, and where I feel it important, I've endeavoured to use their words. You'll find verbatim text in italics. So where are they now? It's time to find out.

MATT

Thinking about the course made me think about how funny life is. Without getting your letter, I probably never would have gone to Japan, trained at Axis, met Caitlin, moved to California or had my daughters! I owe you a lot for setting me off on a path I'm very happy I went down! While my letter started the ball rolling, Matt still had to take the first step. He seized an opportunity and was brave enough to step out of his comfort zone and stay there. *I met my wife in Tokyo and with two awesome daughters I love being a dad. I don't train Aikido anymore. I fell in love with Brazilian Jiu Jitsu during the course. I train regularly in that and have my brown belt.*

Senshusei had a massive impact on my life. In the 'big-picture sense', my decision to move to Japan led to a chain of events. I don't know what my life would be like if I hadn't done the course, but it would be very different! In terms of 'everyday impact', the course just toughened me up a lot and made me realise that you can do pretty much anything if you don't quit. It doesn't matter how tired you are, you just have to suck it up and keep pushing yourself!

The 11 months of the course were absolutely mental and it's really hard to pick one thing that stands out the most. Thinking back about the course, I've realised I had forgotten so many funny stories and memories. Instead of one particular memory, Matt decided to pick out five words that summed up his experience. *In the beginning, it was definitely FEAR that stands out. Before every class we used to sit in seiza not knowing what we would be made to do and whether we would make it out alive! That changed to PAIN and I remember seiza, bruises on my hip and ingrowing toenails.* I'm glad he didn't forget the ingrowing toenails – neither did I – I still smile when I think about his home operating theatre. *Finally, HAPPINESS and RELIEF at completing the course mixed with SADNESS that such a unique experience was over. Looking back now, I appreciate the camaraderie we shared as a group and the way we helped each other through the hard times, as well as having the chance to learn a martial art from people who have dedicated their lives to it. I have a lot of respect for the Sensei that taught us.*

RONEN

Ronen still remembers the buddy system. We've since used these words in every conversation we've had. 'Kind regards' in email, 'see you mate' on the phone, are always replaced with buddy system. We laughed so hard reminiscing that our wives wondered what we were chuckling about while tapping into WhatsApp on our mobile phones. *I'm a scientist, researching new materials for solar energy conversion. Upon my return to Israel after Senshusei, I did an MSc and PhD in physical chemistry and material science, which I completed successfully in 2015. I married Efrat, and we have two children, Yanai and Goni.*

Senshusei made its biggest impact on Ronen in a way I could relate to. *I learnt that I have 'a few tens of percent hidden in an auxiliary battery' that I can switch on when my main battery is showing single digits. I learnt how to draw mental strength from within, in the lowest points, under extreme fatigue, and when everyone around is pessimistic and thinks it's all over. I believe I had this characteristic even before the course, but slightly dormant. However, after Senshusei, I could always find the strength to push forward, in any task ahead of me, as long as I set my mind to do it.* Ronen also learnt an important lesson about six months into the course in a class when the Sensei was teaching yonkajo; a technique he'd been struggling to get right. *The Sensei asked us to perform the technique very slowly on our uke until we felt the lock. I was going through the motions, but I was, of course, tired, in pain, and finding it difficult to do it correctly and to understand what the hell I was doing wrong. I was maybe applying some force to get my uke to lock.* Ronen must have caught Malik Sewanin's attention who came out of nowhere to offer his assistance. *He said 'Ronen, you are doing it wrong'. Malik was correct of course, but I didn't know what to do. I just said 'osu' and listened. Malik continued, 'grab my hand and close your eyes, and do it super slow, on me'. I was starting to lose it. I was holding him, my eyes closed, sweat pouring inside my eyes, it stung. I was tearing up. His voice was making me angry. I was about to snap. He kept saying 'move slow and focus on my voice'. I decided to do what he said, what did I have to lose? I can snap later! Malik kept saying 'you're close, you are going to feel it'. I didn't believe him, but I decided to only focus on his voice and wait to see what happened. Suddenly, without any warning, Malik seized up. He was not acting. I opened my eyes and realised that he was right all along. I was smiling and happy. Until that moment, I would use force when things didn't work. That was wrong. In executing the technique, I immediately understood that it was the same when dealing with people. The level of negative emotions I had and the feeling that I was going to snap, made me want to use force which would have led me nowhere. By going against any natural instinct and doing the opposite, I managed to see that it is possible to do something if you put your mind to it, but you have to do it wisely. Only when there is no other solution, after all of the options have been discussed and tested – stand down, or smash!*

His most prominent memory still haunts him today and was something, despite being his partner for Dai Yon, I never knew. Ronen sucked it up and rarely showed pain. I was shocked to read he'd carried this injury for so long. *About 9 or 10 years after the course, I went to see a physiotherapist to be treated for some pain I was feeling in my neck. Too much sitting in front of the computer perhaps? Because this was my first visit to the clinic, the physiotherapist asked me to take my shirt off so he could check me over and fill in the standard questionnaire. After a minute, he asked me, 'did you ever dislocate your shoulder?' I told him that I once injured my shoulder, but I never went to hospital and that I didn't even remember which shoulder it was. He tapped my right shoulder and said, 'this one?' He continued. 'You must have dislocated this one because it's lower than your left shoulder by one or two centimetres when you stand straight!' I guess I dislocated my shoulder during one of the pre-zagaku 45-minute classes with Laurance Sensei. The class where he marked lines with tape on the mats that we had to perform flying ukemi across. The lines got wider and finished up at about 2.5 metres apart. I smiled at the physiotherapist. 'Thanks, that's good to know. Now, let's fix that neck pain please!'*

LLOYD

I've had a lot of dialogue with Lloyd via email. I always felt a close bond with him since the start of the course. We talked about his brother and although I didn't know Daniel, from what Lloyd shared, it's clear he helped shape my Dai Ichi partner and Senshusei brother. Lloyd is married to Katherine and has three young boys, James, Quinn and Rhys. He works in manufacturing and has just moved positions and locations up to the Sunshine Coast. *Love the title mate 'Suck It Up Or Go Home'. I distinctly remember being across from that expression of intense focus.* He sent me a picture in his Yoshinkan hoodie. I'd forgotten about this. Carlos had them made for us all near the end of the course. I need to dig mine out! He described his hoodie in such a way that I had to share. *It's the toughest most long-lasting item of clothing I've ever owned. It's indestructible! I'm still wondering if it's made out of repurposed dogi material and instilled with warrior spirit nanofibers that Ronen invented and sent into the past somehow!* Lloyd explained how he got interested in martial arts. *In my family there were three of us boys and two sisters. I'm the eldest and Daniel was the second. We were both obsessed with Ninja Turtles and even though we never actually did any martial arts we spent half the time growing up sparring and wrestling with each other. He was the closest person in the world to me and although I still hurt from losing him, I couldn't have asked for a better little brother to grow up with. Daniel certainly is a crucial part of who I was and who I am today. He lived for the day and certainly never let life's worries get in the way of having fun!* Lloyd shared another personal story which gives a clue to a brotherly trait of coming to the rescue of those less able to defend themselves. *Daniel played Rugby Union in high school and one day took a ten-metre run-up to deck some other player who was targeting one of his weaker teammates in a fight on the field. The guy hit the ground and the rest of his team rushed straight at Dan and he's standing his ground there ready to go like it's not even a question he's going to take down all of them at once.* Lloyd stopped training in Aikido within a year of Senshusei finishing, primarily due to work commitments and not wanting another structured environment at the end of the working day. He still likes a rumble. *I've had a few street encounters in the years since but in spite of my best efforts they didn't end up in a physical confrontation. When it came to it, I didn't back down in the slightest and maybe the other guys thought if I was that ready to go then there was something they were missing. One thing I've realised with these dickheads who start things is that they really don't like to throw a punch when you are just standing there ready and looking dead at them. It definitely bothers them a lot.*

Senshusei clearly had a big impact as Lloyd explains. *There is one gift I'd consider unique that I've since found to be the most rare and valuable to me. Over time I noticed that without ever thinking about it, I had a different approach to conflict in the workplace than most people did that let me quietly make progress in a highly competitive and often aggressive environment without having to sacrifice my integrity. Every day and with most people we engage with there inevitably comes conflict because we all see things differently and have our individual priorities. No matter how well meaning, cooperative and collaborative people are, there is always conflict on some level. For all of us, it actually ends up being the people we love and care about most with whom we have the most conflict of all. The depth and quality of these most precious relationships with friends and family, and certainly our ability to maintain and continue to build them over years and decades, requires us to be generous and graceful in all those conflicts that must happen along the way. Aikido is so unusual in the way that a conflict is also that 'meeting of spirits' in a way that is so real and genuine. It allows you to bring all of yourself to engage in a conflict but to also know and appreciate the other person as it happens. This enables both of you to come out of it better rather than just having a winner and loser every time. If we use brute force, or at the other extreme just give up and disengage, it inevitably destroys those relationships we hold most dear. Senshusei was this ultra-high-intensity distilled form of Aikido that we lived every day and I really think because of that it became part of me far more than I was aware of at the time.*

His strongest memory of the Senshusei course is the night he found out about Daniel (BITTERSWEET). *I'd faced and overcome so much but the greatest pain and chaos hit me right at the finish line. There are no easy answers, life is chaotic and complicated and maybe I'm stretching to find meaning. I do think about the fact that he held out just long enough to the day, so that I was able to make it all the way through the course. From then it was like having just those few moments to catch my breath before facing a trial that might have ruined me had I not been the man our Senshusei year had forged.*

GEOFF

Geoff and Vic broke up shortly after the Senshusei course. He didn't go into detail but perhaps the pressures of doing the course together played a part? He runs an apple orchard and trains in a small dojo on site. He was brief on how Senshusei had impacted his life. *It opened me up to Japanese spirit and culture.*

His strongest memory is a class during Dai Ichi. He'd looked at Malik Sewanin the wrong way and was told to do 100 press-ups or get out. *The entire class came over to encourage me and finished beside me.* I captured this story in IT'S NEARLY A KNOCKOUT but hadn't realised what a special moment this was for Geoff – 13 years on it's the one he still remembers. I guess it's a reminder that sometimes the smallest action has the biggest impact. What was a small gesture from the group had a massive impact on Geoff who was struggling at the time.

DAVE

Dave was definitely a character. He was very young back then. With the passing years he's clearly matured, but still retains much of his former self. Dave now teaches Yoga full-time and wrote to me from his current home in South Korea. The last time I'd heard from him was an email he sent to everyone on 8 January 2009 – the round-robin kind people send over the New Year to let you know what they're doing. He was on another adventure at the time and shared extracts from his diary. I had my diary and Dave has his – he needs to write his own book one day. Exploring the Alps, he wrote, *the sky is filled with rock and you get that feeling of dread in your belly. I came across a group of men with a pickup truck, guns and dogs. They asked me what I was up to. I told them and was offered a cigarette and called crazy. Apparently, it's suicidal to climb the Alps in winter. Who would have known?!*

Back to the present day and in response to my second question. *Senshusei doesn't mean that much to me. I did a lot afterwards. It's the distant past now. I know I did it, but I don't really see it as me who did it. I was a completely different person. Really a stranger was in Tokyo in 2006. I wouldn't do it now. It's probably because I did complete the course that I accomplished other things, though – it was the beginning stage. I revisited Tokyo afterwards. Chida Sensei gave me a black belt and asked if I wanted to take a nidan exam. I said no. I was never a martial artist; I was a tourist.*

It turned out I was right; by his own admission, Dave was a tourist after all! From the other stuff he told me, Dave has some bad memories of the course and questioned Aikido's effectiveness and the hierarchical structure that we bowed and scraped to in Japan. On the positive side he recognised the course taught him discipline.

CLYDE

Clyde is still in Japan and is an IT recruiter. He still trains at Axis Jiu Jitsu and has his blue belt. While he no longer trains in Aikido, he recognises that *Aikido has helped with understanding Gracie Jiu Jitsu.* The course made a lasting impression on him. *I now know what 'spirit' feels like. If I see shoes in a mess, I have to put them together neatly with the toes pointing one way.*

He had quite a few memories and remembered Oyamada Sensei's class I described in HOT, HOT, HOT!!! *That one day in July when I was completely exhausted, but my body kept going – 45 minutes into the last class of the day I had absolutely no energy left, but we had another 45 minutes to go. I was flopping around with horrible technique. I was wishing I would just pass out, so I could rest for a few seconds. That never happened. After class, I sat on the floor at the end of the locker room. Everybody let me rest while they cleaned. I have never felt exhaustion like that in my life and I haven't since.* His other memories are of me practicing my Japanese at Dave's expense (JAPANESE FOR BUSY PEOPLE) and the camaraderie we all had. *There is no way I would have been able to get through the course if it wasn't for everyone.*

BOAZ

Today Boaz lives and works in Seattle, visits Israel several times a year and makes recurring trips to Japan. He still practices Aikido and Salsa. *The Senshusei experience has made Aikido an integral part of my life. I often implement and reflect on its principles. The outstanding people, regimen and culture in the course have inspired me to continuously strive to improve and cultivate my spirit and aspire to share our teachers' learnings and make them widespread.*

His standout memory is of the class with Inoue Kancho towards the end of the course (ADVENT-URE), which he described as *a masterclass on sasoi and sensitivity.* I had this experience, too. *While walking amongst us during a 'work at your own pace' window, he stopped by me for just a few minutes. Little did I know at the time that this would become a moment of discovery for me. Thanks to Kancho's amorphous explanation and magnetic touch, for the first time, I began to understand the concept of sasoi. This short personal interaction we had taught me a great lesson on both Aikido principles and teaching style.*

DROR

Dror works as a physiotherapist, a skill we could all have gained benefit from on the course! *I think Senshusei just gave me interesting memories and stories to tell later on and common ground with some people.*

His strongest memory made me laugh. It's probably a lasting memory for most of us. *Geoff farting during the lady cop's hansei.* I told this story in MIND CONTROL? There was a further incident where Dror burst out laughing and momentarily forgot where he was (OVERDOSE).

NEVILLE

I now run a dojo with a permanent base in Lincoln (Eiryukan Aikido). It started in January 2008 in schools and local halls and then grew from there. We had a seminar with Jacques Payet Sensei a few years ago and have had several international visits.

Of all the 16th international Senshusei, Neville is the one who became what the course was designed to create. *It impacted my life and opened up a career, but mainly taught me to persevere through challenging times and make diligent effort which will reap results at a later date.*

His strongest memory really resonated with me. *Being part of a great team of people from all over the world – I did Aikido initially as an individual endeavour but being on the course showed me a great deal about team spirit.*

KAMBARA

Kambara continues to study martial arts. While he still practices kihon dosa every day, he is now learning Owari Yagyu Shinkage-ryu (sword) and Owari Kan-ryu Sojutsu (spear). *Both are old-fashioned martial arts in my hometown Nagoya, and especially Owari Yagyu Shinkage-ryu which has a great influence on modern Kendo.*

He explained why he took the course. *I became a Senshusei to master Aikido. The course where I devoted myself only to Aikido has undoubtedly had a great influence on my life. Until then, I served as a national civil servant to the nation and people. In a sense, I might have been a man who was made that way by society. Senshusei released me and taught me that if I didn't do what I wanted to do, there would be no point in my life. Senshusei changed my life and made it possible for me to live a fulfilling life.*

He had an interesting reflection about the Sewanin. *The Sewanin punished me for going against Senshusei attitude and spirit. Sewanin is Senshusei caretaker but looked like army demon Sergeant!* His strongest memory is about the time he took the Shinkoku diary out of the dojo which is a story I told in AIR CON. *I did something I wouldn't normally do. On that day, I felt very annoyed to write the daily report, and I wanted to finish it immediately and return to my apartment early. I still don't understand why I did such a stupid thing.* He bears no malice towards either of the Sewanin and finished by saying, *as Senshusei I was an Aikido monk and the Senshusei course was a Yoshinkan Aikido bootcamp. I'm proud that I completed the Senshusei course and thank Malik and Graham.*

INAZAKI

Inazaki teaches Aikido and works in the care sector. Senshusei had a big impact on his resilience and ability to keep going. *No matter how painful our daily lives might be, it seems to be no big deal compared to when we were Senshusei.*

His strongest memory of the course was at the hands of Oyamada Sensei. Oyamada's classes were very similar, so it's difficult to pinpoint exactly which one. I suspect it was the class I described in SHINE A LIGHT. *It was jiyu waza, one group at a time in front of everyone. When I was uke Sensei didn't tell me to stop for ever. When I lost consciousness and couldn't stand up, everyone cheered me. At that time, I learned that cheering gives people strong power. It makes me feel nostalgic for those days!* I didn't record this incident in detail in my diary – I must have been too tired myself and missed it!

VIC

Vic is back in Canada and works as a site superintendent with experience in many types of construction. She no longer practices Aikido. *Back from such an amazing year I had to let the reality of life take over.*

It's very evident from our dialogue that Senshusei had a huge impact on her life. *The time in Japan has always had and still continues to have a significant and positive impact on my mind, body, integrity and spirit. I owe so many of my greatest attributes to the lessons learned and knowledge received on the course.* Vic shared a quote with me by Khalil Gibran from the book *The Prophet* that summed up the camaraderie and comradeship we built in our special year. *'You have been told that, even like a chain, you are as weak as your weakest link. This is but half the truth. You are also as strong as your strongest link.'* We were all links in the same chain with good and bad days – we pulled each other through.

Vic had lots of memories and I'm convinced, like me, took comprehensive notes at the end of each day. Perhaps she'll write her own book one day? The week Robert arrived with his camera was one of her strongest memories (THE DOCUMENTARY). In her own words, *it brought on one of the most gruelling weeks of the entire 11-month course. The unwarranted torture was relentless and excruciating.* She also reminisced about the last class on the last day of summer training. The day Ito Sensei announced the gasshuku (VENDETTA), Takashima Sensei advised, *'remember when entering seiza we are entering enemy territory, so be ready!'* We all spent far too long in 'enemy territory' but got through it as a team. Vic had a final message for her 16th international Senshusei comrades. *To my Senshusei brothers, I am honoured and privileged to be your sister and to have shared one of the best years of my life with you. Osu!*

GRAHAM

After Sewanin, Graham became an uchi-deshi. *I lived and worked in the dojo as a professional until the dojo moved to Takadanobaba. I returned to Canada after the earthquake and Fukushima nuclear power plant meltdown in 2011.* In total he spent 10 years in Japan. He is married and has three children (a son and twin daughters) and runs Aikido Ryugikan, his own full-time dojo, in Whitby, Canada. In 2019 Graham was awarded rokudan and the title of Shihan.

The main lesson I learned from Senshusei was to never give up, take the extra step and that life is constantly changing. Japanese 'gaman' is all about the course. Having not come across the word *gaman* while in Japan, I looked it up. It means *to endure the seemingly unbearable with patience and dignity.* Now I remembered – it was a blast from the past and immediately took me back to the TV show I'd enjoyed as a child (SIGHTSEEING).

Graham's strongest memory was the zagaku classes. *David and Dror mostly. David sitting in a puddle of sweat, tears and drool, and Dror rocking back and forth pinching his hand because of the pain.*

MALIK

I wanted to give the penultimate word in the book to Malik Sewanin. It was a difficult year for us, and I suspect also a difficult one for him. We had a number of email exchanges and what he had to say was both poignant and powerful. *I look back on those times fondly. Good, bad or ugly, they are times that none of us will ever forget; not to mention, few will ever experience. Learning Aikido was only a limited part of the course. It was everything else such as the struggle and hardships, living and surviving in Japan as well as the friendships and camaraderie that made it all memorable, special and meaningful. We all have a special connection to one another as well as a suitcase full (or a book full in your case) of life lessons that will stay with us and help us no matter what we encounter.* Like Graham, Malik went on to become an uchi-deshi at the honbu dojo for two years. *I'm currently residing in Tokyo, Japan, but planning to return to the UK in the coming years for my child's schooling. I took a step back from Aikido around three years ago to focus on postgraduate study, marriage and family after running my own dojo in Shinagawa, Tokyo for about seven years.*

Talking about his own course (2005-2006). *The Senshusei course and 'being Senshusei' was always an avenue for me to overcome the death of my parents. The course instilled in me the discipline, strength and fortitude needed to continue to deal with whatever else life had in store. Being a Senshusei continues today, nearly 15 years on from when I graduated from my course, in facing everyday challenges. From putting food on the table to being a good father and overcoming health issues.* Malik in a very reflective mood shared a number of regrets. *One thing about your year from my perspective was that I was never able to let you guys know how it was for me. The way I was as Sewanin was significantly influenced by my Sewanin and the international teachers there at the time. I knew that there was no halfway position when it came to putting you all through hell. It was all in or not at all. There was no way for me to give you the real experience of Senshusei and then have a laugh and drink with you afterwards. The saddest part was that I missed out on the connections that others made with your year when it should have been Graham and I in many of the pictures you're now posting on the Facebook page. We all had a good connection at the beginning, but if I had remained that way the course wouldn't have been what it was, and you may not now be publishing a book. It was either Graham or I to give you the real experience you all came for and it fell to me. I had to be distant and be the way I was. I'm gutted that we all didn't have the connection and friendship that I wanted. I was deeply affected by the fact that others naturally filled that space and a divide to some degree existed between us all. Yes, I made mistakes and could have done some things much better. However, it was what it was. In the end, from my perspective, what counts are the life lessons that came out of the course for everyone and the fact that you all got through everything I put in your way. I hope that I gave everyone hardship and suffering and made everyone struggle, because overcoming these will better prepare everyone to face whatever else in life comes their way. I gave you the Senshusei course as I knew it. Unfortunately, the price I paid was losing the connection. I hope in time your year will come to understand.*

He has two very strong memories of our time together. The first was the weekly zagaku. *It was a rare occasion in the dojo when those called upon could talk freely, and sometimes deeply, in the presence of their peers and instructors about how they felt about themselves, life and training. This was a unique and special part of our training to encourage self-reflection and self-improvement. Zagaku and hansei are sometimes overlooked when people retell stories about the course, focusing more on the pain and suffering each Senshusei experienced.* Talking specifically about those of us who struggled in zagaku. *I would spend much of my time staring intensely at those Senshusei partly to see if they were still alive, but mostly to stop them from being a distraction to the proceedings because of their constant shaking, peculiar facial expressions and bent-over bodies.* His second memory was the YouTube documentary, which I talked about in THE DOCUMENTARY. Malik clearly felt it took a selective and biased 10-minute snapshot of a course that lasted 11 months. *It portrayed me in the light it did to conform to a narrative it chose to follow, without screening the wider collective support the Senshusei received throughout the different stages of the whole year, not only from me but also from Graham, other members of the international teaching division and the Japanese instructors.*

Owari (the end)!

THE LAST WORD

'*These days the differences of ideology, the confrontation of races and conflict between nations, leads to numerous problems from the destruction of the environment to economic frictions. All opposition or antagonism leads to greater conflict. A premise of Aikido is the avoidance of rivalry or any form of opposition. If the people of the world would make an effort to learn how to avoid dissension through the practice of Aikido, I am sure that mankind could realise genuine unification. Therefore, we as instructors must do our best to gain this ideal.*' – **Kancho Gozo Shioda**

I put my heart and soul into writing this book, and whether you're a practitioner of the martial arts or not, I'm happy if you found a little inspiration as you turned the pages. I'd love to hear your feedback and, if you have a moment, would be very grateful for an online review on Amazon or where you bought your copy, please.

I have a dream that on holiday I'll spot someone reading my book by the pool – with Geoff's Ninja skills I'll sneak up and surprise!

To experience more of the Senshusei course, meet some of the characters, see the places, and bring to life many of the stories mentioned in this book, please visit suckituporgohome.com or search *Suck It Up Or Go Home* on social media.

APPENDICES

MATT'S LETTER

27 June 2005

Hello Mate

I thought I would write you a quick letter instead of email, just in case 'Dodger' has forgotten to pay the bills again?! All is good here mate, very hot at the moment, 30 degrees plus and no wind so very, very humid. Just doing the kihon dosa once results in a coating of sweat! Still not found a job yet but have an interview with Berlitz on Wednesday morning for a part-time English teaching job which would give me time to train, too.

Training is good, at the moment tending to do the morning classes, 7am start for an hour then a second class at 8:30am for another hour. It is a bit cooler at this time and also you get to train alongside the Senshusei for one of their classes. This year there are only three international students doing the course, one Canadian, one British and one Israeli along with two Japanese (non-police) which is in addition to about five or six Kidotai (Riot Police).

The training looks quite intense, they get in at about 7:15am and do some cleaning then train 8:30 to 9:30am (class 1), 10 to 11:30am (class 2) and finally 12 to 1:30pm (class 3), so four hours a day in total for five days a week (they have Sunday off and the dojo is closed on Monday).

What I have noticed is that the intensity of their training really drives their spirit, it is awesome mate, I am kicking myself that I didn't enrol on the course this year, I really am! After this training in nine months you grade to shodan and then for an instructor certificate in the last couple of months and you get to train with Chida Shihan, etc.

I graded on Saturday for my first kyu grade (I think either ninth or tenth but not too sure as all in Japanese). I had to do kamae, seiza and kihon dosa on the right side only. It went well so I'm sure I passed but again not sure as all in Japanese!!! I am going to grade again next month so if I have to do more stuff, I will know I passed this month! It was a real experience, they are so much into the detail, I have been picked up on so many points on kamae and kihon dosa, I don't know where to start!

It is not all kihon dosa in the classes, we get to do more advanced stuff but to be honest doing basics is fine by me as this gets you better and better. There are

376

no modules or self-defence classes it is all pure Aikido and taught in a very traditional way.

So mate, I am now going to ask you a very serious question which is also directed at the other Matt, I don't have his address so could you let him read this letter mate (but just keep it between you two)...how about doing Senshusei next year, all three of us??? I can't seem to get the idea out of my head and wish I was part of it now. If you guys did a TEFL (Teaching English as a Foreign Language) online course in the UK, you could get a job as an English teacher out here no problem and work part-time to finance living and training. Japan is so much cheaper than I expected, it is actually cheaper than the UK. If we did this next year it would be a blast. Have a serious think and speak to the other Matt and drop me an email or a letter to:

Simon Gray
Poste Restante
Central Post Office
2-7-2 Marunouchi
Tokyo 100
JAPAN

Other news is that I've joined a Muay Thai gym. Have you heard of 'Masato', he competes in K-1 and is very famous out here, it is the gym where he trains? I try and get down there at least twice a week and got into a bit of scrap with one of the locals which was interesting!

Doing some sightseeing tomorrow, Japan Sword Museum and Tokyo Tower for views of the city which should be good. Have a good think about Senshusei mate and speak to the other Matt, I am deadly serious! Keep it quiet down the dojo, though, mate and let me know if you need any more information, too, on Japan, the course, etc?

I hope your training is going well for shodan mate, keep going with it and it will all be worth it I promise! By the way if you want to read a book about martial arts and Japan get 'Moving Zen' by C.W. Nicol, it is awesome, I read it in two days and in my opinion is even better than 'Angry White Pyjamas'. It is about Karate but is all about, Budo, spirit and Japan.

Anyway mate, to whet your appetite further I've enclosed three photos taken at the gasshuku I went on of me with Chida Shihan, Takeno Shihan and Inoue Kancho, awesome mate. Take it easy bro' and let me know what you think??? All the best and a big Japanese osu!

Simon

I was thrilled that Matt had kept this letter all these years. I remembered writing it but couldn't remember the detail until Matt dug it out and sent it to me in the final throes (or even 'throws') of writing this book. I'd forgotten about Roger 'Dodger', Matt's housemate. The story goes that the Internet was in Dodger's name and because he was always having money problems it was hit and miss whether the Internet bill got paid. I'd sent Matt a letter, just in case his connection to the outside world had temporarily been cut off!

My reference to 'modules' and self-defence related to the syllabus at the Shudokan, which included more street-focused training.

The 'scrap' I mentioned happened in sparring at the Ihara Dojo. I'd jumped in the ring with a Japanese guy who was training for an upcoming fight (I mustn't have learnt my lesson from my first outing in Muay Thai back in Stafford). The guy had an injury to his face, so we agreed I could only hit him in the body. He'd gone full pelt and tried to take my head off. Let's just say the trainer watching had to split us up!

I'd forgotten that I'd also invited another Matt to join me in Japan. 'Other' Matt trained with us at the Shudokan and was a regular at Sensei Michal's special classes. Matt couldn't remember his discussion with the other Matt, but 13 years on confirmed, *'he definitely missed out on something special'*.

I asked Matt to keep things quiet as at the time he was working part-time at the Shudokan. I didn't want to upset Sensei Ken by enticing away one of his employees. That would have been a very bad move!

I encouraged Matt to read *Moving Zen*. I'd enjoyed *Angry White Pyjamas* and it had encouraged me to leave for Japan, but now in Japan, I'd found it quite a spiritual experience. *Moving Zen* communicated more of the spiritual side of martial life, which had really resonated in my new surroundings.

The other thing I noticed about this letter is how much I used the word 'mate'. Some things haven't changed!

DAILY SCHEDULE

<u>Tuesday to Friday:</u>
7:25am – Arrive at the dojo and change into dogi.
7:30 to 7:50am – Cleaning.
7:50 to 8:00am – Roll call and daily meeting.
8:00 to 8:10am – Dojo cleaning.
8:10 to 8:15am – Warm-up / taiso.
8:25 to 8:30am – Seiza.
8:30 to 9:30am – Training.
9:40am – Shinkoku.
9:55 to 10:00am – Seiza.
10:00 to 11:30am – Training.
11:55am to 12:00pm – Seiza.
12:00 to 1:30pm – Training.
1:40pm – Shinkoku.
1:45 to 2:00pm – Cleaning.
2:00pm – Finish.

<u>Saturday:</u>
7:25am – Arrive at the dojo and change into dogi.
7:30 to 7:50am – Cleaning.
7:50 to 8:00am – Roll call and daily meeting.
8:00 to 8:10am – Dojo cleaning.
8:10 to 8:15am – Warm-up / taiso.
8:25 to 8:30am – Seiza.
8:30 to 9:30am – Training.
9:40am – Shinkoku.
9:55 to 10:00am – Seiza.
10:00 to 11:00am – Training.
11:25 to 11:30am – Seiza.
11:30am to 12:30pm – Training.
12:40pm – Shinkoku.
12:45 to 1:00pm – Cleaning.
1:00pm – Finish.

DIARY FEEDBACK

April – Good start to the year. Keep working hard. [Dosa 6.5, Waza 6, Attitude 6.5.]

May – You are picking things up well and progressing nicely. The next few months are the toughest, so stay focused and energetic. [Dosa 6.5, Waza 6.5, Attitude 6.5.]

June – You are continuing to do well and pushing yourself. Keep focused through the summer heat and think hard about the meaning behind each movement. [Dosa 6.5, Waza 6.5, Attitude 7.]

July – Every Senshusei course is different. Everyone in each course is different. That's very amazing. Learn from everyone. Everyone has something to offer. Keep up the hard work! [Dosa 7, Waza 7, Attitude 7.5.]

August – Excellent diary. Keep up the good work. When training, you must always ask yourself why you do a technique a certain way. You must understand the technique. To do that, you must understand yourself. [Dosa 7.5, Waza 7, Attitude 7.5.]

September* – Great job calling at the Enbu! Others are looking to you for leadership and finding it. Nice diary. Try and fit better with your partners and avoid bumping. [Dosa 7.5, Waza 7.5, Attitude 8.]

October – Great diary! You've done well training through and around your injuries. Stretch well in the winter months and have a good winter break. [Dosa 7.5, Waza 8, Attitude 8.]

November – As Senshusei you have gone from strength to strength. Your attitude is always great, your dosa and waza are improving all the time. Keep this up and I hope to see you get better and better. Good job. [Dosa 8, Waza 8, Attitude 8.]

December – A good test. Many people feel that after they get their shodan, they know everything. Shodan is the true beginning. Constantly focus on the basics. With a strong base you can have awesome Aikido. [Dosa 8, Waza 8, Attitude 8.5.]

January – Dai San was a difficult time for you and your partner. I think you learned the importance of working with your partner. The end of the course is near. Enjoy the time with the group and leave the course on a positive note, to hopefully one day open your own dojo. [Dosa 8, Waza 8.5, Attitude 8.5.]

*It's clear from September's entry that the Sensei often took their time in providing feedback. The 51st All Japan Enbu took place at the end of October!

SEWANIN'S 10 TIPS FOR A GOOD TEST

SPIRIT – Energetic, strong attitude, no emotion, no pain. Give everything you have – 125%. Whatever happens during the test, the most important thing you need to show is spirit. It's once in your lifetime, give it your all. No regrets.

KIAI – Loud, make the dojo shake. Comes from the heart. Kiai for atemi, shime and osae. During the osae, project your feeling and hold it for at least a few seconds to show you have controlled uke.

CONNECTION – Keep good connection and timing with your partner. Blend from the first bow, into kamae, sekkin, to the final osae. Shite and uke need to move as one unit. Keep the connection and intensity between you, but be graceful.

CORRECT SHITE – Make sure you know your techniques – ichi and ni. You have to show the Sensei the individual components of each technique. Remember the hand and foot positions for kihon dosa. Project feeling and know your percentages.

CORRECT UKE – Make sure you know the correct foot, body and hand positions for uke and how to take the correct ukemi. As uke, slap hard during the osae.

KAMAE – At the beginning, during and at the end, you have to show an immovable kamae. It's easy to lose your kamae during techniques – DON'T! Make your kamae stand out from the crowd.

ZANSHIN – During osae and especially nage techniques, you have to hold your position for a few seconds to express zanshin. Make your body alignment and feeling powerful and strong.

SPEED – Senshusei should move like lightning, both as shite and uke. Move quickly and with purpose. But don't rush the technique or be hasty. Get up quick from techniques but importantly together.

CONTROL – Project the feeling that you are running things. Don't show you are under pressure. Keep calm, focused and controlled. Don't breathe heavily or keep your mouth open. You should be relaxed at all times, be still in motion, don't shake or fumble around. Be solid in mind and body. Don't show emotions on your face.

SMALL THINGS – Remember the small things like your eyeline, distance between you and uke, keeping your back heel down, suriashi and to move the body, hands, arms and feet as one, and keep your head up – don't look down.

DOJO DICTIONARY

Aikidoka – a practitioner of Aikido.

Dogi – training uniform.

Dojo – matted area for training (in this book I use interchangeably with honbu).

Dojocho – head of the dojo.

Enbu – formal performance or demonstration.

Hajime geiko – repetitive training to the count.

Hakama – traditional Japanese clothing worn by shodan and above.

Honbu – head dojo (in this book I use interchangeably with dojo).

Ippan – regular or general.

Jiyu waza – predetermined repeated attack (uke) and defence (shite).

Hansei – reflection or introspection.

Kamae – ready stance.

Kancho – head teacher / head of school.

Kidotai – Riot Police.

Kihon dosa – basic movements.

Kihon waza – basic techniques.

Kokusai – international.

Mitori geiko – watching training when injured or sick.

Sasoi – invitation to uke.

Seiza – kneeling position.

Sensei – teacher.

Sewanin – assistant teacher and dojo enforcer.

Shido ho – teaching.

Shinkoku – report before and after training.

Shite – the person doing a technique.

Shodan – black belt.

Sho dojo – small dojo.

Shomen – front (the position of the ceremonial shrine).

Shukan – habit or custom.

Uke – the person receiving a technique.

Ukemi – the art of falling safely / the art of receiving a technique.

Usagi tobi – bunny hops.

Zagaku – sit and learn.

Zanshin – awareness.

Printed in Great Britain
by Amazon